THE WORLD ROLE OF UNIVERSITIES

THE CARNEGIE SERIES IN AMERICAN EDUCATION

The books in this series have resulted from studies supported by grants of the Carnegie Corporation of New York, and are published by McGraw-Hill in recognition of their importance to the future of American education.

The Corporation, a philanthropic foundation established in 1911 by Andrew Carnegie for the advancement and diffusion of knowledge and understanding, has a continuing interest in the improvement of American education. It financed the studies in this series to provide facts and recommendations which would be useful to all those who make or influence the decisions which shape American educational policies and institutions.

The statements made and views expressed in these books are solely the responsibility of the authors.

Books Published

Berelson · Graduate Education in the United States
Clark · The Open Door College: A Case Study
Cleveland · The Overseas American
Conant · The American High School Today
Corson · Governance of Colleges and Universities
Glenny · Autonomy of Public Colleges
Henninger · The Technical Institute in America
McConnell · A General Pattern for American Public Higher Education
Medsker · The Junior College: Progress and Prospect
Perkins and Snell · The Education of Historians in the United States
Pierson · The Education of American Businessmen
Thomas · The Search for a Common Learning: General Education, 1800–1960
Weidner · The World Role of Universities

THE WORLD ROLE
OF UNIVERSITIES

25546

EDWARD W. WEIDNER

MICHIGAN STATE UNIVERSITY

1962　McGRAW-HILL BOOK COMPANY, INC.

NEW YORK / SAN FRANCISCO / TORONTO / LONDON

THE WORLD ROLE OF UNIVERSITIES

II

69034

To Peter and Lillian

PREFACE

In 1957, the Carnegie Corporation of New York, long interested in higher education and international affairs, voted support for a study of the international exchange programs of American universities. During the succeeding four years, 11 social scientists contributed to the undertaking. The present author was director of the group. Each scholar contributed to the common pool of data, but in addition was free to publish the data he collected in any manner that he desired. To date, six of their monographs have appeared, and two others have been prepared in manuscript form. Each monograph has concentrated on a certain geographical area.

Thirteen university programs in Mexico, Peru, Bolivia, and Chile were the subject of the work of Richard N. Adams and Charles C. Cumberland, *United States University Cooperation in Latin America* (East Lansing, 1960). The international exchange programs of American universities in Indonesia were reported by Bruce Lannes Smith in *Indonesian-American Cooperation in Higher Education* (East Lansing, 1960). Both volumes were published by the Institute of Research on Overseas Programs which was established at Michigan State University to administer the research grant.

Three monographs were published by the Michigan State University Press. John A. Garraty and Walter Adams, *From Main Street to the Left Bank* (East Lansing, 1959), is a study of student-abroad and faculty-exchange programs in Europe. The same authors collaborated on a study of technical assistance programs of American universities in Europe and Turkey: Walter Adams and John A. Garraty, *Is the World Our Campus?* (East Lansing, 1960). A sample of nearly half the many programs in India was the focus of Henry Hart's volume, *Campus India: An Appraisal of American College Programs in India* (East Lansing, 1961).

The Free Press and the Bureau of Social and Political Research

of Michigan State University have jointly produced Martin Bronfenbrenner's analysis of all the programs of American universities
in two other Asian countries: *Academic Encounter: The American
University in Japan and Korea* (Glencoe and East Lansing, 1961).
Unpublished are the materials on selected countries of the Middle
East and Africa collected by Frederic R. Wickert and the Ph.D.
thesis of Richard Bjork, "The Role of American Universities in
International Relations," which is a study of a sample of 33 American universities, emphasizing the impact of programs on the home
campuses.

For simplicity, throughout the present volume, these monographs
are referred to by author only, such as Adams and Cumberland,
Garraty and Adams, etc.

Two general volumes were projected for the study. The first, an
inventory and a descriptive analysis of all the programs, was published in 1958 by the Institute: Edward W. Weidner and Associates,
The International Programs of American Universities (hereinafter
called "Inventory"). Since the regional volumes gave each of the
authors an opportunity to interpret his regional data, one objective
of the present study, the second general volume, has been to present
an interpretation of the data from all regions. In addition, it is an
attempt at general summary and conclusion.

The present research effort was not designed by itself to lead to
a final evaluation of each of the programs or the programs in general. In addition to data on impacts, evaluation implies the identification of standards or criteria by means of which the impact can
be assessed. Though several sets of possible criteria were identified
in the early stages of the research project during an effort to determine what data should be collected, neither the Institute of Research
on Overseas Programs nor any of its staff is in a position to choose
among them solely as a result of the research. Every organization
and every individual interested in any aspect of the international
exchange programs of American universities may adopt distinctive
criteria for judging the impact. Many have done so. It was the
objective of the present research effort to collect and present data
that would be useful to such groups and individuals in arriving at
their own evaluations. In the present volume, the director of IROP
has attempted to set forth his own criteria, including his definitions
of success and appropriateness of projects, together with the outlines

of an approach to higher education, foreign policy, and university international exchange.

Throughout the manuscript the Agency for International Development (AID) is referred to by the name of its immediate predecessor, the International Cooperation Administration (ICA), since the organization was known as ICA when field research was carried out. Similarly, the International Educational Exchange Service (IES) is mentioned several times, even though it has now been replaced by the Bureau of Educational and Cultural Affairs (CU).

The study would not have been possible without the splendid cooperation of more than 2,000 interviewees. Many of them were gracious enough to say that they welcomed the opportunity to reflect on the programs, yet the time they spent with the cooperating scholars was an inroad upon their busy schedules. Perforce they must go unnamed, but their kindness and help are hereby gratefully acknowledged.

The study has benefited from the services of an eminently qualified national advisory panel, composed of Clifford M. Hardin, Chancellor, The University of Nebraska; Pendleton Herring, President, Social Science Research Council; F. F. Hill, Vice President, The Ford Foundation; Kenneth Holland, President, Institute of International Education; James L. Morrill, President Emeritus, University of Minnesota; Herman B. Wells, President, Indiana University; and Francis A. Young, Executive Secretary, Committee on International Exchange of Persons, Conference Board of Associated Research Councils. Several times these educators individually contributed to the study's outcome, in person or by mail. In January, 1960 a meeting of the advisory panel was held to review several chapters of the present volume. In particular the panel added a measure of depth to the study.

On three occasions in 1957 the research efforts of the Institute were assisted by groups of outside consultants. Several government agencies designated points of liaison for the study, and the Institute was especially dependent upon these persons for assistance during the first year or two of research. At Michigan State University, Frank A. Pinner contributed to the initial research design. Bernard Corman was a member of the planning committee along with the cooperating scholars. Robert Mendelsohn and Steighton A. Watts, Jr. ably performed the role of research assistants. Suggestions and encouragement came from Floyd W. Reeves, continuing consultant to the Institute, and former Vice President Thomas Hamilton, university liaison with the Institute. Without the administrative support of Homer D. Higbee, Assistant Director of the Institute, the project would have broken down at many points. The editorial assistance of George Soule is gratefully acknowledged. Finally, Mrs. Dorothy Young headed a remarkably capable and willing secretarial staff.

The Carnegie Corporation of New York supported the project in its entirety. Indebtedness to Carnegie is far more than financial; several staff members contributed many ideas to the undertaking.

To these, and many others, my sincere thanks. Needless to say, responsibility for the outcome is mine alone, including what shortcomings or errors there may be.

Edward W. Weidner

CONTENTS

Preface   vii

1. *Dimensions of the Problem* 1

   The Roles of Educational Institutions. International Exchange Programs of American Universities. Need for Appraisal.

2. *The Educational Structures of Different Countries* 12

   National Patterns of Secondary Education. National Patterns of Higher Education. Internal Organization of Universities. Relations with Governments.

3. *The Professors and Students of Different Countries* 32

   Faculty Members. Students. Teaching. Understanding of Differences by University Personnel.

4. *American Student-abroad Programs: A Survey* 56

   Examples of Programs. Organizing for Study Abroad. Selection of Personnel. Program Objectives and Accomplishments.

5. *Alternatives in Student-abroad Programs* 76

   The Junior Year Abroad. Other Undergraduate Programs. Graduate Programs. Summer Programs. Alternatives to University Programs.

6. *American Student-abroad Programs: Policy Imperatives* . . 94

   Academic Requisites for Programs. Expansion of the Proportion of Students Involved.

7. *Religious, Research, and Small Exchanges* 112

   Programs with Religious Emphasis. Research Abroad. Small Exchanges.

8. *The Participants: Visitors to United States Universities under
    Technical Assistance* 134
    Illustrations of Participant Programs. Kinds of Programs.
    Selection of Personnel. Achievements. Policy Suggestions.

9. *The University and Technical Assistance Abroad* 153
    Origin of the Programs. Some Examples of Projects.
    Activities.

10. *Sponsors and Advantages of Technical Assistance Abroad* . . 173
    Foundation and Government Programs. Program Advantages.

11. *Formation of Technical Assistance Programs Abroad* . . . 197
    Participating Organizations and Their Role as Originators.
    Identification of Responders. Decision-making. Need for
    Continuous Planning and Assessment.

12. *Selecting the Technical Assistance Team* 223
    Qualities Related to Job Success. Qualities Obtained in
    Personnel. Improvement of the Quality of Personnel.

13. *Achievements of University Technical Assistance Abroad* . . 246
    Accomplishments in the Host Country. Objectives and
    Accomplishments in the United States.

14. *Long-term Goals in Technical Assistance Abroad* 267
    Importance. The Future of University Technical Assistance
    Abroad Programs.

15. *An Agenda for American Universities* 288
    Basis for Participation in Programs. Alternative International
    Involvements.

16. *An Agenda for Foundations and Governments* 314
    Host-country Institutions and Governments. American
    Foundations. The United States Government.

    Appendix: Definitions, Research Model, and Procedures . . 337
    Definitions. Research Model. Research Procedures.

    A Bibliographical Note 348

    Index 355

Chapter 1

DIMENSIONS OF THE PROBLEM

The American sense of mission has been much altered in the last hundred years. Time has had its way, for example, with perhaps the best expression of the dedication of the 1860s—Abraham Lincoln's address at Gettysburg. To Lincoln's hearers the founding "on this continent" of "a new nation" implied that the goal was to be sought within our land—an assumption later vulgarized as isolation. Yet, since the 1860s, real distances between continents have become less than distances within the nation when Lincoln spoke. A "new nation" implied a new beginning for mankind in our practice and example. But now there are many newer nations "conceived in liberty," and some newer beginnings in ideas and institutions.

Propinquity with other peoples has vividly revealed the rich variety of physical resources, human cultures, and institutions. Truths we hold to be self-evident are not breathed in with the air of every cultural climate. Do we try to help others conquer disease, malnutrition, and poverty by methods tested at home? We discover that techniques do not live alone; they spring from a historically determined cultural soil. Isolated transplants often wither and die. Or single exports may engender unexpected trouble, like European rabbits in Australia, or malaria control decreasing the death rate in a country which cannot feed its existing population and cannot curb its increase. We discover that if we are to help others, we must first learn; and indeed the educational process is one of joint discovery.

Nor is learning on our part necessary only in order to help others. We need a continuing reappraisal of our own civilization for our own benefit. We can learn from others—as we have in the past—so that we ourselves can refine and improve upon the American culture. We must avoid the rebirth in the late twentieth cen-

1

tury of a modified idea of the "white man's burden." Our mission
is very much one of improvement and development at home, not
purely political, as many in the 1860s would have had it, but social
and economic as well.

Cross-fertilization of cultural traits is often desirable. Of two
biological strains, each may be strong in qualities weaker in the
other. But if crossing is not to be barren—or to result in monstrosi-
ties—careful analysis and experiment must precede it. No sensible
person would wish to achieve "one world" at the cost of sacrificing
fertile variety. Yet if fertile variety is to be achieved, innovation
and education must be the order of the day.

The Roles of Educational Institutions

The innovators and educators; the originators, modifiers, and
transmitters of idea systems; the researchers and teachers; these
are characteristically found in or about educational institutions.
In so far as cultures condition folkways, the role of centers of
learning is pivotal—as contributors to or distributors of cultural
forms and directions. The academic estate has for centuries engaged more than most other elements of society in international
communication of scholarship and ideas. It would be strange indeed if the colleges and universities had not been enlisted to play
and did not themselves seek a leading role in adjusting the American sense of mission to the needs of a world become so small that
its peoples must live together, if they live at all, peaceably and
with mutual cooperation.

International interest in institutions of higher learning in the
United States has expanded rapidly in the past fifteen years. Although isolation never influenced the intellectual realm as much as
the political, American professors have in the past looked inward
more than they would like to admit. There are still teachers and
students, not to speak of university administrators and governing
boards, who regard their own institutions as independent and
nearly self-contained entities which can let the rest of the world
go by. Yet, in the words of Howard E. Wilson:

Since the beginning of the twentieth century American colleges and
universities have been increasingly influenced by world affairs and by
the rising importance of foreign policy and international relations for the
United States. ... Hardly an aspect of academic life has escaped the

influence of world events and movements. And the changes which have occurred or are now in process seem certain to be followed by additional influences and adjustments through the indefinite future.[1]

American universities responded to world events by increased emphasis on world affairs education, technical assistance, and international aspects of research. At first, activities at home were stressed. To further world affairs education (or international education or the international dimension of education as it is sometimes called), a great increase in the number of curricula and courses in international law, organization, and relations has taken place, and increased, also, have been area studies and comparative or cross-cultural curricula. There has been a trend toward making at least one cross-cultural course compulsory at the undergraduate level. The Committee on the University and World Affairs called for even greater efforts in the latter direction: "A first-class liberal education in the second half of the twentieth century should unquestionably include an effective international component.... During their undergraduate years, all students should get at least an introductory acquaintance with some culture other than their own." [2] Supplementing the lectures and discussions of new courses have been the augmented holdings of even relatively small college libraries. New journals and newspapers from abroad and new books to support efforts at international or world affairs education have greatly enhanced a student's opportuniy to get to know some culture other than his own.

Nor has world affairs education stopped at the campus boundaries. Adult activities in international affairs have been developed across the nation. Be it an extension course for no credit, a night school course, a conference, a public lecture, or the assisting of a World Affairs Council or Great Decisions series, universities and university personnel have been active and in the forefront.

With the development of the Point Four idea from 1949 on,

---

[1] Howard E. Wilson (ed.), Preface to Cyril O. Houle and Charles A. Nelson, *The University, the Citizen, and World Affairs* (Washington: American Council on Education, 1956), p. xi. This is one of eight volumes of a series under the auspices of the American Council on Education and affiliated organizations with financial support from the Carnegie Endowment for International Peace.

[2] *The University and World Affairs* (New York: The Ford Foundation, 1960), p. 17.

private groups as well as government and multilateral agencies became increasingly conscious of their responsibilities in international technical assistance. The less developed countries of the world represented a new challenge to the conscience of mankind, an emerging field for significant social action. American universities were commonly the recipients of requests for help and also on occasion the initiators of ideas for assistance. Despite the widespread involvement of universities and university personnel in technical assistance, fewer institutions and individuals have participated in this aspect of international activities than in the other major aspects.

As fields of knowledge related to international or cross-cultural subjects have become more important or more emphasized, scholars have carried out increased research and study on international themes abroad as well as in the United States. Outside financial help from foundations and government agencies has played an important role, but the resources of the universities themselves have also helped supplement those of the scholars.

All three areas of world affairs impact on American universities have raised a single, major problem: are all kinds of adapting and growing in the international field consistent with the desirable aims and objectives of universities and colleges? [3] Are there conflicts of interests reflecting different goals? Some persons have seen the significance of activity in the three areas as stemming from considerations of foreign policy and world peace. Others have seen the basis for action in the fundamental nature of higher education: the search for knowledge and the strength of American universities. As we shall see in later chapters, these approaches are not always complementary, and may lead to outright policy conflict.

This book does not attempt to describe all the international aspects of American higher education. It has to do rather with activities which cross national boundaries, involving either American students and professors abroad or students and professors from abroad on American campuses. In 1960–61, 53,107 foreign students from 143 countries and political areas were enrolled at 1,666 institutions of higher learning in the United States. Over 15,300 American students were attending foreign universities. More than

[3] The issue is not the ability of an American university "to adapt and grow" *per se,* as the Committee on the University and World Affairs suggested (*ibid.,* p. 1).

3,600 members of foreign faculties were affiliated with 304 American colleges and universities, and over 2,200 members of American faculties were teaching abroad.[4] There are about 2,000 institutions of higher learning in the United States.

Much international exchange of personnel has grown up over the years through individual initiative or activities of small groups. About 30 per cent of the foreign students in the United States in 1960–61 financed themselves.[5] It has long been the custom for a few American college students who could afford it to spend a year or so abroad. Professors have frequently gone abroad on their own resources.

In the past fifteen years, the resources governments and private groups have allocated to the international exchange of students and professors have greatly enlarged. Usually these agencies have developed their own programs, separate from the universities. The United States government has sponsored educational exchange programs under the Fulbright and Smith-Mundt Acts and allied legislation. Technical assistance under the International Cooperation Administration has resulted in a sharp increase in international educational exchange. Great philanthropic foundations have made many grants and have more and more taken initiative in international educational activities. Even small private organizations such as service clubs or professional organizations have sponsored exchanges.

International Exchange Programs of American Universities

Recently, more exchange programs conducted by universities themselves have been initiated. In 1957–58 there were 382 such programs at 184 American institutions. The international exchange programs involve the planned participation in and responsibility for university international exchange by one or more educational units at an American university. It is on these programs that the present study has centered. They represent only one aspect of the activity of higher education in the international sphere and only one part of the total international exchange of university personnel. Yet they have been increasing in number and account for seven or

[4] *Open Doors 1961* (New York: Institute of International Education, 1961), pp. 6, 12, 16, and 17.

[5] *Ibid.*, p. 11.

more thousands of students and faculty members going abroad or coming to the United States each year. The 184 institutions constitute a small proportion of the total of 1,957 in the country as a whole, and 7,000 persons are a mere fraction of the 4 million students and faculty members in the United States. Less than 10 per cent of the institutions participated in these programs and less than one-fifth of 1 per cent of the students. Clearly there is room for growth, and growth is in prospect. University exchange has been growing the world around, and American universities have been participating in its development to a greater extent than institutions from most university systems.

The growth of international programs at American universities has taken place at a wide variety of institutions. Sixty per cent of the larger universities, those with 8,000 or more students, participate in international programs, and nearly all institutions with three or more programs are to be found in this group. Twenty-nine per cent of medium-sized universities and less than 5 per cent of universities with less than 2,000 students have programs. From 15 to 17 per cent of state or private universities, only about 6 per cent of the religious institutions, and virtually none of the city or district colleges participate in international programs. A majority of the land-grant colleges have programs. There is a regular progression between the complexity of an institution and the range of curricula it offers at home on the one hand and the frequency of participation in international exchange programs on the other. Programs are conducted by 1 per cent of the junior colleges, 5 per cent of the four-year colleges, 11 per cent of those offering a master's or second professional degree, and 40 per cent of those offering a doctor of philosophy or the equivalent. Similarly, programs are conducted by 1 per cent of the colleges with terminal and occupational programs only, 5 to 7 per cent of the liberal arts, teacher preparatory, and professional institutions, 11 per cent of the universities with liberal arts and one or two professional schools, and 40 per cent of the universities with liberal arts and three or more professional schools.

The concentration of programs at some of the larger, more complex universities has resulted in many of them having several projects apiece. In 1957–58 there were 17 institutions, each of which had five or more international programs, as indicated in Table 1. The proportion of subunits within a university participating in a program ranges from institution-wide involvement to involvement of only a single department or other educational subunit. The former pattern can be found at a few liberal arts colleges in student-abroad programs, the latter at some of the larger universities in research or technical assistance exchanges.

Table 1. American Universities Having Five or More
Programs Apiece, 1957–58

University		Number of programs
Harvard		18
Cornell		11
New York		10
California, Berkeley		
Indiana		
University of Miami		
Michigan State		
Northwestern	(8)	56 (7 each)
Stanford		
Wayne State		
Wisconsin		
Chicago	(2)	12 (6 each)
Syracuse		
Florida		
Michigan	(4)	20 (5 each)
Puerto Rico		
Tennessee		
Total		127

Source: Inventory, p. 15.

Six major types of university programs are to be found. (1) The American student-abroad programs principally involve world affairs education, higher education objectives, American students going abroad for study, and either large or small numbers of students, depending upon the particular program. (2) Technical assistance abroad programs principally involve help to others, both foreign policy and higher education objectives, American faculty members going abroad for teaching and consultation, and sizable expenditures of money. (3) Technical assistance in the United States includes help to others and world affairs education, foreign policy and higher education objectives, host-country nationals coming to the United States for study, and normally moderate numbers of participants.

Turning from the sizable programs to those occurring frequently but involving fewer exchanges and fewer dollars, two additional types of programs are found. (4) Religious programs are characterized by help to others, religious or proselytizing objectives, and one or a few students or recent students from the United States going abroad to engage in some kind of teaching such as English language instruction as well as the direct or indirect teaching of Christianity. Such programs were at one time much more frequent than they are now. (5) Small one- or two-way exchanges of students and/or staff members between American and host-country institutions are numerous, involve one or at most a few exchangees for study or teaching, with educational objectives, especially international education, paramount.

(6) The sixth program is quite expensive but is no less common than participant and religious programs. Research abroad is usually designed to add to the store of knowledge, with educational objectives predominating, and with American professors going abroad for research in small numbers. Some programs combine two or more of the six major program types.

In addition there are a number of special programs falling outside this sixfold typology, a few of them rather unique in their characteristics. One type consists of the few independent nonpersonnel exchanges. However, generally speaking, nonpersonnel exchange is largely a small and supplementary part of exchange of persons programs. In some instances this type of exchange has provided the basis for a program by itself. Such programs are usually on a very modest, almost insignificant level, although the more active of them provide a steady stream back and forth of books, films, student newspapers, and other educational materials. In 1959, the United States Information Agency listed some 32 university-to-university affiliations largely of this character that it had helped develop.[6] This compares with some 18 identified in 1957–58, apparently reflecting a substantial growth.

Of the six major types of university programs frequently encountered, three are primarily oriented toward the export of knowledge: the two technical assistance programs and the religious pro-

[6] United States Information Agency, "The College and University Affiliation Program" (Washington, 1959, leaflet).

grams. Three have the importation of knowledge as a central objective: the sizable United States student-abroad programs, the research project abroad, and the small one- or two-way student or professor exchanges. Of the 382 programs identified in 1957–58, 136 were of a technical assistance nature (see Table 2). Eighty-four of these provided both for United States staff abroad and host-country students to the United States, 27 others provided only for United States staff abroad, and 23 more provided only for participants (students or staff from abroad coming to study in the United States under a technical assistance program). Equipment or materials provision played a contributing role in some 65 cases and in two others formed the basis for the program. Many combinations of major operations are characteristic of the technical assistance programs.

Of the 246 programs not involving technical assistance, 97 were of the United States student-abroad type and 35 others were of a

Table 2. Frequency Count of Programs by
Major Type of Operation

Major type of operation in program	Number of programs	Total
Technical assistance programs:		
U.S. staff abroad, participants to U.S., equipment provision	55	
U.S. staff abroad, participants to U.S.	29	
U.S. staff abroad, equipment provision	10	
U.S. staff abroad	17	
Participants to U.S.	23	
Equipment-materials provision	2	
Subtotal		136
Programs not involving technical assistance:		
U.S. students abroad	97	
Student mutual exchange	35 *	
Host-country students to U.S.	36	
U.S. staff abroad (teaching)	10	
Staff mutual exchange	15 * (21)	
Host-country staff to U.S.	10	
U.S. staff abroad (research)	25	
Academic materials mutual exchange	18	
Subtotal		246
Total		382

* In some six programs, both student and staff mutual exchange is to be found. These programs have been counted only with student mutual exchange here.

student mutual exchange variety. Almost all the latter and a small proportion of the former were small programs, involving only one or two students. Most of the former involved substantial groups of students, some including over 100. Also primarily of a small character, involving one or two students or staff members either way, were the host-country students to the United States, United States staff abroad (teaching), staff mutual exchange, and host-country staff to the United States. An exception occurred in some programs providing for United States faculty members teaching abroad at branches established by certain American universities; these sometimes included quite a number of staff members. While United States faculty members were carrying on research under the auspices of 63 different programs, in only 25 of these projects was research for nontechnical assistance purposes the major operation.

Need for Appraisal

We ought not to be satisfied with the fact that numerous plans are in effect and more are likely to follow. How well do these plans serve their purposes? How appropriate have been the policies adopted, how effective the execution of the programs? What has been their impact abroad and at home?

In the complex interaction of governmental and private sponsors, of widely varying university practices, of foreign and American customs, what are the most fruitful types of relationships?

In particular, what are the effects on American higher education of these already formidable and expanding obligations? How can the universities fulfill their international undertakings and at the same time perform their unique functions at home? The American sense of mission is not confined to goals within the nation, but without excellence in their principal domestic commitments the American university cannot participate effectively abroad.

This survey was carried out to examine such questions. Its results are here organized according to the following plan.

First to be examined are the wide differences among nations in educational aims and practices, which must be taken into account in any effort at international cooperation in education.

Then follow chapters which assess the programs in which American students are regularly sent abroad, possible alternatives to existing programs, and recommendations of policy governing such activities.

Brief attention is given to three kinds of programs less frequently found or less expensive—religious, research, and small exchanges. University participation in the two major types of technical assistance programs is then discussed.

Finally, the report suggests an agenda for international activities by universities, and related agendas for governments and foundations.

Chapter 2

THE EDUCATIONAL STRUCTURES OF DIFFERENT COUNTRIES

The international exchange programs of American universities encounter systems of education which differ widely from their own. Each country has its own pattern, in some degree unlike that of others, although certain broad types of higher education may be identified. The countries of Continental Europe have universities with many similar features. Another group is composed of the universities in countries especially influenced by the United Kingdom. American institutions have a number of features that are unique, despite some similarities with universities in other English-speaking countries. Whether personnel and material go abroad from American universities or come from abroad, many problems arise from the differences in educational patterns. Are differences to be utilized to benefit the exchanges, or do they lead to frustration? Is national uniformity to be maintained, or are innovations and contrasts prized? The spirit of successful university international exchange programs surely must be one of pluralism, not of obeisance to any single form of university. Yet pluralism involves knotty problems.

National Patterns of Secondary Education

One of the factors that most limits undergraduate student exchange and severely restricts the nature of the existing programs is the variation in secondary schooling among countries. A first-year university student in the United States has not had a background similar to that of his counterpart in Mexico, England, France, India, or Japan. To consider university systems and their

12

participation in student exchange one must begin with the secondary education that helps determine their very nature.

In the United States, elementary and secondary education tend to be on a 6-3-3, 6-6, or 8-4 basis. The four to six years of secondary education in the United States are fewer than in Europe; typically, the French lycée, the English grammar school, and the German gymnasium have seven or eight. In much of the rest of the world, however, the number of years of secondary education is about the same or even less than in the United States. Perhaps more significant, there are great variations even within countries in the total number of years of schooling required before entering higher education.

Most countries may be included in a range of from ten to fourteen years of elementary and secondary education, several European countries having the longer, and many of the less developed countries having the shorter, periods. The United States, with twelve, falls in the middle. Despite the median position of this country in the number of years of prehigher education, undergraduate students in the United States tend to be a year or two younger than comparable students abroad. Graduation from secondary schools abroad usually occurs at a later age than in the United States. In most countries there is more interruption in a student's education than is common in this country. In European secondary education, at least, it is not uncommon to force a student to repeat a year or more of work. The difference in age of beginning university students and in the number of years of their prehigher education has had a noticeable impact on student-abroad programs at the undergraduate levels. In Europe, American undergraduates are typically younger and may have fewer years of education behind them than their European classmates.

In most foreign countries secondary education is divided among sections or programs. One set of secondary schools offers an academic program leading to entrance into a university. There are often, besides the academic schools, several separate series of institutions offering work in fine arts, commercial, agricultural, or technical subjects. Some of these lead to special postsecondary training; the work of others is terminal. These schools are designed for the masses of students who will not go to a university. In countries with systems such as this, a major decision is made at the time a student completes his elementary education: can and should he attend a university? A child's future may thus be determined by the time he is ten, eleven, or twelve years of age. In several systems of education transfer is difficult. Once a decision has been made and a particular kind of secondary education embarked upon, there is only limited opportunity to alter the choice.

The American high school, in contrast, is primarily a single institution, although it may offer various courses of study. Many American high schools permit a student to alter his interests within wide limits. There is no fixed cut-off date after which a student cannot take a college preparatory course. The philosophy underlying the American high school is that children of all possible backgrounds should be brought together and given a broad education. Girls and boys attend the same school. Specialization should be limited, and courses in common should be numerous. Such a system should contribute to the melting pot idea, and give children with fewer advantages at home ample opportunity to demonstrate their real potential throughout the secondary school experience. Many promising university students may be among them. Special institutions such as vocational high schools should be few in number.

In many countries, a progressive identification of a small elite, the members of which are destined to be the few university-educated persons in the society, begins with secondary education. In the less developed countries relatively small proportions of the children of secondary school age go to school at all. The number of secondary schools is exceedingly limited. Only the children of wealthier parents, of parents who themselves went to universities, tend to receive a secondary education in such countries. Even in Western Europe, the existence of several kinds of institutions for secondary education and the fact that a child's future is decided when he is ten to twelve years of age limit access to postsecondary education to the few.

The secondary education designed for those who intend to go to universities abroad is, as a rule, highly traditional and classical in orientation. In the more developed countries secondary school graduates have had intensive work in grammar, composition, classical and modern languages, art and music, philosophy, history, mathematics, and the biological and physical sciences. The proportions of each of these subjects to the whole will vary according to the "classical" or "modern" curricula which are often offered as options. The standards maintained are exceedingly high, and students are regularly dropped out. Discipline is strict, and the students are given substantial assignments for homework. In the less developed countries, the standards of preuniversity secondary education often leave much to be desired, but the basic pattern is the same.

The American high school is more permissive and its subject matter is greatly different from that in traditional European schools. Since it seeks to give all students the benefit of a single, generalized type of secondary education, its standards are less severe. The American courses in driver education, homemaking for boys, and social dancing would not be found at a lycée or grammar school abroad. Nor would much of the instrumental music. The work is somewhat less intensive and less classical in the United States. It lays much greater stress on developing the child socially as well as intellectually. To this end, advising and counseling services are available and extracurricular activities are emphasized.

In countries where a good European-type secondary school system is to be found, students come to a university with a well-rounded background in the fundamental disciplines. They are thought ready to specialize, having completed their general education in the secondary schools. The Continental European type of education has been copied in part by many of the newly developing areas of the world. However, children normally do not receive an adequate grounding even in the fundamental disciplines in these countries, and the universities do not make up for the deficiency, since they proceed under the assumptions of the Continental institutions.

In the United States, children are not assumed to have received a complete general education in the high schools, and increasingly in recent years there have been efforts at substantial general education in college during the freshman and sophomore years, even in technical curricula. Specialization, under the American system, is supposed to be minimal before the junior and senior years. General education courses are offered in the natural and physical sciences, the social sciences, and the humanities—sometimes as a recommended set of courses, sometimes as a compulsory set. Recently, some institutions have introduced courses on non-Western civilizations as part of their offerings at the general education level.

General education has come to take up as much as a full year of academic work and offers opportunities to universities and students for study abroad for general rather than specialized purposes. Increasingly, a four-year liberal arts program postpones vocational or professional specialization until the bachelor's degree has been obtained.

Some of the less developed countries of the world have adopted general education as practiced at American universities. What formerly was meaningless specialization in some less developed countries can be put in a broader context by general education at the university level, and the students can be better prepared for specialization as well. General education can give students a common educational background and can help prepare them for useful roles as citizens. In Indonesia, for example, the former Dutch university system turned out a few well-trained specialists, but currently the objective is to turn out more broadly educated individuals in larger numbers (Smith, pp. 33–37).

Secondary school systems of several countries not only give the students a basic preparation for higher education, but serve as routes of entry as well. In the United States a large proportion of young adults of college age seek admission. Most universities accept as one of their major purposes a broad undergraduate education for as many students as possible. Quality standards are not absent, but the emphasis is on a system that will permit the acquisition of university education by masses of students. The millions of university graduates in the United States do not constitute in any strict sense an elite; they neither function as an elite nor have its status. University education is valued more for its utility than for its status attributes.

Abroad, entry into all postsecondary education is traditionally highly restricted, more so in some countries than others, but generally much more so than in the United States. Universities abroad are distinguished from other postsecondary institutions such as special schools or institutes, and access to the former is particularly limited. Preparation for the university requires years of rigorous effort as well as survival in the selective process. The university accepts no responsibility for graduating as many students as possible. Those that drop out are assumed to be incapable of university education or to be following their own desires. There is a tendency for the graduates of the universities to become an identifiable elite, with appropriate roles and status. In Europe the percentage of the population with university degrees is small by American standards, and it is exceedingly small in many of the less developed countries.

The existence of an educated elite tends to perpetuate the exclusiveness that it enjoys. This, in turn, has affected some American university international exchange programs. Technical assistance projects that aim at a marked increase in the number of university-educated persons encounter strong opposition arising from local cultural values. Another effect of the elite education system is to be found in the case of programs under which American students go abroad. Here, superior students may be identified and university resources concentrated on them. If a cross section of American students are sent to a European country with its highly developed and specialized university system, they will encounter European students who on the average are a year or two older than they, have more extensive academic backgrounds from their secondary education, and are also probably more capable, given their highly selective character and restricted numbers. This is not to condemn American students, but to indicate that American higher education serves different purposes than does higher education in most other countries. It follows that exchange may be difficult because the background of students and the purposes of the university system are so different.

Various countries abroad are coming to embrace the more democratic educational objectives at the university level that characterize American higher education. This fact was illustrated by an Oxford University professor who lamented, "The universities in Egypt and India have really deteriorated since we (British) had much to do with them. The trouble is that they have gone in for mass education. Good standards are impossible to maintain if you let everyone into the universities." India has indeed proceeded along a path of expanding its universities, their offerings, and the number of students in various fields of study. Actually, there is a high correlation between those countries with active national development plans and those countries seeking to expand their universities and the number of graduates from them. Countries that have been active in this respect are among the most frequent users of the university technical assistance contract offered by the United States.

National Patterns of Higher Education

A second factor that affects university international exchange programs is the variation in patterns of higher education within the United States and from country to country. In the case of American universities, this variation has stimulated a number of technical assistance programs and discouraged many efforts for other kinds of exchanges.

The American system is characterized by many large and small institutions with overlapping functions. The directory of higher education of the United States Office of Education listed 1,957 institutions in 1958.[1] The American Council on Education listed 969 accredited universities and colleges in 1956.[2] The institutions included in these directories range from the large, complex undergraduate-professional-graduate universities, through the more modest sized liberal arts colleges, junior colleges, teachers colleges, and a variety of professional and technical schools. Classification is difficult because functions overlap and fuse. The largest universities encompass work similar to that found in any of the other types of institutions. Terminal freshman and sophomore work, four-year liberal arts programs, teacher education, and other vocational and professional specialization are all to be found in at least some graduate universities. Specialized institutions exist, but their offerings are for the most part similar to one part of the offerings of large institutions. Entrance requirements are likewise similar or overlapping, there being institutions with higher and lower requirements in each category. For the student, transfer from one institution to another or from one specialization to another is rather easily arranged, assuming a satisfactory academic record. This overlapping, flexible, decentralized system reflects the pluralism of the 50 states. It reflects a democratic, experimental spirit on the part of public and private education alike. Universities, like high schools, are melting pots, providing maximum opportunities for the student to find the most appropriate outlet for his special talents by keeping alternative courses of action open to him as long as possible.

[1] *Education Directory 1958–1959, Part 3, Higher Education* (Washington: Government Printing Office, 1959), p. 8.
[2] Mary Irwin (ed.), *American Universities and Colleges* (Washington: American Council on Education, 1956), p. ix.

Abroad, the term "university" is usually used in a restricted sense, to indicate those institutions offering education mainly in the liberal arts and such traditional professional fields as medicine, law, theology, and pharmacy. Most of the applied studies are offered by specialized institutions for agriculture, engineering, public administration, or teacher education. Thus, in England there are sharp distinctions between a university and a technological college, and the same situation exists in present or former British colonies in Africa. In Indonesia, traditionally the universities did not include teacher training. In Peru, agriculture has been taught separately. Occasionally, some of the applied or vocational-professional fields are attached to a university as a part of a special institute, but without the status of a regular faculty. Distinct entrance requirements are normally the rule for special institutions. For example, in France the universities require graduation from an approved specialized secondary school, or a *baccalauréat*. The *grandes écoles* in such fields as engineering and agriculture recruit students by competitive examinations which require two years of preparation beyond the *baccalauréat*. Some of the specialized institutions have higher, some lower, entrance requirements. It is not easy to transfer from one specialized institution to another. The degrees or diplomas offered by the more specialized institutions usually differ from the degrees awarded by faculties of the universities.

American practices in higher education, to be sure, are not entirely different from those of other countries. A number of foreign systems lean in the same direction as the American in comprehensiveness of offerings.[3] For example, the University of Indonesia includes faculties of technology, veterinary medicine, agriculture, and other technological specialties. Tokyo University includes faculties of engineering, agriculture, and education. The National Autonomous University of Mexico, while confining its faculties to science, law, and philosophy and letters, includes some 12 national schools in such fields as business administration, engineering, medicine, veterinary medicine, economics, and plastic arts. Indian universities have in particular followed a path similar to that pursued

[3] For information on universities in other countries see H. M. R. Keyes (ed.), *International Handbook of Universities* (Paris: International Association of Universities, 1959), and J. F. Foster (ed.), *Commonwealth Universities Yearbook* (London: Association of Universities of the British Commonwealth, 1959).

in the United States. The University of Delhi, for example, includes faculty members in such fields as agriculture, various branches of engineering, commerce, education, home science, library science, nursing, and social work.

Some members of faculties in European institutions of higher education look down upon American universities because the latter regularly offer so many vocational-professional curricula. These faculty members are disturbed by mutual exchange because they believe that it will involve dealing with persons who specialize in fields inferior in intellectual content. Yet persons in the host country who seek higher status for vocational and technical studies at their institutions and within their countries have often welcomed the exchange. To send to Europe qualified American faculty members in the vocational-professional fields might help to raise the status of some of these fields.

In the less developed countries, changes in the nature of the institutions of higher education may serve national development. If there is need for eliminating illiteracy, raising agricultural production, and accelerating industrialization, for example, progress may depend on encouraging more able young people to go into education, agriculture, engineering, and business administration. At present, such occupations do not command high prestige. If the university, with its distinction, gives recognition and status to students and professors in such fields equal to that in natural science and the humanities, more able people may be attracted to teaching and the applied sciences.

Among the countries surveyed in the present study, India presents a pattern that is unique. Indian universities have regular departments or constituent colleges, but much of the teaching is carried on by affiliated colleges. These are separate colleges that affiliate with the university in whose jurisdiction they fall. They must accept university supervision in matters such as the adequacy of finance, staff, physical plant, libraries, and laboratories. While some universities do not have affiliates, others are almost entirely affiliating bodies.

In territories under British influence, the University of London has established a system known as colleges in special relation. Under this system, a university college in special relation accepts substantial supervision by the University of London over its curricula, examinations, staff, finance, and physical plant. Six university colleges have been established overseas. In 1959, five still retained the status; they were in Rhodesia and Nyasaland, Uganda, Nigeria, Ghana, and the West Indies.

Universities in several European countries have accepted special responsibilities in assisting establishment of universities in colonial territory, such as the Catholic University of Louvain in connection with Lovanium University of Leopoldville in what was the Belgian Congo, or the Universities of Bordeaux and Paris in connection with the predecessors of the University of Dakar. Some of these arrangements are similar to the technical assistance contracts of American universities, although the objective is to create a new university more or less in the image of the European university concerned, while American universities work primarily with already established universities having traditions widely different from those in the United States.

The number of universities in a country and their relative size and prestige are important characteristics of a system of higher education. Small countries may have only one graduate university, if any, while large countries will normally have many. In Peru there are five universities and two specialized institutions; Mexico has some 26 universities and four technological institutes. The three institutions in Ethiopia, including the University College of Addis Ababa and the Imperial Ethiopian College of Agriculture and Mechanical Arts at Harrar, may be contrasted with the nearly 300 universities and nearly 200 junior colleges and teacher training institutions of Japan. Universities are rapidly increasing in number in Asia and Africa. The role a university fulfills varies with the size, number, and variety of the institutions of higher education. In some cases, an entire country may depend for its university graduates on a handful of institutions. Even in countries with several graduate universities, their relative prestige and standing may be such that one of them predominates. Thus, in Peru the National University of San Marcos is central, in Bolivia the University of San Andres. Even in large university systems, one institution may play a central role, as do Tokyo University and the University of Paris.

Such patterns are related to the problem of introducing innovations in university practices. The larger and more diverse a system of higher education, the easier it is to introduce innovations in at least one institution. The greater the prestige of an institution, the less amenable it may be to innovation, at least from the outside. However, changes introduced in a relatively low-prestige institution within a large, complex system of higher education may not have much importance for higher education as a whole, whereas changes in institutions that tend to predominate within their respective systems may have broad influence. It is relatively easy to introduce innovations in medical education in all of Indonesia, beginning with the University of Indonesia, which is predominant in a new and relatively small but expanding system of higher education. It is difficult to obtain similar nationwide changes in agricultural higher education in India, where there are many programs in agriculture at many institutions. Likewise, in the United States, action by many universities is required before any innovation becomes a national trend.

The difference in the number and variety of institutions of higher education in the United States and other countries commonly leads to specialized programs of technical assistance. Yet it also sometimes hinders exchange arrangements because comparable institutions with similar or complementary needs may not be found. Differences can be fruitful, however. It may be desirable for girls from a small private liberal arts college in a small American town to spend a year in close association with the University of Paris just because the academic experience is so different from that at home. Few who do so can expect to progress toward their degrees on schedule, however, unless special administrative arrangements are made by the American college.

Internal Organization of Universities

The differences in the national patterns of higher education are accompanied by many differences in internal organization of individual institutions. The fact that no two universities operate identically must be taken into account in making exchange arrangements.

American professors who go abroad are surprised by the lack of university planning and services (see Smith, pp. 32–37). There are relatively few university services to be found in Latin American institutions, and in most university systems falling within the Continental European tradition. The temporary or even the permanent rector or dean and his secretary and assistant are a far cry from the complicated central administrative organizations found at American institutions.   Compared to their American counterparts, universities in many countries can hardly be said to exist as organizational and administrative entities.

Central campuses do not exist in much of the world.   Instead, one faculty is located in one part of town, a second faculty in a second part, and so on.   There is little occasion for the professors of the different faculties to get together.   Even the deans may see each other relatively seldom.   Central campuses are not by any means nonexistent abroad, and some very handsome ones are being built. Japan, Korea, India, Lebanon, and Mexico are countries in which fine campuses are to be found, and there are many others.   They are in the minority, however.

The lack of university physical unity is symbolic of the lack of central services.   Large central university libraries, so much a part of the American university, are lacking in many instances, or are in such a condition that it is difficult to use them.   When different faculties are widely separated physically, the utility of a central, main facility such as a library is lessened.   Whether on a university or faculty basis, libraries have been exceedingly poorly developed in Latin America, Africa, and Asia.   The always helpful reference librarian, the well-appointed reading and study rooms, the useful cataloguing devices may be missing, even in Europe.

Central health services for the students also are not found at many universities abroad.   That much maligned aspect of the American university, the business office, has few peers abroad in terms of the many services it performs, and the efficiency with which it performs them.   The entire system of university registration and record keeping, often carried on in the United States by automatic data-processing methods, is seldom approached overseas.   Nor is the lack of data-processing equipment the reason.   Record keeping is probably less important in a university system that places almost complete reliance on a final examination in awarding a degree.   In the American system, of course, credits and grades offer a record-keeper's paradise.   Abroad, the inability of some universities to determine accurately the number of students in residence, the length of residence of graduating students, and other elementary facts about the institution contrasts markedly with the extensive records kept in American universities.

In much of the rest of the world universities are regarded as institutions for largely specialized study. Consequently, they lack what to an American institution would be a requisite amount of academic unity. Each faculty tends to be a law unto itself. There are no minimum central curricular requirements. Curricular planning even within faculties is much rarer than in the United States. When every professor controls the work within his own field, it is difficult to obtain adaptation of courses in different fields to the needs of various curricula or groups of students. It is assumed that university education is by nature advanced study, a professionalizing process. Students are introduced to great minds and are expected to study the subjects that have been and are of interest to themselves. They are not "burdened" with general education requirements. Survey courses are unthinkable; students are expected to develop any survey information on their own. From an intellectual point of view, a detailed examination of some narrow aspect of a topic gives a student an insight in depth that he would otherwise miss, and that may be one of the most valuable aspects of his university education.

From the foreign university point of view, American universities are overcentralized. The centralization is related to the assumption common to American higher education that there is need for general education of university students, not merely a desire for university-wide services. In pursuit of this end, central minimum requirements are laid down. Each college and department may have its additional requirements. Work in a major field or subfield is commonly introduced by a general survey course. Specialization is progressively greater as a student goes along, but even as seniors and graduates, students are given opportunity to relate their specialties to knowledge as a whole and to the problems of society.

It is not necessary to choose between these conflicting schools of thought in order to identify some of the difficulties they present to international university exchange. Whether the American purpose in sending students or teachers abroad is related to study, teaching, research, or consultation, the visitor may encounter a system of higher education that is aimed at a different kind of learning. For the American student abroad, it is difficult to meet American university graduation requirements by taking narrowly specialized courses even if he can adjust to the other differences in the host-country university. The American faculty member teaching abroad may have to adjust the content of his courses radically. Those in a consultative capacity may have to examine critically any advice they might give relative to innovations in the university system abroad, since the system is based on so different a plan of education. Host-country nationals coming to a United States university encounter similar problems.

Another contrast in educational philosophy and practice exists between the more vocational approach of American higher education and the more classical, theoretical approach of higher education in much of the world. Even in the United States there is disagreement about the desirable degree of direct relationship between the content of higher education and particular lines of work in society. Some of the universities in the United States represent one extreme, some of the universities in Continental Europe another. The American system usually focuses on general and liberal education with an accompanying emphasis on vocational applicability of knowledge. The Continental systems tend to focus on specialized education with an emphasis on theory. The European arguments in favor of classical education largely center around the development of the reasoning capacities of students, the furthering of their ability to think, and the more limited function of universities. An educated man is one who has a background of theoretical knowledge and can reason effectively from general principles to whatever specific situations he may encounter. If more applied knowledge is necessary for a particular line of work than is available in any of the traditional faculties, it can be obtained through in-service training or separate special schools.

The American emphasis includes a measure of the classical approach but usually aims at practical targets. Among the forms of knowledge with which a university should concern itself, most American faculties believe, is socially useful knowledge. In-service training will always be necessary, but there is little reason for special schools if the universities perform their proper function. Applied knowledge can give a student an opportunity to develop his capacity for independent critical thinking just as well as can knowledge for knowledge's sake. Universities have a social obligation to produce a variety of qualified, educated persons for many different callings in society.

Both American students or faculty members going abroad and foreign students or professors coming to the United States must adjust in varying degrees to the differing emphases in higher education. American technical assistance programs are often concerned with proposed innovations in a host-country university that would move it in a more vocational direction.

Relations with Governments

In some countries all universities are public, and in others the most renowned universities are private. Whether under private or public control, in some countries universities are closely regulated by governmental agencies as to the students they may admit, courses they may teach, degrees they may grant, professors they may hire, and curricula they may offer. Even the university calendars are closely prescribed by outside authorities in a few instances. In other countries, all these matters are left for university authorities to decide. There are varying degrees of financial control or assistance. The structure through which universities are related to government may range from direct parliamentary control to the establishment of quasi-independent university grants commissions or boards of trustees.

The newly independent nations of Asia and the emerging nations of Africa rely predominantly upon public universities in their national development efforts. In a number of new nations, only public universities exist. It is difficult for private institutions to prosper on any large scale in the poorer countries, unless nearly complete reliance is placed on financing from outside the country. Even in the United States, many private institutions have encountered severe financial difficulties, and some have had to close their doors. Private universities are somewhat more characteristic of Anglo-American countries, but they exist elsewhere in significant numbers as well. Private institutions are found in countries old and young, less developed and more developed. Korea, Japan, India, Lebanon, Mexico, and Chile are among the countries in the present study which have a number of private universities. Lebanon places the greatest reliance on private education. The American University of Beirut and St. Joseph University account for nearly all university education in that country. Among the best-known private institutions in Korea are Korea and Yonsei Universities. Japan has a number of private institutions, among which are Keio and Waseda, each with established international reputations, and a relatively new institution, the International Christian University. Private religious or secular institutions with substantial American support are to be found in Turkey (Robert College), Mexico (Mexico City College), Egypt (American University of Cairo), and India (various religious institutions). In none of these countries do they play a predominant role, nor do other private educational institutions, although both Mexico and India have a number of them. In Latin America, Roman Catholic universities are of some importance, especially in Chile, where the Catholic University of Chile is the leading Catholic institution. Italy, Germany, and France present public systems of higher education.

Although systems of public higher education predominate throughout the world, there are sharp differences in the amount of nationwide centralization this entails. First of all, in countries with federal systems of government, often most of the public universities are under the control of the states, not the national government. This is the case in the United States, Germany, and India, and to some extent in Mexico. Occasionally, both national and state governments share in the cost of supporting public institutions as in the United States, Mexico, and India, or cities and states share, as in Germany. France, Italy, Turkey, and Indonesia have public university systems under the control of the central governments, and the well-known national (formerly imperial) universities of Japan follow the same practice.

The way in which control is formally exercised by national, state, or city governments involves varying degrees of autonomy for universities. The pattern of public higher education in the United States typically includes a board of trustees or regents for each institution, sometimes elected and sometimes appointed. This has given rise to problems of coordination in states with many public institutions.[4] Most often the board has substantial autonomous powers, but in practice the powers of boards vary from relatively few to great independent powers, constitutionally derived. In most other countries, parliaments are legally supreme over public universities, although they have exercised their financial and educational policy prerogatives in varying ways. In India, for example, university grants commissions are to be found at the national and state government levels. These bodies are a step removed from

---

[4] See Lyman A. Glenny, *Autonomy of Public Colleges: The Challenge of Coordination* (New York: McGraw-Hill, 1959).

parliaments, and help shape the growth of Indian universities by the grants they allocate. Such a device is unusual. In most countries in the sample that have followed the path of Continental Europe, the ministry of education has general responsibility. Often such an arrangement is combined with the responsibility of the several functional ministries for higher education in their respective fields, especially in limited-purpose colleges or schools. For example, agricultural ministries have special responsibility for agricultural colleges, health ministries for public health schools, personnel agencies for public administration training, and education ministries for teacher education in addition to general university affairs. Such functional supervision, control, and even financial support, in varying degrees, is especially typical of the fields of teacher education and agriculture. India combines its university grants commissions with the functional responsibility of the several ministries. Occasionally, disputes over higher education arise between a ministry of education and other ministries; higher education may suffer, or gain, as a result.

In all countries some legislative or parliamentary action is required, if for no other purpose than the appropriation of money. Often the establishment of new universities must receive parliamentary approval, along with a basic university charter. Sometimes parliamentary control goes far beyond this, to the detailed approval of curricula and other educational details. In highly centralized systems, *ad hoc* innovation as the result of university international exchange programs is less likely to occur in the short run, since a series of approvals is necessary. On the other hand, if change is decreed by a central agency, innovation may be introduced throughout the system. Such decrees seldom result from university exchange programs.

The structure and formal powers of various agencies or bodies does not always indicate the relative autonomy of the public universities. Legislatures in the United States vary in the degree to which they specify the use of funds appropriated to universities and the amount of informal influence exercised. In France, a highly centralized system on paper leads in practice to much autonomy for the universities because the ministry of education accepts the judgments of university personnel on key matters. In Turkey, a somewhat similar system would appear to be operating on paper, but in actual fact the universities have relatively little autonomy because of the heavy hand of the ministry of education in many educational details. Few changes can be brought about, few appointments can be made, without the effective, not just formal, approval of the ministry of education, and often of the parliament as well. In countries such as Turkey, very often the parliament and the ministry of education are bastions for the defense of the traditional patterns in higher education.

The degree of university autonomy is also related to the prevailing political system and the scope of governmental power. The more totalitarian a country, the less possible it is to permit autonomy of any institutions such as universities. But even in nontotalitarian countries, effective governmental power varies widely in regard to higher education. Currently in Italy, faculty members feel that the Christian Democrats are using centralized control over university appointments to further the appointments of party members or sympathizers. Part-time professorships may be rewards for those who contribute heavily, financially or otherwise, to persons in power, or at least rewards for those who support the wielders of power.

Patterns of governmental administration have impacts on universities. Extension and research activities in agriculture and home economics under the jurisdiction of American land-grant universities in a cooperative national-state university-county program is a unique feature of American higher education. Elsewhere, nearly all extension services and most research activities are carried on directly by the ministries of agriculture. In some Latin American countries, the practice of intervention, by which a government takes over an institution such as a university that it does not feel is doing an adequate job, is always a potential threat. Where government tends to be highly centralized and is given a large role in economic and social affairs, there may be little autonomy for universities. In some instances the participation of a foreign government or international agency in an economic aid program may mean either more autonomy or less. The role of the Korean government is such that university autonomy is less than in Japan, for example. Yet the outside assistance that Korean universities receive makes it possible for them to do things they otherwise could not do, in effect increasing their power to act. At the same time, conditions attached to outside assistance may restrict autonomy.

Control of universities by governments is not all of a kind. The effect of some governmental influence may be to strengthen resistance to change. Other governmental action may be designed to facilitate change. Countries pursuing active programs for the acceleration of national development have tried to modify higher education in a manner that would result in a greater contribution to the national welfare. To this end, national planning boards have included universities in their thinking and recommendations, and a number of special temporary commissions on higher education · have brought forth suggestions as to the development or reorganization of entire systems of higher education.

No university system is free from the influence of the prevailing pattern of finding employment in society. This is as true in the United States, with its diversified employment practices, as it is in Japan, with its university senior job examinations and placement, or in Indonesia, with its great emphasis on government employment. Government has a special relation to higher education in the less developed countries, for it is the main employer of university graduates. Universities also adapt to the degree of job mobility and scarcity. In the United States, job mobility is great; in Japan it is small. The greater the mobility, the more important it is to give students a rather broad, flexible education. In India, unemployment of university graduates in certain fields is widespread; in Indonesia, there is a scarcity of educated manpower in all fields. Universities are urged by their governments to turn out students at the rate and in the fields needed.

As American university personnel look outward to universities in other countries, they will find that no system of higher education has a much greater degree of autonomy than their own. Most systems are considerably less autonomous as far as outside control is concerned, whatever the legal theory. These facts have implications for most university exchange arrangements. American university personnel are accustomed to dealing directly with other universities at home or abroad, and are reluctant to go through the intermediary of a foreign government ministry, particularly in regard to programs not financed by the government agency concerned. This fact has had its repercussions in France, where university exchange was handled by government ministry some years ago, but now, for the benefit of university personnel from such countries as the United States, a separate agency with government financial support has been established to facilitate university exchange. Some potential host universities naturally feel that an essential preliminary step to any university exchange is a formal cultural accord between the two countries, although this would not seem important to most American institutions.

Among students and scholars outside the Soviet sphere, the free university freely and vigorously pursuing the truth is unanimously approved as an ideal. American undergraduates, graduates, and professors both abroad and at home are judged closely as to whether they live up to this standard.

Chapter 3

THE PROFESSORS AND STUDENTS OF DIFFERENT COUNTRIES

Perhaps some professors are old, absent-minded fuddy-duddies and some students are gay, carefree, and reckless, but these stereotypes obliterate a host of individual differences. There are also great differences among countries in the roles of teacher and student. To exchange a student from the United States with one from France or Brazil does not mean that equivalents have transferred locations. Nor can professors from different lands neatly fit the same grooves, even if their fields of competence are the same.

Faculty Members

The function of professor varies widely from individual to individual, institution to institution, and country to country, and this poses problems and opportunities for university international exchange programs. In some cases the research function is emphasized, elsewhere a transmission of facts to students, still other places a close relation to community. Whether they find themselves with higher or lower status abroad, professors must ever be conscious of the role they are expected to play and the conditions under which they are to play it as they move from country to country.

Part Time and Full Time. American universities are staffed primarily by full-time personnel, whose sole or major job is to serve the university. In most countries this is not the custom. In Latin America most professors, and sometimes even deans, are on part time. Professorships may be awarded to qualified candidates but, qualified or not, professors are normally persons whose major employment is elsewhere. Turnover in faculty personnel is consequently high. The salaries of professors and the number of hours a week they devote to academic matters are small. Appointments to professorships may bring more increments in prestige than in salary.

Many universities are primarily late afternoon or evening institutions. Professors come once or twice a week for their classes, and then disappear, not to be heard from again until the following week. In Japan, it is possible to study under the same professor at two, three, or even four universities. Multiple academic positions are common as a means of supplementing low academic salaries. In Indonesia, some professors commute by plane from one city to another in order to carry on a series of teaching and government assignments, which together constitute their occupations. Relatively few members of some of the faculties of the University of Florence actually live in Florence; they may live in Rome or elsewhere, as their other employment or their personal convenience directs. The American University of Beirut employs a substantial number of full-time teachers, and so do some of the faculties in the universities of India, France, and Germany. Where academic salaries are high relative to other employments, or where the supply of highly trained individuals is ample, full-time university personnel are more likely to be found.

Part-time professors affect the operations of universities in many ways. They may seldom see their colleagues at the university. The opportunity to develop strong departmental or faculty programs is thus limited, even if the desire to do so is present, though it seldom is when part time is the custom. There may be little time for research, since the two or more employments may occupy all of a professor's time. There may be no departmental or faculty meetings except on formal occasions. There is little time to prepare lectures or to revise old ones. Students cannot see a professor frequently since he is seldom in his office.

The effects of relying upon part-time professors vary in accordance with the nature of their other employments and the percentage of time devoted to work relevant to academic interests. The multiple employment of Japanese professors does not divert the professors from academic pursuits. In Italy, some professors hold special research appointments in private organizations, and are engaged in work which may be relevant to their academic functions. However, professors who can afford only a few teaching hours a week,

offer only a single course, and for the balance of the time are employed by government or business or in private professional practice,
as is the case in many Latin American universities, make minimal
intellectual contributions to a university other than by teaching the
single course. One advantage claimed for the practice is that it
permits the hiring of the best man for each course, rather than having to rely upon one professor to teach several courses, in only one
of which he may be really expert (Adams and Cumberland, pp.
93–96).

Part-time professors are often unable to accept visiting appointments or fellowships to other countries since it is difficult to obtain
leave from their multiple jobs at the same time. When American
professors come to the host university, they often are disappointed
in not being able to associate closely with the host-university professors because of the latter's absence on other assignments. A
number of American professors abroad under university contracts
with the International Cooperation Administration (ICA) of the
Department of State report that the Americans constitute the only
group that is to be found at the university throughout the week.
Part-time professors are not likely to be interested in innovations;
they have little time to concern themselves with such matters.
American students abroad also encounter frustrations in trying to
consult professors who have other employments and are seldom in
their offices.

Teaching, Research, and Extension. The kinds of activities in
which faculty members engage are dissimilar, country by country.
Teaching is the only activity found everywhere. Research on a
very broad scale is confined to relatively few university systems,
mainly in the more developed countries such as those of Europe.
In the Far East research is prominent in Japan, and increasingly in
India. Elsewhere, research may be carried on only by certain professors, but is not systematically provided for. Where faculty
members are mainly on part time, it is difficult for most of them to
engage in research regularly. Money for research or for research
facilities is often lacking; leaves of absence with pay for research
purposes are unknown in most countries. There is also a simple
lack of interest in research in many instances, a looking backward
rather than ahead. One of the resulting difficulties for exchange
programs is that it is difficult to organize and carry out a research
project with mutual participation by American and host-country

professors. Another is that supervision of the Ph.D. theses of American students by host-country professors may not be feasible. Nor will it always be possible to place undergraduate field or laboratory research under host-country professorial direction.

The many advising-consulting-extension activities in which American faculty members participate are lacking abroad, at least in the form they take in the United States. There is no general acceptance of university responsibility in this field, in most instances. The extramural activities of some of the universities in Africa following the English tradition are partial exceptions among the countries in the sample for the present study. Extension and consultation are not considered integral parts of university work abroad, but they occasionally are undertaken by quasi-independent institutes or other units attached to universities. Typically such units do not have the status or prestige of regular faculties.

The lack of acceptance of university responsibility for advising-consulting-extension activities does not mean that university faculty members are aloof from the communities in which they live or from the governments or public policies of their countries. American university personnel abroad have often been seriously mistaken in regard to this matter. The part-time university professor may be, in another capacity, a government official or employee, and as such he may have much more influence on public affairs than his American counterpart. Or he may play an important role in some private company or in the affairs of some professional association. He often accepts private consultantships, thus extending his influence in the area of his expertise. He will give many speeches and lectures to community groups. His contribution to public policy may be substantial, since his opinion is valued; he is a member of the professorial elite. It is true that, being a member of the elite, he may be unwilling to participate in teaching, demonstration, or writing aimed at simplifying and applying his professional knowledge for the general public. The professor in an ivory tower is to be found abroad more frequently than in the United States. Yet the ivory tower is less isolated abroad than an official listing of university activities would seem to indicate.

In many countries great importance is attributed to the distinction between individual participation in advisory, consultative, or extension activities and university sponsorship of them. If the university were to sponsor such activities as an organization, university autonomy might be threatened. Unnecessary involvement with the government and community groups at the official level is discouraged. Professors in most parts of the world do not make a sharp distinction between academic freedom and official university aloofness from the community or government (the freedom not to become involved). They prize their official independence, much as the students prize their freedom. Technical assistance programs may thus be adversely affected, because technical assistance usually requires at least some direct relationship with governmental agencies.

Roles and Statuses. American universities are probably more administered, and place greater power in the hands of administrators and boards of trustees, than all but a few foreign universities beyond the iron curtain. Legal responsibility for the American university normally rests with boards of trustees on which the faculty members are not represented and with administrative officials whose aptitudes and training are not necessarily academic. Although matters of strictly academic concern are the prerogative of faculty members at major institutions, at some others academic policies are regularly determined by nonfaculty groups. Administrative officials and employees are numerous, and they usually are appointed with indefinite tenure by the boards of trustees or by other administrative officials. Seldom do the faculty members choose them, although faculty advice may be sought.

Abroad, control by the faculty, at least in theory, prevails in Continental-type systems. Deans and even rectors are commonly elected by the faculty members or their representatives. In many countries it is the practice to change deans and rectors every few years; elsewhere they have longer tenure or are normally re-elected. The rector and dean have few staff assistants; on occasion they are part-time officials, and cannot carry on extensive administrative planning or direction. In any case, where their tenure is short or uncertain, they remain scholars who are temporarily occupying administrative posts. This system does not necessarily lead to democratic control by all faculty members over all matters of concern to the university. The power of the ministry of education from without and the rank and prestige of the full professors from within are usually very great. Yet consent of at least the senior faculty is normally obtained on educational policies, and they or their representatives also constitute the general university governing body or a major portion of it. In comparison with American universities, there is little central leadership in university affairs.

Universities affected by the British tradition fall somewhere between the American and Continental patterns. For example, the vice chancellors of Indian universities are normally chosen by the chancellors, who are usually the governors of the respective states. Furthermore, the chancellor's approval is frequently required on certain items before the action of a university governing body becomes official. The general governing body is usually a senate or court, with a large membership representing many different interests, including university professors.

The relationships between full professors and lower-ranking faculty members vary from a spirit of equality to one of near-authoritarianism, from one of mutual exploration of matters of interest to one of extreme deference to the full professor. The Anglo-American tradition of higher education calls for a group of staff members of different grades, together representing the competence of the university in a broad field. Departments normally have more than one full professor, and there is no necessary correlation between the number and specializations of full professors and the number and variety of fields. In Anglo-American universities, lower-ranking staff members are often put in charge of lower-level courses or sections of courses, much as a full professor might be. There is much give-and-take among the members of the staff, and in general the atmosphere is that of a group of equals more than of inferiors and superiors. Department meetings are free interchanges between faculty members of all ranks, with equal voting privileges, actually exercised, for all. Although recruitment to academic posts is much more formally organized in the United Kingdom than in Canada or the United States, the standard minimum qualification for academic appointment is a doctorate and the effective decision on personnel selection is made by a special committee of qualified academics or some representative(s) of the department concerned. The young instructor can look forward to early promotion if he proves his competence. Most departments do not have a fixed quota of full professors.

An opposite extreme is represented by most of the university systems of Continental Europe and Latin America. Very often there is only one full professor per field, and in several countries the subject fields of the professorships and their number are determined by the ministry of education or by parliament. In Latin America, new professors are typically approved by the university council. In any event, a small determinate number of full professorships exists. Entry even to the lower ranks is restricted. Furthermore, for a junior staff member who has spent years in the lower ranks there is no assurance that he will ultimately become a full professor if he performs creditably. Someone from without the system may be appointed instead.

The status accorded full professors is in direct proportion to the restriction on entry into the rank. There is a sharp distinction between professorial and nonprofessorial levels. The full professor exercises almost complete control over all the work in his field. Those in the lower ranks do his bidding and carry on his work as he sees fit. Nothing is done without his consent. To put it more crudely, the professor is king; he can do no wrong. Those in the lower ranks are treated as supplements to the full professor. If the professor decides not to attend his class, no one compels him to do so. The class may not meet, or he may send in his assistant or some lower-ranking faculty member. Faculty meetings, when they are held, are often purely formal, and the full professors make the effective decisions.

There are many variations from country to country. In some cases professors are not necessarily distributed one to a field. In others, junior staff members are assigned to courses that they can handle with some freedom. The French and Italian systems present a less extreme picture than the German or Spanish. Yet the over-all pattern is similar. There is a long, hard road for a young instructor to travel from the time he receives his final degree to the time, if ever, when he becomes a full professor, and throughout this period he is treated as obviously inferior, being forced to give deference to his betters. Asian and African university systems tend to approximate either the Continental or Anglo-American patterns, depending on which pattern exerted special influence in past decades.

The difference in the role of faculty members within their universities and the difference in the relationship between full professor and junior staff members have many consequences for university international exchange programs. To mention only two: If the American professor's function abroad is advisory and consultative as in the ICA contract programs, the impact of the advice may be small. Innovation may threaten the established hierarchy of status: professors and occasionally even junior staff members may feel threatened by accepting something new, the consequences of which are uncertain. When a host-country professor comes to the United States to teach, he may be unprepared for some of the demands that are made upon him by his new colleagues. Some visiting professors will like the new role, others will be uncomfortable; the great majority of them adjust remarkably well.

Students

The objective that students seek and the means that are available to them in the pursuit of these objectives are many. Even more than in the case of faculty members, equal numbers of students cannot be exchanged with the casual assumption that equivalents are exchanging places. Students in each country are accustomed to roles that are distinctive of their own culture. To migrate to another culture often requires of the student major adjustments in the role, function, and objectives to which he is accustomed—aside from the difficulties of language barrier and differences in standards.

Relations with Professors. The relationship between the full professor or junior staff member and the student varies internationally as does that between professor and junior staff member. In the Continental systems, the student tends to be the low man on the totem pole. He is privileged to attend classes, but the classes are not occasions during which the professor is to be questioned or student-professor discussion is to take place. Interrupting a professor during a lecture is considered impolite; disagreeing with him during a seminar is usually impolitic. Classes are often so large that discussion is impractical. Faculty members may be in their offices a few hours each week, but only a handful of students actually go to see a faculty member. Even for those who do, the occasion is not one for discussion of some point of interest to the student, but for the inferior to ask the superior a question to which he is likely to get a short reply. There is so little contact between professor and student in some university systems that a student coming up for the final examination for his degree may find that the professor does not even recognize him. However that may be, in some Continental systems such as the Dutch, an individual professor may be a student's sole examiner, with rather unrestricted power to determine whether the student is to get his degree. Such a system is not designed to develop close professor-student relations based on mutual respect and mutual intellectual inquiry.

The student is expected to "sink or swim." Students are not given advisory or counseling services. Spending professorial time on individual or even personal problems of students is thought to be wasteful. Orientation programs for new students are usually lacking. Students are expected to work out their own problems by themselves. This results in some drifting, especially in the first year or so; those who fail to adjust or who drop out are considered to lack qualifications for university study. Placing a student on his own will teach him self-reliance and show him the path to independent study and critical thinking. In actual fact, the great majority of students do adapt to university life.

Social and academic controls over students are either nonexistent or minimal. The equivalent of the American dean of students is not found. Extracurricular activities are not promoted or highly developed. There are no restrictions on late hours for women students or regulations on student drinking or automobile driving. Either dormitories are absent or the available rooms are very few, and student housing is dependent on student initiative unless, as is often the case, universities are urban institutions and a high percentage of the students live at home.

Academically, specific requirements are few except for final or yearly examinations. What a student reads and when is his own affair; there are no weekly or even monthly assignments, no due dates. Attendance at class is purely voluntary. Recognizing this, many European universities provide classrooms with fewer seats than the number of students registered for a course. A person may remain a student almost indefinitely. If he chooses to waste his university years, that is up to him. After the rigid discipline of secondary school, his freedom includes the freedom of doing nothing.

The Anglo-American tradition places the student in a markedly different role, although the American system is the most extreme. The years at the university are not years of strict discipline, but some restrictions as to student conduct are imposed. In the United States, the office of the dean of students promulgates the many rules of personal or social conduct for students while on the campus. Through the same office, extensive counseling and advising facilities are available. Orientation programs for new students are common, and information on almost all details of university life may be had for the asking, if indeed it is not given without a formal request. Academic advisers are assigned and curricular outlines and requirements are present to guide the student further. There is a presumption that the student will attend class.

The classroom atmosphere is often that of mutual respect in the process of learning. Ideally, the attitude of the faculty member is that he may learn more than the students during the classroom sessions. Questions are put to the professor with little hesitation. Discussion is taken for granted and is informal. Students are permitted, even encouraged, to disagree with the professor. Outside the classroom, the professor may have many contacts with the students, in the hallway, over coffee or tea, in his office, or during some student club meeting. In short, each student is the center of a university effort to produce as good a finished product as possible. At the extreme, according to its critics, the system leads to coddling of students. As a consequence, in the United States there has recently been a trend toward developing programs under which a student is freer to pursue studies on his own, taking more responsibility for them than he does at present.

The Continental and the American systems of higher education are based on different assumptions and philosophies. The American system in part reflects the Protestant ethic. Students and the universities have an obligation to see that the maximum number of students makes a maximum contribution to society. This can be assured only if certain controls are established. Drifters are social outcasts, and have no claim whatsoever on university facilities. Each student must apply himself to the task at hand, looking forward to increasing his potential productivity as much as possible. In Europe, a student has a right to be left alone. Society has no claim on him. He vigorously defends his freedom of action or inaction. The work philosophy being less intense, his contribution to accelerating productivity is of less concern.

The American system is rooted in the democratic spirit, the European in a privileged class concept. Consequently, in the United States requirements are laid down to facilitate education of vast numbers of students. The professor-student relation is a democratic one. In Europe, the presumption is that the student either is from or is about to join a privileged class. University education is for the few, and the responsibilities of the elite are something that they should determine for themselves. Specific assignments interfere with the academic freedom of the students. The professor is the living symbol of the elite.

The less developed countries that are actively implementing programs for accelerating national productivity have increasingly found that the American philosophy is more congenial to their aims than the European. They cannot afford the luxury of a university system that trains only a few elite members, nor can they afford to have potential intellectuals drifting along for a period of years without apparent social utility. They must produce vast numbers of trained persons devoted to developing their countries.

The differences in the relationship between the faculty members and students within the several university systems have posed difficulties for the international exchange programs of American universities. The American student who goes abroad to study at an institution modeled on one of the Continental European systems finds few of the usual services to which he has become accustomed at home. He feels lost. The university seems a cold, impersonal institution where less interest is shown in exchange of ideas than in the memorization of old lectures. Only the most unusual undergraduate can adjust easily to such a different system. This difficulty has given support to some who have urged that study abroad be limited to advanced graduate students. The student from a Continental-type university system is likely to find adjustment easier in the United States than his American counterpart who goes abroad, if for no other reason than that he has more contacts with his professors, more services placed at his disposal.

Student-professor relations in the Continental universities naturally place an American teacher who goes abroad on an exchange program in a role different from that to which he was accustomed at home. The American professor teaching abroad confronts students who may not respond in question or discussion periods. His whole method of teaching may be challenged, directly or indirectly, since it is likely to require a more informal relationship between faculty members and students. Problems of adjustment also arise for the European professor coming to the United States. He may not find the deference to which he is accustomed. Students may be restive under the lectures he delivers, even though the lectures would be warmly appreciated in Europe. He may not be prepared for the interaction with students that the American system demands. His contribution may consequently be less than Americans expect.

Student Roles. In some countries students are usually on part time—a tendency that is commonly related to local economic conditions. In countries that are especially poor, the only way in which a student can attend a university is to work full time and go to classes in his off-hours unless his parents are exceedingly rich. Poor countries also are usually those in which a scarcity of trained manpower exists, and there is likely to be great pressure on even well-to-do students to work before they graduate.

Conditions such as these sometimes have unexpected impacts on the granting of local scholarships. The obtaining of a scholarship may be an important source of income for a student, so important that he may try to extend his education over a longer period of years in order to continue to receive the scholarship. In effect, attending the university thus becomes a part-time job. If scholarships are substantial enough, a student may find it possible to attend the university on a full-time basis. If the scholarships awarded for local study are available only for certain fields, an enterprising student may register in such fields solely to satisfy the requirements of the award, but in addition take work in another field of dominant interest to him. In Europe, Japan, India, and many other countries, full-time students are common, though often they work at part-time jobs in addition, just like their American counterparts. In these areas, part-time students are found more frequently at universities in large metropolitan centers.

Students vary in seriousness of purpose from institution to institution. One American professor found a great difference between the students he taught at one South American university and those he had had in India:

The experience here is totally different from that in India. There the students were the most devoted, eager, interested lot, hungry for every scrap of information, and anxious to make every moment count. Here there seems to be an indifference that is frustrating and disappointing. There seems to be no *esprit de corps*. The individual seems to be looking out only for himself, and who cares about the other fellow? Childishness and immaturity, the inability to see down the road and around the corner seem to be the rule rather than the exception.

At a number of universities, the student plays some direct role in determining the nature of the educational system, its rules and regulations, and its procedures. Strangely enough, this is especially true of some of the university systems in which students give the greatest deference to professors. Classic examples of student influence in university affairs are found in Latin America and Asia. Student organizations are strong in Latin America. Students, as well as professors, are represented in the governing body of the institution. Traditionally, students are concerned with what they term their rights. When the rights are violated, the academic freedom of students is threatened. In practice, student participation in the governing of a university is a force for conservative higher education policies. Student groups tend to be against change. The proposed introduction of a new requirement or an additional examination may be viewed as violating the academic freedom of the students. Substantial outside reading may be opposed; students may believe that they have a right to expect everything of importance to be contained in the lectures. Basically they are against control, and such changes represent control to them. The power of student groups in Latin America is not solely academic; it is also political. They carry on many political activities, often constituting a major activist element in opposition parties. They may be joined in their political activities by certain of the professors. Thus, whenever the students take an interest in any educational matter at the university, the mixture of higher education, politics, and student rights becomes rather involved.

In order the more effectively to exercise their prerogatives, the students develop extensive organizations. Sometimes there are competing organizations of nearly equal strength; in other instances there is a single predominant organization. One of the most famous of all student organizations is found in Japan (Bronfenbrenner, chap. 2). The Zengakuren is a student organization usually dominated by Trotskyites, although it also has a strong Stalinist or Communist faction. It is active in pursuing its political objectives, and also in opposing any threat to what it regards as Japanese university autonomy. Student organizations such as the Zengakuren need effective leaders. Positions of leadership are highly prized and competition for them is often extensive and even rugged. In such countries as Japan, Indonesia, and Mexico, the same student leaders remain in control year after year, extending the period of their status as students for the purpose of controlling the student organization. Some university officials have given thought to restricting the number of years a person may be classified as a student, but little has been or is likely to be done in this respect.

The impact of student organizations on the international exchange programs of American universities has been extensive in Asia and Latin America. The ultimate weapon of the student organizations is the strike, and student groups have used it on several occasions against American university international programs. For example, the ICA–Texas A and M contract of Antonio Narro in Mexico was one of the issues in a student strike. So was the ICA contract of the University of Michigan at Waseda University in Japan. There are many techniques of opposing exchanges with American universities other than the strike. Where students are represented on governing bodies, they may have a direct voice in determination of policy. Professors who are in alliance with them may be of help. A variety of propaganda techniques are available, including the distribution of handbills outside the classroom in which an American professor is to lecture. Zengakuren tends not to object to the presence of individual American professors or students on Japanese campuses as long as they do not threaten the organization or oppose the things for which it stands. Exchanges of student leaders may contain a threat and are therefore opposed. Professors in some of the social sciences may bring anti-Marxist or pro-United States ideas and therefore may be opposed. Any ICA university contract is opposed as representing the hidden hand of the American military and the capitalist philosophy. Scholarships to the United States are not considered an honor by Zengakuren members and this point of view is well publicized. Changes in the practices of Japanese universities as the result of international exchange programs with American universities are opposed as a threat to Japanese university autonomy.

Teaching

The method of teaching may be as different from country to country as any aspect of higher education. Here is where the professor meets the student most intimately. The many differences in the roles of professor and of student are compounded in the interaction in the classroom. These differences are prominent

among the factors impeding study-abroad programs, yet they are
the focus or *raison d'être* of many technical assistance programs
of American universities.

Techniques. There are three main techniques of presenting material to students, namely, by use of the classroom, reading, and
laboratory and field experiences. Higher education in the United
States has typical patterns in regard to each of these, in comparison
with university systems elsewhere. The number of classroom hours
per week is limited, even for undergraduates, to about fifteen. Although the size of some of the beginning basic or survey classes is
rather large, many university classes are small enough so that class
discussions and recitation are possible. Formal lectures are mixed
with a liberal proportion of informal discussion, and the whole of
class work is closely interwoven with reading assignments, term
papers, and laboratory and field work. Textbooks are available for
most courses and are required reading. In addition, extensive use
of university library facilities is required for almost all courses beyond the beginning level. Reading assignments do not duplicate
but complement the work in the classroom. The student is held responsible for both. Numerous courses require field or laboratory
work, in order to relate classroom and reading knowledge to data
personally and empirically obtained. Field and laboratory work is
to be found in many subjects, not just in the physical and biological
sciences.

Perhaps the most extreme contrast to the techniques of presenting material in the American universities is to be found in some
of the less developed countries with systems of higher education
that have been influenced heavily by the Continental European
patterns. Indonesia and Bolivia are examples. In countries such
as these, the lecture system predominates. Classes are very large,
attendance is not compulsory, and virtually the sole technique of
the professor is a lecture, uninterrupted by him or by the students.
The lectures tend to be repeated year after year, and sets of lectures are occasionally published so that students can either read or
listen to them. If a student were to attend all lectures, he would
be in class twenty-five to thirty hours a week. Textbooks are often
unavailable—for economic, language, or other reasons. University
or faculty libraries are virtually nonexistent and probably under
lock, the professor having the only key. There are no librarians.
The students are not often required to do outside reading. Term

papers are rare. Laboratory or field work is at a minimum and in many fields nonexistent. There is little emphasis on empirical verification of statements by the lecturer.

The university systems of most countries fall somewhere between these two extremes. In Continental Europe, there are great libraries, and a portion of the students make use of them on their own initiative, although most university libraries are not as accessible as those in the United States and most university students confine themselves to the reading lists required for examinations. Nevertheless, reading is a major aspect of university work in Europe, although less use is made of textbooks. There is laboratory and field work, although not as much proportionately as in the United States. However, discussions in class are infrequent except at very advanced levels. Where the European system has been transplanted elsewhere, especially in the less developed countries, much less emphasis on reading and field work has occurred. The instructional techniques in English universities are much more similar to those in the United States than in Continental Europe, and this is reflected to some extent in present and former British territories in Asia and Africa.

The techniques of instruction are related to cost. Large lecture classes are cheaper than small discussion sections. In many countries in Latin America, Asia, and Africa, there are few persons with qualifications for professorships, and little money to allot to universities for salaries, classrooms, or offices. An individual professor must be "stretched" over as many students as possible. Furthermore, the basic physical facilities for library and laboratory work are inadequate in the less developed countries, including laboratories, equipment, books, and library space.

Additional money would help to provide the human and material resources needed for a different system of instruction. Yet money is not the sole or basic need. Economically, the Netherlands, Germany, and France are not any poorer than England. The Philippines is not richer than some of its neighbors. Yet within these groups of countries with relatively equal resources different systems of instruction prevail. Fundamentally, systems of instruction reflect philosophies of and approaches to education. For example, in some of the less developed countries, the professorial and future university-educated elites would lose face if they carried out any extensive laboratory extension or field work. It is not the kind of thing in which a gentleman scholar engages. Where a more inductive philosophy prevails, an empirical approach will be more likely, with its emphasis on laboratory and field work.

Evaluation of Student Performance. The evaluation and examination methods of higher education around the world depart from any single pattern, as do the degrees to which they lead. The American system is the most detailed. A grade is given for each course a student takes, typically based upon an examination, term paper or project, class participation, and such other tests or assignments as may be required. Usually a certain number of credits is given a student who completes each course, and is applied toward the total number required for graduation. The bachelor's degree normally does not involve a comprehensive final examination. Theses and comprehensive written and/or oral examinations as well as individual course credits and grades are usually associated with advanced professional and graduate degrees. Course examinations are developed, given, and usually graded by the professors in charge of the class. Written or final examinations at the graduate level are evaluated by a group of professors with whom the student has worked.

The European Continental-type systems do not involve course credits, nor are there examinations or grades given for individual lecture classes or seminars. The student stands or falls on the year-end examination, as in France, or the final examination for the degree, as in Germany. He may elect to take the examination in any year when he feels prepared. These examinations are normally oral, and may be given by one or more of the professors in a student's field.

Countries falling in the British tradition of higher education present a third pattern of examination and evaluation. Though intermediate and final examinations are found in these countries, much more reliance is placed on written papers than in the Continental pattern. At the undergraduate level, work in organized classes is important. In many instances, the grading of papers and the giving of oral examinations is carried on by professional personnel hired especially for the purpose and not by the professor who gives the course. This means that he is not in a position to determine the questions asked of his students or their grades. Universities with outside examiners find it difficult to change the content of their curricula and courses, since the examiners represent a force for tradition, as well as possibly a force for objectivity and high standards.

The American professor who goes abroad cannot expect as much attention to be paid to his lectures as the visiting professor who teaches at an American university. The European student in his own country may feel certain that he will never be asked any questions in his yearly or final examinations on material covered by an itinerant. The American student at home knows that the visiting professor will give him a grade like any other member of the staff.

Understanding of Differences by University Personnel

The success of university international exchange programs depends to a great extent on appropriate behavior of professors and students. This behavior, in turn, is conditioned by their views of the differences between the university systems of the two countries concerned. Actual differences may not be so important in this regard as perceived differences.

Differences in systems of higher education are perceived by various individuals and groups in varying ways. Perceptions depend in part upon the actual differences, partly on the information available, and partly on the value framework of the viewer. Perceptions can be accurate or inaccurate representations of real differences, and they can be favorable or unfavorable. They vary in accordance with the expectations of individuals and groups.

American universities are perceived abroad as especially strong in science and technology, be it chemistry or physics, botany or zoology, public health or medicine, agriculture or engineering. Somehow the development of the United States, its high productivity, its excellent health standards, and perhaps its addiction to modern mechanical conveniences, have helped fasten attention on these aspects of university work. Other nationals are acquainted with United States achievements in these fields, and they therefore have an initial receptivity to university exchange in regard to them. In general, visiting scholars have been skeptical of the state of liberal arts, the humanities, and social science in the United States, although social science, basic and applied, is becoming recognized as a field of special strength of American universities, at least in the eyes of persons not committed to any antidemocratic philosophy.

Professors from abroad, as well as some students, often think of higher education in the United States as based on secondary schools and undergraduate colleges which have low standards and a vocational emphasis. Little note is taken of the insistence of the system on regular work for course credit or of the liberalizing elements of American higher education. It is felt that fundamentals are ignored while extracurricular activities are emphasized, that there is too little respect for the professor, too much for the academic administrator, and too many poorly qualified students who waste the time of faculty members. The large number of institutions of higher education in the United States is confusing to the foreigner, and he tends to believe that the only institutions of higher learning which maintain standards and reputation are a few well-known private institutions such as Harvard, Yale, Princeton, Columbia, and Chicago. The role of the small liberal arts college or the large state university in American higher education is not generally understood.

American universities are thought of as wealthy, and every American professor abroad is supposed to offer an avenue to fellowship awards. The perception of higher education is not clearly separated from the perception of the United States as a whole. The United States is a world power, often viewed as imperialistic. American universities are sometimes seen as instruments of that imperialism, as representing an extension of American influence abroad in their exchange activities. Among the items often favorably perceived are the democratic atmosphere, the spirit of problem solving, and the emphasis on hard work on everyone's part, from the full professor to the undergraduate. American graduate education and research are widely respected.

American personnel in higher education have their own perceptions of higher education abroad. Americans frequently criticize the aristocratic and classical bent of universities in other countries. They also often feel that there is a lack of competent people at universities in much of the world. Scarcity of personnel abroad, together with a general lower level of material assets, has helped to create this impression. Host-country professors understandably resent this attitude. It hinders exchange activities and also causes Americans to overestimate the need for American professors abroad (Branfenbrenner, chap. 7).

Favorable or unfavorable perceptions of American higher education may have little to do with the success or failure of many American university programs, if involvement of host-country nationals in them is mainly indirect. Some of the international exchange programs of American universities do not involve much official connection with higher education in the host country, although personal contacts may be frequent. Many of the undergraduate student-abroad programs are run essentially by the American university, with little direct participation by host-country institutions, although certain personnel may be borrowed. One reason for this is that European and most other university systems do not have the equivalent of the American undergraduate college. Research programs abroad also are often carried out without involvement of host-country universities, in part because of a lack of interest or a lack of time of university personnel. A number of foundation and ICA university contracts call for consultation and advice to nonuniversity groups such as government agencies. Here the reason is that universities in the host country are not interested or active in such work or do not have the resources to carry it on. In any case, a majority of the programs are related to higher education in the host country, whether they are formally connected with a particular institution or not. In such instances, the favorable or unfavorable perception of American higher education may be important for the growth of the programs or for the problems encountered, and the favorable or unfavorable perception of host-country higher education by Americans equally important.

Even where there is a close relationship between a host institution and an American university, the fact that the American higher education system is perceived as different may not have much to do with the success or failure of university programs. Differences or perceived differences in the systems of higher education are not related to the receptivity of the international programs of American universities in any one way. There is not necessarily a high degree of receptivity even at the cultural level just because there are similarities. Nor do differences necessarily reflect a lack of cultural receptivity. Whether receptivity will be greater or less in such circumstances depends basically upon the goals sought.

For example, the strong ties of the United States with Europe politically, economically, militarily, and intellectually, provide a broad base upon which to build programs of university international exchange. This is particularly true of programs designed to bring about accretions of learning or innovations in regard to the student's knowledge. In many respects, however, Continental Europe is less congenial to American higher education than are many underdeveloped countries, especially in regard to programs that might imply changes in a university system. Europeans place great value on their cultural and, more particularly, their university traditions. They are proud of their centuries-old systems of higher education. Their universities are not seriously considering modifying roles or practices to any great degree. Consequently, it is to be expected that substantive innovations in Europe from exchanges between European and American universities would take the form primarily of accretions to individuals' knowledge, rather than of alterations in social practices or even in the practices of universities, and that European universities would be primarily receptive to programs of the former type.

Furthermore, Europeans view the American system of higher education as a recent arrival on the educational scene, and as a potential threat to their own dominance in and contribution to higher education in various regions of the world. Leaders of higher education in Europe have been especially sensitive about the development by American universities of close relations in former colonial territories. France has been alarmed about what is viewed as the challenge from American higher education in replacing the French cultural tradition in Latin America and parts of the Middle East and Asia. It is not only proud of its own culture, but is conscious of the fact that the French cultural tradition has helped keep nations close to France, even after formal political power has disappeared or where it has never existed.

In contrast, leaders of higher education in the less developed countries, particularly those that are making the greater efforts to accelerate national development, may look to the United States for possible patterns that will help them achieve their goal. The United States has developed its human and material resources more recently and further than most other countries, and higher education has played a role in this development. As a consequence, host-country nationals in the less developed countries may welcome international exchange programs of American universities, and may be interested in the various innovations that they can introduce in such areas as the activities of universities, teaching techniques, examination methods, and the content and scope of the work offered.

India, for example, is, like the United States, a huge nation, and at least equally pluralistic. Its atmosphere is a congenial one for American university personnel in so far as American higher education fits well into an open, diverse society, with autonomous institutions like universities playing an important role (Hart, pp. 34–35). India has also come to embrace increasingly the objectives of large-scale education at the university level. It is a country that officially looks more and more to the future, not to the past. Stress is placed on accelerating national development. It is in a problem-solving mood. Not all university personnel in India are caught up in the new spirit, or see any application of the new national objectives to their work. Furthermore, the class structure and the reluctance of the educated groups to carry out field work and laboratory experiments are strikingly unlike practices in the United States. Yet the general direction is similar, and exchange is likely to prove of more mutual interest and benefit as time goes on.

As for the cultural receptivity of American universities themselves to university international exchange programs and innovations flowing from them, it is apparent that although many innovations are introduced from time to time, relatively few of them come from abroad. American universities strongly believe in their basic philosophy and approach. Rightly or wrongly they feel they are leaders in such an approach, and hence as far as university programs are concerned they are most receptive to exporting innovations in university practices, and to exchanges both ways that result in accretions to the knowledge of individuals rather than to institutional changes at home.

Broad social goals or purposes help to determine cultural receptivity, yet there is no doubt that within limits similarity of university practices also facilitates university international exchange. For example, there is much exchange among universities falling within the French system and much exchange among those falling within the English pattern. The United States is somewhat hampered in developing exchanges because most of the world has a widely different pattern of higher education. Consequently, the exchange of many students at anything below a relatively advanced graduate level is impossible, unless such exchange involves special programs for the students concerned. Professorial exchanges are also somewhat limited by the different systems and the varying expectations as to professorial competence, activities, and methods, let alone differences in underlying facilities, university courses, curricula, and calendars.

Finally, cultural receptivity depends on a number of variables other than similarities or differences in university systems. The political, economic, and religious systems are examples. Language is also important. One advantage United States universities have in international exchange is their use of the English language. Not only is English the language of a large proportion of the scholarly literature in the various academic fields, but it is also the medium of instruction, or the second language, of much of Asia and Africa and of numerous countries elsewhere. Geographical proximity has some influence on exchange. The wealth of the United States and the fact that a substantial amount of money for the exchange programs of American universities from government, foundation, and other sources is available help to overcome one of the handicaps of United States universities—geographical distance from other countries. The color barriers in the South are a disadvantage to exchange with African countries. American capitalism is a disadvantage in the eyes of the supporters of the left center and the extreme left abroad. The complete listing of such factors would consume many pages.

It is easy to overgeneralize about the difficulties facing the international exchange programs of American universities as the result of differences in the roles of professors and students between one system of higher education and another. Some exchanges, both technical assistance programs and other types of programs as well, have developed precisely because the American system is different. Some have found these differences to be obstacles that the program must overcome. Furthermore, problems of receptivity have been connected with university exchange programs even in those instances in which similar university systems are involved.

In comparison with universities in most parts of the world, the American university is a flexible institution, relatively unhampered by tradition. The experimental nature of American universities is undoubtedly related to their great number, their relative prosperity, their variety, their decentralized status, and their more or less democratic aims. One of the many institutions of higher learning in the United States is usually willing to try any given promising idea. Experiments that prove successful are quickly copied. So it has been with international programs.

Chapter 4

AMERICAN STUDENT-ABROAD PROGRAMS: A SURVEY

Study abroad was an accepted part of the higher education of a few American young men and women even before the founding of the Republic. The best universities were, of course, in Europe. In the latter part of the nineteenth century—long after universities with renown had arisen in the United States—it was still customary for certain wealthy families to send their children abroad for a while, but for a somewhat different reason: they felt it was a desirable means of completing their education. Living and studying abroad was broadening, and it brought prestige. All this activity was carried out on an individual basis.

The feeling that "there ought to be an organization" mounted after World War I, especially in some of the more exclusive women's liberal arts colleges, among whose student bodies were many whose parents could afford European trips. These institutions took the lead, although the honor of the first junior-year-abroad program went to the University of Delaware in 1923. The idea was soon taken up by Smith (1925), Mount Holyoke (1926), and later by others. The number of institutions with junior years abroad has increased in every decade since the 1920s, and reached a new height in the 1950s.

Two other kinds of American student-abroad programs appeared about this time. Overseas branches of American universities began with the opening of Marymount's Paris branch in 1923, Rosary's Fribourg branch in 1925, and Marymount's Rome branch in 1930. Branches were never established by many universities, although recently the plan has attracted renewed attention with the

Johns Hopkins Center at Bologna (1955) and the Stanford branches in Germany (1958), France, Italy (1960), and Japan. Summer or short-term study tours with or without credit developed a few years after the junior years abroad or overseas branches began. Among the early programs that still continue are the Texas Technological College (1935) and the Indiana University (1939) study tours to Mexico. Short-term study tours have substantially increased in number in the last ten years.

In the 1950s student-abroad programs grew rapidly. A partial tabulation indicates about a dozen or so programs at the end of the forties. The number doubled in four years, doubled again in another four or five years, and in 1959 and 1960 increased at the rate of 15 to 20 a year.[1] Actually, these figures understate the number of programs, especially those involving small numbers of students. In the academic year 1957–58 there were 132 programs which primarily involved study abroad under the auspices of American universities (see page 9, Table 2). Thirty-five were primarily small two-way student exchanges and 97 were one-way American student-abroad programs, most of which involved many more students. In addition, 25 other programs sent students abroad as a secondary part of their operations. Together, these programs provided opportunities for thousands of students, estimated at 3,500 in 1957–58 (*Inventory*, pp. 39–40). At least some of the programs are to be found in almost every geographical area of the non-Communist world, and even the Iron Curtain has not proved an insuperable barrier.

At least in the past, the significance of these programs has been less than these figures suggest. They have been concentrated in Europe. Furthermore, though the number of programs and persons participating is considerable, and the device is widely used by American universities, these programs are not the major factor in study abroad by American students. Of the 10,200 American students reported at foreign institutions by the Institute of International Education in 1957–58, 3,500 students were associated with American university programs including summer programs and special American-administered student programs.

In some few universities, the student-abroad programs are unusually significant. At institutions such as Oberlin, Smith, Stanford, or Lake Erie College, a substantial part of the students go overseas. Even at other universities, such as Syracuse or Antioch, the programs may play a central part in academic plans, even though smaller proportions of students take advantage of them. A large majority of institutions do not have student-abroad programs and at most institutions that do have them the programs are small in size and modest in importance.

American universities have thus accumulated nearly forty years of experience with student-abroad programs. Yet there has been a surprising lack of experimentation with various forms of the device except in the past few years. The bulk of the programs that are now operating are products of the 1950s, and so most of the universities administering them have had relatively little experience to evaluate. Partly for these reasons, the strengths and weaknesses of each program are not so evident as might be supposed.

Examples of Programs

The use of the term "student-abroad program" may imply that there is only one kind of program or that all the programs have much in common. This is no longer true. The programs vary in basic purpose and objectives, the type of relation with host-country groups, the kind of students they attract, the size of the group, the fields of study—indeed, in every characteristic imaginable. Consider the following five illustrations.

Earlham College is a small, church-affiliated, liberal arts college with high academic standards. In 1957, after lengthy discussions and studies, Earlham embarked upon a plan of group study abroad; France was the first country chosen and Mexico the second. Unless unforeseen circumstances intervene, in alternate years groups of students will go to France and to Mexico. Mexico City College will be the cooperating institution in Mexico. Earlham's basic objective is to give better instruction and wider experience to its students. A small institution with a limited faculty and limited library facilities, Earlham cannot give on campus, as a part of its regular instructional program, a sufficiently large number of courses dealing with foreign areas to provide for its interested students the opportunities available to students in larger institutions. Furthermore, the faculty and administration are convinced that living abroad, quite aside from the formal instruction, is valuable for the students. The basic educational values sought through the program are high.

As far as the Mexican part of the program is concerned, there is no formal contract between Earlham and Mexico City College; nevertheless, a detailed understanding exists. Earlham College selects 15 students, all of whom have had previous classes in Spanish, for participation; the minimum grade in Spanish must be in the high B's and the general academic grade no lower than a high C. The selection of students is made carefully, with attention to such qualifications as aptitude for smooth adjustment to foreign living patterns and other characteristics which might affect the success of the program. The students register at Earlham for a normal academic load during the semester to be spent in Mexico; two of the courses are taught by the accompanying faculty member, and the remainder are given by Mexico City College. All fees, including tuition, travel, and board and room, are paid to Earlham by the students; Earlham, in turn, pays to Mexico City College the tuition charge for each student and a small fee to cover medical and other such services, in addition to a fee for the use of classrooms in courses taught by the Earlham faculty member. Housing for the students is arranged by Mexico City College, but payment for lodging and food is sent to the proprietors by Earlham. Travel arrangements are made by Earlham, but Mexico City College meets the student group in Mexico City and transports them to their lodging places.

Since Earlham practices the semester system and Mexico City College the quarter system, the students arrive at Mexico City College during the middle of a quarter if they leave Earlham at the beginning of the second semester. Mexico City College undertakes to supply a series of orientation lectures and Earlham to give intensive language training during the period. At the opening of the new quarter, the students attend the regular classes previously selected. During the session the Earlham faculty member acts not only as instructor for specific courses, but also as general adviser for the students, who remain a cohesive group through the mechanism of the seminar, in spite of their dispersion in the classes. Although Mexico City College retains general administrative and disciplinary control over the students, all official acts with regard to the students are taken after consultation with the Earlham adviser. Toward the end of the session, the Earlham students preregister for the succeeding semester on their own campus (adapted from Adams and Cumberland, pp. 746–747).

Another program is that of Johns Hopkins in Bologna. It has established a Center or branch in Italy separate from any Italian university, although in close proximity to the University of Bologna. At this site it conducts a graduate school program in international relations. The 40 students, half from the United States and half from Europe, live in a series of apartments. Frequently an American and a European room together. Johns Hopkins administers the entire Center by itself, without participation by Europeans. Some four full-time staff members are sent to Bologna by Johns Hopkins, and their work is supplemented by part-time and guest European professors or visitors, giving courses or special lectures. American seminar methods are used throughout.

The Smith College Junior Year in Paris is illustrative of some of the junior years:

The students leave New York together on a French liner early in September. From Le Havre the group goes for one day to Paris, then proceeds by train to Aix-en-Provence. In Aix they are boarded in private families while they spend six weeks in concentrated drill in the French language. They attend classes in French grammar, composition, and phonetics, taught by local professors and *lycée* teachers, and write, in French, a formal paper on some subject dealing with the art or literature of southern France. They also attend a series of lectures and take field trips to nearby centers of local art and culture.

After this period they have a five day vacation, usually spent in independent travel, ending about November 1 in Paris, where they are again boarded in families. The girls take four courses during each semester. Usually one of these is a regular lecture course at some branch of the University of Paris. The others are special classes organized by Smith in such subjects as phonetics, seventeenth-century French literature, and modern art. For each regular university class attended the girls take an extra hour a week of work with a special tutor, who fills in the background, explains points that were unclear in the lecture, and so on. At the end of each term the girls take examinations prepared by the instructors of the special courses and by the professors or the tutors in the regular university courses. The grades, on a scale of zero to twenty, are then "converted" into letter grades in the American manner. A student successfully completing two semesters receives twenty-four credits. (The additional six usually covered in an academic year are granted for the work done in Aix.) The girls are then free to tour Europe on their own during the summer, or to return home at once (Garraty and Adams, pp. 204–205).

Summer programs vary as much as those during the academic year. Annually, Hope College conducts a six-weeks summer session in Vienna, in cooperation with the University of Vienna and the Institute of European Studies. Courses in German, history, music, art, and other subjects are taught by Austrian instructors specially appointed for the Hope College summer program. In each course an American faculty member serves as "Associate Instructor" to help in planning course outlines, selecting texts and materials, and determining final grades. Students reside in Austrian homes during the six weeks in Vienna. In conjunction with the Vienna Summer School, students take part in a noncredit, two-week study tour which is designed to introduce them to contemporary Europe through a series of high-level briefings and conferences.

The program is designed to offer students intensive academic work in subjects in which the European location can substantially add to the understanding of the material covered. It is also intended to acquaint students with European culture, to provide for academic growth and social maturity, and to inform them of the complexities of international relations and United States foreign policy. It is anticipated that the program will provide an increasing number of Hope College faculty members with an opportunity to spend a summer in Austria coordinating courses in their respective fields with their European colleagues.

The program of Howard College, Birmingham, Alabama is quite different. It arranges a summer tour for students in languages, art, music, and history. The tour begins at the Sorbonne or the Alliance Française in Paris, depending upon the choice of the participating students, and covers most of Europe and part of the Near East. The tour may or may not include formal lectures. Elaborate briefs which discuss the places to see and study are prepared for the students prior to leaving. The tour lasts for three months. Students are tested upon their return. The largest group was 20 in 1951. Six professors are engaged in the program on the Howard campus, two in languages, two in art, and one each in history and music.

These faculty members prepare the instructions, brief the students, and test and grade them when they return.

Organizing for Study Abroad

The American student-abroad programs are almost always originated at the American university, since participation by host-country institutions is often minimal and outside financial support is normally a supplementary rather than a major factor. Frequently, study-abroad programs are completely or nearly completely financed by fees charged the participants. Some universities make available one or more scholarships. It is difficult for any university to obtain outside financing on a continuing basis for these programs. Government agencies and foundations are reluctant to finance specific university programs of indefinite duration. However, some of the more enterprising institutions have received support from a variety of sources, varying from year to year. The Johns Hopkins Bologna Center has obtained grants or assistance from several European and American sources, for example.

That initiative is in the hands of American universities is natural, given the programs' one-way nature. The advantages to be gained from sending American students abroad are primarily on the American side. This is particularly true for those programs that have little relationship with host-country institutions, and a substantial majority of the programs are of this nature.

The relative degrees of responsibility for American student-abroad programs taken by the American and host universities, respectively, extend from virtually none at all by one of them to complete dual operation and policy control. The involvement of host universities is greatest where American students go abroad to obtain a regular foreign degree, diploma, or certificate. Arrangements such as these, with few exceptions, fall outside the American student-abroad programs, although some individual Americans seek these degree on their own. A number of Americans are enrolled in universities in the Netherlands for medical degrees, for example.

American student-abroad programs really begin with a lesser degree of host-university responsibility. A few of the programs send American undergraduates or graduates abroad to take regular work at a host-country institution, but the students return home and get their degree from the American university. Credits are transferred. The Fordham junior year is a good example of this kind of program. It is part of a three-year honors program, and only a few students go abroad in any one year. Fordham establishes the general outline of the program and selects the students, all of whom are outstanding in their work. It also provides general information about the experiences the students are likely to encounter while abroad. Once the students leave the shores of the United States, however, they are on their own. There are no program directors to help them out. They are like any other student at a European university, finding housing, registering in the same manner as others, and taking the same courses. Fordham evaluates their work abroad for American university credit by means of a series of papers which are graded at Fordham in competition with those who have stayed at home. Obviously, a program such as this is suitable only for a few exceptional students. For these, the program offers the most thorough immersion in European universities and culture possible, short of staying on and receiving a European degree.

European and some Mexican universities have such large quantities of foreign students that they have established special courses for foreigners. Often, these courses are not offered by regular universities at all but by special institutes or organizations which may or may not have a distant relation to a university. The *Cours de Civilisation* is one of these in France. Many of these special courses are looked down upon by European scholars because of their low standards. American student-abroad programs have often made extensive use of these courses, sometimes modifying them by adopting their own system of evaluating their students' progress or arranging for special courses established for only their students but taught by instructors of the institutes. For the most part, the students of the Sophie Newcomb junior year concentrate their efforts in offerings of the *Cours de Civilisation* or other special institutes. Some of the problems encountered are illustrated by a young woman from Sophie Newcomb who said, "the *Cours* is at about the level of the secondary school courses I took in Mississippi." [2] In a program such as that of Sophie Newcomb, the American university selects the students, arranges for any briefing,

[2] Quoted in Donald J. Shank, "The Junior Year Abroad: A Critical Look" (New York: Institute of International Education, n.d.), p. 3.

sends the students abroad as a group under a resident director, provides for special language training, obtains suitable housing, and determines grades.

There is only a short step from the Sophie Newcomb type of program to that involving no host institution initiative or responsibility. Some American universities have established student-abroad programs under which they have set up special courses entirely under their own supervision and responsibility, though they hire persons from the host country to teach the courses. The logical progression of events leads also to a number of courses taught by the resident director of the program, normally an American university professor. Where all of this is done on a large scale, the result is an overseas branch of an American university, like the Johns Hopkins program in Bologna or the Stanford programs in Germany, France, Italy, and Japan. In these programs no host institution is involved at all.

Selection by an American university of the kind of relation to a host institution it prefers is not easy. All the advantage does not lie with one form. Language barriers may argue for special courses. Desire for cultural immersion may argue for regular courses of foreign universities. Large numbers of students may argue for overseas branches. And a few of the newer student-abroad programs concentrate on research or field work, not courses. The advantage of close affiliation with a host institution under such circumstances is greatly reduced, and there may be disadvantages if host-institution professors are not accustomed to research or field work.

Partly the decision may rest upon the kind of institution with which an American university can affiliate. If the objective is to find an institution that matches the American university, difficulties may be encountered because of the many differences in institutions of higher education, country to country (see Chapter 2). For example, in Continental Europe, where many student-abroad programs are located, there are relatively few private universities. Consequently, there are many American private universities associating with public institutions abroad in student-abroad programs. Relationships between private or religious universities such as two Roman Catholic institutions, as is the case with Fordham, are not found frequently. If the characteristics to be matched are extended to size of institution and courses of study, additional difficulties occur in finding a similar or "twin" institution.

There is also the matter of prestige. Student-abroad programs that do affiliate with a host-country institution often find that it is not possible to develop a relationship with the most prestigeful universities of a country. Even where that is possible, an affiliation with one of the most prestigeful faculties of the university is almost out of the question; a special university institute, perhaps yes; a regular prestigeful faculty, no.

Furthermore, all parts of host institutions are seldom equally involved in cooperative programs with American universities. In American student-abroad programs that have close affiliations with host institutions, only a small part of a large host institution is likely to be aware that any such program exists. There may have been formal approval by a rector or some other university official, but few professors are aware of it, even though they may have American students in their classes, because of the large number of all students, host country and foreign, attending the lectures. There may be an officially approved relationship, but it causes little change in university practice, and concerns few. Most of the summer-abroad student programs that use otherwise vacant university facilities involve few persons beyond the special staffs assigned to them. Though there are exceptions, as a rule the American student-abroad programs have little relation to host-country universities as total institutions or to any of the regular faculties.

Under such circumstances, it is only natural that some American universities exercise careful choice concerning which host institution, if any, they wish to affiliate with, and under what conditions. That more have not done so in a manner that would maintain high standards for the programs is one of the principal indictments of the programs. Even some of those that have exercised care have found that the host institution cannot, in fact, offer courses of a quality equal to that on the home campus; the Oberlin music junior year abroad is a case in point. Certainly some institutions would do better to get extensive advice on the matter from universities running programs of high quality or from such organizations as the Council on Student Travel or the Institute of International Education. It is important to select a host institution on the basis of its suitability for the objectives of the program, its technical competence, and the availability and adequacy of its resources. If an acceptable host institution cannot be found, it is better to organize a program without one or drop the idea entirely.

It is apparent that extensive planning must precede any new program and continually accompany an existing one so that it can adjust to program realities. A wide difference exists in the care with which continuous planning has been undertaken between those projects reasonably successful in reaching their objectives and those not very successful. Two examples of excellently planned programs are the Smith and Fordham junior years abroad. In these cases planning has been the work of a number of persons with effective central leadership. One example of good advance planning is that undertaken by the University of Kansas under former Chancellor Murphy.[3]

Selection of Personnel

Each subvariety of student-abroad program has its own distinctive set of personnel. The larger programs typically send 10 to 100 students overseas at a time, recruited from one or several American campuses. An American field director—an academic person —accompanies them, gives over-all leadership, serves as adviser, and may even teach a course. Assisting the field director in a few instances is a host-country national who may be hired by the American university or attached to a host-institution's staff. The local assistant performs many detailed services for the group on a part-time basis, such as the making of local contacts and arranging for housing and transportation. In some instances outside organizations such as The Experiment in International Living contract to perform these services for the student-abroad programs.

Under programs such as the Oberlin music junior year abroad at the Mozarteum in Salzburg, Austria, where there is dependence on regular courses at a host institution, the selection of host-country staff is, of course, made by the host university. Most large student-abroad programs have special courses for the students, the staff members of some of which are selected by the American university. At home, the American university designates someone as on-campus

[3] See *The University and World Affairs,* a report to the Chancellor of a faculty committee of the University of Kansas, 1960.

coordinator of the program, and in a large number of cases he will be assisted by an advisory policy committee.

Five kinds of personnel choices may thus be made by the larger study-abroad programs: the field director, his host-country assistant or liaison, host-country teaching staff, American students, and the campus coordinator. Of these, two hold key positions. The campus coordinator gives continuing long-range policy guidance, helps select students, and coordinates the program with academic work on the home campus. The field director sets most of the standards of the work for each group (Garraty and Adams, p. 78).

The American university branch overseas has a somewhat different structure. The field director is the central figure since he is, in effect, dean of a university branch with all the responsibility for students, staff, and physical facilities that such a position carries. The American university must select the entire staff of the branch, most of whom are Americans, although a small proportion may be host-country nationals. Personnel requirements also include American students (in the Johns Hopkins Bologna Center a matching group of European students in addition) and a campus liaison or coordinator. In the Johns Hopkins case the field director is in charge of all aspects of the program. A field director is normally dependent on a campus coordinator for help in staff recruitment, selection of students, and dovetailing of overseas education into the long-range academic plans of each student and the university as a whole.

A few of the small student-abroad programs such as Fordham's provide no field or resident director. In addition to the fact that small programs are typically based on the philosophy that students should take care of themselves while abroad and register for regular courses at a host-country university, there is the additional consideration that without a sufficient number of students paying fees it is impossible to support a field director.

Depending on the kind of program, the field director, the campus coordinator, or both, largely determine the success or failure of the program. Few other persons will have so deep an involvement. The coordinator usually is the major factor in selection of students— sometimes the sole judge, while in other cases the regular academic departments play a role. The field director is the person who sets the tone for the period of study abroad. A field director for a student-abroad program should know how to fit the experiences of American students, in a host-country system of education, into a pattern meaningful in relation to their experiences at their home universities.

It is somewhat easier to select coordinators than directors. Coordinators often are the persons who take the initiative in setting up the program and, in effect, select themselves. In any event, the position is normally part time and requires a minimum amount of adjustment or accommodation. The field director's position requires that he absent himself from the campus for a long time. A shortage of able field directors is not uncommon for programs that have been under way for some years. The most frequent solution for shortages of faculty members is to recruit from outside the university on an *ad hoc* basis. Most of the student-abroad programs have recruited field directors in this manner year after year. The Hamilton practice of rotating field directors among members of the French department is a signal departure from standard practice, although it is uncertain whether Hamilton can continue this policy after its program has been in operation as long as some of the other junior year undertakings.

Host-country assistants should primarily be selected on the basis of their ability to make suitable local contacts and arrangements, thus relieving the American resident director of many details with which he may not be familiar. Some programs have overlooked the usefulness of the host-country assistant and have failed to appoint one. Host-country teachers or faculty members, in addition to meeting the usual academic standards of competence in their fields, should understand something of the American university system and be sympathetic to study-abroad objectives. Many programs have failed to apply the latter two criteria to host-country faculty members.

In most programs, the selection of American students proceeds by means of a few more formal criteria than are used with faculty members, perhaps in part because there are often more applicants and a greater number to be selected. For example, a certain grade average may be specified, such as a C plus or B average. Minimum language qualifications are often set for junior-year-abroad programs. Certain courses may be prerequisite, or advanced standing required. An image of an ideal student may be conveyed in a brochure for the larger student-abroad programs. The designation of desired qualities in students is rather meaningless when all students are required to go abroad as at Lake Erie College, or where a program has difficulty in filling a quota sufficiently large to make it financially feasible.

Experience indicates that the most important quality to be sought in students who are to go abroad is academic competence, assuming program objectives are primarily academic. Are the students of a high caliber in terms of ability and academic accomplishment? Have they had suitable subject matter, area, and language courses? For students who go abroad for academic credit or to work toward a degree, these questions are obviously of the utmost importance. For those who go abroad on noncredit programs, such as the Smith Africa summer program, academic competence is also an important quality, since academic objectives are not confined to credit or degree activities. For example, a nondegree academic objective may be acquisition of knowledge, such as learning about other countries and peoples, even though not for credit. Nondegree academic desiderata may include the ability to engage in activities of a semi-teaching nature, such as giving talks about one's country abroad.

Dedication and enthusiasm are other important qualities. Students going abroad are often enthusiastic, but the direction of their enthusiasm is another thing. It is important that they have enthusiasm for the major purposes of the program. Their objectives should be clearly formulated and academically relevant.

Cultural empathy may be crucial to what a student learns during his stay abroad. Those who fail to understand or who simply reject the culture in which they find themselves close their minds.

Personal adjustment abroad should be easier for students than for faculty members, for two main reasons. Normally they are not married and thus they do not travel with families and are not bothered by family problems. Being younger, they are perhaps more flexible than faculty members. To be sure, the living conditions American students face when abroad are quite different from those enjoyed by American faculty members; perhaps greater adjustment is necessary because of this factor. For example, host-country dormitories, even where they exist, are often inferior to those in the United States. Private housing near universities often falls below minimum standards. On the other hand, many students in Europe live in local middle-class homes and have close contact with European families; adjustments are required if living with another family under strange conditions is to be successful. In addition, adjustment to different educational procedures and content is necessary.

Just because a student is undertaking honors work is no sign that he may be successful abroad in a plan of studies. Academic qualifications are a necessary and even the basic criterion, but not a sufficient one. Because it is difficult for universities to reject applicants who have favorable academic records, some of them have relied upon the Experiment in International Living for screening candidates for adjustment factors after the university has reviewed them for academic qualities.

The qualities of a group of students for study abroad can be considerably strengthened by suitable preparation and briefing. Preparation extends back over several years. Students can prepare for going abroad by the courses they take for a year or two previously, as in the Western College for Women study tour abroad. Courses in the culture and language of the country to be visited and courses in American institutions as well are a necessary background. Students who know little of their own country cannot interpret it very adequately.[4] Nor do they have a standard of comparison.

Briefing materials and/or sessions, some adequate and some quite inadequate, are also used by most programs. The programs sometimes specially contract for briefing services abroad, or hold briefings of their own. Some of the year-long student-abroad programs incorporate briefing into the beginning of the year by taking the students to a provincial town for six or eight weeks of intensive area and language training.

The results of the efforts to select, prepare, and brief students properly have been disappointing to date in nearly half the programs and have been spotty in some others. More than one of the student-abroad programs in Europe have developed host-country criticism because of the poor quality of students. American students abroad have tended to be C plus to B plus in quality: the A students have tended to stay home; the poor students are usually not selected. Most have had some area and language training be-

[4] See *American Students Abroad: Goodwill Ambassadors?* (Syracuse: University of Syracuse, Maxwell Graduate School of Citizenship and Public Affairs, vol. 28, January, 1958), 8 pp.

fore going overseas, although some went in search of it. As a rule, the academic preparation and experience of American undergraduates are less than those of the highly selected European university students. Though the majority of American students did not have severe personal adjustment problems abroad, cultural empathy was characteristic of less than a majority.

There were difficulties in harnessing enthusiasm and dedication for academic purposes in many instances. Specific academic objectives were found in a majority of undergraduates overseas, but they were not necessarily the sole or principal motivation. Some students went abroad for liberal education purposes, others to work on their subject matter specialties. Nonacademic objectives were present in most instances, and were conspicuous among students in some programs. Students went abroad because they did not have defined academic interests, and they thought that traveling would be a pleasant way to spend a year. Some had friends or relatives in Europe they wished to visit. Others went because someone offered the opportunity. The most frequent motive given by American students for going abroad was a thirst for travel, adventure, and new ways of looking at life. Such an objective may be related to academic goals, in that it can lead to new lines of inquiry and be a spur to learning, or develop new experiences that will help adapt present and future knowledge to later life; but it is not central.

How do the students sent abroad compare with those at home? The better study-abroad programs probably send students with academic motives typical of at least the average run of comparable undergraduates at home (those of C plus to B plus quality). There are many students at home who fail to have clear-cut academic objectives as their sole or principal motivation. The policy question is whether typical motivations form an adequate criterion for students going abroad for study.

Program Objectives and Accomplishments

To an American institution considering adopting a student-abroad program or to a student considering whether he should participate in one or another program, go abroad by himself, or stay at home, the objectives to be achieved are (or should be) of major importance in reaching a decision. Objectives have often been vague and ill-conceived, but uniformly the programs have emphasized the contribution of the program to the American students and the American university, more than any contribution they may make abroad.

Among the substantive innovations flowing from these programs at American universities have been curricular and course changes. Special curricular provisions for the large student-abroad programs and overseas branches have been made at the universities undertaking them. Where only a few students have gone abroad from any one college or department, the problem has largely been one of determining the credit to be given and the on-campus courses, if any, to which the overseas experience is equivalent. However, in programs where a large number or proportion of students go abroad, basic curricular replanning has been necessary, as at Lake Erie where the whole junior class spends a term abroad or at Oberlin where the whole junior class in music spends a year overseas. Since student-abroad participation is often confined in practice to humanities and, on occasion, to social science majors, curricular problems may not be institution-wide.

Enrollment in regular or special language or cultural history courses before students go abroad is common for students in many programs. Thus Hollins has a one-semester pro-seminar for girls planning to go abroad. On return, some students have found their interests modified and so have selected courses that they otherwise would have passed by. As a whole, enrollment in courses in the humanities, social sciences, and foreign languages that focus on the country or area of the program has increased. Emphasis has been on the understanding of a single culture rather than on courses with more generalized objectives. The impact on courses and curricula is negative as well as positive. The selection of certain courses before going abroad and after returning means the omission of other courses. And study abroad for credit means many fewer courses on the home campus, a situation that has led to criticism and lack of support of programs that require a year abroad.

Several of the student-abroad programs expect the recently returned students to relate their experiences to the other students through class participation, talks before campus groups, and informally through dormitory living. This can be particularly effective at small liberal arts colleges or other small institutions where students get to know one another well. It is likely that such impact may be greater if the students return for the second semester or winter or spring quarter as at Hollins College rather than coming back in the fall when so much is new on the campus.

Although objectives of the programs are not always clear, and vary greatly, most programs have included at least three objectives for American students, namely, to develop language competence, to make friends, and to acquire knowledge of a foreign culture and at the same time a greater insight into one's own. To some extent, all three objectives have been achieved. Sending of American students abroad to non-English-speaking countries greatly augments their language ability. On return, the students are far ahead of those that stay at home in ability to use the language. The programs stimulate interest in language instruction. There are more majors in French, Italian, and Spanish at Smith as a result of its several junior years abroad. Language competence is one of the main substantive results of student-abroad programs.

As for making friends, the testimony of observers and participants is overwhelmingly that many friends have been made. After returning home, students report continuing correspondence with families with whom they lived in the host country. Continuing peer friendships are also common. A few international marriages occur. Some American students make almost no acquaintances in the host country, and a few actually have unpleasant experiences. The latter are largely confined to those who had severe adjustment problems or who had less than adequate academic backgrounds before going abroad.

The effect of the programs on the American students' perception of other countries is not uniform. Some become more defensive about the United States and develop an antipathy to the country they visit. Good international relations are not necessarily the result of the programs. Yet, as a whole, students return with a greater interest in world affairs in general and in the country they have visited in particular. Also, there is a greater likelihood that they will participate in international affairs activities in their home communities and evidence a greater interest in foreign visitors and students on the home campus. At the very least, most of them have learned much about another culture. There is a general desire of students to return again overseas. Their experience has been encouraging to them. (See also Garraty and Adams, pp. 146–147.)

More difficult to determine is what effect the programs have on the total academic experience of a student. A student gets behind in certain work as a result of going abroad unless he adds an over-seas experience to a complete curriculum at home. What is the balance of the gains and losses?

Are students who go abroad those who tend to be more interested in world affairs to begin with, so that subsequent participation and interest in world affairs is not derived from being abroad but a reflection of self-selection? Self-selection does take place and re-flects the original interest of the students, but such interests are nurtured and developed during their stay abroad. Both students and their professors reported this to be the case.

Some of the students reported being more serious in their studies on their return to the campus. The experience was a maturing one, and their value systems had been altered and developed. Human values were more important to them, cultural differences appreci-ated. Higher education had more purpose, more relevance to their personal objectives.

Women students in particular felt able to afford such an experi-ence; men were more concerned with their vocational-professional objectives and tended to stay at home in order to pursue them more vigorously and directly, even though more narrowly. The impact was greatest in such fields as literature, language, history, music, and art. In most other fields, there was a net failure to accumulate knowledge that would have been acquired at home. Even within the area of humanities, the knowledge accumulated abroad was a special kind of knowledge, not equal in scope to that which would have been obtained at home in an equal period of time.

The student-abroad programs varied considerably in the extent to which they immersed the students in foreign cultures and foreign university systems. Undoubtedly, those programs that presented more opportunities for cultural immersion were also those that had a greater cultural impact on the students. The Fordham junior year abroad maximizes this immersion factor. Some of the over-seas branch programs or closely supervised junior years abroad minimize it. With special, independent courses and with their personal and social behavior supervised quite closely (often, it is said, in order to protect the good name of the program and assure the parents of the students that their children are being properly taken care of), the students see a minimum of the host country aside from the usual tourist attractions unless contacts are specifically en-couraged and provided for by project design.

Few of the student programs, large or small, have had as an objective substantial impact on host-country persons or institutions other than the vague statement that international friendship and understanding of the United States are desirable. Some student-abroad programs have helped to reinforce host-sponsored activities for foreign students such as those of Mexico City College for American students. The Johns Hopkins Bologna branch, although formally it does not have host institution-building among its objectives, has enjoyed the compliment of imitation paid by those who have proposed an Italian international relations center at Milan. The Johns Hopkins long-range goal of European unity also has institution-building implications, but it cannot be said what small contributory effect, if any, the program has or will have. The problem of overcrowding or straining the facilities of host universities has been serious in only a minority of instances, since up to now little use has been made of regular courses in most programs, and even where regular courses have been attended they have often been large lecture sections where extra students are hardly noticed.

In the long run, the student-abroad programs must be judged by the effect on the American students who participate. This is or should be the prime objective. In arriving at an assessment, the total education pattern of a student must be considered. For example, a student-abroad program may result in students learning more facts about a given country, better retention of the facts over a period of time, and more influence of such facts on their lives after leaving college. Yet the program may be a minor influence on the participating students even in regard to international affairs, and it may have almost no influence on students who do not directly participate—the vast majority of students, in most cases. The better programs have had impacts on a substantial portion of the students who have participated, impacts that would not have occurred at home, impacts that are considered of high value in the total pattern of their educational experiences.[5] However, a majority of the programs have had disappointing results to date in this and other respects.

[5] A summary of the findings of other studies of the impact of student-abroad programs is to be found in Irwin Abrams, *Study Abroad* (Washington: U.S. Department of Health, Education, and Welfare, 1961), pp. 15–17. In general, the findings of other studies confirm what has been reported herein: the more substantial impacts are in the areas of general cultural values, political-international attitudes, and personal maturity. See also Garraty and Adams, chap. 9, and Adams and Cumberland, pp. 249 and 256.

Chapter 5

ALTERNATIVES IN STUDENT-ABROAD PROGRAMS

Do the obvious opportunities in undergraduate study abroad over-balance the disadvantages of missing an academic year on the home campus? This is the crucial question for any individual or institution that may be considering the choice. Universities in other countries have great merits in their own environments. When another system of education is involved these merits may be of less importance than they are at home, and comparative disadvantages may be present. Most universities abroad do not offer the coordinated planning of courses, the variety of electives, the central campus with its possibility for association with other students and faculty members, the excellent equipment, the relatively small classes, the readily available and well-stocked libraries, and the extracurricular activities that typify American universities.

The main objective of a student-abroad program is to give students academic and educational experiences abroad that they could not reasonably expect to receive at home and to assure that there are advantages to these experiences that offset the disadvantages of being away from the home campus for a substantial period of time. Most of the programs are centered on classwork, since classwork is the normal means through which academic credit is received. At one extreme a few university programs, such as the Stanford branch in Germany, use transplanted American professors almost exclusively in rather standard American university courses with only American students. A few other programs, such as that of Fordham in Europe, rely entirely upon regular courses at European universities taught by European professors, in which the American student is the foreigner. Most programs fall somewhere in between.

Devices include regular host-country institution courses with special tutors for the students in the group, special host-country institution courses for foreign and perhaps only American students, and special courses for students of the group only, taught by host-country nationals.

Language barrier aside, the overwhelming experience is that few institutions will find it possible to permit their students to take *only* regular courses at a foreign university without falling behind in their academic work in this country. The basic reason for this lies in the many differences between the system of higher education in the United States and educational systems overseas. What has meaning for one system may have no meaning for another. There is much more possibility of transference between some than others; for example, the English and many of the Commonwealth university systems are similar enough to the system in the United States so that participation in regular classes by American students will be valuable without any supplemental work. But this may be far from true of the Continental higher education systems or those which they have most influenced, such as universities in Latin America and some Asian countries. In countries where the professor is king, where he may or may not appear for his classes, where he teaches whatever appeals to his special interest rather than attempting any systematic survey of a topic, where there are no course examinations or American-style term papers, where the professor is seldom seen outside of class, where give-and-take discussion in the classroom is unknown, and where classes number several hundreds and sometimes a few thousands of students, it is understandable that American student-abroad programs tend to favor special classes for their students or at least the arranging of special class sessions devoted to going over some of the material in the regular classes.

In study-abroad programs, there are distinct limitations to the assignment of reading and the use of books in furthering the education of students. The counterpart of the American university library with its open shelves, excellent catalogue, able reference librarians, and ample well-lighted reading rooms is not to be found in many countries. Despite the excellent national and university libraries in Europe, most American student-abroad programs have been forced to provide an essential minimum library from their own resources. While the multitude of host-country periodicals and newspapers overseas may be an advantage, on the whole, there are fewer available reading materials for the undergraduate in most other countries than he would find at his own home campus. However, advanced students, especially graduate students, can find valuable and unique collections abroad ín their fields of specialization.

While some distinctive opportunities for study-abroad programs lie in making available to American students certain classroom opportunities not possible at home, in field work, research, and observation the unique experiences possible are almost unlimited. In the humanities, this type of activity has been fairly well developed: going to the theater, attending concerts, studying at art centers, or writing term papers on localities of historical interest. Yet there are many unexplored possibilities for field work, research, and observation in other subjects, such as the social sciences, education, agriculture, biological sciences, geography, geology, communication. It could involve observation of institutions in action and discussions or interviews. Antioch places its students in jobs abroad, just as it does in the United States. Research or other work in the field requires presence in the field, whereas information derived from reading or lectures about foreign countries can often be obtained just as well at home campuses.

Temporary immersion in a foreign culture is a valuable experience. Though it scarcely results from mere attendance at the university, it can be promoted by contacts away from the lecture halls, and such opportunities are provided by most programs. Joint meetings or social gatherings are held where the American and the host-country students can get acquainted with one another. What American students miss by not living in dormitories may be replaced by living with families, most of which have intellectual or professional interests. It is almost impossible to arrange social intercourse with host-country professors. Yet mingling with the population outside the universities matures most students and may give them a different awareness of their own country, its shortcomings and strengths.

The Junior Year Abroad

American study-abroad programs have emphasized the junior year. Though there are many variations, a typical junior year abroad includes nine to fifteen months overseas for college credit, with class and field work in the humanities and languages. The program is supervised by an American professor, although it normally involves some regular or special courses taught by host-country professors as well. The stress on humanities and languages has meant that the junior year abroad has appealed to a distinct group of students at American universities. Those who are following a general liberal arts curriculum often find that a year abroad can contribute effectively to their educational objectives. The requirements for majors in these areas are not so restrictive as those in fields such as the sciences, engineering, education, or even some of the social sciences. A year abroad does not interfere with rigid course sequences in liberal arts since few exist. Because of the general nature of major requirements in fields such as the humanities or languages, it is not always clear just what academic work the students are giving up at home during their stay overseas. Many of the majors in these fields are not highly job-motivated; often they are young women of better than average means who expect that marriage and family life will have the first call on them in the future.

The better junior-year-abroad programs such as the Smith and Hamilton junior years have made a real contribution to students in these fields. The programs have given foreign-language specialists an opportunity to use the language under rather exacting circumstances in a country in which it is the native tongue. Students in art or music have gone to countries where great men have made and are making unique contributions. Majors in history have visited places where great events have taken place. Such students have made distinct academic progress.

The better junior-year-abroad programs tend to have clear-cut objectives for limited groups of students. Yet the term "liberal arts" has many meanings in American higher education. Those who have been in charge of the less successful programs have often not distinguished between the specialized needs of majors in humanities, languages, or the general liberal arts and the more basic needs of majors in other fields for a liberal education. Some program sponsors have tried to promote the traditional junior year package to students majoring in any field, perhaps partly because of a feeling that liberal arts are good for any student, and partly to increase the number of "takers" so as to assure a strong financial base for the program. To say that a liberal education is important for all university students is one thing; to say that a liberal arts specialization in the junior year is appropriate for all students is quite another.

The junior-year programs have made occasional concessions to majors in fields other than the liberal arts. A biology major may be steered to a specialized course in his field at Munich by the Wayne State junior year, for example. A student in the Fordham junior year can take work in nearly any field offered at a foreign university. The more typical programs do not permit their students to take a wide selection of courses: at least in practice the students do not do so. For example, the Syracuse semester in Italy offers courses only in fine arts, history, Italian, and political science. The programs are geared to a relatively few courses in the humanities and languages which, with minor variations, are taken by all or most of the students. Where electives exist, as in the Syracuse program, they usually fall within relatively few fields. Even under some of the most diversified programs, humanities and languages normally constitute three-fourths or more of a student's work for the year.

In this situation, a student majoring in some other field will be hard pressed to graduate on schedule if he joins the program, even though he receives full credit for the work he has completed. In American higher education, the junior and senior years are those in which progressively greater specialization in a major takes place. Liberal arts electives are few at these levels; general education requirements have been met in the sophomore and freshman years. As long as this practice continues, the traditional junior year formula will be useful only to a limited group of students.

There are two possibilities for expanding junior-year-abroad programs. One is increase of the number of American universities participating, the other is emphasis on other subject matter. It would be undesirable and indeed unnecessary for all the nearly 1,500 institutions of higher education in the United States that offer work in the liberal arts to sponsor a junior-year-abroad program for humanities, language, and general liberal arts majors. Yet if the advantages of participating in the better programs were presented to liberal arts students in all colleges and universities, thousands of additional applicants would be forthcoming. The junior-year movement is still concentrated in the East, although there are at least a few institutions with such programs in every part of the country. It is concentrated in private institutions, although a few public universities have organized student-abroad programs. A more representative group of junior-year-abroad institutions, public as well as private, in the South, Middle West, and West may be desirable, providing that the new programs profit from the experience of the projects over the last thirty-five to forty years.

Humanities, language, and liberal arts majors are but a small part of the total student population in higher education in the United States. Does the formula provide a pattern that could be utilized more fully in other fields? The social sciences, education, and business administration seem to be three areas that might be suitable for year-abroad programs. The social sciences are already represented by a few programs, such as the Smith junior year at Geneva. Teacher education is represented by the program at Adelphi. Majors in a number of other fields occasionally join one or another of the existing programs. It would be preferable to have a number of programs specifically tailored to the needs of students in these several fields, since any program that does not rely almost completely on the offerings of a foreign university must have a severely limited number of course alternatives for its students. In American higher education the courses appropriate for students with different major fields of concentration vary widely, especially at the junior and senior levels. In these years, only one or two at most out of four or six courses per year are likely to be available as liberal arts electives. An important contribution to the junior-year-abroad movement would be new programs with courses specifically developed to meet the needs of students in some major fields of concentration other than the humanities and languages, at the same time relating the content of the courses to the culture or resources of the host country. In addition to courses similar to those that could be taken at home, classwork, field observation, and research in social, economic, and political institutions and practices in the host country could be arranged for social science students. Education majors could delve into comparative education systems. And those in business administration could concentrate on foreign trade, American business operations abroad, and host-country practices.

Even with such adaptation, the junior-year formula does not seem appropriate to fields of specialization such as the sciences, engineering, and most of the undergraduate work for the professions. First of all, these are realms in which liberal education electives in the junior year are exceedingly limited and in some cases nonexistent.

Second, such study involves many laboratory courses, or courses in which expensive equipment is necessary. To build suitable laboratories or purchase duplicate equipment for junior-year programs abroad is beyond the financial resources of American universities. European, Latin American, or Asian universities usually have a shortage of such facilities. It would be impossible to rely upon their equipment for any sizable junior-year programs. For a few highly superior students who already have fluency in the language of the host country, specialized study abroad in these fields in the junior year is possible and may be desirable. The Fordham program, relying on host-institution courses entirely and being highly selective of the students it sends, is an instance.

The shortage of educational resources abroad in comparison with those at home is illustrated by the Oberlin School of Music program under which all juniors are required to spend the year at Salzburg. On the surface, this program would appear to benefit from the strength of European higher education. Perhaps it does so in regard to music theory, composition, and education. But "the students who wish to become performing musicians say that the coaching resources of the Mozarteum and musical resources of Salzburg cannot compare with those of Oberlin and Cleveland." [1] Garraty and Adams observe, "It is questionable whether Oberlin's music majors have much to gain academically from their junior year at the Mozarteum in Salzburg, for the opinion of unprejudiced observers is that the level of music education there is not as high as it is at Oberlin itself" (p. 78). For these reasons, Oberlin is considering making the program purely voluntary.

Other Undergraduate Programs

The junior year is only one of four undergraduate years. Obviously the senior year has not appealed to the sponsors of student-abroad programs or the student participants. It is the capstone of the undergraduate experience, and most American universities require residence on the home campus throughout the year. The freshman year also seems inappropriate for an experience abroad, since the student is just becoming acquainted with a university and beginning his course of study.

[1] Donald J. Shank, "The Junior Year Abroad: A Critical Look" (New York: Institute of International Education, n.d.), p. 5.

In American higher education, the first two years of undergraduate work are devoted largely to general education, the last two years to work that is considerably more specialized. The Universities as a rule either require general education courses of all students or impose a distribution requirement under which the student chooses several courses in diverse fundamental disciplines. As a result, students usually take, among other work, basic courses in humanities, foreign languages, English, social science, and natural science. For the most part these requirements are met during the freshman and sophomore years; in total they amount to about a year's academic work. Without in any way hindering their academic progress, sophomores enrolled in a wide variety of curricula could go overseas for such general education experiences. General education could be strengthened thereby. Instead of speaking a foreign language in class only, students could use it in everyday situations. Instead of looking at photographs, they could visit buildings of classic architecture. Instead of reading about a foreign culture, they could observe it at first hand, and indeed participate in it. The problems of effective communication and clarity of expression in English could assume new meaning and importance. Such immersion in a foreign culture could be a telling academic experience in the lives of sophomores. It could be as useful to a future engineer as to a social scientist, to a future chemist as to a teacher of foreign languages.

In order to profit most from an academic experience abroad, any student, graduate or undergraduate, needs to have some elements of a general education before he goes. In the case of a sophomore study-abroad program there is a double basis of general education, that which is obtained before going and that which is obtained abroad. This situation produces some difficulties if a large increase in general education requirements is to be avoided. If the host-country language is other than English, an advantage of studying abroad would lie in the furtherance of language facility. Yet other aspects of the general education abroad, such as some classwork, reading, and certainly field work and out-of-class contacts, require some language facility on arrival abroad. Again, study abroad may be valuable in terms of learning about another system of government or a different economy or social system. Yet in order to understand fully that with which he comes into contact, a student should have a good deal of knowledge of the host country, its institutions and people, before going abroad, as well as a knowledge of the United States. Some background in the fine arts and the cultural history of the host country would be desirable before going there, although special knowledge in this field can also be obtained abroad.

No single measure can solve these difficulties. As far as language preparation is concerned, the requirements are clear. If the aim is to send sophomores abroad with basic foreign language competence, some combination of secondary school language instruction, instruction in the freshman year, or special intensive summer language work must be found. This is far from impossible. With the renewed emphasis on foreign languages in the secondary schools and with the language laboratory methods now available at most major universities, the average competence of sophomores in a foreign language may rise sharply. For those who reach the sophomore year without language competence, study abroad in an English-speaking country would be a useful alternative. English is the principal international language and is the language for university instruction in many countries around the world. Because student-abroad programs have been so closely associated with learning a language, it has often been overlooked that lack of fluency in a foreign language need be no barrier to effective experiences in countries where English is widely used.

It is also essential that students going abroad for study have before leaving a minimum amount of work in the humanities and social sciences as applied to the United States and the host country, if study abroad is to be of much academic value. Assuming that the usual American university requirement of about a year's work in general or liberal education is to remain, perhaps half of it could be taken before going, and half abroad. This immediately suggests the possibility of a sophomore semester of six months abroad, rather than a year as is more typical of the junior level programs. Such a shorter period would also ease another problem, that of sequence and laboratory courses in the beginning sciences. Lecture courses in these areas might be offered abroad, laboratory work being postponed until a return to the home campus. Or sophomore sequences in sciences and related fields could be concentrated in a shorter period just before or after the study abroad.

Three to six months abroad of general education at the sophomore level are in accord with the findings of several recent surveys and reports. Donald J. Shank found that "most students testify that the contributions of foreign experience are in general education rather than progress in their major fields."[2] The special January, 1960 conference at Mount Holyoke College to explore academic programs abroad concluded that "the sophomore year has some definite advantages over the junior year for programs emphasizing general education" and that "in general, shorter terms of foreign study are better suited to 'general education' goals, while the longer terms of a year or more are better suited to advanced study and technical specialization."[3]

Sophomores are of course younger than juniors, and some adjustments must be made as a result of this fact. At most European universities, the first-year students are a year or two older than American sophomores, on the average. European universities may be regarded as senior colleges and graduate schools in comparison with American universities. A further complication lies in the fact that at the undergraduate level most systems of higher education abroad serve neither mass education nor general education, both of which are central to the American system.

Nevertheless, the difference in maturity between a second-semester sophomore and a first-semester junior has probably been greatly exaggerated in the student-abroad movement. As a matter of fact, the second-semester sophomore is probably better prepared to go abroad for general education than the junior for specialized study. The latter part of the sophomore year is likely to be the capstone of a student's general education, the junior year the beginning of specialization. In any event, various adjustments can render sophomore study abroad meaningful. Fewer regular courses at host-country universities will be appropriate for the younger students, and those that are taken will have to be supplemented by tutoring. There can be concentration on special courses, taught by host-country instructors and offered by universities, institutes, or special associations. While some special courses have been of inferior quality, this is not inevitable; high quality can be insisted upon. Special efforts can be made to bring the sophomores into close association

---

[2] *Ibid.*, p. 4.
[3] *Academic Programs Abroad*, Report of a Special Conference (New York: Institute of International Education, 1960), pp. 12–13 and 17.

with host-country students of their own age, attending either universities or advanced preparatory institutions. If the American students are young, somewhat inexperienced, and with inadequate backgrounds, it is possible to establish a branch of the American university overseas and to provide a more complete set of American-type services and courses. However, if this is done, the academic advantages of studying abroad are minimal, the students are isolated, and the process of immersion in a foreign culture greatly limited unless vigorous efforts are made to bring the students into contact with the local culture outside the classroom.

A semester or quarter abroad can be offered in the junior or senior year. Lake Erie College provides a quarter abroad for the entire junior class, Adelphi a summer and the first semester of the senior year. The short period makes it possible for a somewhat greater number of students at these levels to go abroad for purposes of rounding out their liberal education or pursuing their major fields of study with special courses, although curricular requirements will still prevent students in many fields from participating. The possibility of enrolling for regular work at host-country institutions in such a short time is almost nil. For most students, a single term is inadequate for mastering new courses at a strange university.

The short term abroad need not center on classwork, however. Field work at the undergraduate level is possible. This has been tried in only a relatively few instances. Field work, appropriate for either general education or specialized study and for students at any level, would require at least two or three months abroad, emphasizing internship, research, or observation rather than classwork. Such a program could combine maximum contact with people and conditions abroad in as short a time as possible, and in addition could use the academic program and facilities of the home campus to as great an extent as possible. Classwork could be completed in the United States, and field "laboratory" work related to these classes could be done abroad. Special advantage could be obtained if the field work were supervised by selected host-country personnel. The Colgate-Columbia-Princeton-Rutgers-Swarthmore program in Europe provides two months of field research after two weeks of seminars at the Institute for Social Studies in the Hague. The program terminates with two weeks of seminars at Oxford. Material for the senior theses is obtained.

Graduate Programs

Formal programs of study abroad for American graduate students have not been numerous. Graduate study can be carried on easily by individual students, and therefore an organized program is often unnecessary. Institutional programs, however, can be a useful supplement to individual study. Examples are the Middlebury language programs and the Johns Hopkins program at Bologna in international relations, both largely at the master's level. Under the latter program, graduate students that are sent from Johns Hopkins to its branch at Bologna study with an equal number of European graduate students, and student give-and-take is extensive. European professors give some of the courses and many individual lectures. This program demonstrates that a branch of an American university overseas need not isolate its students from host-country or host-region professors and students. On balance it is an effective means of study abroad for students having an international bent and an interest in the area. While at the master's level, the Middlebury program is similar in outline to many of the junior-year-abroad undertakings. Reflecting the needs of graduate study, it permits greater freedom to its members both academically and personally than most junior-year programs. Institutionally sponsored study-abroad programs at the master's level can be especially useful in the same fields in which junior-year programs can be most effective—humanities, languages, the social sciences, education, and business administration.

Individual study is of course necessary for the doctor's degree. In many fields, the student who wants to pursue his major abroad is probably well advised to wait until he is a doctoral candidate. At this level a student has a background that more readily qualifies him for specialized courses, for study under a selected professor in his field of interest, or for a research project for a thesis. Differences between university systems are less a barrier to doctoral work than to studies at lower levels. Formal accumulation of credits is less important in the American system at this level. The doctoral student may make a contribution to the students and professors with whom he comes into contact, as well as being able to profit from his experience abroad. In view of the emphasis on individual study for doctoral candidates, it would be inappropriate for universities to sponsor large group doctoral student-abroad programs, but assistance to individual doctoral study abroad could be much more extensive than it is at present.

There have been some valuable experiences in relating doctoral thesis research to faculty-directed group research overseas or technical assistance programs. The Cornell group research projects in Peru, India, and elsewhere have permitted doctoral candidates to complete field research for theses. Several American universities with technical assistance contracts in Asia and elsewhere have provided opportunities for a few of their own graduate students to carry on research for doctoral dissertations. Such programs provide valuable incidental benefits for graduate students. A more extensive system of doctoral research abroad, partly under the supervision or guidance of professors in the host countries, should be possible in the future, especially as the internationalization of the several disciplines proceeds further. In such cases the American professor can provide the graduate student with the appropriate introduction to the host-country professor. In time, a semiformal exchange of graduate students and staff may develop between the respective faculties at the two institutions, to the benefit of doctoral students and also to the benefit of the professors and the universities.

Summer Programs

Every year there are dozens of exchange summer programs for credit, some under the auspices of American universities, some under host-country institutions, some jointly run. One of the more ambitious summer programs is the two-way exchange of Monterrey Tech with 10 American universities, involving 100 students. Students between their junior and senior years are the most common participants in programs such as this, although some lower classmen and graduate students also elect them. The normal objectives of the programs that extend college credit are those of liberal education. A combination of lectures, interviews, and opportunities for observation and elementary research is typical.

Summer programs have two noteworthy advantages. They render overseas study in the liberal arts compatible with even the most rigorous curriculum. No sequence or laboratory courses need be missed. In most cases a student can pool some of his liberal arts electives and offer the summer experience as a substitute. A second advantage is that in the host countries the facilities of regular universities are available during the summer, whereas they tend to be fully used during the academic year. The summer student-abroad program has a greater choice of physical facilities, and laboratories and other equipment are far more readily available. Yet they suffer a disadvantage as well. Summer programs abroad are almost without exception special programs held at special times. Consequently, American students participating in them do not come into contact with many host-country students. In many countries, it is exceedingly difficult to involve local professors in summer programs since they prize their holidays and are seldom at the university during vacation periods.

There is no fixed line between the credit and noncredit summer programs which is recognized by universities. Some programs combine both objectives, giving credit for the academic work and no credit for the tour or work-camp experience. Hollins and Western Michigan have programs of this type. A combination of work-camp experience and academic objectives may be especially suitable for some less developed countries in Asia, Africa, and Latin America. The danger in such programs is that credit will be extended for the nonacademic portion of the work as well.

A noncredit program may include graduates, undergraduates, or both. The best of the programs offer most of the same supplemental, extracurricular opportunities as do the longer-term student-abroad programs, and in some cases even more. Short immersions in selective aspects of a foreign culture may occur. A few noncredit programs are run by student groups; a few others are administered directly by universities. The Smith summer tour to Africa is not for credit, and is educational, not simply touristic, in its objectives. The girls have an opportunity to talk with some of the important leaders in the emerging nations of Africa. Noncredit summer experiences such as this can be, and sometimes have been, highly integrated with a university's general or liberal education objectives. However, most summer programs, whether for credit or not, are not closely integrated with regular academic activities; this is one of their shortcomings at present.

To some extent, the summer programs, especially those not for credit, range more widely in geographical area than do the longer-term junior programs. The program sponsored by the Western

College for Women is a case in point; it operates on a four-year cycle, visiting in sequence Latin America, the Middle East, the Far East, and Africa.

Alternatives to University Programs

There are opportunities for study or travel abroad for any student who does not participate in a program under the auspices of an American university. He may go abroad on his own or join a study-abroad plan undertaken by some other group. Many private associations offer study-abroad experiences and an increasing number of overseas universities offer special programs that are often recognized for college credit in the United States. Among the former are such projects as The Experiment in International Living, the Institute of European Studies, Scandinavian Seminars, and the American Friends of the Hebrew University. Among the latter are programs of the International Christian University (Japan), Mexico City College, American University of Beirut, the University of Oslo International Summer School, University of Stockholm, and the University of Aix. Such programs relieve American universities of the administrative burdens of study-abroad programs and bring a student into close contact with host-country personnel. However, with courses for credit the problems of assuring high standards and integrating the program with a student's regular work at home are troublesome.

While there are many serious nonuniversity programs for study abroad, the good name of student-abroad programs has suffered from the so-called educational travel programs for which academic credit is given but which are in reality guided tours. Typical of the approach of such travel programs is this ad, sponsored by Air France and appearing in many university student newspapers in the Spring of 1961:

HAVE A BALL IN EUROPE THIS SUMMER (and get college credits, too!) Imagine the fun you can have on a summer vacation in Europe that includes everything from touring the continent and studying courses for credit at the famous Sorbonne in Paris to living it up on a three-week co-educational romp at a fabulous Mediterranean island beach-club resort!

It is unlikely that any program which requires students to move from place to place every few days, sampling the major tourist spots, can be seriously academic. There is a place for tours and for many other activities abroad that do not earn academic credit. Most of these will be educational in the sense that they give the student new experiences, but there is no reason why every new experience should be recognized for credit.

Reacting to "dubious commercial connections" of some of the programs, the special Mount Holyoke conference stressed that "faculty members should not operate study programs abroad as a commercial sideline, or cooperate with agencies run for profit and with no educational interest." To this end, academic credit should "not be granted unless the program is officially sponsored by an institution," and "colleges should warn their faculty members of the danger of being victimized by irresponsible travel organizations."[4]

As for bona fide, well-administered noncredit programs, given their nondegree objectives it is appropriate that most of them are administered by private associations or travel agencies. Such programs represent an alternative for students who desire overseas experience, and specially for those who do not want to interrupt their undergraduate work. They vary in purpose all the way from completely touristic trips to thorough living, working, and educational experiences abroad. It is entirely appropriate that they should be called to the attention of university students. In this manner, a student can be given the widest of choices in deciding whether an overseas experience is a useful supplement to his education. Little student counseling touches on such matters at present.

Quite a different nonuniversity program approach to study overseas is independent study. Independent study abroad can lead to a foreign degree. This requires the ultimate degree of immersion of an American student in the host-country university system and society. Another alternative common at the undergraduate level is independent study abroad for a short time such as a year. Those wanting an American degree will find that because of the extensive differences in the educational systems of various countries, the transfer of credits, in the American sense of the term, is difficult to arrange on an individual basis, although on occasion it can be done. Extending one's formal education a year may be the only possible alternative. If not pressed for time or money, students may find this a happy course of action. They can go abroad, register at a

⁴ Ibid., pp. 15 and 20.

foreign university, and fend for themselves for a year. Perhaps there is no better way to learn the frustrations of trying to adjust to a foreign culture. At the same time, such an approach gives a student a maximum opportunity for autonomous study, allowing him to concentrate upon what he wishes, and to engage in independent inquiry. One of the most valid criticisms that many student-abroad programs must meet is that independent study by the students is minimized. Many of the programs rigidly channel the students in predetermined paths, whether appropriate for a particular student or not.

To some extent there is a great division between the "classicists" and the "modernists" of study abroad. The classicists argue that complete immersion in a foreign culture is necessary if study abroad is to have value. This requires a year or two abroad at the very least during which American students take regular university courses, live as host-country students do, and encounter and overcome all the personal problems of participating in a foreign culture. The modernists argue that immersion is not the sole objective of study abroad and that if it is overemphasized, other values may be sacrificed. A student who spends many days or several weeks trying to locate satisfactory housing may be immersing himself in another culture, but to what academic advantage? A student who goes through the frustration of trying to figure out how to register at a foreign university may be immersing himself in comparative academic administration, but to what end? A student who sits through a year-long series of lectures at a European university on an aspect of a single humanist's life may be immersing himself in a foreign university system, but does that have meaning for him if his background is in American secondary and higher education?

Learning by immersion is of academic value only if the immersion is related to academic objectives. The student who must solve all the problems of living and studying abroad by himself may have less time to observe parts of the culture of relevance to his academic interests than the student for whom some special arrangements have been made in advance. It is far better for the teacher education major to immerse herself in the teacher education system of a host country than to worry about minutia of everyday living or university red tape. The political science major should concentrate on studying government and politics, the economics student the economic system, and so on.

Upon these latter arguments, the entire movement for study-abroad programs rests. Essentially a student-abroad program provides selective immersion. The principle of selective immersion is sound and undoubtedly necessary in most cases if the students are to receive American degrees. The challenge confronted by the student-abroad programs is threefold:

1. To permit (and require) students to become immersed in the most meaningful ways in the aspects of the host country most appropriate for them from the standpoint of the academic objectives of the program.

2. To identify those ways and aspects clearly, so students and faculty will be aware of the specific aims and objectives of each program.

3. To counsel students to participate only in those programs, if any, that further their individual academic objectives.

Chapter 6

AMERICAN STUDENT-ABROAD
PROGRAMS: POLICY IMPERATIVES

The potential contributions of student-abroad programs to young adults in search of education, and to world-wide understanding, are great. The more successful programs have had impressive results. The fact that a majority of the programs have been disappointing is a sharp reminder that a good idea is not enough.

Academic Requisites for Programs

The results achieved depend in considerable degree upon the academic standards of a program and the extent to which its content is related to the student's university work. A well-conceived program with low standards of performance is of little advantage. An isolated experience will have less meaning than one related to a student's education as a whole. Only if high standards prevail is a program likely to be accepted as an integral part of university work at quality institutions. If student-abroad programs are accepted as integral parts of university work, an additional force for maintaining high standards will be present. Currently, many, perhaps most, programs fail on both counts. Both a cause and a consequence of this failure is the fact that faculty cooperation has often been lacking.

Faculty Cooperation. A major obstacle to adoption and success of student-abroad programs at American universities is the lack of regular involvement of departments, schools, and the central administration of the institution in the initiation and policy control of the programs. This lack of involvement reflects a lack of confidence in the project on the part of the administration and/or the faculty members. Where programs have been proposed or are operating there is often outright faculty resistance and administrative passivity. Where the issue has not been raised, faculties usually show little interest.

Faculty support of, or interest in, student-abroad programs has been wanting because of traditional conservatism, because the programs in some way threaten established values, and because in many cases the programs have not been of sufficiently high quality. Without faculty support, students will not be encouraged or permitted to participate in a program. Every group wishing to alter educational patterns sooner or later must come to the faculty members concerned, to seek approval of its ideas. Over the years faculty members are asked to consider many proposed plans for which fine values are claimed. After listening to a number of them, a certain skepticism sets in. No one plan is the solution for the major problems of higher education; there is no panacea. Resistance to change develops. Student-abroad programs have been no exception.

Some proposals have few implications for a given department. However, if student-abroad programs were developed on a wide scale at a university, the impact on the department might be great. Such programs require the absence of some or all of the better students. Teachers who work hard to identify serious students and then seek to give them the best possible educational opportunities naturally hesitate to recommend to them an unproved program abroad, with unknown staff members and professors, under somewhat uncertain circumstances. It is not unreasonable for a teacher to conclude that it would be far better to keep the student at home where his destiny lies in known, capable hands. Perhaps the student of just better than average abilities may find a year abroad suitable, it is often contended, but the best students should remain at home, where a concentrated program of assured quality can be chosen.

Students tend to echo these sentiments, according to program directors. The outstanding student will probably have an educational plan in his mind and will not desire to be diverted from it. The student who is not highly motivated or who has unclear academic objectives may find in a year abroad a pleasing change of pace. Most noncompulsory programs report difficulty in attracting the very best students. The C plus to B students may be enrolled, and perhaps even some with B plus averages. But the outstanding students usually remain at home.

Faculty members see financial as well as educational objections. It is often argued that to send students overseas is not much more expensive for a university than to educate them at home, and in a growing institution, the absence of a large part of the student body means that additional expensive facilities do not have to be erected. To university administrators this may be a cogent argument, but it may confirm the worst fears of a faculty department. The department that sends most or all its majors abroad for a considerable time stands to lose enrollment, and eventually to lose staff members. To some extent at least, foreign professors are being substituted for American professors. In a student-exchange program there is no guarantee to a department that even in the long run the number of its visiting students will equal the number it sends abroad. Nor is there any assurance that a department will get the same proportion of students from added American enrollment of the university that it sends abroad. In its own plans for staff development or in competition with similar departments at other universities, a faculty feels in danger of suffering professional disadvantages. If university funds are expended for the program, faculty members can appropriately raise the question whether these funds might not be better spent on higher faculty salaries or additional faculty members at home. The quality of education received by a student may be improved more by keeping and attracting capable faculty members than by developing student-abroad programs.

Faculty cooperation may be lacking for other reasons. The person directing the program, be he professor, department chairman, or dean, is occasionally not a highly respected member of the staff. He may be someone who has never written a book, who has not succeeded in the world of scholarship, and who has accepted this administrative assignment as his kind of contribution.

In addition, many of the programs for study abroad remain largely the concern of the program director or a small committee and not in any way tied into regular department activities. Occasionally a program is so isolated that the president or vice presidents of the institution have little consciousness that it exists as a university program. This may be true of programs such as that of

Wayne State, which recruits many from student bodies other than its own.

If the student-abroad idea is ever to be widely and warmly accepted in American higher education and is to be elected by a large proportion of the students, the prime requisite is to bring programs into close association with the regular departments and colleges, under general university approval. The opinions of individual faculty members must be taken into account in formulating policy. Independent islands or empires of foreign study must go. Persons of distinction must be placed in charge, and must account to both the faculty members and the administration. Faculty members themselves must freely accept the academic value of study abroad, with the emphasis that this requires on faculty exchanges and internationalization of the disciplines. If, in addition, the university can assure a department that it will not suffer financially either by loss of staff members or by failure to obtain salary increases, a basis will be laid for consideration of revising the curricular and counseling patterns to include student-abroad activities.

Close Relation to Regular Academic Work. Only if curricula are revised can student-abroad programs come to play an important part in higher education generally. In some manner, the overseas experience must be related to the courses a student takes before and after it, as at Hollins and the Western College for Women, where there are courses compulsory for all students going abroad. At present, most such adjustments are made on a purely *ad hoc* basis. Participation in the study abroad by a larger proportion of the student body would require more general adjustments. For example, it would be necessary to see that a participating student had appropriate preparation in the humanities, languages, and social sciences. If the purpose in going abroad is general education, the general-education segment of a student's program should be recast with that possibility in mind.

If the purpose be the pursuit of specialized knowledge, contributing to a student's major, more extensive revisions in curricula would be necessitated. Consideration of needed revisions might provide the occasion for rethinking the entire pattern of higher education in some fields. The student-abroad concept is primarily one of liberal education, not of narrow professionalism. Perhaps acceptance of a program for study abroad would contribute toward basing more undergraduate education on broader, more liberal, subject matter, and postponing narrowly professional training until graduate studies are reached. This could be the outcome in such fields as education, business administration, and engineering, and even in such traditional liberal arts areas as the social sciences, which have become more narrowly professional in recent years. If this is to be the result, many would welcome it.

It would be advisable to adapt study-abroad programs to the curricular needs of individual students as well as to the over-all curricular pattern of a department or university. Since needs vary widely, a flexible set of choices for study abroad should be available, including programs of general and specialized education, at undergraduate and graduate levels, for credit and not for credit, for short or long periods abroad, and in different language areas and regions of the world. At present, most of the student-abroad programs suffer from a lack of individual adaptability. It is one thing to embrace the idea that a student should have an overseas experience. It is quite another to say that he should have *the* overseas experience provided by the program that happens to be administered at his university. That particular program may not meet his needs at all. No single program, however adjusted to individual needs, is likely to meet all requirements.

Sound Standards and Academic Criteria. The programs requiring residence abroad for a semester or two disrupt curricula that have long been established, after painful compromises. To ask faculties to develop new curricula based on long absence of many students is to encounter the wrath of nearly all faculty members, to challenge values long accepted as valid. Unless the quality of the student-abroad programs can be demonstrated beyond question, faculty acceptance will not be forthcoming. The demonstration as a rule has been unconvincing.

The most serious objections relate to the feeling that students' work in the programs is of low academic quality. Many do not maintain standards equivalent to those on the home campus. The reasons for the discrepancy in standards are many. First, there is more direct competition for grades among a large group of students on the home campus. The student abroad is deliberately somewhat isolated from his American contemporaries, but there is less group pressure on him as a result. For some students the outside distractions are greater abroad than in the United States. The glamour of being in a strange land, the desire to see and do things, may divert them from academic paths rather than encourage them to follow a worn trail.

Many foreign professors or special instructors, not being acquainted with standards at the home campus, give the American students the benefit of the doubt, much as some foreign students in the United States receive the "foreign-student B." Some of the special instructors from the host country engaged under the programs are of doubtful ability, especially if compared with the faculty at home. The special courses sponsored by certain host institutions sometimes lack adequate standards (Garraty and Adams, pp. 69–75). The problem of standards in these programs is similar in some respects to the problem of standards in field work at home. Students are likely to receive higher grades in field work than in other college classes unless rigorous steps are taken to ensure equivalent grading.

To keep the grading under the control of the faculty members of the American universities would not solve all the problems of evaluation. Since students are carrying out work, at least a part of which is difficult to evaluate on the same basis as course work at home, standards are not easily defined. There is a tendency for those instructors who believe in study abroad to grade high, and those who are skeptical to grade low. This has been Adelphi's experience.

Objections as to the quality of the student-abroad program are heard on the campuses of the institutions sponsoring the best programs as well as on those sponsoring some of the worst. For example, at Smith, objections to the junior-year-abroad programs come from faculty members who, having received at least one of their degrees abroad, believe that the junior-year programs should, like their experience, involve complete integration with a European university.

A more serious question of standards is whether the academic content of the work the student carries on abroad is at least equal to the academic content of work at home. It is difficult to answer this question since an answer would involve an evaluation of the academic program at home—a task not attempted in the present study. Those institutions that have student-abroad programs with the best academic content also are likely to be those that have the best academic reputations at home, and vice versa. But does the excellent program abroad of a college such as Smith equal the work carried out on its own campus? The answer to the question depends upon the criteria of judgment. Students abroad have an academic experience different in kind from that which their contemporaries get at home. Students going abroad will naturally fall behind in the type of work required at home. Program directors have stressed the values of study abroad in terms of general education and extracurricular activities, while faculties at home have been more interested in achievement in specialized fields and hold more traditional academic values.

Most of the confusion concerning the criteria of judgment has arisen from too many loose and sweeping claims as to the advantages of study abroad. If academic credit is to be extended to students participating, the programs must be judged on the basis of specific academic criteria. Some programs, such as those at Fordham and Adelphi, are rather directly related to academic objectives, but most are at best only generally so related. Few would question that international understanding and good will should be encouraged, and that students should mature, but there is no reason to give academic credit on such grounds. Those responsible for student-abroad programs need to distinguish clearly between formally academic and extracurricular aims, between general and specialized education. If these distinctions were clarified, it would be clearer at what level, if any, a student might appropriately go abroad, how study abroad would be related to his formal educational objectives, and whether academic credit should be extended.

Expansion of the Proportion of Students Involved

If the opportunities for study abroad, in all their variety, were made available to every student, there would be few who could honestly respond that they were not interested in some form of the experience. The time could be utilized, if not for undergraduate purposes, then for graduate; if not for specialized objectives, then for general education; if not for a year, then for three or six months; if not for classwork, then for field research; if not in the Western world, then in the non-Western. The possibilities are so numerous, the objectives to be achieved so diverse, that almost any student would find some combination that would fit his needs and interests.

No university comes close to offering any of its students the range of choices for study abroad that is desirable if the programs are to be adapted to individual needs. Without such diversity of choice, most students will not derive advantages from participation. The decision of an individual university to develop a single study-abroad program can be based largely on the considerations outlined in the previous section and the previous chapter. If many institutions do so, and if they desire to send large proportions of students abroad, an additional set of considerations is encountered. Should most or all students be encouraged or required to participate sometime during the college years? If so, how can a more or less balanced package of alternatives for study abroad be made available to them?

Interinstitutional Cooperation. To explore the second question first: few universities have resources sufficient to administer or underwrite several programs of diverse types. Furthermore, weaker institutions should probably allow the others to take the lead, both for purposes of strengthening their home program and for the good reputation of the student-abroad movement. A number of the directors of student programs in Paris felt strongly on this score. They reported a desire to slow down the increase in programs. They believed that only the more reputable and stronger institutions should conduct them; other institutions might participate in the programs so administered. They argued that standards would be higher if this could be accomplished. This suggestion raises the question whether cooperation among American universities is to occur among equals or by leadership of a few institutions. Probably the most desirable course would be for stronger institutions mutually to supplement one another's programs by providing alternatives for their students, while at the same time they offer opportunity for study abroad to students at smaller or weaker institutions. At present, many student-abroad programs, such as those of Adelphi, Hollins, Earlham, Elmira, Oberlin, Sarah Lawrence, and Stanford, restrict participation to their own students. Problems sometimes encountered are illustrated by the Hollins program, under which low admissions standards prevailed in its early years for the reason that there was an inadequate number of applications from the Hollins campus. Other institutions, such as Smith, occasionally admit outsiders.

A few universities administer study-abroad programs which are specifically designed for students from as wide a sampling of institutions as possible. Sweet Briar and Wayne State follow this practice.[1] Informally, Fordham has extended the benefits of its program to students at other Jesuit universities. Princeton, together with Rutgers, Swarthmore, Columbia, and Colgate, has recently inaugurated an interinstitutional program. An older cooperative program is located at Minnesota, which, in cooperation with eight other Minnesota colleges, conducts a study tour each summer.

Interinstitutional arrangements would seem to have real advantages, although experience with them is still limited. The Sweet Briar, Fordham, and other programs indicate that recruitment from several universities is compatible with high academic standards, and may even encourage them. A measure of responsibility is needed on the part of each of the participating institutions in relating the program to its own curricula and the respective needs of its students, together with the assumption of administrative responsibility on the part of one institution. Such a pattern will not place an undue strain on the administrative or faculty resources of any of the institutions and will provide enough students to assure the financial success of the program at the same time that standards can be kept high.

Interinstitutional cooperation can be fruitful in a variety of other ways. There are several examples of cooperation among the junior-year-abroad programs in Paris. Some have offices close to each other, and others jointly arrange some of their classes. Each helps the other out in times of emergency in such things as student housing. The interchange that takes place among the directors of the junior-year programs in Paris is a force for upgrading the quality of the programs as well as for solving administrative problems and serving as an information clearinghouse.

Relation with Host Institutions. With expansion of American student-abroad programs, there would be a need to consider carefully the relationship with host institutions. At present, the smaller programs involving one or two or three students, often in the form of a two-way exchange, normally rely completely upon the host institution for courses and professors; there is no other choice in

---

[1] For a tabulation of institutional practice in admitting outside students, see *Programs for U.S. Undergraduates in Other Countries* (New York: Institute of International Education, 1960), pp. 9–20.

these instances. One or two students may be found who can adjust to the marked differences in educational systems and who have language competence, but large groups of students are not likely to share such capacities. The small programs provide a useful one- or two-way exchange, but they cannot play a substantial role in making it possible for large numbers of students to go abroad. In addition, if large groups go abroad, they might well overcrowd the facilities of the host-country institutions if complete integration with host universities were attempted. One factor making the Monterrey Tech arrangement possible is that it is a summer program.

On the other hand, a study-abroad program carried out in its entirety by an American university has limited value if it unnecessarily isolates the student from contact with host-country professors, students, and courses. One of the main reasons for going abroad may thus be sacrificed. However, a branch abroad of an American university is a device that may be essential if study-abroad programs increase in number or if they are extended more widely to certain Asian, African, and Latin American countries. Most countries have exceedingly crowded universities, and American students would be looked upon as unwanted intruders if their presence denied host-country students adequate access to university facilities. It may be necessary for American universities to construct dormitories for their students, and even classrooms on occasion. Yet nearly everywhere it should be possible to bring American students into some regular contact with host-country university personnel or courses. One means to this end is to invite host-country students into American-organized courses and American-built dormitories, as Johns Hopkins does in Bologna.

The appropriate relation to a host-country university does not depend only upon the size of the program or the number of students. It also depends upon the nature of the objectives of the program and the nature of the host-country university. For those programs that are oriented toward field work, less contact of the formal university type will occur, and more contact with other aspects of the host country. If the program objectives are such that they can be best achieved through the employment of the lecture-discussion technique, most host-country universities of the Continental type would not have much to contribute. Likewise, many universities in the world would not share a concern for general-education objectives of large numbers of students at the university level. A looser relationship with a host institution would seem called for in such instances. Specialized undergraduate education would more often fit in with study at host-country universities and graduate instruction would be most compatible of all.

Location of Programs. Most of the student-abroad programs of American universities have been located in Europe and Mexico; a few are scattered in other regions. Two queries are thus raised. Is there likely to be an excessive number of students in these locations if the student-abroad programs are expanded? Secondly, are there even greater unrealized values for American students in locations other than Europe and Mexico? There is little likelihood that Europe or Mexico will be overrun with American students in the near future. With occasional exceptions, the student-abroad programs do not generally place an excessive burden on host-country universities or upon scarce local personnel. Partly this is due to the European pattern of lecturing, partly it is due to the fact that programs make use of nonuniversity resources, and partly it is explained by the few demands on host universities for laboratory or other work requiring expensive equipment. Even in Paris, where the largest number of programs in any one city is to be found, American university students do not overcrowd higher education facilities. It is probable that the first sign of overcrowding will not be a strain on local facilities nearly as much as an excessive fraternization of American students with their fellow Americans. If the student-abroad programs expand in number, some will be forced to locate in provincial university towns; there is still large opportunity for expanding student-abroad programs in Europe and Mexico, especially outside the main population centers.

The history of the programs accounts largely for the current European-Mexican emphasis. They began as, and up to now have largely remained, programs emphasizing Western languages and culture. This objective was the central orientation of liberal arts education in the 1920s and 1930s, when the earlier programs got their start. Without sacrificing these laudable objectives, universities can extend student-abroad programs to accomplish other aims as well. In the world of the 1960s there is need to devote more attention to non-Western countries if we, as a people, are to understand the world and find our way in it. The cultural differences encountered by an American in Asia and Africa, for example, are much more extreme than those encountered in Europe. The student-abroad movement can play a unique role in helping future generations of university-educated Americans meet world-wide problems with some degree of world-wide understanding and experience. Locating student-abroad programs in underdeveloped countries would be tangible evidence of genuine American interest in them, evidence that we were anxious to learn about their culture and that technical assistance, with its emphasis on giving, was complemented by cross-cultural education in which American students and professors were in part on the receiving end. General education programs at the sophomore level, noncredit summer programs, and advanced graduate research would be particularly suitable in these areas.

The problems to be overcome in organizing a student-abroad program in Asia, Africa, or Latin America south of Mexico are not much greater than those encountered in Europe or Mexico. Some additional expense would be incurred because of the greater distance to be traveled. Since the programs are almost all under the direction and supervision of an American university and rely upon host-country universities and personnel for only supplemental help, the burdens placed upon American universities should not be much greater in the case of countries outside Europe and Mexico. In order not to strain local facilities in the less developed countries, American universities would probably have to supply a larger proportion of the physical facilities and professional personnel than is done in Europe and Mexico. The part-time character of both professors and students in many of these host countries would pose a problem; it would be difficult to bring American students into close touch with them.

Students have an interest in the non-European world, and if given an opportunity to make a choice, they demonstrate their interest effectively. For example, the University of California, Los Angeles, program in India has many times more applicants than it can accept. There is great enthusiasm among the student body for participation in this venture. The University of Minnesota SPAN program found much student interest in the Philippines. The international programs of American universities began in the early twentieth century with programs involving recent graduates or students in China and other Asian countries.

Administrative Problems. Difficulties concerning transportation, briefing, housing accommodations, registration, vacation tours, and special cultural and social opportunities, to name but a few, would be greatly accentuated if many more students should go abroad. In the larger group programs, almost always the American university takes responsibility for some or all of them. These difficulties, peripheral to academic matters though they are, can nonetheless thwart academic accomplishment if not handled adequately. If local cultural and social activities are overlooked, a student may end up with a most limited experience and with few contacts of value in the host country. The student who spends all his time looking for housing is academically deprived. The program director who spends all his time on these problems is less an academician than he is an administrator. Some universities have rather laboriously solved all these problems by themselves. On occasion this has led to an overadministered program, where the student is not left with any problems to solve for himself—hardly an experience of cultural immersion.

If the number of programs and the number of students going abroad increase, more universities will be looking for ways of easing their administrative burden so that they may concentrate upon the many inherent academic problems. Fortunately, there is an increasing number of organizations that provide some of these services. Their number and scope could be greatly enlarged. Some of the host-country institutions provide excellent briefing services. For example, both Monterrey Tech and Mexico City College have briefing programs, and there are a number of special briefing programs available in France, Italy, Austria, and elsewhere. Briefing before a student leaves the United States and while on board a ship to Europe may also be contracted for, along with help on travel plans, from such organizations as the Council on Student Travel. A variety of host-country organizations promote special social and cultural programs for American or other foreign students and their host-country contemporaries.

Housing is always a bothersome problem. Particularly is this true if accommodations in the homes of host-country nationals are desired. Fortunately, the services of The Experiment in International Living have been made available with increasing frequency. Engaged in placing students in homes abroad for nearly thirty years, The Experiment is now cooperating with several American universities. That housing is no easy matter to arrange is exemplified by the Hamilton group in Paris. During its first year, 23 changes in housing assignments had to be made for a total of 32 students. If study-abroad programs are increased, administrative services of outside groups will become of greater importance.

Financial and Advising Resources. Many students cannot afford a year abroad. Although the cost may not be much greater than the cost of study in the United States for a student who is attending a reasonably expensive private university, who lives away from home, and who does not engage in part-time employment, a majority of students do not meet these stringent conditions. It is the rare university that is able to put aside general funds for subsidizing student-abroad programs. To the extent that students who go abroad continue to pay fees to the home university, the use of some general university funds is justified. Lower fees may be warranted if the American university performs fewer services for students overseas than those at home. Some special scholarship funds may be raised, and certainly should be raised, to help those who cannot go abroad because their own financial resources are inadequate. A number of programs already depend to a large extent on scholarships, such as the Earlham College program in Mexico.

University scholarships will help a few additional students to study abroad, but short of large-scale scholarship or program support from foundations or the United States government, especially the latter, it is simply not possible to envisage a time in the near future when most of the students of American universities who may be qualified for study abroad will be financially able to take advantage of the opportunity. Such support is urgently needed. A prerequisite for substantial foundation or government support is to improve the present programs.

American universities need to modify their advising systems so that opportunities for study abroad will be regularly brought to the students' attention. In order to assist the student and his adviser in identifying appropriate programs, better information needs to be available. As a permanent service, information on the many programs for group and individual study needs to be assembled on a comprehensive, national and world-wide basis. Some beginnings have been made, such as the Institute of International Education's *Handbook on International Study: For U.S. Nationals* and *Group Study Abroad,* and UNESCO's *Study Abroad* and *Vacations Abroad,* and the Institute of Research on Overseas Programs' *International Programs of American Universities.* However, to be most useful, the data need to be more carefully organized as to the purposes of overseas study so that a student can more readily see how his objectives may or may not fit into the objectives of the various programs. In turn, each university needs to adapt these general data to the special circumstances of its own students, curricula, and study-abroad programs, if any. Supplemental informational brochures would prove useful in most instances. With such data available, university advisers would be in a position to bring to the attention of the students the ends to be attained by study abroad and the opportunities that exist, just as they now do in regard to their on-campus curricula.

More, Most, or All Students? The major question concerns the desirability of encouraging or requiring most or all students to participate in study abroad. Some universities do require all their students to participate in this activity. Lake Erie College sends its entire junior class to Europe for about ten weeks. At Oberlin, all juniors who are majoring in music are sent to Salzburg, Austria, to study at the Mozarteum for a year. The policy of these institutions is exceptional. Students are not required to participate in most university-sponsored programs, and consequently the program sponsors engage in rather extensive recruiting campaigns to get an adequate number of applicants. Some universities are not always successful in this effort and must cancel plans for the year abroad for lack of students.

The number of institutions that require all students to go abroad is few. In such programs the results achieved are dependent on the standards of admission and of academic instruction on the home campus. A basic difficulty in requiring participation is that there is no necessary correlation between the admission requirements to a university or to one of its curricula and the aptitudes appropriate for membership in a study-abroad group. Unless the selection procedures for admission are to include judgments as to the fitness of a potential student for study abroad, universities will not find it wise to require all students to study overseas.

The experience of compulsory and noncompulsory programs alike is that only selected students should go abroad. It is useless to send students with less than C averages in the hope that they will become better students. The Hollins program has discovered this. It is useless to send a student abroad who has a positive dislike for things foreign, in the hope that he will develop cultural empathy. He is likely to return confirmed in his attitude, as in some study-abroad programs in Mexico. It is useless to send the personally maladjusted person abroad in the hope that he will somehow find himself; neurotic traits may be reinforced abroad. It is useless to send a student abroad who has no enthusiasm for study overseas; the person who prefers to stay at home ought to be left there. It is not only useless to do these things; it is positively harmful to the program, to its acceptance by American faculty members, to the reputation of American universities, and to friendly relations of the United States with other countries. Just as American higher education is not for every person of college age, so study abroad is not for every university student.[2]

Herein lies an opportunity for the student-abroad programs at American universities. Until now, there has been surprisingly little experimentation in the programs with methods of selection and with measurements of the results achieved through study abroad. With all the research talent at American universities, it would be a rather simple thing to experiment with procedures for selection and evaluation which, when related to each other and validated, might be suggestive of selection and evaluation procedures for many overseas assignments other than those of student-abroad programs. It appears from experience to date that the central criterion for academic programs is academic competence on the part of the students—at least a C plus average for students seeking general education, at least a B minus average for those pursuing specialized work.

It should never be forgotten that there may be solid academic reasons why some students should *not* spend a year abroad. The capable student who changes his curriculum is pressed for time. The outstanding student who has made a special point of coming to a university to study under a particular professor or department hesitates to leave for long. Many curricula are so replete with

---

[2] For arguments in support of making opportunities for study abroad available to all students, see Harlan Cleveland, Gerald J. Mangone, and John Clarke Adams, *The Overseas Americans* (New York: McGraw-Hill, 1960), pp. 207 and 296. The authors devote most of the book to identifying bases of selecting personnel that would make for success abroad, yet do not apply them to the selection of students, since students go abroad to learn, not to be employed.

requirements that no student can take time out for study abroad
without falling behind. And there are always some students who
simply prefer the advantages of the curriculum at home to the
advantages of the curriculum overseas.

Most programs are young and only limited experience has been
accumulated to date. Because of this or other factors, many programs have vague or diverse objectives, lack academic orientation, have poor standards, are inadequately tailored to the problems facing an individual student, and too often are not brought
to the attention of students who could benefit from them. Though
relatively few students should go abroad for specialized study,
large numbers would find it advantageous to go abroad for purposes of general education or in connection with noncredit programs. The programs need to be integrated into the regular university departments and curricula, and into a student's educational
objectives. Since there are many such objectives, study abroad
choices need to be numerous so that any one student is likely to
find a program that meets his distinctive requirements.

American universities have been uncertain as to the educational
implications of the ever more interdependent world. The number
of foreign students has increased on American campuses; the course
structure and curricula in international subjects have been altered;
and student-abroad programs have multiplied. Yet there has been
little thought given to the manner in which these and other developments are related to objectives of higher education. As a
gradual re-examination of objectives occurs in higher education in
the light of the needs of the 1960s, the student-abroad programs
will be found well suited for serving a part of the aims. Far from
being a limited, inflexible device, study abroad is adaptable to a
wide variety of academic needs and purposes. It can give a large
number of students what will be their first experience abroad in
a country of their choice, for the purposes that they desire, and
for the length of time they can devote to it. In preparing themselves for the world of tomorrow, in which they are likely to be
increasingly involved in cross-national affairs, whether they are located in the United States or abroad, students will find no substitute for experience in living in a foreign country. If the initial
experience is an academic one, it can be additionally valuable.
Substantial immersion in a culture other than one's own is highly
educative. Learning by doing, the laboratory technique, the em-

pirical approach—whatever the label—student-abroad programs are in the mainstream of the traditions of American higher education and the typically American approach to knowledge. In participating in them, university students will be preparing themselves for many challenging vocations as well as for useful lives as citizens.

Chapter 7

RELIGIOUS, RESEARCH, AND SMALL EXCHANGES

In the current trend toward more university international-exchange programs, the "fads" are the large, numerous, and well-publicized student-abroad, participant, and technical-assistance-abroad programs. Some universities find, however, that their own distinctive characteristics point to the suitability of other types of programs. Most of these programs individually involve few exchangees. Three kinds of them are programs with religious emphasis, research abroad, and a wide variety of small exchanges for study and/or teaching.

Programs with Religious Emphasis

Programs with religious emphasis are the oldest form of international exchange by American universities; they date back to the nineteenth century. Initiative came largely from missionary groups, who turned to the establishment of educational institutions abroad as a method of assuring Christian influence. In the latter decades of the century, they paid increasing attention to higher education. Whatever the level of education, there was always an urgent need to find staff members from the United States who could help the host-country institution during its early years or decades. A qualified host-country staff was not easily or quickly assembled. At first the contact did not involve direct affiliation of American institutions with colleges abroad. Missionary boards approached teachers at religious and other American universities to solicit interest in assignments at religious colleges and secondary institutions overseas. Personnel at institutions with close church connections were especially receptive, since the objectives normally included proselytizing as well as secular education.

Examples of Programs. Mutual religious interest, although not of the traditional missionary type, provided the basis for the oldest continuing program, a Roman Catholic institutional affiliation between Benedictine colleges in the United States and the Collegio di Santi Anselmo in Rome, begun in 1887. The countries in which missionaries were welcome were limited. Since most of the distinctly American missionary efforts in higher education were Protestant, they were not warmly received in Catholic areas such as Latin America. China and Japan, however, were especially hospitable, and some of the English colonies permitted entry. The Middle East proved to be fertile ground. In 1865 the Syrian Protestant College, later to become the American University of Beirut, was opened as the result of efforts by missionaries even though it was independently organized.

It was at the turn of the century that the first exchange programs with religious objectives took definite shape and developed in one of their most common present forms. In these early university programs, the persons who had participated in missionary groups abroad and host-country nationals who had come to the United States for their education played an especially important role. They helped establish formal institutional programs by which such universities as Princeton (1898), Yale (1901), Carleton (1903), and Oberlin (1907) sent teaching personnel to China and a few other countries. Often the programs related to secondary schools and were confined to instruction in English and Christianity. Recent graduates of American universities were able to carry out these assignments abroad.

Several such programs began in the decade from 1900 to 1910, and a marked increase took place after World War I. Few have been added since the 1920s, although several transfers in the location of programs took place in the 1950s with the rise of Communist China.

The religious element in many of the programs begun in the 1900s and 1920s was considerable, whether or not the formal objectives included proselytizing. The early decades of the century were an era of moral uplift, of resurgence of political and social reform. The experiences of the missionaries in the nineteenth century had its influence, but so also did a general feeling of moral responsibility to others that pervaded American society. One of the leaders in developing university international programs was Dr. John R. Mott, president of the International YMCA, who promoted sister relationships between American universities and those abroad. Two programs begun in the 1920s with moral and religious overtones were the Amherst relationship with Doshisha University and the Rockford relationship with Kobe, both in Japan.

Recently, one or more programs with religious overtones have taken forms similar to those in the nonreligious area. Similar in many ways to the summer student-abroad programs without college credit is the University of California, Los Angeles, program in India. Actually this program is sponsored by the University Religious Conference, a recognized student group, not by the university itself. Otherwise the program appears to follow a familiar plan. Students visit India for the summer, where they go to several universities, spending about four days in each, and engage in talks, songs, and discussions with Indian students and other Indian personnel about their respective countries and customs.

An illustration of religious programs which combine the student-abroad idea with technical assistance is the Oberlin program, begun in 1907 in China. Administered by the Oberlin Shansi Memorial Association with the assistance of the administration and students of Oberlin College, the program now operates at Tunghai University in Taiwan and at two colleges in Madurai, India. Aided by alumni and student funds, it annually sends graduating seniors of Oberlin College as short-term English (and Christianity) teachers to colleges in these two countries. During 1957–58 there were nine former students in the two countries. Besides the short-term English-Christianity teachers, the plan calls for assignment of a permanent American staff member and the granting of capital funds to build a student center at each site. Participant training for host-country staff members is also included in the plan (Inventory, pp. 277–278). In India the problems encountered by the student representatives include the danger that they might deprive qualified Indians of badly needed jobs. Consequently, student representatives have done supplemental teaching only, such as remedial work or tutoring students with special interests. Student representatives, not being classified either as faculty members or as students, have often desired a clearer definition of their status.

Small programs with religious overtones such as the Carleton-Doshisha program in Japan send one or two advanced students or recent graduates abroad for a year or two to a university's secondary or middle school, where they teach English and emphasize Christianity. Doshisha middle-school graduates are encouraged to attend Carleton College for undergraduate study; in 1957–58 two such students were enrolled at Carleton. In addition to teaching English, the United States students abroad are expected to carry on informal study of Japanese culture and history. The personal contacts which result from the program are supplemented by an exchange of books and other educational materials. From 1903–1951, this program was conducted in China, but international conditions caused its locus to be changed to Japan. Although programs such as that of Carleton's are designed for the participation of only a few students, they nonetheless provide a rather wide educational, primarily academic, experience in a foreign culture (Inventory, p. 105).

Within a religious or proselytizing framework, several variations are found such as programs under which American faculty members are sent abroad in a capacity that helps them establish or reinforce competency in a subject matter area. Examples are the several medical missionary programs, such as that of the College of Medical Evangelists with the Christian Medical College in Vellore, India. For some years one or more of its faculty members have served for varying periods of time on the faculty of the Christian Medical College. Two such faculty members were in India in 1957–58. The program is primarily financed by Christian Medical College. In addition, religious colleges have carried on a variety of technical assistance work directly with governmental or community agencies abroad, designed to alleviate depressed conditions. Here again, medical programs are prominent.

Still another pattern, that of a faculty member who is affiliated with both the American and the overseas institution, is illustrated in the Amherst-Doshisha University relationship, a much older one than that of Carleton-Doshisha. The program was preceded by a series of informal relations. The founder of Doshisha University was an Amherst graduate, and some degree of affiliation between the two institutions therefore existed from the beginning. In 1922 recent Amherst graduates began teaching English at secondary schools affiliated with Doshisha University. The program was further broadened in 1932 with the building of Amherst House at the Doshisha campus. Now, Amherst College appoints an Amherst faculty member to teach on the staff of Doshisha University in Kyoto. When in the United States on leave from Doshisha, he teaches Japanese culture and history at Amherst. In Japan, he teaches English literature, American history, and American studies. He receives an appointment of indefinite duration at Doshisha. While in Japan he lives at and directs Amherst House, a small dormitory where about twenty students reside (Inventory, p. 82). In addition, a recent graduate of Amherst—on occasion a divinity student on leave—helps the faculty member at Amherst House. The activities of the House include some of a religious nature.

Although few of the religious university programs abroad were initiated by American educational institutions, some of the transfers of these projects to other countries after China's fall to the Communists were arranged by the universities. The financing of the several kinds of programs is varied; funds come from religious and private organizations, individual donations, some host-country support, and even on occasion from foundations and United States government agencies. However, the initiative in financing, too, has been primarily from religious groups. Missionary groups sometimes provide administrative services to the program in the field.

Each of the several programs with religious overtones in the sample has developed its unique system of selecting and briefing its personnel, according to its own structure. Superficially it appears that the programs are simply organized. A committee or chairman at the American university selects the American participants—either students, recent graduates, or faculty members. Beneath this seemingly uniform and simple procedure are many complications. Some of the programs with student representatives require approval by a missionary board of the university's choice—a requirement that has been highly controversial in some instances. One program nominated a non-Christian student who was rejected, and this caused major criticism of the program at the American university.

The UCLA student program in India illustrates the outstanding results that can be obtained by a carefully executed selection procedure (see Hart, pp. 153–159). Recruitment begins in the September preceding the summer program, with campus appearances of those who have just returned. The University Religious Conference organizes the program, and accepts applications in October. Applicants numbering as many as 200 for the 14 posts go through a long series of screenings, including three group interviews by members of the previous year's group, a written test prepared by the university testing service, participation in discussion groups, special seminar reports, observation of behavior in a culturally strange situation, and a weekend of intensive concentration on India during which the candidates rate each other. Briefing and background training are made an integral part of the selection process. Profiles of the strongest candidates are prepared by the university counseling center, and final selection is made by a leader of the religious conference. This selection and preparation process, the most extensive and intensive series of screenings by any project studied, is in large part responsible for the outstanding success of the program and for its favorable reception in India. The program enjoys high prestige on the UCLA campus, in part because it is so difficult to join.

Unlike the UCLA program, most religious programs have little or no briefing period. Some of those using student representatives arrange for short briefings by a missionary board in the United States. Student representatives from at least one program have informally utilized a summer area-studies program of an American university for necessary background information.

Achievements and Prospects. The objectives and achievements of the programs with religious overtones are difficult to measure as a group because of the programs' diversity. The Amherst program at Doshisha is well-received and can play a continuing role as far as the Japanese are concerned. It has maximum impact on those who live at Doshisha House, and some impact on the students of the Amherst professor. Some enrichment of the Doshisha University community has occurred.

Better English-language training has been the result of the work of student representatives, but the number of English-language teachers in host countries is so great that the relative contribution of these programs is small. To be sure, the programs with religious aspects have normally helped support a Christian college or university in the host country and in this respect they have helped to build institutions. This has been their most important objective. A special aspect of some religious programs such as that by Oberlin in India has been the development of extracurricular activities at host institutions by student representatives.

For their size, the programs with religious aspects have had important consequences for American universities and personnel. Returning American students or student representatives often give talks or write articles for campus newspapers. The Carleton representatives sent letters to Carleton while abroad and spoke at convocations on their return. The Oberlin representatives in India systematically reported on their experiences on their return. The UCLA Project India also includes campus speaking engagements on return. The speeches not only help give the program publicity and provide a good means of recruiting for another year, but also make a contribution to the knowledge of foreign areas. The potential contribution to the American university of such activities is so great that Carleton, for example, would like to develop a Far Eastern studies program and use its Japan program as one element in the larger picture. Financial support has yet to be found.

American students who have participated have received benefits from all the programs with religious aspects. In the Oberlin program in India two out of seven student representatives used their experience to gather data for their M.A. theses. Student representatives abroad for one or two years have learned host-country languages, almost all of the so-called exotic types. They have become thoroughly immersed in a foreign culture.

If it is immersion in a foreign culture that is desired, the UCLA summer program in India has few peers among the programs of short duration. The students live in Indian student dormitories and engage in constant discussions and debates with the Indian students. Here is a program that should be copied in many another university. Yet it is a noncredit, extracurricular program under the auspices of the University Religious Conference.

Religious-oriented programs have increasingly run into difficulty in Asia and Africa because the spreading of Christianity has not always been compatible with the spirit of equality of peoples that pervades the newly independent countries or with the emphasis on indigenous religions that comes with increased national consciousness. This feeling is stronger in some countries such as India than in others. Taiwan and Japan remain at least tolerant of

Christianization programs, even though the people are predominantly non-Christian.

A tendency that has worked toward de-emphasizing the religious aspects of programs has been the secularization of many colleges in the United States that formerly had religious ties, and the liberalization of theology at many of the remaining Christian colleges. One result has been great dissatisfaction with the programs on the part of struggling fundamentalist religious colleges abroad, since the representatives sent by American institutions have had much less fervor for spreading Christianity than the leaders of the host-country college. The latter maintain a fundamentalist zeal, in part to keep their identity in a predominantly non-Christian atmosphere. They are distressed when arriving Americans are reluctant even to teach Sunday School, let alone openly proselytize among the student body. There is a parallel conflict between the American college and the mission board in the United States. The board often acts as a liaison between American and host institutions, and its personnel are much more religious than the student representatives of the American university. Some of the student representatives and their faculty advisers are even loath to admit that their programs have any religious orientation whatsoever.

The day of the evangelical missionary abroad is drawing to a close. Most of the university programs with religious overtones have either changed in character or have gradually disappeared. No longer are countries willing to participate in cultural exchange or technical assistance under any and all conditions. Basic national purposes must prevail, and where they conflict with the religious objectives of outside groups, the latter must give way. The "nationalization" (i.e., complete control by host-country nationals) of former religious educational institutions, some of which were run by American boards, has been taking place rapidly. The secularization of university programs having religious backgrounds is coming about quickly, also. Furthermore, the centers of cultural exchange and technical assistance have become national and international, reaching dimensions far greater than are possible under private religious activities. Religious-oriented programs may continue to be of importance to a few host-country religious colleges, but they will not be of national importance either to the United States or to the host country.

Research Abroad

American scholars have been carrying on research overseas since the early days. In this century, some group research projects have been under the responsibility of universities. Often programs of group research abroad have been of only a few years duration, and consequently it is difficult to identify their growth in number. Research abroad arrangements on a considerable scale had appeared, at the very latest, by the 1920s. The University of Chicago began its Egyptology research in 1924, and other institutions such as Harvard and Pennsylvania were active in the same area. In the same year Tulane began a research program in Central America. More recently, especially after World War II, many research programs have been carried out abroad.

The research projects examined in the field during the present study included those focusing on several Asian, African, and Latin American countries: Japan, Indonesia, India, Egypt, Liberia, Mexico, Peru, and Chile. A majority of the projects were in the social sciences. Several of them were officially classified as technical assistance projects while others, often performing much the same function, were not. The latter were uniformly financed by foundations.

ICA has not regarded research as squarely within its sphere of responsibility. Some research has been worked into multipurpose university contracts overseas rather informally and in recent years by direct reference. In the few instances in which ICA has supported projects whose sole or major purpose was research, it has been cautious and even hesitating and has referred to them as highly applied and centrally oriented toward technical assistance. The International Educational Exchange Service has supported evaluation research undertaken by some nine American universities, a part of it including field research abroad. Most of these projects have been of brief duration and none are examined herein. The United States government has been at best a modest supporter of research projects abroad; foundations have more than equaled the government's contribution.

In one project, Cornell extended legal assistance to the government of Liberia. The project involved the preparation of a code of laws for Liberia and supplements to the code, as well as the revision of some laws and the preparation of the reports of the Supreme Court of Liberia. Almost all the work was undertaken at Cornell by two nonfaculty staff members (Inventory, pp. 119–120). The initiative for this program came from Liberia, which supplied much of the money and was anxious to get the job done, in part to attract foreign business. Legal codes render the action of a government more predictable and systematic.

In Mexico, the School of Veterinary Medicine of the University of Pennsylvania conducted a research program in cattle diseases, largely on its own initiative. In this instance the money came from several sources; Squibb of Mexico, Olin Mathieson (chemical companies), ICA, and Mexico were among the contributors. The program centered on the research efforts of a husband and wife team who were not members of the regular faculty of the university.

Cornell's several research programs in social anthropology in Mexico, India, and elsewhere were good examples of foundation-supported social science research projects. In Peru, under a grant from the Carnegie Corporation of New York and with the assistance of the Peruvian government, Cornell helped introduce a change in a rural village from hacienda to independent status. The purpose of the research was to study the problems of introducing such a change, the various innovations flowing from it, and their effect on Peruvian indigenous culture in such areas as economics, health, and education (Inventory, p. 120).

The methods by which research was carried out varied according to whether a host group initiated the idea for the research or actually collaborated in carrying it out. On occasion, as in Liberia, American research was contracted for. More frequently, the American university initiated the project. Nearly all these research projects involved either administrative liaison with the host-country government or with a host institution. Although host-country nationals were often employed in carrying out the research, they were not, in most instances, equals or genuine collaborators. For the most part, those projects which did not involve host-country nationals to an extent or at a level that the nationals believed appropriate encountered severe difficulties and were unable to reach their objectives effectively.

One of the difficulties in involving host-country nationals was in some instances their inability to collect acceptable research data on schedule. Not all Americans complete research assignments, of course, but a somewhat lower rate of successful performance was obtained from host-country nationals in many of the programs. At least one program in India tried to avoid this difficulty by paying researchers a lump sum upon completion of an assignment.

Except in those few instances where research is contracted for by a host organization, the American university normally decides whether it desires host institutional involvement and selects the institution with which to deal. In Japan, Indonesia, India, and Chile, universities were selected as host institutions; they worked with Michigan, Johns Hopkins, Cornell, and Chicago, respectively. Nonuniversity host organizations participated in Mexico with Pennsylvania, in Peru with Cornell, in Egypt with Chicago, and in Liberia with Cornell. In some cases government agencies and in other cases special institutes served in such capacities. Some research programs, such as the Cornell-Lucknow program in India, were connected both with a supervising host-country government agency and with a host university. A group research project is now seldom without some host organization, especially in the less developed countries.

Normally, the selection of a university or nonuniversity organization as host is dependent upon the nature of the research project, its relation to host groups, and their interest in it. This fact was underlined by a publisher of social science books in Italy, who commented:

Italian universities are entirely too conservative. They have hardly anyone in the social sciences so far. They look down their noses at any real social science research. Consequently, social science research should be promoted independently of the universities in Italy. To try to go through the universities would result in frustrations on at least two counts. First of all, there would be the difficulty of trying to get acceptance within the university; this would be almost impossible. Secondly, it would almost be impossible to get any support from the university on a continuing basis. And experimenting along new lines would be frowned upon.

The younger people are those interested in social science research and they do not control Italian universities. The situation in Italy is typical of conditions in many countries, at least for the time being.

A research program is often the result of the efforts of one man —a senior scholar at an American university who is interested in a certain problem. Consequently, planning depends upon his ability to set up a research project effectively. Among the several research projects that were effectively planned, the Chicago-Chile technical assistance research project and the MIT-India research project, both in economic development, stand out as excellent examples.

Given the long-range research interests of scholars, any group research project is normally preceded by one or more years of individual research in the host country by the project director. For example, some of the senior research personnel of Cornell and the Massachusetts Institute of Technology spent several years in India before their respective programs of group research abroad were launched. Long acquaintance with the host country, however, facilitates but does not guarantee effective planning. The Cornell-India program in anthropology was one of the more poorly planned projects and for that reason, among others, had minimum results.

One senior American professor usually directs the project and often serves as the initial field director. It is he who recruits the Americans and, in over half the programs, the host-country staff, and who serves as liaison with the financing organization. The Cornell research programs in cultural anthropology in Peru, India, and Indonesia followed this pattern. Senior professors were also responsible for the Chicago-Chile program in economics, and those of Pennsylvania-Mexico in veterinary medicine, and of MIT-India in economic development. The senior American research professor is such a central figure in these projects that its success or failure is highly related to his professional and personal qualifications and the amount of time he can devote to the undertaking.

Research-abroad programs are difficult to staff by the American faculty concerned. One reason for this is that research undertakings requiring extensive investment of personnel such as long-continuing and comparative research projects are often desired so that broad social trends can be more effectively discerned. Then, too, few faculty members can or will desire to stay abroad indefinitely. An institution needs to plan in advance for personnel needs after the first group has returned. Many relatively small departments, though excellent, cannot meet program requirements over a period of years. Cornell, an outstanding university in the international area, illustrates the point. The Cornell anthropology research projects in several countries, including Peru and India, were a daring and ambitious venture undertaken by an excellent but small group of Cornell anthropologists. But university resources were spread too thinly. There was a lack of personnel to support the senior professor in charge of research in each country. Shortage of regular personnel has naturally forced some research programs to place emphasis on outside staff members; the Pennsylvania-Mexico, Chicago-Chile, and Cornell-Peru efforts relied on special recruitment heavily, while the MIT-India program did so less extensively.

The results of research abroad must be judged largely on the basis of publications flowing from it. At best, the record is erratic. Substantial publication came from the MIT-India project in economic development and the Michigan-Okayama project in area studies. The University of Chicago archaeology program in Egypt has been a good producer. On the other hand, there are projects with slim publication records, as with the Cornell-Peru anthropology project. Of the nine programs in the sample with major basic or applied research objectives, about half have produced at least one substantial published work. It is difficult to compare this record with that in similar types of research in the United States for lack of data, but it would appear to be somewhat lower than the average expected publication result in United States-based research, even allowing for the fact that on-going rather than completed programs were being observed.

In the host country, definite increase of interest in research and in the ability to execute it occurred among a few individuals as the result of most of the research projects, whether or not the programs had formal connection with technical assistance. However, the long-range importance of this fact is dubious since host universities or other special host institutions do not normally give adequate financial support and attention to research. In order for research to play a more important part in higher education in host countries, major changes must occur within higher education. Research should bring some reward to the researcher.

As for American universities, their institutional research objectives have been reinforced by the programs. Cornell's anthropology department, MIT's Center for International Studies, and Michigan's Japanese center have all used international programs to further institutional research aims rather directly. Chicago has developed its specialization in Egyptology through its program of research in the field. It is apparent that those disciplines or aspects of disciplines that depend upon area or regional research have been furthered by international exchange programs far more fully than those where research may be equally well carried out anywhere, or those that depend upon expensive equipment.

It is probable that scholars will increasingly be required to get permissions from host governments to carry on group research, and that one condition involved will be that a host university or other institution participate in the project, as well as an American or other foreign group of scholars. India probably has the most elaborate procedure for screening prospective foreign university research (Hart, pp. 140–141). The National Planning Commission has decided that social science research in India by foreign groups should be carried on only under procedures established by it, including prescribed forms of collaboration with Indian institutions. Under this policy, a foreign university group proposing to do research is required to have a host-country institution as collaborator, and to make the selection only after consulting the research programs committee of the commission. Though the Indian government has permitted by-passing of this rigid procedure, as in the case of the Massachusetts Institute of Technology research in economic development, the procedure serves as a warning to American and other universities that substantial social science research is to be done only with some Indian collaboration and approval. MIT found that even the informal procedures took a long time to work out, although they did avoid selection of host-country institutions or collaborators by the research programs committee. One of the disadvantages of the latter procedure is that the committee would have to consider the prestige of and competition among Indian universities in advice concerning a local institution, whereas effective research as well as technical assistance requires that the collaborators select themselves to a large extent. Enthusiasm for the enterprise rather than a desire for prestige or competitive advantage is the most important ingredient.

The steps taken by India should not go unheeded by American scholars. Aside from making the subjects of research abroad at least consistent with a government's goals, American scholars must take appropriate steps to allay any nationalistic fears or suspicions concerning their research, its objectives, its methods, or the personnel undertaking it. The university research projects have not been noticeably more successful in this than have individual scholars. The reason probably lies in the larger scope of university projects and their more readily felt presence in the host country, and in the failure of most projects to involve host-country scholars in the research in a substantial way.

The quality of scholarship abroad is equal or superior to that in the United States in a number of fields in some countries, especially in Europe, and will shortly be equal in many others. Organizations such as UNESCO have played a leading role in this rise of scholarly ability. To ignore local scholars not only is rude and impolite, but it also results in less effective research in many instances, or even the duplication of research. As host-country scholars come to share common interests with American professors, a new era of international scholarly cooperation is developing.

Small Exchanges

The exchange of one or two faculty members or students has been a custom of higher education for centuries. Usually these exchanges, whether mutual or one-way, have been on an informal basis. Throughout the nineteenth century American students and professors went abroad for advanced and specialized study, and an increasing number of students and faculty members from abroad were attracted to United States universities. Some of these latter exchanges were encouraged by scholarships arranged by members of advisory missions or religious groups abroad. Others were carried out by individual means, or by governmental or university scholarships. There were few continuing arrangements; scholarships were largely *ad hoc*. Gradually, more formal, long-range arrangements emerged.

The small student or faculty exchanges took more regular form in the 1920s. Institutional responsibility for programs emerged. Among the programs, the most frequently encountered were the exchange of language or literature students or faculty. The Western College for Women hired a former or present student from Chile to teach Spanish (1928) and Buffalo brought a professor from France to teach French civilization and literature (1930). Augustana College brought a Swedish student to serve as an assistant in the Swedish language (1938). Book exchanges were also present in the early decades of the century. One of the earliest was that between Gustavus Adolphus College and Upsala (1912). There has been a steady but unspectacular increase in these "small exchange" arrangements over the years. The number and variety of the small exchanges is truly surprising.

One-way or two-way student exchanges are common.[1] Stanford has had a two-way exchange with Japan since 1955. Through a reciprocal arrangement the students of Stanford and Keio University provide financial assistance for the exchange of students between the two institutions. One student from each university studies at the affiliated university each year. The program is sponsored and directed by students at both institutions, and in the case of Stanford, is an activity of the Associated Student Government. Fields of study are not specified and special study programs are not a feature of the program. Instead, the visiting student may select work from a field of interest to him, and is further encouraged to make contacts with nationals of the cooperating country (Inventory, p. 267).

American or host-country students normally take regular academic work, although frequently not for credit. The small exchange usually lasts a year. A special effort is made at a number of institutions, especially smaller ones, to have the exchange student give talks both on and off campus; a regular student may be designated to stay with and help the visitor. Where the exchange is student sponsored, special events may be scheduled or housing arrangements made, as with the Stanford-Keio exchange, in which the visiting Japanese student stays at several student housing units in sequence. Exchangees very commonly have special interest in languages or area studies, and this has led to their use as part-time language instructors. Augustana College brings a Swedish student to the campus who acts as a teaching assistant in the language and helps promote interest in Swedish culture. On American campuses there is frequently more interest in the small exchanges than in the larger participant training programs. This is especially true at small institutions with few foreign students or colleges where the exchange is officially sponsored by the student body itself.

Another form of small exchange concentrates on faculty members and emphasizes teaching. The effects of sending American

[1] American student-abroad programs are discussed separately in Chaps. 4 to 6.

professors abroad are in one respect quite different from those of sending foreign professors to the United States. At an American university, the visiting professor gives a course for credit much like any other member of the staff. American professors abroad teach courses that frequently do not count toward degree work. In European-type universities, examinations at the end of the three or more years of university education are given long after the American professor has returned home, and are little influenced by his previous presence. Furthermore, the American professor may teach a course not recognized for degree purposes at the host university. There are problems of conflicting academic calendars in some countries, making it difficult for American professors to teach regular courses during the academic years abroad. In two instances in the sample of programs studied, the courses of American professors counted toward degrees, as the result of unique arrangements. The Amherst-Doshisha and Georgetown-Frankfurt programs each involved a single professor who was a permanent member of both the American and host-country staffs, spending somewhat more time abroad than at home. The professors would be resident at examination time.

Often professorial and student exchange are combined. Since 1957, Reed College and the University College of North Staffordshire, United Kingdom, have had a two-way student exchange; similar faculty exchange began in 1958. The plan is for one undergraduate pair and one faculty pair to exchange places each academic year. The student is usually a sophomore or junior.

Temple University and the University of Hamburg are affiliated in a faculty- and student-exchange program, which began in 1955. The faculty exchange is periodic, depending upon availability. A Temple University professor was in Germany in 1956-57. The faculty members teach courses for which regular credit is given. The student exchange functions every year, one student in each direction. The student from Temple may be either a senior, as in 1957-58, or a graduate. The student from Hamburg is always a graduate, but no degree is conferred by Temple. The exchange is for one year (Inventory, p. 278).

Fellowships from an American university for Americans to go abroad or overseas nationals to come to the United States are common, but normally the American comes from, or the foreign national comes to, the awarding American university. A few universities have accepted small grants or endowments for exchanges of students that do not necessarily involve the American university in any activity other than making the award. In such cases, the American university engages in a service operation for a host institution or a financial sponsor. Competition is open to all applicants, who may select universities of their choice. Such an administrative function is also approached in two or three of the junior-year-abroad programs, by which only a small part of the students come from the home campus, and the field director is recruited from outside.

Similar services exist in faculty exchanges. Some universities abroad seek to have an American university act more or less as agent in the United States to recruit visiting faculty members. Sometimes American universities are willing to furnish such services, as in the case of Harvard, which acted as recruiting agent for the host institution in its nutrition program in Peru. Stanford recruited non-Stanford faculty for a technical assistance program in the Philippines, and provided qualified experts in American studies, largely not from Stanford, for seminars at the University of Tokyo. Stanford's interest in the Far East is a substantial one, and servicing or arrangements of this sort may help Stanford to maintain its scholarly stake in the region. Though the Stanford-Tokyo American studies program has been discontinued, Stanford remains interested in Japan and still cooperates closely with Tokyo University.

Exchange of information not involving personnel movement is quite different from the activities previously discussed. Such exchanges have resulted in shipment and receipt of student newspapers, books, periodicals, radio tapes, films, catalogues, curricula statements, syllabuses, reading lists, and many other items. Apparently such programs seldom lead to an exchange of personnel, although in one or two cases this has occurred. They have been especially promoted by the United States Information Agency, under the "people to people" policy. European universities engage in information exchanges much more frequently than American institutions. The Stanford-Keio exchange originally was confined to information and then was extended to include students.

A major issue is raised when American universities provide fellowships, recruiting services, or equipment, and little more. These programs help universities in other countries without prospect of direct gain to the American institutions. Such programs require servicing organization or offices. It may be questioned whether scarce university resources should be used in this manner. To involve the regular departments of universities in such activities is difficult. There is little professional incentive to participate unless they can foresee some tangible benefits for their personnel or department, or unless they desire contact with a host institution or country for future, long-range reasons, as did Stanford in Japan. Where two-way recruiting services can be rendered, as in some small two-way student or professorial exchanges, the case for university affiliations of this type is much stronger.

The degree of mutual participation in the small exchanges by a host institution and an American university is not uniform. The small one- or two-way exchanges of students and professors are originated in at least three different ways: by the American university, by a host institution, and, occasionally, by the sponsoring individual or group. Small exchanges often involve formal clearance with a host institution at least, if not outright collaboration. The University College of North Staffordshire initiated the exchange with Reed College. The initiative for the Stanford-Keio student exchange came from Stanford, particularly from the Stanford students. Joint initiation led to the Stanford-Tokyo program and University of Arizona-Sonora program. The University of Arizona and the University of Sonora in Mexico had informal relations over five or more years that, in 1958, culminated in a formal program in social science, humanities, biological science, and agriculture. Individual donors have often suggested the establishment of small exchanges.

Extensive interinstitutional relationships in the host country characterize the program at the Instituto Technologico y de Estudios Superiores in Monterrey, Mexico. In a large summer program, 10 universities from the United States exchange students with Monterrey Tech; it is by far the largest mutual-exchange program, involving about 100 students each way. From the standpoint of Monterrey Tech, cooperation with a group of American universities means lower costs, a more complete program on its own campus for American students, and the possibility of sending a greater number of its students to the United States. From a United States university point of view, facilities of a single institution are made available to several universities, thus making competition among them quite unnecessary and maximizing the number of American student participants.

Small exchange programs are financed sometimes by those participating in them, sometimes by the host or American universities. Yet a majority of them have some supplementary assistance from a donor, a foundation, or a Fullbright or other United States government grant. Multiple financial sources are common, and the role of the financing organization in policy determination is somewhat proportionate to its financial contribution.

The small exchanges have simple organizations. Selection of American or host-country students is in the hands of each of the two affiliating institutions. A committee or chairman of the program is then designated, who needs to spend only a few hours each year on the task. After the selection of a participating student or faculty member and the reception of the selectee from abroad, few persons allocate time to the program, since the regular facilities of each institution handle any problems that arise. Where two or three American professors are abroad at the same time, as in the Michigan and Stanford American studies programs in Japan, one of them is normally designated as chief of party. Some of the small programs center on special seminars or lecture series in which a visiting student or professor participates; the chairman of these undertakings may be a key person, along with the visitor.

There are fewer major shifts in the role a professor plays in many of the small faculty exchanges than in other projects. He normally teaches in the area of his specialty. Yet in some of them, he may play a role similar to that played by an American professor in a technical assistance abroad project, that is, a combination of teaching, research, and formal or informal consultation.

Recruitment problems have plagued some of the programs. In the Michigan-Doshisha-Kyoto American studies program, the Japanese tended to prefer persons with good reputations whom the Michigan people considered somewhat old-hat in their approach; reputations have a way of lagging. A few two-way exchanges have become one-way over the years because of inability or lack of interest on the part of one of the institutions to continue its share of the undertaking. Some of the small professor exchanges have had to make use of outside recruitment as a result of lack of interest in the program by part of the university. Stanford's American studies-Japanese studies program with the University of Tokyo was beset by such a situation. The social science departments co-operated, while others, at least originally, were not much interested. Stanford administrative officials thought that the faculty should carry on research rather than overseas teaching and advising. Still, the involvement of Stanford in its American studies program in Japan was more widespread within the institution than at Michigan, in part because Japanese area studies at Stanford are less isolated from the regular departments. As with larger programs, two problems in small exchanges have been uncertainty of the quality of faculty members or students to be sent from the partner institution and a mutual hesitation to enter into a long-range agreement which either institution might in the long run neither want nor be able to afford, through lack of funds or personnel. Normally, a few faculty members or students have most contact with the exchange, although in other cases the exchange receives campus-wide attention as in Swedish and general European exchanges at the Illinois campus of Augustana.

Among the objectives of the small exchanges, curriculum and institution-building have been prominent. Several small programs in law, designed in part to build up the study of American law abroad, were launched after World War II. The focus of several programs has been American studies for host countries. Sometimes this focus has been challenged by host-country professors. A Japanese professor at Tokyo University insisted, "What we want out of such a program is not just to learn about things American. We want to learn about the basic progress and thinking that is going on in our fields in your country." Despite reservations such as these, American studies have grown at universities in many countries in the last ten or fifteen years. American university programs have been only a part of American cooperation in their development. In turn, American cooperation has been only one of the factors accounting for their rise. In regard to the growth of American studies in Europe, Sigmund Skard concludes,

This progress is primarily due to the simple pressure of events. Discrepancy between the position of the United States in the world and its place in syllabuses and curricula had long been growing; after 1945 it proved intolerable. Direct support on the part of the Americans could only be a contributory factor. The radical change was brought on by the need for reorientation among the Europeans themselves.[2]

[2] *American Studies in Europe: Their History and Present Organization* (Philadelphia: University of Philadelphia Press, 1958), vol. 2, p. 641.

However, he adds that both financial assistance and professional collaboration from the United States will be necessary for their continued development.

Some American universities, colleges, or departments have used international exchange programs to promote and reinforce existing regional specialties. Stanford and Michigan with their permanent interests in Japanese studies are classic examples, combining professor and student exchanges, research projects, and technical assistance programs. Foreign-language departments have brought a number of teachers to the United States. On the student side, in the Monterrey Tech program with 10 American universities, heavy stress is placed upon American students acquiring a knowledge of Spanish and Mexican students acquiring a knowledge of English.

Friends and long-term professional acquaintances have been made; there is ample testimony to this fact. A good example is the joint law program in Japan where American law specialists are welcomed among Japanese law scholars, and Japanese collections on American and Japanese law are readily made available.

Small exchanges have been of special help to small institutions such as Rockford in assisting students or faculty to get abroad or in bringing students or faculty from abroad. Even though the visitors to or from a small institution may not exceed one or two a year, the exchangees may have a marked impact on the home campus because of its modest size and because of the few exchanges of other types.

Although the number of small exchange programs of long-range or indefinite duration is not great, there are some in this category. It is apparent that small exchanges are a form of university international program that is suitable for long-range affiliation and their numbers may increase for this reason. The increasing importance of small exchanges at all American universities is perhaps symbolized by the fact that in November, 1960 Arizona amended its constitution to permit aliens to be faculty members in state colleges and universities.

Chapter 8

THE PARTICIPANTS: VISITORS TO UNITED STATES UNIVERSITIES UNDER TECHNICAL ASSISTANCE

As popularity of the "Point Four" idea grew after January, 1949, the number of students and trainees from abroad greatly increased. All told, over 53,000 foreign students are in the United States during all or part of an academic year. One response to this great inflow of students from overseas was increase of foreign student services on American campuses. There were several other impacts. So many short-term trainees were sent to the land-grant colleges by the United States Department of Agriculture that each agricultural college appointed special contact officers with whom the USDA might deal. As governmental and international agencies and, later, foundations began to bring larger numbers of students to the United States, they saw advantages in arranging for a group of students to be sent to a single university under a single contract rather than paying individual tuition fees on an *ad hoc* basis. The contract would be of mutual advantage: it would give the university a basis on which to plan, offer special services, and cover its costs, while the organizations which financed the project or sent the students could be assured of the university's receptivity and, presumably, its attention to the students' needs. In other instances universities assumed the initiative to establish special programs for groups of participants financed from several sources. In such cases, fees have been used to reimburse the university and it has solicited several groups for participants for its program.[1] These

[1] For a description of the numerous government agencies and private organizations bringing visitors to the United States for higher educational purposes,

134

two types of programs have come to be known as university participant programs and the students as participants. About 2,000 of the 43,400 foreign students in the United States in 1957–58 were participants under formal university programs or contracts, and the proportion has grown steadily since then. Though this may seem an unimpressive fraction of the total, participants often account for a majority of the foreign students in a particular department or school, such as the School of Public Administration at the University of Southern California.

Illustrations of Participant Programs

There is no typical participant program. In practice, each program has been tailored to the resources of the university, the needs of the participants, the size of the group, and the time available. Thus, Indiana University, under an International Cooperation Administration contract, offers a special training program for foreign nationals in audio-visual education (utilization, administration, and production). The study program occupies eleven months and is conducted annually. The students spend 75 per cent of their time on the Indiana campus and 25 per cent in off-campus training. During 1957–58, 30 students from various countries participated in this program (Inventory, p. 163).

From 1956 to 1958, Wayne State University's Department of Political Science conducted a training program in public administration for Indonesian public officials. The trainees observed United States practices, particularly those that might apply to their administrative problems. They remained for eleven and one-half months; their work did not lead to a degree. Approximately one-half of the training was off campus. Fifteen participated in 1957–58 (Inventory, p. 300).

Quite a different program is in operation at the University of Puerto Rico. The Labor Relations Institute of the University carries out a resident leadership training program for Latin American trade unionists. This program, which was originally the outcome of an agreement between the University of Puerto Rico and the Latin American branch of the International Confederation of Free

see Reuben Lorenz, *Problems of Cost and Programming of Foreign Visitors on the American Campus* (Washington: Commission on Education and International Affairs, American Council on Education, 1961), pp. 3–7.

Trade Unions, now operates within the technical assistance program of the International Cooperation Administration and with the collaboration of the Office of International Labor Affairs of the United States Department of Labor. Designed as a leadership training program for young trade unionists the program aims to teach the techniques of labor union organization and administration, to give an understanding of the role of trade unions in a free society, and to examine the ways in which democratic governments administer labor-management relations. Training combines classroom and field work in the labor union movement in Puerto Rico. Upon completing the three-month training period in Puerto Rico, the teams go to the United States for two months to observe union activities there. Three 3-month programs are offered each year. Instructors are drawn from the faculty of the University of Puerto Rico, government labor agencies, and the trade unions (Inventory, p. 248).

Some of the participant programs are affiliated with technical assistance abroad programs. The University of Minnesota has a multidiscipline ICA contract to assist the Seoul National University of Korea. Minnesota sends some of its staff abroad, and participants come to Minnesota from Korea. In 1957–58, 52 Korean faculty members were working for advanced degrees at the University, 13 in agriculture, 17 in engineering, 9 in medicine, and 13 in public administration. The average length of these study programs was one year and six months. A total of 135 Koreans had already received some participant training (Inventory, p. 201).

Kinds of Programs

The methods used in technical assistance participant programs can be classified in several ways.

1. Is the participant program one aspect of an overseas technical assistance project or is it separate, without any overseas involvement of American university personnel? Most of the programs are of the former type, although more than one-fifth are of the latter type. Programs related to overseas projects restrict themselves to participants from the country involved, while many of the programs independent of overseas activities include participants from many countries. A majority of the overseas technical assistance programs (discussed in Chapters 9 to 14) have state-side participant

training aspects to them; they are examples of the former type. Examples of the latter are many: Indiana University handles for the ICA most of the training of participants from numerous countries in audio-visual education. The United States Office of Education has used a number of teachers colleges or colleges of education at large universities to give participant training to groups composed of persons from several countries. A new context for participant training has begun at the East-West Center of the University of Hawaii. Under a large multimillion dollar United States government grant, the university is giving awards to hundreds of Asian students to study at Hawaii. The program is much larger than its participant aspect and provides for visiting Asian scholars and United States mainland students and scholars interested in Asia as well.

2. Is the program designed to develop persons qualified for specific positions or is it designed to add to the general pool of trained manpower? Participant programs with overseas connections are more frequently of the former type, independent participant programs more commonly of the latter. The former implies building of institutions abroad, and may relate specifically to the training of counterparts of visiting American professors. A few programs train counterparts abroad, a few at American universities, and a larger number in both places. The programs with the greatest success in institution building in the less developed countries have followed the last pattern, combining both experiences for the counterparts. Participant training gives visitors to the United States an opportunity to see an entirely different system of higher education in operation and to feel the full impact of a different culture, and training counterparts abroad permits adaptation of ideas to their own environment and the creation of a climate favorable to acceptance of innovations. The training of participants who are not destined to be counterparts fulfills two functions: development in the participants of a desire for particular changes in a host country where no such changes have been wanted before, and, in advanced countries where institutional frameworks are well developed, the transmission through the participants of innovation, which can be built into existing structures by the participants themselves after suitable adaptation.

3. Do participants take regular courses at the American university or are special activities arranged for them, or do they have a

combination of both? The majority of programs with overseas connections enroll most of their participants for six months to two or three years, and mainly in regular courses, supplemented by special classes and by occasional field trips to points near and far. The majority of independent participant programs are shorter-range, and utilize special courses or seminars, supplemented by a few regular classes sometimes and by field trips. The leader-specialist program of the Department of State has contracted with several universities to conduct special four-month programs for personnel from abroad. The Harvard Business School, journalism at Indiana, and radio-television at Syracuse are among these. Through a subcontract with the Governmental Affairs Institute, Pittsburgh has conducted a similar program in public administration for specialists brought by the State Department, as have Michigan State and Wisconsin in the labor field through subcontracts with the Department of Labor. These programs have been multinational, combining tailor-made noncredit courses at the university with field observation or experience and travel.

4. Are the participants working for degrees?

5. What rank do they have at home—that of a regular graduate student or that of a faculty member or other professional person? Most independent programs are arranged for participants who do not seek degrees, and such participants are often senior professionals or others who do not wish them. The programs with overseas connections include both junior and senior personnel as participants, the former usually seeking degrees. There have been important disagreements among American universities, visiting nationals, and ICA concerning the desirability of obtaining degrees. American university staffs have normally favored regular degree work, but ICA until a few years ago hesitated to permit participants to stay longer than a year in the United States. Different purposes underlie these positions. American universities have wanted to increase the academic standing of institutions abroad; junior participants have sought advancement and prestige; senior participants have been fearful of losing prestige; and ICA has desired to emphasize short-range objectives.

6. Are the participants in a program located at a single institution? Although almost all participant programs provide for short visits to several American universities, among participant programs connected with a technical assistant project overseas, practice is

divided between sending all participants to the home campus of the American university which carries on the work abroad for the basic period of study, and apportioning them among several American universities. The latter practice leads to a greater variety in the education received. This result may be valuable if the participants all come from a single foreign institution in which innovations are planned. The former practice facilitates the arranging of special courses and services for the participants.

Sending participants to a variety of universities can result in the administering university becoming merely a distributing agency for participants coming to the United States. The original intent may or may not have been that all or most participants would remain at the administering university, yet the overseas institution and the participants often exert pressure on the American university to permit the visitors to go where they please—to an Ivy League university, to one with favorable climate such as California, or simply to one that offers the best work in the field in which the participant is interested. Frankfurt faculty members wanted to be free to come to any American university, not just to Chicago. Hokkaido University desired to send its participants to a wide group of American universities, not just to Massachusetts. Indonesians and others have sometimes said they wanted American universities to look upon the participant program as a sort of trusteeship, not as an institutional monopoly. The university contract may become merely the source of funds and the American university merely a liaison with students who come to the United States.

7. Is a special organization established at the American university to administer the program? The probability of a special organization is great when at least several participants are located at a single institution. The special organization may provide all academic and nonacademic services to the participants, as in some of the programs designed to brief participants or to improve their competence in English. In such instances, the program may have little to do with the regular academic units of the American university. More commonly, the special organization is limited to providing special services, such as assigning American assistants or students to participants, making available special reading or study rooms, helping to locate needed books, and even planning for the courses they will teach on return. The Indiana University program in education with Thailand is one of the more elaborate pro-

grams of this type, including a special building for the participants and related staff.

8. Is the training at the university a small part of the participants' training while in the United States or is it the major program focus? Several universities have entered into formal programs for minor parts of the training. Universities in the Washington, D.C. area have provided refresher English courses and other briefing-type programs for a wide range of participants, for example.

Selection of Personnel

The principal persons in participant programs are, of course, the participants themselves. But in order to make their stay effective in the United States, a number of others are involved in the programs. Included are the program director on the campus (who often is the campus coordinator if overseas and campus programs are combined), the regular staff of the American university, and a series of persons abroad—some host-country nationals and some Americans—who help select the participants.

Standards for selecting the participants go far to determine the success of a program. Academic ability is essential, but a special quality sought is that participants be willing or eager to return to their country and accept employment in the institution which sent them. The institution abroad, in turn, must be prepared to hire them. Maturity is of special importance, since unless a participant has made a start on a permanent career and intends to stand by his choice, he is not likely to make maximum use of his education abroad on return home.

Because of the length of time spent in the United States, those participants who are candidates for degrees need to be closely screened for aptitude to make adjustments. A participant who seeks a degree must remain one to four years in the United States; some stay six or eight years, although not often in a single program. He must make both a program decision and a personal decision as to the length of stay and the level of the degree to be sought. The best fitted participant may have to be prepared to extend his stay if he proves himself equal to obtaining an advanced degree.

Being away from home for several years has alienated some participants from their own cultures. A maximum stay of two years at a time in the United States has been suggested by some foundation officials. An initial period of two years should be adequate for obtaining a master's degree. After a period back home, a second two-year period should be adequate for passing preliminary examinations. In many cases, the doctoral dissertation could be completed most appropriately at home. It has also been suggested that degree candidates who are married should bring their families with them if possible, at least after proving themselves successful in the initial six months or so.

For the more long-range participant programs, the selection procedures tend to be extensive. Selection normally takes nine months to a year from the time of announcement of openings to the arrival of the participants in the United States. Applications are solicited, interviews held, English and sometimes other proficiency examinations given, and various guarantees as to future employment obtained. In a few instances, future participants work for a year or so as assistant to the American professors in their own country, obtaining special training before going abroad. The overseas institution is often involved in selection. In India, the university agricultural technical assistance programs begin selection procedures at regional joint meetings attended by American professors, Indian agricultural college personnel, and state agricultural agencies. Goals are set and criteria established, such as which departments most need strengthening, in what areas Indian colleges can profit most from American graduate training, and what kinds of individuals are mature enough to adapt, not adopt, American methods to Indian conditions after their experience in the United States. ICA representatives also play a role. The principal of the college is perhaps the central figure.

A special problem in some less developed countries is how to involve domestic institutions in the selection of participants and yet keep applications open to as wide a group of qualified nationals as possible. Two dangers to avoid are the selection of friends and relatives on the one hand, and of those who are wanted out of the way on the other. Some countries take into consideration special factors, such as the religious quotas applied to participants in Lebanon. The worst abuses occur where institutions in effect select the participants but have little interest in the program itself. Some American universities have resorted to exercise of a veto of prospective participants or unilateral selection, as would be the procedure with regular foreign students applying for acceptance at an American university.

The quality of participant obtained by the more successful programs has been high, but there have been problems in some programs such as poor language ability of the participants or their inability to adjust. In order to minimize language difficulties, participants enroll in intensive English-language courses before leaving home. Adjustment is often furthered by briefing in the home country by American university personnel, if any, or occasionally by other Americans, while the long process of appointment is under way. Such briefings typically include a few formal sessions and informal discussions on the United States, American higher education, and living conditions at the university. Visits to American homes in the home country may be arranged.

Some motives of participants do not favor the likelihood of success. Participants often want to come to the United States for the travel experience and to improve their English rather than for academic reasons. Improvement of skill in the English language may lead to a good job. Participant programs are frequently designed to train persons for academic posts at home. Since academic salaries or promotion prospects are low, grantees may take the opportunity to advance their education in the United States though they do not plan to stay in academic employment on return, if alternative job opportunities are available. For example, in the Tennessee public administration program in Bolivia, some returned participants look forward to the time when they can be released from their commitment to teach at the public administration school of the University of San Andres. In Indonesia, a required commitment to work at low salaries in government service or teaching on return tended to divert the more able students to other employments, so that some of them never became participants in the first place. Only one out of three to five participants in American university programs actually stays for a long time in the employ of the cooperating institution after his return.

In the case of Keio University in Japan and its business administration program with Harvard, a decision to begin a program was largely made by the president of the university and certain influential alumni without consulting the faculty. There was considerable resentment among faculty members when the agreement was consummated—an inauspicious way to develop sound motivation.

In contrast to the careful selection of participants is the casual designation of American staff members to work with them on the American campus. No special selection is appropriate for the instructor of regular courses taken by participants. If special courses are arranged, more often than not a staff member who can be "spared" is found. Several programs, however, choose their best personnel for special courses. One such case is the University of Minnesota, where the regular public administration staff offered a seminar for Korean participants.

American staff members at home, working with participants, satisfied fewer appropriate criteria than their colleagues in technical assistance programs abroad. They definitely had less enthusiasm for or dedication to the task, and normally less cultural empathy. Their professional competence was about as high, although in some cases less specifically related to the task at hand. Personnel at home generally spent only part of their time on the programs, with the limitations of attention to the programs that this implies. Campus coordinators who had visited their program in the field or who were former project members performed their tasks more effectively.

Achievements

Being a technical assistance program, the participant program must be judged by its impact on the personnel and institutions of the country involved. Many of the participant programs have as one objective the introduction of change in the home universities. One difficulty in attaining this objective is that faculty members usually serve part time overseas. Universities in British and former British colonies in Africa and South Asia tend to have a higher proportion of full-time personnel. About a fourth of the technical assistance abroad programs had some effect in stimulating more full-time service through the device of a concomitant participant program. Usually guarantees were obtained in advance from the home institution as well as from each participant that at the very least a period of one to three years of full-time employment would follow the training period in the United States.

The utilization of participants on return has varied markedly country to country. It has been greatest and most appropriately related to the objectives of the projects in Japan and India. At Waseda University the president was instrumental in getting some 25 faculty members, mostly younger ones, to come to the United States for a year's work in economics, business administration, or engineering. Since they were already faculty members, their use in an appropriate capacity on their return was assured. Much the same situation exists in the Keio University arrangement with Harvard. In India, the 11 faculty members trained at the University of Tennessee in home science and the participants trained at Kansas State and Illinois in agriculture were well used on return. In both Japan and India, there is a scarcity of jobs for well-trained persons, and this is reflected in a tendency for participants to remain with the home university and to be employed on a full-time basis, with or without supplementary jobs. Also, participants from Japan and India tended to be persons already established professionally with positions awaiting them on return; they had committed themselves. Japan and India are also countries with extensive existing institutional structures.

Participants from these two countries accepted many innovations and some of these innovations were reflected in their teaching on return. In home science in India, the returned participants were involved in such matters as special summer teaching, planning curricular revisions, and advising on building layouts. The Kansas State–Illinois participants had interested themselves in new research in agriculture and experimented with new teaching techniques such as term papers and class discussions; two had started quizzes in their classes. In general they were applying themselves to the more practical problem of agriculture in their regions. The programs did not create important frustrations among the participants, rather, a satisfaction with the additional learning and discovery of new capacities. The success of participant programs in Japan and India led field observers in both countries to observe that there is better payoff in the participant programs than in those sending American professors abroad (Bronfenbrenner, chap. 6; Hart, pp. 53–59).

Participant programs have not been so successful with Europe or Latin America. Academic participants have not been able to overcome the handicap of the predominant pattern of part-time professors and comparatively low salaries; alternative job opportunities have often taken them far away from assignments with the institution from which they came. Furthermore, there has been a sheer lack of permanent career opportunities at the university. In Italy, only one out of four returned participants actually stayed with public administration at the University of Bologna. In Turkey, New York University had a record of five out of twelve, Harvard only one out of six, and Georgetown none. In Latin America, participant attrition varied from rather low to very high.

Personal impact of the participant program was often high, but institutional impact was low (Adams and Garraty, p. 93). The number of persons trained in the United States is growing larger, but may have no significance for an institution. Many government agencies and universities abroad have never accepted the idea of participant programs involving institutional changes. Neither participants nor other staff have fully embraced it. Where this objective is accepted, the participant program has a much greater impact; where it is not accepted, personal impact or a contribution to the pool of United States-trained personnel is the only major result in the short run. In the long run, institutional receptivity to innovations adapted from the United States may be increased by the existence of such a pool of persons, especially as they rise in their occupations.

Impact on the American campus, while of secondary concern in participant programs, has not been great in most instances. American university innovations arising from them have been largely accommodative. Where enough participants have been present, one or more special courses have been developed, but few institutions look upon these special courses as anything except temporary expedients. Once the participants no longer come, the courses will disappear. The number, size, and frequency of participant programs on several campuses has caused disruption of regular teaching schedules, but these inconveniences may be temporary. Professors have been transferred from regular courses to special noncredit training assignments. A few institutions have developed continuing specializations as the result of participant programs or return of staff members from abroad. Examples are Vanderbilt in economic development and Harvard in the teaching of business administration abroad. Discussion of developing similar specializations has occurred at several other institutions.

Few other impacts can be observed on the American campus. American universities which have developed participant programs for certain host countries do not find a great increase in the general foreign student enrollment from those countries. Thus Minnesota with its large multifield Korean program has not experienced any great increase in the number of nonparticipant Korean students. Michigan State, with its large program in Vietnam, has not found that Vietnamese students come in any larger quantities. Temporarily, the university with a large participant program may become a headquarters for students from the host country. In this sense, Indiana with its two participant programs for Thais has become a kind of center for Thai student activity in the United States.

Talks to community groups in urban areas by foreign students who are able speakers are so numerous that some institutions have had to take measures to prevent excessive speaking engagements, such as requiring a fee of $5 or so to be given to the student, or requiring transportation to and from the campus. This is more an aspect of foreign student activity on American campuses as a whole than it is of the participant programs in particular, however. Where participant programs have been located at universities with few other foreign students, they have helped overcome the disadvantages of isolation of American students from other cultures. However, the majority of participant programs have been located on campuses where foreign students abound.

Policy Suggestions

Every university participant program involves the assumption that American higher education has something from which foreign students or trainees can benefit. What is this "something" and who are the foreign students or trainees that can most benefit from it?

The wide range of program activity is illustrated by university participant programs that are unconnected with university technical assistance abroad and which constitute over a fifth of all participant programs in higher education. There are many practices: the use of regular or, more commonly, special courses; the centering of attention on briefing new arrivals or, more commonly, the meeting of the needs of a group specializing in a certain subject; a group from a single country or, more commonly, one from several countries. For example, some universities have undertaken to sponsor sum-

mer briefing programs for newly arrived State Department exchangees from several countries. The main problem of most independent university participant programs lies in organizing special
nondegree training activities. Some of this training is similar to
regular adult education. Some of it is hardly at a higher education
level or seldom brings the participant to the campus, field observation being emphasized.

Nearly all participant programs have involved special program
features, but there has been overemphasis on field trips to points
near and far, or on watered-down versions of university courses not
for credit. Such special program features fail to reflect adequately
the need for giving the participants something more than an opportunity to acquire subject matter competence and techniques in
a narrow sense of these terms. Although some special seminars
have been held on problems of countries from which students come,
there has been insufficient emphasis on placing subject matter and
technical knowledge in the context of higher education and of national and international development. An outstanding exception is
the program in teacher education for Thai students at Indiana University, where regular courses are effectively supplemented with
work relevant to Thailand's needs. Another exception is the program of the Harvard Business School designed to meet the needs
of teachers of business administration from other countries.

The argument is not that all special program features should be
eliminated. Even among foreign students studying for a degree,
some special courses are desirable. This is especially true in such
areas as "English as a foreign language." Special service courses
might be extended to an examination of American political, social,
and economic institutions "as foreign institutions." However, such
special arrangements are supplemental or peripheral to most students' major interest.

There is less justification for special courses in the degree-participants' major fields of study. If a university has a participant program, presumably there is some desire that the participants apply
their particular branch of learning to their home environment for
national development purposes. With this in mind, universities
should review their courses and curricula to see that the following
aspects are included:

1. If the student is a future professor or teacher, he should understand something about an educational system and the way his par-

ticular discipline relates to it both in the United States and in his own country. Most American university curricula include no attention to university or educational systems. For example, the merits and shortcomings of the relatively integrated American university, its central services, and the presentation of knowledge in socially useful ways, especially in elementary and secondary education, are aspects that need attention, particularly as they relate to a student's field of study.

2. The student who is going to apply his field of knowledge on return home, at the university level or in a government agency or private business, needs to know the relationship of his discipline to various national development goals. There thus can usefully be an emphasis on economic, social, and political development and the way particular disciplines fit into development goals and processes.

3. Similarly, it is important to give the students some notion of how higher education as a whole does and can fit into economic, social, and political development both in the United States and abroad. With this background the student on return can make a much faster adaptation of his new knowledge to development programs.

4. In some fields of study there are special applications depending upon the physical, climatic, or other characteristics of a country. For example, there is the study of tropical agriculture or tropical medicine. Even in the field of engineering there are certain problems peculiar to tropical engineering. These subfields are of special importance to some participants.

5. As a whole, a broadly comparative approach rather than merely a host-country and United States approach should be followed in order to give deeper meaning to the participant's experience.

None of these suggestions lead one to conclude that special curricula are necessary. In all cases, the courses would be as appropriate for American students as they would be for foreign students. They would be excellent preparation for someone intending to spend part of his professional life abroad as an American in a technical assistance program, for example.

It is thus largely in the noncredit, nondegree area that American universities must develop special program features. The field of special noncredit courses in any American university is indeed a rough uncharted sea. There are few markers to help the university ship as it makes its way across the vast expanse. The question is not whether the university should offer noncredit courses and curricula. Every large university is doing so in many different fields, although not all do so for participants. The question is what kind of criteria can the university establish so as to delimit its responsibility in this area? Furthermore, what kind of personnel shall be used for these special courses and curricula, regular university staff or special staff from outside the normal university resources?

Participants often have nonacademic objectives as their primary center of interest while in the United States. Some may wish to engage in extended on-the-job observation or work while here. Some may be on a quick inspection tour. However, many nonacademic training objectives can be facilitated by limited exposure to courses with real academic content, even though the courses are not given for credit.

The university can develop a series of courses and/or curricula that build upon its academic strength and areas of interest for presentation to foreign trainees that are not registered for work for college credit. The standard of work in such special courses and curricula need not be low. Very often participants are perfectly capable of doing work of college level, but their limited time or interests are such that they do not desire college credit. It would seem wrong in principle for a university to accept technical training in areas that are less than of an advanced nature. Government agencies, the Washington International Center, professional groups, secondary schools, trade schools, and other nonuniversity groups can give technical training on a nonuniversity level. But a university, faithful to the standards of higher education, can give a wide variety of work to the intelligent layman who does not desire a degree.

Just as participants coming for nonacademic purposes can profitably work some programs of academic merit into their busy schedules, degree-participants (as well as American students) can supplement their classroom activities with internships and on-the-job observation. Complementary contributions can be made by the university and the community for both kinds of participants. However, universities must realize that meaningful on-the-job observation can only take place with adequate supervision both from the university and from the business or agency involved. The experience of practice teaching in schools of education or field work courses in social work is appropriate. Most participant programs have failed in providing adequately conceived and supervised field training.

Universities can usefully engage in preparation and briefing activities for foreign trainees coming to the United States. However, here again a university must be careful to engage in that kind of work which is most appropriate for the university rather than to take on any and all preparation and briefing activities simply because they somehow relate to one or another aspect of international exchange. Universities are especially equipped to engage in programs that relate to cultural, social, economic, and political matters, with special attention to education and language training.

There are many kinds of participants who can benefit from such a wide variety of programs. Two general categories of participants are junior (or future) staff members of a host institution, usually by far the larger in numbers, and senior staff members. It is preferable that the former be given status as regular graduate students who are working for degrees and take regular courses supplemented by some special work and a few observation trips. For senior staff members, special nondegree programs need to be arranged during what will usually be a shorter stay, and the status of visiting scholars ought to be accorded them. Harvard made such arrangements for the visiting participant professors and judges from Japan under the joint law program. The difference between the two categories of participants is marked, and has unfortunately often been overlooked at American universities, with consequent aggravation of status difficulties.

Unfortunately, distinctions between junior and senior participants are not so clear-cut as they might seem. Even the junior participants may be older than the usual American graduate students. Furthermore, on occasion the desire for special status has been a desire not to engage in classroom, laboratory, or field work, for fear that such activity would be demeaning. The conflict between the American and other systems of culture or higher education in such instances is sharp.

Some participants come to American universities individually, with no university program connection. Though they fall outside the present study, it is relevant to point out that to the extent that they register for regular courses few problems are presented, but if they come for a short visit, special programming is necessary which in some cases has placed a heavy burden on the universities.

Some universities have appointed special assistants to the president simply to handle short-term foreign visitors, and the state agricultural colleges have each appointed a staff member as liaison for the same purpose. There is little balance of the visitors among universities and fields, some institutions or fields being inundated and others rarely seeing a foreign visitor.

Participant programs often bring financial resources to a university that permit the organization of special field trips. The more serious of these should be continued, but their benefits should be extended to all foreign graduate students to the extent that resources permit. The Harvard Business School program in the teaching of business administration includes classwork, research, and appropriate field trips for foreign nationals from any country.

For the most part, universities have allowed other agencies such as the United States government to take the initiative in designating nondegree participants, where no overseas university project exists. If nondegree participant programs are to be placed on a more systematic basis and on a higher plane, universities must exercise more discretion in the short-term trainees they accept. This is especially important for on-the-job training programs and special seminars.

Every participant program will encounter a difference between group and individual objectives, particularly those that are directed toward helping build a particular institution abroad. Even with the most solemn of assurances before his selection, an individual participant may have motivations that are not consistent with the objectives of the program. This is also a situation that has been aggravated by a lack of group planning, both on the part of Americans and on the part of overseas nationals. Participants cannot fit their personal plans into group objectives when the latter are at best uncertain. Even with the most definite of group objectives, conflicts will arise. For example, in countries short of highly trained personnel, as are most of the less developed nations (India and Pakistan being notable exceptions in some fields), the participants on their return find themselves in a favorable job market. No guarantees or assurances are going to prevent tempting job offers from being made and, frequently, accepted. Aside from taking formal precautions against this hazard when specific institution-building objectives are of major importance, American universities might well bring to the United States for training three or four persons for every position to be filled at the home institution(s), and thus make allowance for those who accept other employment. The training of those who accept jobs elsewhere is not wasted if a country-wide point of view is taken, as long as they do not leave the homeland. They will be a part of the pool of educated individuals.

Universities should make sure that participants spend an amount of time at their institution adequate to the educational objectives in view. Last-minute requests from Washington or elsewhere should be turned aside: advance planning is needed. And in this planning, there should be a maximum amount of university initiative in establishing a meaningful program for the participants.

Chapter 9

THE UNIVERSITY AND TECHNICAL ASSISTANCE ABROAD

Not all international exchange programs of American universities focus on individual educational or scholarly objectives as much as those discussed in previous chapters. Since World War II another type of program has grown rapidly—technical assistance, largely to underdeveloped countries. The focus in this kind of program is less the effect on participating students or faculty members and more the impact on the nation to which the assistance is extended. This and five subsequent chapters discuss activities and problems which have arisen under technical assistance abroad.

Programs of technical assistance abroad have differed from those hitherto considered in several other respects. First, the work has been carried on mainly in Asia, Latin America, and, more recently, Africa rather than in Western Europe. The countries concerned are more widely varied among themselves and in comparison with the United States than are the Western European nations. Second, they usually involve much closer relations with governmental agencies both at home and abroad. Also, public and private sponsors play a more important role. Third, they have created additional internal problems for the American universities which are called upon to assist in the work.

The sheer magnitude of these programs, for one thing, weighs more heavily on university resources. There are more than 125 American university programs of technical assistance abroad. For example, in Brazil, Johns Hopkins University is assisting the government in public health, the University of Michigan is working with the University of Sao Paulo in education, Michigan State University and the University of Southern California are engaged with

153

several Brazilian institutions in the fields of business and public administration, and Purdue is helping a rural university in agriculture and home economics. These projects are underwritten by the United States International Cooperation Administration to the extent of over $3.6 million. In addition, the Brazilian government and private Brazilian institutions have contributed liberally.

In one country alone, Indonesia, the University of California has undertaken projects in medical education and engineering at two universities, Indiana is assisting the government with a public administration training program, and Kentucky is helping two institutions in engineering and agriculture. These projects cost the United States government more than $5.8 million. There is a local contribution. The Ford Foundation also is underwriting the dollar cost of several university contracts in Indonesia, including the University of California and the University of Wisconsin in economics, and the State University of New York in education. Under still different auspices, Johns Hopkins University has been assisting an Indonesian university in political science and international relations.

Brazil and Indonesia are not isolated examples. University assistance for India is far greater than for any other country in the world; ICA alone sponsors 13 projects there. Many other countries have or have had three or more university contracts each, including Chile, Mexico, Peru, Liberia, Nigeria, Turkey, Iran, Pakistan, Japan, Korea, the Philippines, Thailand, and Vietnam. Europe has had the fewest. Africa has had the most rapidly increasing number of programs.

Origin of the Programs

During the nineteenth century, when the great expansion westward took place in North America, this nation encountered many development problems. Colleges were called upon to contribute to the new society. As they undertook this task, they found that the European model of higher education, followed to a considerable extent by colleges near the Eastern seaboard, was of limited relevance. Thus there began a series of improvisations and experiments in higher education which were to lead American universities in a direction different from that taken by European institutions. The ever-present frontier was long the predominant influence. The frontier dwellers and those who followed them were democratic and pragmatic. They seemed to have little use for the aristocratic and theoretical bent of the private colleges and universities of the East. Their need for knowledge concerned aspects of rural life such as agriculture, forestry, and problems of living in new environments. They wanted knowledge that would contribute in as short a time as possible to the needs of the new West. With the onset of the industrial revolution and the development of industry in the West, a further requirement emerged—advanced training in the mechanic arts.

The movement of population westward was so rapid that private institutions of higher education were not established fast enough. The needs were too great and private benefactors too few. Thus began the era of publicly supported institutions of higher learning. The Morrill Act of 1862 subsidized each state in creating at least one college "to teach such branches of learning as are related to agriculture and the mechanic arts . . . in order to promote the liberal and practical education of the industrial classes in the several pursuits and professions in life." The land grants set aside for this purpose and subsequent additional Federal assistance resulted in the establishment of at least one land-grant college in every state. The Morrill Act was only one legislative step toward a system of public higher education, but it came to be of major significance. Emphasis on the liberal and practical content of higher education and on its availability to all interested persons, not just to a small elite, became central in American public higher education by the twentieth century, and has strongly influenced most private universities.

Early Assistance Abroad. The experiments in higher education in the United States began to attract attention from abroad in the latter half of the nineteenth century. Even Europe was interested. England sent a delegation to look at the land-grant colleges as possible prototypes for extending its own system. Canada took note. With the opening of Japan, educational leaders of that country turned to the United States for help, as well as to certain European countries. The experience of the United States in relating universities to the problems of development of the American West seemed particularly relevant to the Japanese.

The number of countries in which American higher education attracted attention was limited, for several reasons. Most of Asia and Africa, being under the sovereignty of European nations, was closed to the United States. Colonial governments or local leaders in education were not free to request help from the United States even if they had wished to do so, and the United States government did not offer such services. Europe was not active in requesting missions since it believed itself to be more advanced than a newcomer to the political and educational world. Occasional requests came from Latin America, although in higher education Latin America looked primarily to Europe.

Several technical missions in higher education went from the United States to countries interested in development, such as Japan, in the latter half of the nineteenth century. These early advisory missions were for the most part initiated and paid for by the host countries. They gave advice on establishment of entire systems of higher education, on special fields such as medical or teacher education, and on establishment of single universities. The membership of such missions was individual; institutional arrangements with American universities were not involved. However, among those who participated were prominent staff members on leave from American universities or alumni who were still closely associated with their alma maters. Increasingly, American universities became aware of a need and of an opportunity.

Despite these early ventures, not many American university programs of technical assistance developed until after World War II. The technical advisory missions in education in the later nineteenth and early twentieth centuries signified a willingness to give assistance abroad, but academic participation was limited to individuals, usually without responsibility by their institutions. One instance of institutional responsibility stands out. Beginning in 1876, the Massachusetts State College of Agriculture, now the University of Massachusetts, helped in the development of Hokkaido University in Japan. Although the affiliation had long since lapsed, in 1957 these two institutions again became associated with each other, this time through an ICA contract. The early program was a factor in Hokkaido's selection of Massachusetts.

Point Four and After. In the 1940s the many technical assistance activities of the United States government and private groups in Latin America foreshadowed events to come. Substantial dollar underwriting accompanied these efforts, but again the missions were staffed at first by experts individually recruited.

As Americans came to play a growing role in world affairs, it was natural for them to turn to the universities for assistance, as they had in internal affairs. This they did gradually, without considering the implications or making broad policy decisions. Most of this assistance has been, and probably remains, individual and informal. Yet the early precedent set by Massachusetts State College of Agriculture, unusual for its time, was to become the model for post-World War II developments.

One or two university programs of technical assistance abroad began in the late 1940s. For example, in cooperation with the inter-American public health servicio, Harvard University in 1949 informally began a research and training program in nutrition in Peru and some other Latin American countries, although a contract was not forthcoming until a few years later. Nearly all government-financed university technical assistance programs began after 1949, and foundation-financed programs were not numerous until the middle 1950s, although foundations had been carrying on their own technical assistance for many years.

President Truman's message to Congress in 1949, with its Point Four passage, was to have extensive implications for the universities. It aroused so much interest among academic circles that the services of the Association of Land-Grant Colleges and Universities were offered to the President in carrying out the proposed program. The offer was not immediately accepted.

By 1950 three agencies administered government technical assistance: the Institute of Inter-American Affairs (IIAA) in Latin America, the Economic Cooperation Administration (ECA) in Europe and the Far East, and the new Technical Cooperation Administration (TCA) in Africa, the Middle East, and South Asia. For the most part, the United States Department of Agriculture, the United States Public Health Service, the United States Office of Education, and the Bureau of the Budget carried on the several aspects of technical assistance under these agencies. The USDA has traditionally turned to the land-grant colleges for help in its programs, and programs in the foreign field were no exception. Many members of the state agricultural colleges, on leave, participated in foreign agricultural assistance—so many that by the early 1950s it was becoming difficult to recruit able persons. One way to solve the problem was to give the colleges contracts for a part of the program so that staff members would not need to take leave in order to participate.

Meanwhile, the president of Oklahoma State University had been appointed director of TCA. Well known in the Association of Land Grant Colleges and Universities, he and leaders of the association, with USDA members, helped to develop plans for college contracts. As if acting together, officials of IIAA, ECA, and TCA began to work out college contracts for their respective geographical areas, although there was little contact among them. IIAA completed arrangements with Michigan State University for Colombia (1951) and with the University of Arkansas for Panama (1951). TCA signed contracts with Oklahoma State for Ethiopia (1952) and with Arizona for Iraq. ECA worked with Cornell (1952) and Michigan (1952) for the Philippines. Five of the six contracts were primarily in agriculture; one, the Michigan program, was in public administration.

It remained for someone associated with governmental technical assistance to promote vigorously the use of university contracts. This Harold Stassen did when he became director of the Foreign Operations Administration (FOA) in 1953, the first year in which all technical assistance was unified under one agency. He saw many advantages in the procedure:

There were three main reasons why I supported the university contracts idea. First, I felt that there was an important potential in the long-term relationships between an American university and a university of another country. Second, I felt that, given the educational nature of technical assistance, a university was a most natural institution for carrying it out. Third, universities were important repositories of excellent personnel which had to be tapped if an acceptable program were to be carried out.

His friends have suggested that there was an additional factor in his thinking, namely, the political advantage to him personally and to the mutual security program of state university participation and support.

Although Stassen was eminently successful in involving universities, it was much easier to convince them of the desirability of university contracts than the FOA bureaucracy; easier to convince the subject matter specialists in FOA than the legal and controller's offices; easier to influence the Washington bureaucracy than some of the field units. Support of FOA (later ICA) for contracts with universities has varied both with the top leadership and with the working subunits. After 1954, the USDA and other subject matter agencies of the United States government no longer played an important role in technical assistance activities abroad. FOA handled them directly. The universities thus were forced to deal solely with FOA, unable to use the familiar channel of professional contact of the regular subject matter agencies. The FOA bureaucracy had not had experience in working with the universities. Some FOA personnel actively opposed university contracts, others as actively promoted them. At least one of Stassen's successors was exceedingly cool to the universities. Despite such opposition and coolness, the number of contracts increased until in 1961 it reached 100, exactly the number that Harold Stassen had set as his goal some eight years earlier (see Figure 1). Forty per cent of ICA advisory personnel overseas is obtained by contracts rather than by direct hire, and university contracts make up a substantial proportion. University contracts are likely to increase still further under the

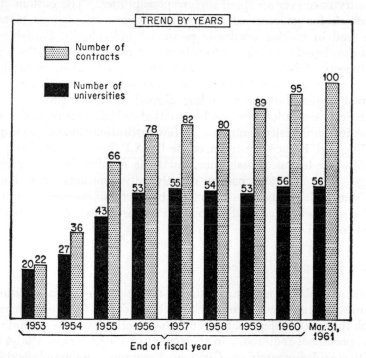

Figure 1. ICA University Contracts in Operation. (Source: Office of Statistics and Reports, ICA.)

Agency for International Development (AID), which succeeded ICA in 1961.

American foundations also increased their technical assistance activities during the 1950s. Like the government, they turned to American universities as instrumentalities to carry out some of the work. In the latter part of the decade, the Ford Foundation began to operate increasingly by means of university contracts overseas. Several of the other foundations supported one or more similar efforts.

The programs of technical assistance abroad for which American universities accepted *institutional* responsibility numbered 111 in 1957–58 (Chapter 1, Table 2). Some of these programs also provided for the training of host-country nationals in the United States, but all were principally centered on teams of American professors sent abroad. The number of university contracts increased to somewhat over 125 by 1961. Few universities from any other country have ever accepted such responsibilities. The custom elsewhere is for government agencies or private associations to take the lead in making academic personnel individually available to less developed countries or to others that request them. Even the University of London, with its well-known program of universities in special relation and its external examination system, has not assumed responsibility for sending abroad teams of professors for technical assistance comparable to that which occurs under the American university contracts. A few institutions in such countries as England, France, Australia, or the U.S.S.R. have accepted responsibility for technical assistance, but their number has never been large. The American pattern of university contracts for technical assistance abroad is consequently of interest and concern to universities everywhere as well as to those in the United States and the host countries.

Some Examples of Projects

There probably is no such thing as a "typical" technical assistance contract of an American university. Each differs from the others in such things as subject matter, objectives, activities to be performed, and personnel required. In the course of four years of study, the Institute of Research on Overseas Programs conducted field research in regard to 35 technical assistance projects in 14 countries. A few examples well illustrate the variations.

The University of California has undertaken important responsibilities in Indonesia in the field of medical education:

Under an International Cooperation Administration contract, initiated in 1954 and extended to 1960, the California and Djakarta medical schools cooperated in modernization of the medical school at Djakarta, in the training of future teachers in medicine and public health, and in medical research. About 10 American professors per year were recruited by the University of California for the project (about three from the University of California and seven from other institutions in the United States). With contract funds, California procured several hundred thousand dollars' worth of equipment. Though the contract did not provide for participants to study in the United States, a number did so through coordination of this program with other United States government and Indonesian government assistance. In addition, the China Medical Board (an affiliate of the Rockefeller Foundation) contributed equipment and the salary of the group leader. Among the important results of the program were rounding-out and expansion of the faculty of the University of Indonesia Medical School, a modernization of its curriculum, and creation of opportunities for the rapid training of additional Indonesian professors of medicine, so that establishment of a second well-rounded medical school began in 1960. To this end, the University of California Medical School entered into a second affiliation in 1959, this time with the Airlangga University in Surabaja. This second affiliation is being developed along similar lines and also will last about six years (adapted from Smith, pp. 121–122).

In an entirely different field, the Spring Garden Institute of Philadelphia undertook a program in Turkey:

This program, starting in May, 1955, and financed by ICA, was designed to bolster Turkey's automotive repair and maintenance schools. During the 1957–58 academic year, eight Spring Garden instructors were assigned to the Automotive Repair School at Izmir. Their primary mission was to train teachers rather than automobile mechanics. They were to help modernize the curriculum of the Izmir school, introduce American teaching methods, and give students more practical training on equipment supplied by Spring Garden. Ultimately, Spring Garden was to assist in the establishment of other automotive repair schools (i.e., in Adana and Ankara) and to plan similar projects for training electronic and electrical technicians. The program consisted mainly of sending American experts and equipment to Turkey, and did not involve the training of Turkish teachers in the United States. Its annual dollar budget in 1957 amounted to $200,000. In addition, there was a local-currency budget (adapted from Adams and Garraty, pp. 170–171).

In Peru, North Carolina State College participated in a project to further textile engineering education:

The scope of the project was "broadening and improvement of the curriculum in textile engineering, the accompanying improvement in teaching methods, the introduction of teaching aids, the establishment and equipping of textile engineering laboratories, guidance in a program of applied textile research, and training of Peruvian teachers, both in the United States and at the National School of Engineers in Lima." A textile education program was to be provided, geared to a level to fulfill the developing textile needs of Peru. To this end, North Carolina State College was to provide services in teaching and research, demonstration projects, consultative services, training of college faculty and other staff, special conferences and training programs, training aids, professional associations and publications, and books, materials, and supplies. "Under the contract NCSC agreed to maintain in residence in Peru a 'staff specialist' to represent the NCSC and act as liaison between the [National School of Engineers]—designated representative and the short-term consultants of NCSC. NCSC would also then provide short-term consultants, some of whom were limited by contract to a period of four months in Peru, who were specialists in the various fields to be operative in the project work. These included textile chemistry, instrumentation, quality control and testing, etc." (adapted from Adams and Cumberland, pp. 171 and 173).

Although each project has had its distinctive aspects, they all have involved sending one or more American staff members abroad to help bring about some change in the host country. Most of the projects have fallen in the fields of teacher education, technical education, engineering, agriculture and home economics, business or public administration, and public health, nursing, and medical education. A team of from 5 to 10 specialists is most common, but the number of staff members abroad under a project at any one time has varied from 1 to over 50. The duration of an individual's stay has been from a few weeks up to four years, but the most frequent term of duty has been one or two years. Among the more common objectives has been the introduction of changes that will be permanent through building a new institution or substantial modification of an existing institution in the host country.

Activities

To some extent, every member of a technical assistance team abroad acts as an agent of change. Underlying this basic role are several activities, such as that of administrator, teacher, consultant, or research specialist. The two most common activities in which American staff members overseas engage are teaching and consulting.

Teaching. Three kinds of teaching have been frequent: (1) direct teaching while acting as a substitute teacher, such as teaching undergraduate students in Indonesian programs or in-service trainees in engineering programs; (2) direct teaching in a demonstration class; and (3) teaching of intermediary groups such as teachers or the teachers of teachers. In general there is agreement that priority should be given to the latter two. However, American professors are often faced with the fact that there are no teachers or counterparts to train in their field or there are no personnel who will watch demonstrations. Which should come first: to make a beginning at teaching students directly or to develop host-institution personnel who can teach after the American professors have gone home? In part, any training of student groups can be considered a demonstration, and most American universities faced with a lack of actual or potential counterparts have resorted to direct training. Where the staff members of the host institution have lacked interest in innovation, or where evidence of immediate results is desired by ICA, the tendency to train students directly has been reinforced.

The results have been rather disappointing, particularly in those programs where nearly all teaching in a new field has been carried on by American professors. Building of institutions has not progressed rapidly, and some American universities, such as the University of Pennsylvania in Pakistan, have almost forgotten about training counterparts, so busy have they been with other teaching problems. Only if a host institution has made an initial commitment to the training of counterparts, in addition to accepting the direct teaching of student groups, has this system contributed much to building up institutions in a short time, as with the University of Michigan in the Philippines. Without such a commitment, the legal, administrative, and financial difficulties in getting a counterpart system established, together with the lack of prestige of the new field among host-country professors, virtually prevent any early start toward building a permanent institution.

In countries such as Bolivia and Indonesia, where educational structures are not as well developed as in some neighboring countries and trained personnel are extremely scarce, it may be necessary to begin with undergraduate groups and hope that some among them will become future intermediaries. This is a process which requires a decade or two, however, and the hazards confronting such a program are exceedingly great. In countries with even moderately developed educational structures, it is probably best to begin by working with existing or potential intermediary group members. If they cannot be identified, the usefulness of the project itself is open to serious question.

There are two prime aspects of demonstration teaching in a host country: subject matter and teaching techniques. In subject matter, the tendency has been to demonstrate American practice without extensive modification. The course content has been so nearly 100 per cent American on occasion that courses without local application have been copied from American university catalogues. Most often, however, selected courses have been introduced in the hope that they would prove to have long-range applicability to the local situation after adaptation by host-country nationals. In Bolivia, students complained that courses taught by Americans had too much content which did not apply to the Bolivian situation. Courses in some fields such as chemistry and physics may not need much adaptation.

For the most part, the teaching techniques that have been demonstrated have been modified from those found in American higher education because local conditions have required change. For instance, if an American professor begins by using a textbook written in English for American students, he will usually find that this procedure does not work. Still more important has been the lack of receptivity to American teaching methods in the host country. For example, field work and laboratory methods have been emphasized in the demonstrations. These have often collided with prestige values. The local educated elite do not want to condescend to engage in such work, although American professors have not suffered loss in prestige by using these methods with host-country students.

Teaching techniques which demand close relationships between professor and student have been demonstrated, such as seminars, discussion, and the case approach. In a substantial minority of programs, emphasis has been placed on educating students, not training them, on how to develop a problem-solving approach to knowledge, rather than on transmission of knowledge. Such techniques have encountered the obstacle of the high status of a host-country professor and his traditional aloofness from students. Anything contrary to cultural mores tends to create some opposition and to lack prestige.

There have been other sources of opposition as well. Some of the methods are expensive in terms of the required equipment or personnel. As Bronfenbrenner (chap. 7) observes:

> Visiting Americans are not characteristically informed as to the reasons for the Japanese and Korean preference for the large lecture system in undergraduate teaching and the relative neglect of textbooks, cases, libraries, laboratories, and discussion groups. It is not that "they don't know any better" or "they like to hear themselves talk." There are sound economic reasons for the differences. Japanese and Korean universities are too poor for small classes, large libraries, case research, and extensive laboratory equipment, especially for undergraduates. Textbook prices are also too high for students, particularly if the text is an authorized translation of a standard foreign work.

Thus some new methods have been sterile; the host country cannot afford them. A number of the American professors have been overly enthusiastic about specific techniques, and have created opposition because of excessive claims. The proponents of the case method in business administration have been especially open to this criticism. They have sometimes forgotten that techniques are means, not ends (Adams and Garraty, pp. 43–44). Demonstrations of required or expected attendance in class and numerous examinations have not been frequent because of opposition on the part of host-country nationals, professors as well as students. This practice has been contrary to local mores. Teaching conditions abroad have not been so favorable as at home, as a rule, and this has made the demonstrations less effective on occasion. Lecturers must speak a foreign language, use translators, or speak at a very slow rate to ensure comprehension in non-English-language countries. More use of mimeograph lecture outlines and fewer reading assignments are also consequences of the language barrier.

In both course content and teaching technique, Americans, like other nationals, are prisoners of their own experience. They do not know what in their experience is appropriate for adoption or adaptation in a host country. At best it is difficult to determine applicability. In a third or more of the programs, American professors have become involved in teaching and other activities before they could seriously examine suitability of the content and teaching techniques in their courses. They have taught courses and used teaching techniques with which they have been most familiar. Gradually adjustment has taken place, but there has been much rigidity in many programs. To some of the problems of adaptability there are no easy answers; the question is primarily whether answers have been sought. In a few programs in the sample, answers to these problems were seriously being sought for the first time only after the program had been under way for four or five years.

Advice and Consultation. Advice and consultation are a by-product of almost any gathering of professors from different countries, but all the technical assistance programs specifically provide for advice and consultation by the American staff. The scope of the advisory function is great. In one program or another, American universities offer advice on almost every aspect of higher education: intake of students, and obtaining employment by students; basic teaching and research, and applied extension activities; professional functions and administrative functions; operation and organization. No matter how narrowly construed a program was in origin, after a period of time it usually becomes involved in many aspects of higher education.

Advice and consultation have not been confined to higher education. Numerous university contracts provide in part for consulting services to host-government agencies such as the nutrition program of Harvard in Peru. Some American faculty members are experienced in consulting with government agencies at home, and so it is not unnatural for universities to undertake such an assignment abroad. However, the advisory activities abroad have much wider scope. American university personnel often advise at a somewhat higher level abroad than at home. Consulting with ministers is usual and even consulting with prime ministers or presidents may be found.

Most professors sent abroad have not had previous experience in consulting about higher education as a whole or with government at high levels. Of necessity, their approach has thus had to be experimental at best, and amateurish at worst. Where the American university has sent a team abroad, practice has varied from taking a firm team position and making team recommendations to taking individual positions and making individual recommendations. The latter practice has frequently resulted in open disagreement among American faculty members. Although such disagreement has on occasion caused concern, especially among faculties at the host institution who more frequently tend to develop a "country position," it has at the same time demonstrated to them the antihierarchial attitudes of American professors and the free exchange of views in which they engage.

Because of their common background in American higher education and their common interest in the project abroad, American professors have agreed on many recommendations; a team position has readily evolved. One of the more frequent team positions is a recommendation that the host institution adopt what is termed "the land-grant philosophy." Application of knowledge in teaching, research, and extension activities is stressed. Host institutions are urged to advise and consult with governmental agencies or other community groups. In agricultural programs Americans believe that the extension and experiment station functions should be placed under the university's jurisdiction. Jurisdiction over extension service and experiment stations is thought essential to a land-grant institution. Such a recommendation is not in accord with the usual practice abroad; extension and experiment station activities are almost always under the ministry of agriculture or some other government agency. Whether or not such a recommendation is justified in any particular situation, it has been almost uniformly ignored. American university personnel have usually not come up with suitable alternatives.

Suitable alternatives require more than superficial knowledge of host-country practice. Host universities and personnel are not all or exclusively ivory-tower oriented just because land-grant patterns do not prevail; their activities suggest alternatives.

The state of contact between university and outside world in Japan or Korea varies from campus to campus and department to department, quite as in America. Contact is generally quite active, though admittedly less so than in an American land grant college. It is however easily missed, since it is not organized in the paraphernalia of "contact institutions" such as Extension Divisions, Farm and Home Weeks, Institutes, affiliated Experiment Stations, and so on. Rather it is individual teachers or groups of teachers who consult for outside agencies, teach extension classes, or work on practical problems in research stations unaffiliated with their universities (Bronfenbrenner, chap. 7).

To some extent, the land-grant recommendations illustrate a confusion of practice with philosophy, of application with principle, common in consulting work. The principle that a university should be involved in agricultural extension and research, which is highly important, does not necessarily mean that involvement must take the same form as in the United States. Exclusive jurisdiction over extension and experiment station activities is not essential. Where American university personnel have sought agreement on principle and have worked out the specific applications, they have been more successful in achieving their objectives than where the application itself is given the status of a principle.

Working out specific applications takes time and requires the collection and analysis of data. Some American universities, with their host-country colleagues, have made thorough studies before reaching recommendations, and others have not done so. Collection of data takes time and money which have not always been available. Field trips are not easily arranged in some countries; the host institution and American faculty members have sometimes not been eager to make them in any event. Where careful research has preceded advice, both the appropriateness and acceptability of the recommendations have been strengthened.

Advice and consultation have taken numerous forms. Formal or informal personal discussions, group conferences, demonstrations, observations and suggestions in letters, and regular or special reports have all been used. Development of laws, plans, organization charts, curricula, courses, and reading lists have served advisory purposes. In this process, informal channels of communication and decision-making have been used as much as possible. This has not always been easy. Since staff members of institutions abroad often are only on part time, and since the membership of American teams may change over a period of several years, the opportunity to get together has been limited. Furthermore, social patterns being what they are, Americans have been more willing to invite host-country nationals to their homes than vice versa. If the housing conditions of American professors were less pretentious in some instances, two-way social exchange might be more natural. Where host-country staff members have been on full time and their institutions have been located in smaller cities, close contact between them and the American professors has usually resulted, as at Jimma and Alemaya in Ethiopia under the Oklahoma State contract.

Although almost every technique has been tried, from the weakest informal suggestion to the threat of canceling a project, it cannot be said that any one degree of forcefulness has been superior to others. There is a correlation between the successful use of force-ful suggestion and the fundamental agreement of host-country with American personnel (Hart, pp. 76–78). Assuming an agreement on the objectives of a program, firmness may be welcomed by host-country personnel, because it helps them accomplish what they desire. The prestige of a respected outside group may be useful in bringing pressure to bear at the right points. But if there is little agreement on objectives, forceful techniques may result in rather complete alienation of American professor and host-country national.

There are many alternatives to forcefulness. Senior staff members at the host institution are often less interested in innovations than are their younger colleagues. American universities have sometimes recommended extensive use of new or supplemental staff in the host-country institution, who would presumably be more amenable to suggestions for change. The preponderant practice has been to proceed at a deliberate pace, without use of severe sanctions. The emphasis has been on "getting together" and on defining objectives and methods little by little.

Teaching and consulting have normally been closely interrelated, as the following account of the California program in agriculture in Chile illustrates:

Viehmeyer provided groundwork and materials for the irrigation cur-riculum (at the agricultural school at Chillan), and Schultis tried to hold two of his courses at the school. Various staff members spent consider-able time in giving short courses to ministry personnel, and in many cases directly to Chilean farmers. The specialist in irrigation, Frank

Viehmeyer, devoted over 150 hours to such courses, and the specialist in farm management, Arthur Schultis, gave 9 one-week courses on Chilean farms, thereby combining analysis of the farm economy with the teaching. Over two hundred people were in attendance at these courses. Informants in Chile felt that the work in irrigation may have had considerable impact since among his listeners were the technical staffs of the ministry and engineers responsible for the development of irrigation work. The farm management work involved providing many workshops and conferences over Chile, but the lack of follow-up makes long-term impact difficult to estimate. . . .

The most effective extension efforts were put forth in the fields of irrigation and farm management. . . . The specialist in extension, Roy McCallum, contributed to the improvement of the extension service in the Chillan area, worked on the general coordination of Chillan technicians, and contributed to the formation of a private farm management consultant organization, the *Agro-Servicio* (Adams and Cumberland, pp. 215–216).

Other Activities. Most technical assistance projects of substantial size included among their activities research and obtaining educational equipment and books. Research has been primarily aimed at the preparation of teaching materials or the collection of documentation and statistics. However, whether or not it has been the central activity of a program, research has usually been more characteristic of the activities of American professors than of host-country nationals. Partly this is because many host-country professors devote only part time to their tasks. Partly it is because in many underdeveloped countries research is not a high-prestige activity, or is almost unheard of.

Research has often had a low priority in technical assistance projects. In the University of North Carolina program in sanitary engineering in Peru,

. . . the inability to initiate or stimulate research activities, stemmed in part from priorities given to other aspects of the program, and hence, sheerly from a lack of time; in part from the bad luck with the fellowship students; and in part from the lack of laboratory facilities during the first two years of the project. It seems likely, also, that the decision to give priorities to other activities, such as curriculum improvement, was related to the sanitary engineer's general orientation towards education and extension activities. Considerable time was devoted to the introduction of field training, short courses, and particularly to the integration of laboratory courses, and the time spent on these activities reflects a professional preference as well as a problem of time. Another factor in this problem, however, is probably traceable to the philosophy of the dean of the sanitary engineering faculty in Lima. His original interest in this project was in the acquisition of materials for the improvement of teaching. He was not personally interested in research, nor necessarily in promoting it within the faculty. As the work of the North Carolina engineers progressed, he did take an interest in this area, but it still did not reflect a basic desire on his part. Since the direction of the faculty basically reflects the dean's propensities, the lack of emphasis on research, and indeed the present indecision with respect to promoting the establishment of a research center, doubtless can be traced to this source (Adams and Cumberland, pp. 179–180).

One of the major needs of universities in less developed countries is educational equipment and books of all kinds. Most of them do not have the foreign exchange necessary to obtain an adequate supply. Requests for equipment are more frequent than requests for other kinds of assistance; the reluctance of financing organizations to underwrite costs of equipment without American faculty members to advise as to its use has led some host institutions to request, reluctantly, visiting American faculty members. In two instances, an American university technical assistance program has been confined to the provision of equipment and materials, no faculty member exchange being intended. For example, Rutgers University under an ICA contract advised the Royal Technical College of East Africa in Kenya on library acquisitions, engineering equipment purchases, and building plans without presence in Kenya of any of its personnel. Money for the purchase of materials was included in the arrangement. More commonly, equipment purchases are a part of a regular multiphase technical assistance contract. However, there has been little integration of the provision of equipment and materials with other phases of the contract. Rather than being related to a proposed work project, a request for equipment is likely to be merely duplicative of the kind of equipment found in American universities (Hart, pp. 64–65). This tendency is augmented in far-away countries by the fact that ordering and shipment of equipment from the United States may take so long that an American university faculty member who could have advised as to its use may have returned to the United States before the equipment arrives.

University staff members who are sent abroad to head up large university technical assistance projects may spend almost all their time in administrative responsibilities. This is particularly true in those instances in which new host institutions are being established but for which the top level personnel are not yet available. In such cases, the chief adviser may be *de facto* director of a host institution for some time, as the University of Pennsylvania chief of party was in Pakistan.

Some countries expressed a desire to have an American university serve as a resource gatherer and recruitment agency under a technical assistance contract. Thus, some persons in Indonesia would like an American university to make a thorough study of the host-country's long-term educational requirements and to take what steps it could to meet them, whether with home-campus facilities or by calling upon other institutions for assistance (Smith, p. 116).

American universities, having gradually developed the concept of a socially useful university in the middle and late nineteenth century, were contributing members of their staffs to technical missions abroad before 1900. Since World War II, many of them have extended their services overseas through formal institutional contracts. Though the activities of staff members have been primarily teaching and consultation, the underlying role has been one of being agents of change. The ability of staff members to play this role has been an important determinant of the success of the programs.

Chapter 10

SPONSORS AND ADVANTAGES OF TECHNICAL ASSISTANCE ABROAD

During the past ten or fifteen years, several kinds of sponsors have offered to finance American universities participating in technical assistance. "He who pays the piper calls the tune." To a considerable degree, the programs of universities have varied with the source of the financing and the objectives of the sponsor. Since the largest financial sponsor has been the United States government, foreign policy objectives have been prominent.

Only a few programs have been initiated and financed primarily by a host-country government or a host-country institution. The countries that can most easily afford them are those that do not need them. Those that cannot afford them turn for financing to some third party such as a government or an international agency or a foundation.

Since university projects financed by the country to which the assistance is rendered do not involve third parties in the United States, the host government or institution deals directly with the American university. The Johns Hopkins–Gadjah Mada University program in Indonesia is financed by the two universities concerned and the Indonesian government. There was a marked shortage of professors in Indonesia after it gained independence. A number of university staff members from abroad were hired on individual contracts. Such individual recruitment was difficult and time-consuming; it yielded less than satisfactory results. The president of Gadjah Mada, being a Johns Hopkins alumnus, turned to his alma mater for help. The American university assumed institutional responsibility for recruiting staff members and for carrying on a program.

This kind of program usually suffers from inadequate financing. Also, the host-country government has not usually understood the need of an American university group for local support. Provision of housing, customs arrangements, cost-of-living allowances, and many other facets of any technical assistance operation abroad are potentially divisive forces between host and guest. International agencies, the United States government, and some foundations have worked out these matters in principle for all programs in which they are active. The individual American university is seldom in a position to deal so effectively on a one-program basis. In short, the financial and administrative problems of such programs are so great that not many more may be expected in the near future.

A few American university international programs in technical assistance are primarily financed by business interests abroad. In most cases these are programs designed to introduce American methods of graduate business education in developed countries. The IPSOA program at Turin, Italy (Instituto Post-Universitario per lo Studio del' Organizzazione Aziendale, a management institute), financed in large part by Italian business interests, is a case in point. IPSOA has called upon three American universities in succession to recruit staff members for it, beginning with Harvard. The fields in which private business will pay for technical assistance under a university contract are exceedingly limited, and the countries in which private business is organized on a large enough scale to meet the expense are also rather few. Some expansion of business administration programs is likely, if for no other reason than that there are persons in some host countries who are looking for a key to American business success.

American corporations with overseas interests have sponsored university technical assistance in employee training or in research. For example, the research in cattle diseases of a University of Pennsylvania team in Mexico is of interest to Olin Mathieson and Squibb and is financed in large part by them. Only a few American corporations use this device; for the most part they concentrate both training and research within their own companies overseas. Some American-owned corporations have been instrumental in getting host-country organizations to apply for help from ICA, and in this manner they have avoided spending their own money. A common criticism of some ICA-university contracts, especially those in engineering or business administration, is that the training is received largely by personnel that are or will be employed by the overseas units of American corporations. Though such concentration is rarely found, it remains true that as long as programs in such fields can be financed with ICA help there is little incentive for American businesses to support them directly. Some expansion in American business-financed training and research overseas is likely, and some of it may come through American university contracts.

International agencies have not made use of the facilities of American universities, except in rare instances. One exception was a program financed jointly by the Inter-American Institute of Agricultural Sciences and the Carnegie Corporation of New York. It involved Michigan State University in a program of research aimed at testing various approaches to community development. Most international agencies have not considered using American university programs since an international agency must normally make use of resources from more than a single country. Use of the university contract by international agencies probably will be restricted to a few situations in which the university helps the international agency itself.

Foundation and Government Programs

Most of the American university technical assistance programs are, and probably will be, financed by agencies of the United States government and American foundations. Government agencies and some foundations have resources sufficient to cope with the many administrative problems in technical assistance overseas. They provide important administrative support to host government, host institution, and the American university. Also, their financial resources are such that they are in a position to give large-scale assistance. In the long run, of course, government agencies and foundations are supplementing the efforts of host institutions. Yet in the short run, host governments and institutions and business corporations often play a supplementary financial role, merely rounding out the support of programs basically underwritten by government agencies and foundations. In the past twenty years United States government agencies and foundations have become increasingly concerned with the role of higher education in the less developed countries, and thus university contracts for technical assistance are a natural complement to their work. Being American groups, they do not regard calling upon American universities as inconsistent with their objectives, as some international agencies might. One or more of their interests affects nearly every subject matter in higher education in nearly every country outside the Communist bloc.

Within the government, the International Cooperation Administration has been the leader in the university contract field, but the Department of Defense and the United States Information Agency have also been active. By March, 1961, ICA had some 100 contracts with 56 universities in 37 countries for technical assistance work overseas. As for the foundations, many of them have made grants involving American university participation in technical assistance programs abroad. Some of the grants have been directly to American universities while others have been to the host-country university or the foreign government, which in turn has contracted with the American institution. The Ford Foundation has supported more university technical assistance programs than any other foundation, especially in Pakistan and Indonesia. No program of equal scope anywhere in the world relies so markedly on the university contract as the Ford Foundation program in Pakistan; except for the country representative and his assistant, the entire Ford group is composed of personnel hired by universities under technical assistance contracts. Ford even relies upon some of the universities for its staff planning in that country.

A government agency is an entirely different type of organization from a private foundation. Experiences of universities with contracts has varied accordingly. ICA is a government agency attached to the State Department, to whose policies it is completely subordinate. Technical assistance is a part of the United States foreign policy, closely interwoven with economic and military aid as well as the general position of the United States in each region and country of the world. In the field, the director of the United States Operations Mission (USOM; ICA field organization) reports to the ambassador. At home, ICA is responsible to the Congress, with the many demands that arise in consequence. Its financial and legal affairs are governed by the General Accounting Office, the Bureau of the Budget, and the Congress. It is a huge organization, part of the vast government bureaucracy.

A foundation, on the other hand, is a private association created for limited purposes as set forth in its charter. Foundation officers are usually few. Only a handful of foundations have more than 20 professional staff members permanently attached to their offices in the United States; the smaller foundations have only a part-time representative or one or two full-time staff members. Foundation officers are responsible to boards of trustees that are composed of persons who serve for many years as members. Even the larger of the foundations have funds narrowly limited in comparison with those of the United States government. Each of them formulates its own policies and establishes its own administrative and financial procedures. Their policies have no necessary relation to the public policies of the United States. Being private organizations, foundations do not have to operate as much on a country-by-country basis as ICA. This is of particular value in such areas as Africa and the Middle East, where foundations have helped establish regional programs; for example, that of Chicago and UCLA in Africa, south of the Sahara. Foundations are not under as much pressure to establish programs in every country.

University Relations with Sponsors. The respective characteristics of ICA and foundations have led to important differences in their relations with universities in technical assistance programs. Since ICA has to relate university contracts to the requirements of a rather extensive and inflexible government policy, it has tended to supervise universities more closely both in professional matters and in financial and administrative details. Individual country directors for the government technical assistance agencies have felt a need to maintain close control over the entire operation for which they were responsible. Members of the bureaucracy in Washington and to a lesser extent those in the field have not known how they would fare if universities were given a substantial role in technical assistance; to some extent the universities have posed a threat to them in so far as they represent an alternative to direct ICA technical assistance.

Furthermore, the kinds of activities in which universities engaged often required day-to-day liaison with government agencies. Universities did not confine themselves to long-range projects in higher education of an advisory, consultative, or research nature. Then, too, in the early years of university technical assistance contracts there were no clear guidelines as to how to work universities into the technical assistance picture abroad. For whatever reasons, the close association of the universities with ICA and its predecessor agencies produced a number of unpleasant clashes. Whether over issues of selection of personnel, publication of articles by faculty members, detailed supervision of university contract accounts, or other matters, many universities found their relations with the government agencies to be unhappy.

The irritants caused by close supervision resulted in a groundswell of reaction from universities in 1955 and 1956. It was in these two years that the newly-formed Committee on Institutional Projects Abroad of the American Council on Education (CIPA) held its first two annual conferences. They were attended by university professors, contract coordinators, deans, presidents, and government representatives, all involved in ICA university technical assistance work. The sessions were exceedingly bitter, the universities charging that the government agency was not even regarding the universities as responsible bodies. Said one member of the CIPA at the 1955 session:

... whether they intend to do so or not, officials of FOA-ICA place innumerable obstacles in the way of the interuniversity programs, and ... the basic relationship between ICA and the American universities is an intolerable one from the point of view of the universities. ICA insists on keeping much too close a check on the execution of the interuniversity contracts, and the result is that university coordinators, or at least some of them, find that they have to turn to ICA for approvals on many decisions which should be left wholly within the province of the university, under the general provisions of the contract. And they feel that they are engaged in an endless war with people in ICA, especially people behind the scenes whom they seldom, if ever, see.[1]

American universities have been opposed not so much to accepting ICA funds or to accepting the idea of participating in any technical assistance programs as to submitting to ICA administrative red tape. Some universities, for example California, have threatened to cancel ICA contracts unless administrative red tape is reduced, but have hesitated to act on the threat. Rejection of technical assistance contracts has occurred on other grounds. Yale,

---

[1] Norman D. Palmer, "Evaluation of the Policy Statement of the Committee on Institutional Projects Abroad" in Richard A. Humphrey (ed.), *University Projects Abroad: Papers Presented at the Conference on University Contracts Abroad, 1955* (Washington: American Council on Education, 1956), pp. 21–22.

Princeton, Iowa, and Iowa State do not have programs financed by ICA, but neither do they have foundation-financed programs in technical assistance. Both ICA and the Ford Foundation report some difficulty in inducing appropriate American universities to respond favorably to technical assistance contracts overseas. Perhaps a near maximum has been reached. The Massachusetts Institute of Technology turned down a contract in management engineering in Austria even after the Austrians had agreed to MIT's strict conditions; MIT felt it could not do an adequate job. Negotiations with Georgia Tech for a contract in industrial productivity in Japan fell through in part because of the objections of the Georgia textile industry. Most large universities have rejected at least some invitations to participate in technical assistance programs.

Since 1956, important improvements have been achieved in ICA-university relationships. After a number of changes in top ICA personnel, it was announced in 1957 that no longer would ICA field units try to censor the professional writings of faculty members serving abroad under the projects. Furthermore, a new model contract was developed that helped solve some of the problems of contract interpretation, financial accountability, and audit. Contract negotiations still take many months of hard work, however. After the idea for a contract has been initiated, at least six months elapse and often a year or more before contracts are signed. In recent years there have been fewer objections by ICA to university nominations of personnel for overseas assignments, although interference on this score has not ceased entirely.

For the most part, the antagonisms of yesterday have been succeeded by cooperation today. Positive supervision has replaced the former negative emphasis. Increasingly, the chief advisers of the university teams in the field are invited to the staff meetings of the USOM. Policy decisions facing the university teams are discussed with appropriate USOM staff members, and a considerable measure of professional exchange of views occurs. Nonetheless, control is exercised by means of this liaison, sometimes on a day-to-day basis. The main exception is found where a university project is physically isolated from USOM field personnel, where the site of the university project is distant from the capital of the country or the main regional centers. In Uganda and Sierra Leone, American university personnel have preceded USOM personnel into the country, and in Ethiopia, Oklahoma State itself was, in effect, USOM for some years. In these instances, university personnel of necessity proceeded largely on their own.

University relations with foundations have been much more informal than those with government. Negotiations proceed more rapidly. Once a foundation grant is made, the university has been relatively free in selecting methods of administering the program and in determining items of expenditure. The foundations have taken the position that universities are responsible bodies and can be trusted to carry out a program to the best of their ability. Little contact between university and foundation occurs after a foundation grant is made, except on a rather irregular basis. Policy matters are in the hands of the universities and the host institutions. Foundations being smaller, more adaptable organizations, their operations are considerably more flexible than those of ICA.

Relations with the universities are affected by the size of the respective bureaucracies. With extensive agency personnel in Washington and the field, ICA is in a position to supervise the universities closely, and to be in daily contact with them. Foundation personnel simply cannot be in close touch with the universities for the most part. Lack of field personnel and few central office employees make this impossible. An exception is the overseas development unit of the Ford Foundation. Its staffing pattern includes country representatives abroad and a sizable staff in New York. Though most foundations obtain a first-hand impression of projects they are financing overseas only through an occasional brief tour by one of their officers, the Ford overseas development unit is in a position to obtain frequent information on activities of universities to which it has made grants. Yet even in this case, foundation personnel do not supervise the activities of universities as closely as does ICA.

Effect on University Relations with Host Institutions. The most important consequences of differences in foundation and ICA-financed programs lie in the effect these differences exert on the relations between American universities and host institutions. The greater tendency of ICA to insist on restrictive contracts and engage in close supervision affects these relations adversely in some instances. Host personnel see the close supervision and conclude that American universities are mere instruments of the government technical assistance agency rather than free and independent institutions of higher learning. The universities seem subject to all the restrictions and red tape of the technical assistance agencies. University personnel check with appropriate USOM staff members before any major policy is decided and even on minor policy matters so that a united front is presented to the host country. In the words of an ICA conference report on university contracts,[2]

The contractor [university] becomes the agent/partner of the Mission in terms of a specific service to be performed. . . . Within Mission policy, the contractor should have maximum freedom. This was construed to mean freedom for *professional* action, but even here it was stressed that there is a need for policy guidance from the Mission. . . . A contract team should consider itself—and be so considered by the Mission—as an integral part of the whole Mission operation. In spite of some unavoidable differences between contract and non-contract personnel (income tax exemptions, certain allowances, passport type, etc.) the major point here involves the building and maintenance of total Mission "team spirit."

University personnel and United States government personnel attend the same parties, ride in the same large American cars (occasionally with the same diplomatic license plates), buy their food from the same commissaries. An American professor under a university contract in Japan, says the president of a prominent Japanese university, is viewed by the Japanese no differently from the regular employees of ICA or other agencies of the United States government. "After all, they are always together, and the university cannot make any major decisions on its own."

In the long run a project will usually be judged on the basis of the quality of the persons associated with it and the merits of their performance, regardless of the means of financial support or other "extraneous" factors. But the merits of the performance are influenced by the receptivity to the project in the host country. In turn, the receptivity to *university* projects is often less when there is a close identification of university and ICA personnel, especially in the early years of an undertaking.

By being closely associated with ICA and sometimes losing their separate identity, universities and professors give up some of their distinctive initial advantage in the technical assistance field. In most countries universities and professors have great prestige, far

---

[2] "Regional Education Conference, South Asia and the Far East, New Delhi, India, December 2–6, 1957, Conference Report" (Washington: International Cooperation Administration, mimeo.), sect. IV D, p. 2.

above that of government agencies and their employees. Indeed, ICA uses the university contract partly to take advantage of the nonpolitical "front" and prestige of a university. Private foundations or international agencies have political neutrality and a high prestige of their own, not associated with the prestige of governments.

Any technical assistance program must be adapted to the national aims of the host country. To the extent that an agency of a foreign government, such as ICA, engages in technical assistance, adaptation may be difficult. The advice of a person not regarded as an agent of the United States foreign service may be more effective in technological change because his counsel will be thought disinterested, and hence more objective. The suspicion that may arise about professors who are believed to be intimately associated with government agencies is illustrated by the remark of a well-known Egyptian educator who somewhat heatedly exclaimed, "Some American professors simply become tools of the United States government. They try to push American culture on other cultures. Their interest is neither in the host country nor its technological or educational improvement."

By being closely identified with ICA, universities and professors are subject to the advantages and disadvantages of all bilateral government technical assistance. Because ICA is a government agency it must always report to Congress. It emphasizes immediate, demonstrable results and claims credit for what its contractors do, in order to justify appropriations. Yet in technical assistance, anonymity is an advantage; nationals of the host country should have credit for achievements. Also, long-range programs that do not yield short-range results may be advisable, especially in higher education. Under ICA-university contracts anonymity and long-range programs have been less frequently and forcefully found than under foundation university grants, and less effective relations between the university and host institution may ensue.

Countries vary in the extent of their agreement with American foreign policy. In some instances technical assistance financed by ICA may be more effective simply because it does come from the United States government. The prestige, power, and/or dollars of the United States may be persuasive forces for those reluctant to change or for those needing a certain kind of recognition and support at home. A university contract may be accepted primarily because it will improve the host-country's relations with the United States government or lead to other, more advantageous grants. United States technical assistance may be viewed as inevitably related to the foreign policy of the United States. In a country such as Turkey, a host institution does not reject a university contract simply because it is financed by ICA. The advantage of a foundation-financed university contract in such a case may be slight or nil.

In countries such as India, where there is an agreed national plan, the universities look to the national planning commission and other national agencies for help to implement the plan. It may be a matter of small moment whether the government suggests assistance from an American university through ICA financing or through foundation financing. Similarly, where a university or a faculty is intent upon some project for change, the choice between ICA or foundation financing may not be determining. For example, in Peru, the National Engineering University badly wanted assistance in sanitary engineering and was glad to accept assistance from North Carolina even though it was ICA-financed.

Finally, there are countries or groups that view all assistance by American groups, government or private, as part of the same conspiracy of American capitalism. No distinction is made between government, foundation, or university. Marxist or Communist groups especially adopt this line, but others also object to ICA university programs. Many persons associated with universities wish no involvement with the policy of any foreign country, especially an extremely powerful nation.

Furthermore, governments both domestic and foreign are identified with red tape and restrictions. The dean of one of the major faculties of an outstanding Italian university states the point clearly. "We refuse to have anything to do with any program financed by ICA in our faculty, no matter what the reputation of the proposed American university may be. We are involved enough with the government of Italy; we don't want to get entangled with a foreign government as well." The difficulty experienced by ICA in convincing an Italian university to accept a public administration contract a few years ago was not just Italian resistance to the American idea of public administration. It centered on Italian university reluctance to become associated with American foreign policy and the United States government.

A number of countries and institutions at one time or another have refused to have anything to do with ICA projects. Universities of the highest prestige in the host countries are among them, such as the University of Rome, the University of Florence, the University of Tokyo, and the National Autonomous University of Mexico. At times Mexico, Burma, Indonesia, and some other countries have been reluctant to accept ICA aid. They have wanted to avoid ICA red tape, the influence of a foreign government in their internal affairs, criticism from local Communists or other leftists, and entanglement with their own government which an ICA contract would require. ICA cannot do much about the latter two items, but it could simplify procedures and free American and host institutions from close policy supervision without congressional action. Finally, some host institutions refuse to accept ICA financing simply because it means accepting a technical assistance program; they reject the entire idea that they need technical assistance.

Many host institutions prefer foundation-financed projects, at least as they approach the idea of technical assistance. Foundations have maintained their identity; they are not entangled with United States governmental agencies. The Ford Foundation has established its own offices abroad, making use of direct grants to host-country groups, consultants, and universities as has seemed best from time to time. The Rockefeller Foundation has undertaken direct technical assistance projects abroad for which it has hired its own personnel, often from university faculties. It has also been active in giving grants directly to foreign groups, and to American universities for work abroad. The Carnegie Corporation has relied completely on independent grants to universities in the United States and groups abroad; it has had no personnel of its own overseas. Most foundations have followed either the Rockefeller or Carnegie pattern, the latter being the more common. Foundation-financed university personnel abroad do not have the privileges of government employees, and they are not subject to government red tape. They may make major decisions on their own, independent even of foundation officials, let alone congressional or State Department policy. As a consequence, host-country personnel often perceive them more favorably, at least initially.

The evidence of preference for foundation-financed activities is impressive. For example, throughout Latin America, the direct-hire agricultural programs of the Rockefeller Foundation are well known and universally respected. They carry no implication of the "big stick." Events in Mexico in 1955–56 effectively underline the point. Mexico became strongly displeased with United States government-sponsored technical assistance. The displeasure reflected in part strained political relations and Mexico's traditional fear of its big neighbor to the north. The activities of USOM were curtailed severely. At the time, ICA had undertaken two substantial university contracts, still in the early stages, the Texas A and M program at Antonio Narro and the Columbia University Teachers College program in Mexico City. Both programs were canceled. Yet throughout this same period, the Rockefeller Foundation continued its excellent direct-hire agricultural program in Mexico without interruption. Evidently the Mexicans involved made a sharp distinction between the ICA-financed and foundation programs.

Some host-country governments and institutions of higher education have accepted ICA university contracts in largely nonsensitive areas, but not in areas in which there might be any overtones of political or economic policy. Mexico has been exceedingly cautious in discriminating among ICA programs. It is highly wary of undue North American interference. The two small university contracts that have existed in recent years are of a purely technical or research nature, with no impact on Mexican universities whatsoever. In Indonesia, the ICA university contracts relate to engineering, medicine, and similar matters, but the Ford Foundation has sponsored two university contracts in economics. The Ford Foundation is helping the national planning commission in Pakistan through a university contract, but ICA contracts in that country are for technical help to universities. In Peru, the most "sensitive" program was the Carnegie Corporation-financed Cornell program, affecting land tenure and the Indian problem; here also ICA contracts were concerned with narrow technical subjects.

Not only do the host-country governments and universities desire to keep some areas outside the influence, direct or indirect, real or imagined, of the United States government and its foreign policy, but ICA itself tries to keep American universities out of fields that it regards as sensitive. Business and public administration, agriculture and veterinary medicine, public health and medicine, engineering, education, and home economics are the principal fields of ICA contracts. Foundations do operate in many of these fields, but also have sponsored contracts in law, economics, national planning, and American studies—fields in which ICA hesitates to use the university contract.

It is remarkable that an agency such as ICA, which is responsible for contributing to the economic development of other countries, does not place more emphasis on economics in its university contract program. The University of Chicago program in Chile is a major exception. For the most part, ICA has refrained from encouraging or permitting American universities to engage directly in technical assistance in economics or economic development.

The experience of Michigan State University in Vietnam is a case in point. When contract details were being worked out for a program in public administration, the Vietnamese told a university representative that they thought public administration was closely related to economics, and desired to include economics in their public administration institute as a major emphasis. Michigan State was asked to include some economists among the professors it would send. The University agreed, but USOM immediately objected on the ground that economics was not relevant to a program in public administration. It reluctantly agreed to a contract provision for a small number of economists, but when the first two arrived, USOM again questioned the relevance of economics to public administration. Even if economics were a part of the institute, USOM argued, American economics professors should not teach or freely engage in research. "They might recommend something contrary to ICA policy," said a ranking USOM official. A moment later he added that if the Vietnamese and the university insisted that the economists teach, at least the economists should submit detailed syllabuses in advance to USOM for clearance. This requirement was never implemented, but USOM remains sensitive on the matter of including economists.

The most serious problem that arises under ICA-financed projects and not under those sponsored by the foundations concerns the relation between government and university in a free society. In their own country, American universities accept responsibility for bringing the benefits of knowledge to the community, and therefore work closely with government, business, agriculture, and other community groups. They study problems that are of immediate, practical import, yet resist attempts to force them to study only such problems, or to study them at the expense of other activities with other values. They follow a policy of involvement but not entanglement, concern but not servility. The American university's relationship to government and the community is not one of subordinate and superior. The university maintains its independence and integrity. In technical assistance work overseas, American universities seek to demonstrate the nature of this relationship, and encourage host-country universities to make a more substantial contribution to their communities.

In most underdeveloped countries, work with one's hands is not honored. Field or laboratory research in any area of specialization, if not relegated to lowly assistants, is ignored. University work is highly theoretical and classical. The medieval conceptions of what subjects were proper for a university to teach have survived. The scholar is removed from society and its concerns. The university professor may teach only a few hours a week and the rest of the time work for a government agency or a private concern, but in his capacity as a professor he does not believe it wise to mix his teaching with the concern of government or of business. He, along with his full-time associates, fears further intrusion of government into university affairs, often with reason. He believes that one way of encouraging such intrusion is to become interested in problems in which the government is interested. Distance from the government is the best way to assure proper academic freedom, and to minimize government interference and regulation.

The ICA-university contract program is at its weakest in this area. It has not permitted an American university to demonstrate its seeking socially useful goals and at the same time remaining independent. Rather, faculties in the host country have seen or have thought they saw an American university carrying out the foreign policy of the United States government and subject to its detailed supervision. They have observed universities treated like any other ICA contractors. They have watched American universities at odds with ICA on many issues, including some that affect academic freedom, such as the selection of personnel and the determination of the content of syllabuses and professional writings. Some ICA officials have not respected the traditional relationships between government and universities in free societies. They have not understood the role of a university. All this has constituted a demonstration of what universities abroad most fear. It confirms their resolution not to get involved with ICA and not to get involved with their own governments in local technical assistance, lest their freedom be curtailed.

Program Advantages

The multiplication of university contracts for technical assistance is taken to be adequate testimony to their usefulness and perhaps also to their appropriateness. However, the programs have involved a real cost to the universities, the host institutions, and the sponsoring organizations. They have demanded allocation of scarce university resources to the assistance programs. Are American university programs necessary to the achievement of certain technical assistance goals or desirable instruments to these ends?

Individual Consultant and Team Alternatives. University contracts are not *necessary* to achieve any technical assistance goals, at least not necessary to those that have been laid down so far. There are several alternative devices that have been used, with favorable results in many instances. Individual advisers or consultants employed by governments, foundations, or others have been effective in the same areas in which university contracts exist. Though the Ford Foundation in Pakistan relies exclusively on university contracts to carry out its program, the Ford Foundation in India has relied almost exclusively on other devices. It is not clear that the first policy has been superior to the second. Both have had about equal success, given the marked differences in conditions in the two countries.

In India, grants were made directly to the Indian government or to other Indian institutions, including money to bring individual foreign experts to India to advise on special problems, many of whom have been American university professors. The foundation has had a few experts attached to its own staff in India from time to time. Fewer American experts were brought to India by the Ford Foundation, directly or indirectly, than the number brought to Pakistan, and the experts sent to India have been of far greater renown on the average than those sent to Pakistan. Their role has also been basically different. In Pakistan, institution-building has been necessary, and it has seemed desirable for a university team to help in the institution-building process. The needs have been more numerous and of a different order, perhaps not requiring as high an average level of expertise. In India, the basic institutional structure has been built, and the role of the foreign expert has been to advise and consult with Indians in charge of going institutions.

Experience in Japan, European countries, and other highly developed countries tends to confirm the view that where the institutional structure is highly developed, the need is not as much for a team from abroad, such as is provided by a university contract, as for an occasional outstanding foreign expert who can bring outside experience to the attention of the persons concerned. This is as true for the United States as it is for other countries. We, too, benefit from the foreign expert who comes to our shores and shares his insight with us. The greater the pool of trained manpower in a country and the more extensive its institutional structure, the less useful will be a team in technical assistance, and the more useful will be individual experts on occasional assignments.

Some university contracts have been used to send single experts abroad, but over 90 per cent of the university technical assistance programs employ teams. If a team is sent, a defined segment of work must be set aside by the host institution or sponsoring organization for the team's special attention. Where such separate emphasis is not either feasible or desirable, the team method has grave shortcomings.

Universities have no monopoly either in the team approach or in assumption of responsibility by an institution. There are foundation teams, consulting firm teams, teams recruited by professional groups or various private associations, teams of international agencies, ICA teams, and teams from government agencies such as the United States Department of Agriculture or the United States Public Health Service. All such teams have, from time to time, engaged in effective institution-building in technical assistance programs overseas, and one or more of each type of team has specifically engaged in helping to develop institutions of higher education.

Special Competence of Universities. In comparison with other organizations that can assume responsibility for technical assistance activities abroad, universities have a certain uniqueness of competence in a few areas and share competence with other groups in many additional areas. No other organization is so experienced in higher education as the universities themselves. By definition, only universities offer courses of study leading to advanced degrees. However, American universities engage in many kinds of activities more or less related to their central function that are also carried on by other types of organizations. For example, university faculty members consult with governments, businesses, and private associations, but universities have no monopoly in this field. They sponsor thousands of educational conferences each year, but again have no exclusive jurisdiction. Nor do they have a monopoly in extension or research activities. Many organizations engage in them.

A school of thought in ICA and elsewhere argues that universities, in their technical assistance activities, should be confined to helping other universities with degree programs and closely related activities. They should not, it is intended, engage in consulting activities with government or other agencies. The argument is a poor one, if it has reference to the total area of competence of universities and university personnel. It is a good one if it has reference to the areas of their unique competence. There is scarcely a university staff member overseas carrying on an assignment that cannot in some way be paralleled by the assignment of a university staff member in the United States. (However, it is frequently true that the particular person carrying out the assignment overseas has not had comparable experience in the United States, and the same can be said for universities or colleges or departments within them.) Yet persons in a wide variety of other employments are equally well qualified to carry out most of the tasks required, and a number of other organizations are equally well qualified to assume institutional responsibility. For example, the University of Michigan has a contract in Mexico for the training of operators of heavy equipment, especially road construction and repair equipment. There is nothing in such a project that makes it uniquely a university project (Adams and Cumberland, p. 422). Most university assistance projects abroad are largely technical, and technical competence does not reside exclusively at American universities.

One important aspect of a university contract is that through its employment a host organization may be able to draw upon varied resources and a kind of resource not so readily available in any other way. An engineering program at a host university may be confronted by problems of records, admissions policies, or library resources. A college of engineering at an American university can quickly turn to personnel in other parts of its institution for the appropriate assistance. Most of the programs have made at least limited use of unique university resources such as these.

Closely related to the use of supporting resources at the American university is institution-building. One of the special competences of a university in technical assistance is its experience in running an institution of higher learning. It should be able to do a job in helping to establish or develop such institutions or parts of them superior to that of commercial contractors or government teams.

Recruitment of Personnel. The predecessor agencies of ICA or the United States Department of Agriculture or some other government department recruited teams for technical assistance assignments overseas. Frequently they turned to university staff members for some of their recruits. There was difficulty in securing leave, paying rates equivalent to varying salary scales, and ensuring that the professional future of the recruits would not be the less bright because they accepted such a noncampus assignment for a year or two. Such difficulties led to the conclusion that it would be more effective to let the universities themselves recruit the teams and accept institutional responsibility. A university would have some advantages in attracting its own personnel to its own overseas program, as well as in recruiting personnel from elsewhere. In addition, contracting would avoid personnel ceilings in ICA.

In practice, universities do possess certain advantages in recruiting university personnel to be sent overseas. Yet most universities have not restricted themselves to university personnel in selecting teams for foreign service. They have recruited also from government, private business, and the professions. Although universities may be able to offer a higher salary, somewhat better working conditions, exemption from income tax, and the prestige of university employment, their competence in this field of recruitment is not unique or necessarily superior.

Many another organization, private or public, has had far more recruiting experience for overseas positions. For most universities, a technical assistance contract has been a new experience. Even where this has not been true, to say that a *university* has had experience in overseas technical assistance work is usually highly misleading. It may be only the department of agricultural economics, the school of business administration, or a particular program coordinator. There is usually little or no transfer of experience from one department or school to another.

ICA, the foundations, or other groups can and do obtain for

their overseas programs able and experienced individuals who are in academic employment. If there is any deficiency in their recruiting mechanism, the most obvious solution is to improve their recruiting practices rather than to turn to university contracts. In ICA, salaries need to be raised and recruiting of professional personnel should be carried out to a greater extent by professionals. Personnel ceilings should be adjusted. Yet many capable people who understand American higher education are turned up by the present system of recruitment. "After all," said a USOM education director, "don't forget that all of us in ICA are products of American universities. We should be able to bring some of the benefits of higher education in the United States to these countries." A person from academic employment is not necessarily better in quality. ICA and foundation personnel were found to be noticeably more capable and better chosen than those sent abroad by a few university programs and equal in quality to those sent abroad by some others. Examples of this were found in Turkey and Pakistan.

Interuniversity Affiliation. A few long-range interuniversity affiliations will probably result from technical assistance, and will be of value to both American and host institutions. Yet the number of such affiliations is not likely to be large. The cost, scope, and nature of a technical assistance program are too large to be continued by a pair of affiliated universities. The more successful affiliations have begun in a more modest way, on a much more reciprocal basis.

Often there is no genuine institution-wide involvement at either the host or the American universities, and thus the bases for long-range institutional affiliations are not laid. Most of the programs are limited to one or two fields. In such instances permanent professional friendships and interests may be more stimulated than formal, permanent institutional ties, but it is too early to be sure since the programs are in their first decade.

Some contract programs are quite isolated from the regular faculty members and departments of the American university. Perhaps only one or two staff members or administrators are interested in such a program. Stanford University has had a contract in the Philippines in a subject matter area that is not even offered on its campus. Tampa had a similar one in Cuba. Such a program by its very nature is an isolated one. On other occasions the program coordinator is provided with no mechanism of liaison with the regular colleges or departments. Even the interest and concern of university presidents and top officials is sometimes lacking. Such conditions are not likely to make permanent affiliations a probable outcome.

Even without affiliation, closer relations between American and host institutions can develop as the result of the programs. But too much may be claimed in this regard. Making friends at the host institution, helping it to understand the United States, and maximizing the impact of the United States are not the major justifications of university contracts. The first two of these objectives are associated with any exchange program. Pushing the influence of this country, in its extreme form, would jeopardize the very integrity of universities if it were accepted as an aim. University faculty members are not soap salesmen. Their recommendations and actions must be governed by the criterion of knowledge rather than by the degree to which they expand United States influence. To act otherwise would be to forfeit their claim to membership in the fraternity of scholarship.

Administrative Liaison Problems. University contracts may be disadvantageous to the sponsor and the host organization because of liaison problems. Contract negotiations and renewals may be painstakingly slow. Both professional and personal jealousy may arise between university personnel and government or foundation employees. An ICA conference listed seven disadvantages of the university contract device: [3]

1. Greater cost per technician
2. Possibility of "free-wheeling" on the part of the contract staff
3. Lack of clear-cut line relationships
4. Existence of contract may be construed as requiring that budgetary cuts—when they become necessary—be made exclusively or largely in non-contract projects
5. Staff morale may be damaged by difference in status between contract and non-contract personnel
6. Contract technicians frequently have less foreign experience and greater insularity than non-contract technicians
7. Lessened direct control

Enlargement of American University Resources. Those who have been most hopeful about the impact of technical assistance

[3] *Ibid.*, sect. IV D, p. 1.

programs on American universities have felt that through the contract device a new national resource would be developed at the universities, a kind of new expertise. In all fields in which technical assistance programs have been at work there has been greater exchange of information between American and foreign scholars, more internationalization of disciplines. In fields where regional knowledge is of special importance, such as the social sciences, tropical medicine, or agriculture, expertise has been developed at American universities. Many professors in the relevant disciplines have been abroad in a technical assistance capacity and if called upon to go again would benefit from their initial experience.

Experience abroad has been reflected in the content of the articles in professional journals and the papers delivered at professional meetings. It has contributed a depth of comparison to many of the courses. Talks to campus and community groups have been given by participants and their wives. New areas of research have been identified.

Results such as these have been limited by the fact that only a few universities have taken advantage of the technical assistance projects systematically to build their resources at home. Any impact has been incidental, not institutionally encouraged. The extensive use of nonuniversity personnel or personnel from other universities has reduced the likelihood of much benefit.

Many technical assistance projects are of such a nature that a university's resources could hardly be enlarged through them even with formal planning. By definition, a technical assistance project places the emphasis on export, not import, and the enlargement of American university resources is derived, not central. Many of the financing agreements, especially ICA contracts, provide only for the most necessary expenditures for exporting know-how, none for importing or self-development of the American university.

If an institution is in a position to choose, it can develop new areas of competence best by a direct approach, not through the complications of a university technical assistance contract. So, too, for the individual professor there are many opportunities to go abroad for teaching or research purposes. On the whole, professors who have returned from overseas under university contracts do not feel that *from a professional point of view* their time was as well spent as it would have been under alternative arrangements. For example, a number of them believe that a single year abroad as a research professor probably would further them professionally much more than three or four years abroad under a technical assistance contract, especially where research and teaching have not been the prime activities.

The technical assistance programs actually place a strain on American university resources, especially at a time of staff shortage. To the extent that a university's own faculty members are recruited to join the teams, departments are deprived of badly needed help. Regular teaching and research programs have been disrupted markedly in some cases.

Departments have on occasion prospered by using the contracts as devices to expand their staffs, keeping on some of the added personnel after those sent abroad return home. This is possible for departments at any one or a few universities. It is not possible for all or most departments in a given field. Persons qualified for university employment are in limited supply. The supply is highly inelastic. Some fields suffer more from the shortage than others. Though some expansion of university contracts could take place without serious consequences, a large expansion in the next decade or so would necessitate the sending of inferior personnel abroad or the accepting of inferior personnel on the campuses at home.

A report by the committee on Utilization of College Teaching Resources concludes, ". . . even the most optimistic estimates leave little question that higher education will face a critical shortage of teachers within a few years." It goes on to quote a report of the United States Office of Education as follows:

In the last few years, when the ranks of teachers with doctors degrees should have been swelling and swelling fast, they have been actually thinning. The number of people earning Ph.D.'s has been falling off from 8,903 in 1955–56 to 8,756 in 1956–57 and 8,380 (estimated) in 1957–58; and of each year's total only about half have gone into college teaching. In certain fields—science and engineering, for example—the proportion has been even less. In 1953–54 about one-third of the new college teachers were Ph.D.'s; last year, less than one-fourth. In recent years colleges have been adding about 3,000–4,000 new teachers with Ph.D.'s every year; but additions like these will be utterly inadequate for the future. Conservative estimates say that in the coming decade colleges must recruit between 15,000 and 22,000 teachers a year.[4]

[4] "The Guide to the National Defense Education Act of 1958," Circular no. 553, quoted in Committee on Utilization of College Teaching Resources, *Better Utilization of College Teaching Resources, A Summary Report* (New York: Fund for the Advancement of Education, 1959), p. 7.

American universities are going to have to choose between augmenting the personnel shortage that faces them or restricting the number of professors they are sending abroad under technical assistance programs. Already, some universities have accepted responsibility for technical assistance programs but have failed to send a single regular staff member of their own overseas, relying on nonacademic personnel. The personnel shortage will be with the universities for many years to come. At a time when university resources in the United States are overburdened and becoming even more so, it is a waste of national resources to send university personnel overseas if others can do the job satisfactorily. A distinction needs to be drawn between situations in which universities are *necessary*, and situations in which they are *desirable* or only *convenient*.

Technical experts can be found from many sources. In the present manpower shortage of higher education, it would be tragic if university faculty members were diverted overseas for purposes other than those unique to a university. It seems strange that sponsors of technical assistance programs have not been concerned directly with doing something about the university manpower shortage in the United States, a shortage which they are augmenting and which may prevent their achieving their goals abroad.

Chapter II

FORMATION OF TECHNICAL
ASSISTANCE PROGRAMS ABROAD

The several parties to a possible technical assistance project must
first reach agreement on the need for a program and then develop
a suitable system of decision-making for its operations. Each
project has its own distinctive background. [A program is the
culmination of a series of events, often over several years.] The
nature of the background forms the context within which project
personnel must work, and this preliminary work may create or
avoid problems or pitfalls.

Among the backgrounds favorable to success of a program is
long acquaintance between key representatives of the American
and the host-country institutions. The ICA-financed programs of
the University of Michigan in Japan (business administration and
industrial productivity) and in the Philippines (public administration) followed long familiarity with the two countries concerned
on the part of some University of Michigan faculty members and
acquaintance with many scholars there. Some Michigan State
University personnel knew ranking Vietnamese prior to the ICA-
financed public administration program in Vietnam. The Chicago-
Chile program in economic development followed after personnel
had become acquainted.

A second element favorable to the achievement of chosen objectives is knowledge of American concepts of higher education by
the host institutions and, in turn, familiarity with host-country
ideas by the American university. The more accurate the understanding of each other's university systems, the more likely the
project is to avoid trouble. Such knowledge can come about in
many different ways; through observation trips to the United States

or the host country, books, or conversations. Field representatives
of ICA and foundations have sometimes done an excellent job
of explanation to representatives of the host institution. Over
several years, they have pointed out to host-country personnel the
limitations and possibilities of cooperation with an American university. In India, the Ohio State–ICA project in teacher education benefited from advance knowledge of American universities by
the host. A Ford Foundation adviser and an ICA official paved
the way for the development of a specific program.

Contact with Americans before the formulation of a project does
not guarantee favorable conditions for the programs. For many
years agencies of the United States and the United Nations worked
with Bolivians in the field of public administration, pointing out
the great needs. Some Bolivians seemed to agree. Even so, the
Bolivians did not think that their needs were such that the University of Tennessee program was particularly appropriate.

American officials had many contacts in Germany and Japan
after World War II, and some of the activities in which they engaged led to American university programs. Occupation efforts
were nominally aimed at democratization, and involved the adoption of some elements of the American legal system, such as decartelization. In Germany, the first program was that of the University of Chicago with Frankfurt, established in 1948 with funds
from the Rockefeller Foundation, and later financed by Ford.
Extensive exchanges of professors and the establishment of interdisciplinary seminars at each university were arranged to bring
German universities back into contact with American, with the
expectation that among the results would be an adaptation of some
of the American ways by German institutions. The Georgetown-
Frankfurt program in part was focused on decartelization. In
Japan, the joint law school program financed by the Ford Foundation was developed in 1954, in part to assist Japan in adjusting
its legal structure to American innovations. Some of these programs in Germany and Japan began with real enthusiasm. But
desire to imitate the United States waned with the passing of the
years, and the contacts during the occupation days were not de-
cisive.

As a part of the activities that followed the Marshall Plan in
Europe, the European Productivity Agency, with American support, encouraged the several national productivity centers to stimu-

late education in business administration. United States universities were held up as examples. There were extensive contacts with individual Americans, including some American university officials. Despite such contacts, American university business administration programs in Europe have not been very successful.

The probability of success in a program is dependent not so much on contact alone or on the duration of contact as on mutual identification of purposes. Enough time is needed for the two parties to make certain that there is agreement on objectives. In this process, the staff of the proposed financing organization and other Americans may play an important role. Such a procedure is neither a sufficient nor a necessary condition of program success, but it is closely related to it. Programs without such backgrounds involve large risks. Forced agreement or agreement on the device but not on the purposes is seldom adequate.

Participating Organizations and Their Role as Originators

A program may be originated by a member or members of an American university, a host institution or government, a financing organization, or an outside group. The responders may be members of any or all of the three participating groups—the American university, host institution, or financing organization. The source and manner of origination and the method of selecting the respondents not only reveal something of the purposes behind the international exchange programs of American universities, but also affect the problems encountered and the success of the program.

The Number of Participating Organizations. The usual technical assistance program of an American university includes one or more host institutions, one or more financing organizations, and the American university. On rare occasions the host institution and the American university go it alone. The Gadjah Mada–Johns Hopkins program in Indonesia in political science and international relations involved only Johns Hopkins outside Indonesia.

In about half of the programs, there are several financing organizations. The American university may search for two or more sponsors or, more commonly, a major sponsor such as a foundation or ICA may insist on financial participation by others as a condition of its own support. ICA is normally the dominant financial factor in the programs it sponsors, even though costs payable in currency of the host country are often underwritten by host governments or institutions. An exception is the University of Pennsylvania veterinary medicine research program in Mexico, where ICA financing plays a minor part and the contribution of a Mexican chemical company bears most of the expense. The interests of sponsors are both varied and limited; an American university frequently finds that if it is to carry out the kind of program it desires, several sponsors are desirable. Special grants for research or fellowships often supplement the main source of financial support.

In the host country, several institutions participate in almost half the programs. Often one of them is designated as the central organization, but sometimes they have equal status. A technical assistance program in teacher education may include the central ministry of education and a group of teachers colleges. In the ICA–Ohio State contract in India, the All-India Council for Secondary Education of the Ministry of Education serves as a host organization, through which OSU works with teacher education institutions. Ohio State, Illinois, Kansas State, Missouri, and Tennessee each conducts an ICA agricultural contract in a region of India, working with local agricultural colleges, the Indian Council of Agricultural Research serving as coordinator. The New York University program in Turkey involved two faculties of the University of Ankara plus a separate training institute for commercial education. The reason for including several host institutions is that innovations are sought at each of them.

Association of several American universities with a program occurs much less frequently. The State University of New York conducts a Ford-financed teacher education program in Indonesia and draws on its many campuses for support. The joint law school program in Japan represents a collective effort of the law schools of three American universities—Harvard, Michigan, and Stanford, and seven Japanese institutions—Chuo, Keio, Kyoto, Tohoku, Tokyo, and Waseda universities and the Judicial Research and Training Institute. The Institute of International Education handles the financial and logistic arrangements of the program. The reason for involving several American universities is usually that a single university cannot supply enough teachers, as in the case of the American law schools in Japan.

A single host-country organization may have relations with two or more American universities in separate programs; the financing organization may support two or more programs at a single host institution or American university; and the American university may be administering several programs involving various combinations of host countries and sponsors. Thus Indiana University has two separate programs financed by ICA in Thailand; North Carolina State has two separate programs in Peru; and the University of Indonesia and Gadjah Mada University each have programs with different American universities, financed in varying ways.

Involving several participating organizations in one program is from one point of view a complication, but it may be essential. Though many organizations are involved, if the resources of several institutions are desired or if innovations are to be made at several institutions, it may be simpler to combine the institutions in one program than to have several programs. The proliferation of separate programs in some countries has led staff members and others to suggest more pooling of American university efforts overseas. ICA officials have stressed the possibility of pooling as one means of making available the resources of smaller institutions. To take advantage of field experience, ICA has encouraged institutions to accept additional contracts in countries in which they already have projects.

When host organizations include government agencies as well as institutions of higher education, special problems arise. In those instances where a government agency acts as a coordinator for higher education there may be no problem, as in the case of the Indian Council of Agricultural Research. However, where an American university is expected to render consulting advice to government agencies as well as to extend help to universities, two kinds of personnel may be required. If the American university appears to be a government consulting agency with nonacademic personnel, it may lose some of its rapport with a host university. Several ICA programs have suffered from this difficulty.

When a number of host universities with varying prestige are included, other problems arise. Selection of the institutions is difficult. What should be the basis of a decision to include some universities and exclude others? Injured feelings may follow the exclusion of some, as in the joint law program in Japan. Still worse, within the group selected, unequal status may mean that participation in the project is shared by inferiors and superiors. If the superiors are active, the inferiors may be forced to accept a minor role. If the inferiors are overly active, the superiors may stay in the background. The joint law program in Japan illustrates the former situation, the University of Tokyo and the judicial institute being predominant.

The most serious difficulty of a project with numerous participating organizations is agreement on objectives and keeping up equal interest in achieving these objectives. Agreement at the beginning is likely to be rather general and based upon different expectations. As the project evolves, interests of each organization are defined more precisely and change from time to time. Some degree of conflict is almost inevitable. A somewhat long preparatory period before a program is launched may help to identify and clarify goals, and perhaps lead to compromise. Good communication and occasional review of objectives are useful. It is important to provide simple means of discontinuing membership in a program by an organization, once it deems its interests are no longer furthered. With arrangements such as these, there is no reason why multiple organizations cannot seek their main objectives—supplying adequate resources and diffusing the benefits of the program in the host country and in the United States.

The Role of Originator. The originator of a project may be any one or any combination of the participating organizations, or an outside group. Technical assistance programs under ICA and other government agencies are initiated by American universities in perhaps 20 per cent of the cases, and not much more frequently by host institutions and outside private groups. ICA and host-country governments initiate a majority of the programs. Foundation technical assistance programs follow much the same pattern, the foundation replacing ICA. Of nine technical assistance programs in Mexico, Peru, Bolivia, and Chile, two were initiated by ICA and three by host-government agencies (Adams and Cumberland, pp. 4–5). The Seoul National University–Minnesota ICA contract in several fields was developed primarily because of the initiative of the Korean government. A proposal for help to a private institution was changed largely by the Korean government, to one for help to the public Seoul National University. The Cornell-Liberia project was also originated by the host-country government. President Tubman approached the American ambassador about the idea. The importance of this project in the eyes of the originators is illustrated by the fact that the Liberian government financed it directly when ICA financing ceased after a few years. A substantial number of programs have been initiated by the metropole governments in Africa. Outside private groups such as American and foreign business concerns have originated projects, as in the case of United States-owned textile companies in Peru, which were aided by the ICA-financed North Carolina State College textile engineering program.

Most programs have been originated by Americans rather than host-country nationals. American financial resources are primarily employed and American universities have a more adequate supply of personnel. The proportion of host-country initiations varies greatly among countries. Mexican organizations took the initiative in five of six programs, while Peru, Bolivia, and Chile together accounted for less than half the originators of some seven programs. India, Indonesia, and Japan are countries with high proportions of locally originated American university programs.

Some countries are especially sensitive to what they view as potential United States interference in their internal affairs, and in these countries a project is more likely to get under way and be successful if it is originated locally. Mexico and Indonesia are examples, and to some extent Japan also. Because the joint law program in Japan was largely American in concept, Japanese criticism was encountered. Countries also vary in the degree to which they follow definitive national development plans. Programs in less developed countries without active national plans will frequently be initiated by American groups. The more specific the national plans and the more actively they are implemented, the more likely it is that programs providing for advice and consultation from American universities will be originated locally. India is an outstanding case in point. On the other hand, a special, limited need may lead a host country to initiate a program, whether related to a broad national plan or not. In Liberia, when President Tubman initiated the Cornell program, he knew that he wanted a codified set of laws and that Liberian law was patterned after United States law. In the more developed countries, programs requiring active participation and some sharing in the costs are originated almost as frequently by the host country as by the United States.

Identification of Responders

In almost all university programs, a group originating an idea for a project and developing it to some extent must seek the participation of other organizations. To select responding organizations requires criteria of selection, applying them, and obtaining acceptances. Selection may involve a series of decisions. For example, in the Cornell-Liberia program, the Liberian government approached the United States government, which in turn approached Cornell. It is common for a host country to approach an American university or an American financing organization and for that group, in turn, to select the third participating organization. A sponsor or an American university which originates a project approaches the other two groups.

Matching American and Host Institutions. One of the most frequently used criteria for selecting the cooperating universities in America and the host country is to try to obtain matching institutions. Characteristics for matching vary, but include type of control—private or public, size of institution, composition of student body, and relative prestige. When the host organization is not an institution of higher education, such matching is not possible. A public institution in the United States usually associates with a public institution abroad; this is the case in many ICA-university contracts. There are exceptions; the University of Southern California and New York University have had ICA contracts for work with public universities in such countries as Iran, Turkey, and Brazil. Matching universities according to their public or private character does not have much relevance to the probability of success in a project, although it may have much to do with the nature of the stated objectives.

Matching universities according to size has also occurred; a university large for the United States affiliates with an institution that is large for the host country. Major exceptions are technical assistance programs that relate an American university to a special school or institute rather than to a general university. A university with high prestige in the United States is likely to be matched with a university of comparable prestige abroad. However, comparability in terms of size or prestige is far from close or universal.

Geographical factors have had a noticeable effect on the selection of American and host-country institutions. American Western institutions tend to look to the Pacific and the Far East and Southern institutions to Latin America. ICA and foundations have on occasion tried to match geographical conditions in the United States with those in the host country, especially in agricultural programs. Similarity of geography is to be found in the University of California program in Chile, the Arizona program with Sonora, and the former Texas A and M program at Antonio Narro.

Another kind of matching involves the desired future characteristics of a university rather than those it has. In technical assistance programs on occasion a model is constructed of the kind of institution which the originators would like the host institution to become, and an American university is selected that best meets the requirements of the model. It is no accident that there are many land-grant colleges in the ICA university contract program. Not only have land-grant institutions been willing to participate, but they also represent a model which, with the necessary adaptations, many persons in ICA would like to see followed overseas. Relatively few Ivy League institutions are active in ICA work abroad, not merely because they refuse to participate, but also because they and ICA believe that they do not present an appropriate model for host universities in less developed countries.

Other institutional characteristics are on occasion matched, as in the case of Prairie View A and M, a Negro college, and the Booker Washington Institute in Liberia. Matching of language competence was mistakenly thought to have been achieved by relating the Delgado Trades and Technical Institutes to the École des Arts et Metiers of Beirut. Matching as a criterion for selecting respondents is limited by the fact that there are many characteristics to match in order to find comparable institutions; anything beyond a rough approximation is impossible in most instances. Probably for this reason, attempts at matching have had very little relation to the success of a program. Matching also implies that the functions which the host country and American institutions are to perform are similar, and that the characteristics matched are related to the functions to be performed under the program. These assumptions are usually false. Where they have been well founded, matching has served its purpose well.

Criteria for Selecting American Universities. Although matching has had little to do with the success of a project, it is closely related to something more relevant, namely, the competence of the institutions to carry out the tasks assigned them under the program. Each institution has its own kinds of competence. For example, it may have certain kinds of subject matter competence, area competence, competence in carrying out an overseas program, and adequacy of resources.

Furthermore, a distinction between competence and established reputation is important. Selection of an American university as a respondent normally is undertaken by a host institution, a foundation, or a government agency which has little detailed knowledge of American higher education. The originators are often overseas and are concerned with regional or country matters. They are likely to have a general impression of established reputations of American universities rather than a knowledge of actual or potential competence, more likely to know of competence in an area than in subject matter, in contact with those universities that carry on numerous overseas programs but not with those that might have unused resources. Often the international reputations of American universities are quite different from their reputations within the United States. For example, the outstanding private American institutions are much better known overseas than the outstanding public ones, as was illustrated by the voting at the American exhibit in the Brussels World's Fair in 1958. Private institutions were overwhelmingly favored by Fair visitors. A special business administration institute in Italy which relied upon visiting American professors for its staff had, up to 1958, selected only professors from private institutions. African institutions, like many others around the world, want to associate only with a Harvard.

Universities which have achieved the objectives of their programs, and have become involved in them by responding to an invitation, are for the most part institutions marked by *subject matter competence* and *adequacy of resources;* they may or may not be known by international reputation, area competence, or competence in carrying out an overseas program. The University of California (Berkeley) medical school in Indonesia, the University of Nebraska in agriculture in Turkey, and the University of Michigan in engineering in Mexico had neither area competence nor experience in administering overseas programs, and yet they carried out programs that are generally regarded as more successful than some others in these countries. Undoubtedly area competence, experience in overseas work, and established national reputation do facilitate program success, provided the more relevant requirements are met.

Apart from these factors, originating organizations and especially the sponsors look for American universities which *agree with the proposed program objectives,* have real *enthusiasm* for the enterprise, and present some prospect of *continuing interest.* At best, enthusiasm and continuing interest are difficult to determine, yet they are as essential to success of a program as agreement on objectives. Sponsoring groups prefer that some of the details of the objectives be worked out by the two institutions concerned, but preliminary objectives are formulated by the originators of a program and it is exceedingly important to select an American university sympathetic with them.

Inevitably, personal or political considerations affect the selection. The game of "who knows whom" is universally understood and is played frequently. The number of universities chosen in part because of personal acquaintance of someone in the host institution or sponsoring organization with someone at the American university is large; personal acquaintance may be a factor in a majority of the selections. There is nothing necessarily illegitimate in such a procedure; indeed, it may result in a good selection if the selector knows what he is about. Yet it places a premium on whom the faculty members of a university know rather than on what they know. At its worst, the practice may border on patronage handouts or selection primarily for political reasons. Some of the most obvious selections of this kind occurred during the early days of the Foreign Operations Administration, predecessor agency of ICA. The university contracts awarded throughout the country to the various state and land-grant institutions were intended to increase support of the agency in Congress and help the political aspirations of top agency personnel.

Criteria for Selecting Host Institutions. In contrast to criteria used for selecting American universities, host institutions are selected more according to expected future competence, and more for their willingness to innovate than for current availability of resources. Technical assistance is given to universities at many levels of development, some of them without staff in the subject area of the program. To develop its resources a host institution must join in seeking the program objectives and the host government must be willing to give necessary assistance. The more actively a host government tries to accelerate national development and relate universities to the process, the more likely it is that such assistance will be forthcoming. Especially sought are host institutions that will participate in pilot projects, serving as demonstrations for other host institutions so as to multiply the effects of technical assistance in the long run. This does not always result in selection of a university with the highest prestige, since a prestigeful institution is often a citadel of tradition.

American universities may choose to work with one of three kinds of academic units abroad in technical assistance projects. A program may be attached to a regular part of an institution of higher learning, to a special department, school, or institute within the institution, or to a special separate institution. The success of the program may be affected by the choice of academic unit and by its reputation among other academic units.

Where a qualified and receptive regular academic unit of a host university is to be found, it has been preferred by both American universities and sponsoring organizations, as a rule. Affiliation with such a unit carries prestige and is likely to involve the best of host-country personnel and other resources. But qualified and receptive regular academic units may be hard to find. They are often the least receptive to innovations desired by originators of technical assistance projects; the personal future of the faculty members is very much bound up in the existing order of things.

As a consequence, special institutions of higher education, separate from the universities, have been selected under or created for many of the projects. This course of action was followed by the Michigan-Mexico project and most of the others concerned with technical education. The aim was to expand training facilities and to create model demonstration institutions. In some programs the intention to build a model has led to the establishment of entire new universities, borrowing from American practices. The major difficulties have been the low prestige of the new institutions and the defense of vested interests on the part of those associated with the old-style institutions. The Nebraska experience with Ataturk University in Turkey bears on both points.

A compromise has been followed in certain other projects by selecting as a host institution a special institute or school within an existing host-country university. The technical assistance programs in business and public administration have usually chosen this course if they have not selected an independent organization; for example, Tennessee in La Paz, California in Bologna, and Harvard in Istanbul. This pattern was defended by the director of USOM (ICA field office) in a large Latin American country, who said, "Our only chance is to build institutes around the main university structure and hope that after many years they'll have an impact."

Choice among the three major policies depends upon long-range objectives. If it is desired ultimately to obtain the benefits of co-operation with regular academic units of host universities or to have an impact on them, it is not yet clear that working with special or independent schools or institutes will be a means to that end. The programs have been going much too short a time for any such impact to be evident. On the other hand, if the main desire is to work with any group that can provide suitable resources or that can give special training to host-country personnel, quite aside from the regular university faculties, the other two courses would seem perfectly satisfactory and in many cases highly preferable.

Application of Criteria. Except in a few instances, the negotiations with selected participating organizations have been rather simple. A member of the originating group communicates with some member of a prospective participating organization in person, by telephone, or letter, and the process continues until a conclusion is reached, one way or another. Such contact is normally preceded by one or more planning sessions of members of the originating organization. Because of the great distances that may separate American universities from host-country institutions, personal conversations may require one or more expensive field trips. As a rule the selection for each new project is an *ad hoc* matter at American and host universities. Almost no universities or their academic units have developed general criteria for selecting program respondents. Most often the process is rather casual; in a few it has been more formal. Criteria usually are worked out by the persons or subgroups immediately involved in a program. Some universities have appointed coordinating officials for several international programs, but all-university criteria for selection of other participating organizations have yet to appear. It may be unrealistic to expect them in the larger institutions.

Extensive selection procedures have been followed by a few host-country governments in identifying host institutions. In a technical assistance program, the financing organization or the host-country government, not the American university, usually selects the responding host university. The financing organization often defers to the wishes of the host government, since local interest may be greater if the host government has an opportunity to participate in the selection and feels involved. However, the role of the host government may be merely formal. Government approval is obtained after a tentative selection of a host institution has been made, particularly in countries that do not have active national development plans or a high degree of nationalistic sensitivity. Most host governments, however, are cautious about technical assistance, and wish to keep it under their control. It is in such instances that elaborate selection procedures by the host government are likely to be found. In Indonesia, the National Planning Bureau in the prime minister's office has the function of planning the growth of Indonesian universities and the relations of foreign university personnel to them. It is so understaffed, however, that it acts as a bottleneck; it has never been able to assemble entirely adequate data. Much the same can be said about the Coordinating Bureau for Higher Education in the Ministry of Education. In India, the Planning Commission plays a major role in channeling all technical assistance programs.

Problems of selection have been especially difficult for the financing organization. Both ICA and the major foundations officially prefer that at least one of the other participants take the initiative. In practice, as the Ford Foundation and ICA have developed large programs, they have sought to find the most likely combination of host institution and American university for the ends in view. They have become the originators, not the responders. This is a natural course of action for any group with an active program, but it involves dangers. There may be insufficient knowledge about institutions in the host country; the host institution may be selected because of its prestige and status, or because of who knows whom, rather than on the basis of genuine enthusiasm and other qualifications for the task at hand.

Furthermore, a certain rigidity is likely to be introduced as large groups of programs are sponsored by an agency—rigidity of purpose or objective, rigidity of form of agreement, inflexible arrangements for participation. It is not necessarily desirable for financing organizations to avoid these dangers. There may be real advantage in unified policies for large groups of programs. The sponsor may even be desirous of gambling on the chance that a university, American or host country, may become highly motivated during the course of a program though it may not be so at the beginning. Any program is likely to involve some maturing of purpose, some modification of goals. There is a fine line between reckless and intelligent risk-taking. In any event, in those instances where the financing organization selects one or more of the other participating groups, selection is conditioned by the program emphasis of the sponsor.

Both the Ford Foundation and ICA, having appropriate liaison with government agencies, also have extensive contact with potential host institutions. This contact has curbed any tendency to select on the basis of status or prestige alone. Sometimes such relations are the result of the initiative of the host institutions, sometimes the result of host-government suggestion. Sometimes they arise from the initiative of the sponsors themselves (for example, during a field trip or conference), and occasionally spring from the suggestion of an American university. The problem is not how to find institutions that will accept money, but how to identify institutions that will be interested in using the money for innovations that fall within the sponsor's interests. There has been too ready an assumption that host institutions willing to enter into an agreement are also those that embrace, potentially at least, the proposed goals.

One technique tried in order to avoid this difficulty has been to bring an exploratory consulting mission from a prospective American university to the host country for a survey. The Ford Foundation in Pakistan has followed this procedure. The system seems to work best when the mission can spend some months in the field, working with an appropriate group of host-country nationals. A visit of a few days or a week or two by a university official, as was the practice in some of the early ICA contracts, has been of some value in helping to select a suitable host institution. However, the value of a short trip is dependent upon the adequacy of the background work of the field representatives of the sponsoring agency and representatives of the host government and potential host institution. Relatively short trips preceding the Chicago-Chile and Tennessee-Bolivia projects were useful.

A second technique has been joint inquiry into an area by an American and host-country team, the American side being composed of representatives of the sponsoring organization in the field. In several countries in Latin America, servicios or joint American-Latino administrative organizations exist in fields such as health, education, or public works, and these groups may be vehicles for helping to identify appropriate host institutions. The servicios themselves are host institutions in several instances, as with the Harvard nutrition research and training project in Peru. The world-wide ICA field organization permits a cooperative approach; in India there have been joint Indo-American teams in advance of the formalization of several ICA university contracts. The mere presence of a field official from a sponsoring organization does not assure a concentrated period of inquiry, field research, and discussion before a program begins, however. Nor does it provide for participation by a prospective American university, as does the consulting team approach.

Selecting American universities by sponsoring and host-country groups has been relatively casual. Because the sponsor has a United States office and its staff members are Americans, there has been a tendency for the sponsors to let each individual program officer in the United States choose cooperating institutions on his own, with appropriate suggestions from and clearance with staff associates. The Ford Foundation has often permitted its field representatives the principal initiative in selecting an American university. Since officials of the sponsoring agency attend professional meetings and make occasional trips to American universities, these procedures are more rational than they may seem. Furthermore, Washington and New York, where government agencies and many foundation offices are located, are frequent stops for academic persons. Numerous informal conferences take place. The central offices of a number of professional associations are also located there; contact with them is common. When specific criteria have been chosen for the selection of an American university, informal application of them is adequate in many instances. Many universities that have been so selected are carrying out their tasks with enthusiasm and success.

Such a selection procedure falls short on two grounds, however. First, it places a premium on those institutions with established national reputations and those that have contacts with the officials of the sponsoring group. Second, it does not provide an opportunity for the prospective host institution to participate effectively in the selection. To meet the first shortcoming, it has been suggested that ICA and foundations work mainly through professional organizations or associations of universities or their special committees. The suggestion has been rejected by both ICA and the Ford Foundation, since they feel that no membership organization can be objective in recommending universities for participation. The Ford Foundation has considered the use of a series of consultants that would keep it informed in the several fields of its overseas interest. Such consultants, attending professional meetings and spending a few weeks each year at a selected group of universities, would have the function of turning up possibilities among universities whose reputations are less well known and those which do not have easy access to the foundation. They could also check the enthusiasm at working levels of institutions with reputations in the international program field. This procedure would probably prove helpful to foundations generally and to ICA.

One of the signal failures of ICA and foundations alike has been, in effect, to exclude host-country institutions from the selection of the American university. Representatives of host institutions of course have been asked for their suggestions and they usually formally approve the final choice. But they cannot really participate without making an extended trip to United States universities. In none of the Latin American programs in the research sample did any Latin American academic representative make a survey trip to the United States before the program was approved. This was true also of the majority of programs in other regions. ICA has begun to alter its practices in a few instances, especially in the more nationally sensitive countries, but the new idea is not spreading rapidly. A two-man Indonesian team, accompanied by the local ICA public administration adviser, visited a group of United States universities prior to the selection of Indiana University for a public administration contract. A joint Indo-American team visited United States agricultural colleges in an effort to choose four that were qualified and willing to accept ICA university contracts which, along with the already existing Illinois contract, would cover all of India on a regional basis. This visit was later followed up by two-man exploratory missions to India from the American universities.

Decision-Making

From the first effort to establish a technical assistance program, an American university and host institution are faced with choices as to how they are to carry out the arrangement. Choice of methods and modification of policy goals confront program administrators throughout the life of a project. These choices are often conditioned by the sponsors and occasionally made by them but essentially most decisions are the product of the American university and/or the host institution. The host-country government may also play a significant role. There may be one or two main centers of decision-making and one or two smaller centers.

Actually, the patterns of decision-making are even more complicated. It should not be implied that each participating organization is unified in its approach to a program. Of course, this is not often true. Within each organization there may be originators, responders, and those who refuse to be involved or are at best reluctant responders. And there are likely to be those who oppose a program as well as those who hold varying points of view on any one matter of policy.

The two most important individuals in major projects are the American chief adviser and the host-country director. When these two persons are in agreement, a project may move ahead with specific priorities and plans. Where the two do not agree or fail to pursue a common policy for one reason or another, a project tends to lag. They condition the entire atmosphere in which project personnel work.

The American University. At the American university, a member of the faculty without any other administrative responsibility may serve as coordinator of an international program. Often a middle-level university administrator assumes the role; many coordinators are also department heads or deans. The coordinator usually reports directly to the president or vice president of the university. "Nearly half the programs provide the campus coordinator with committees with varying functions of advice and policy decision-making. The variety of composition of these committees is great, but departmental, school or college representation, and occasionally representation from the general university administration, are all common" (Inventory, pp. 43–45).

Occasional advisory committees do not alter the fact that most technical assistance programs involve small parts of the American institutions at which they are located. They are not institution-wide efforts, but the efforts of specialized units. The major exceptions are some programs at small institutions or an occasional large program at a medium-sized institution. The Peabody program in education in Korea has attracted widespread interest and support at Peabody. The Oklahoma State University–Ethiopia program has gone as far as any at a sizable American institution in involving many units of the university. No program at universities such as California, Minnesota, or Harvard has ever been institution-wide, even though some do cross college lines.

Furthermore, faculty members at home are busy, and often have little time for interest either in special on-campus activities or in university programs overseas. If a project in which a university is engaged falls outside the humanities and social sciences, as it often does, faculty members of the foreign area studies center sometimes have had little or no interest in it, even though the project is located in a country of the area with which they are concerned. Some faculty members in the humanities and social sciences have lacked interest even in programs within their fields since they have felt there was too much emphasis on one country. Both of these situations have existed at Michigan in its several programs dealing with Japan.

Faculty and even administrative opposition to many of the projects exists. Where there is not opposition, at least much apathy is likely to be present. It is difficult to evaluate this fact, since opposition and apathy are to be found in relation to many university programs and policies having nothing to do with international programs. Nevertheless, many of the most respected and best qualified faculty members have severe misgivings about some of the technical assistance programs. This is as true at larger institutions or those that are known for their participation in such programs, such as California, Indiana, Minnesota, and Cornell, as it is at smaller institutions or those less well known for their international bent.

The opposition at American universities arises in part from

traditional professorial skepticism. Partly it is based on a belief that the programs are not appropriate to academic objectives. And partly it is a consequence of the fact that the programs tend to be special administrative offshoots, in which the faculty members are not active. (Coordinators, it will be recalled, normally report to the president or vice president.) Programs may be promoted by one or a few persons whose personal property they more or less remain. Though many programs are organized at a university level through some special administrative device, even some of those administered by departments do not give faculty members a feeling that they are part of the enterprise. A department chairman or a faculty member designated to carry out the task may make all the decisions.

Once a program gets under way, the differences in support for it are accentuated. If staff members are sent abroad, their interest becomes far greater than that of their colleagues at home. They find it difficult to understand why more support is not forthcoming from the home campus. After a program is launched, administrative university officials turn to other matters and appear unconcerned about its fate, leaving everything to the program administrator.

Faculty opposition or isolation should not be overstressed. Substantial interest on the home campus exists at a departmental level in perhaps a quarter of university technical assistance programs. Such programs often receive advice from faculty members, especially those programs that have been operating long enough to have staff members on the campus who have returned from the project abroad. Faculty involvement is especially marked in programs organized by departments and in those at small institutions. Wide involvement in decisions at an American university is not a requirement of success, but it does help to ensure that the programs will have academic relevance and will tie in with other university activities.

Campus liaison with the field has been promoted by short trips abroad by campus coordinators or other administrative officials. Occasionally these visits offer opportunities to review project methods and objectives, but usually they are too short for much to be accomplished, especially if the coordinator serves on a part-time basis, as he usually does.

Despite these and other arrangements, it has been difficult to involve persons on the home campus in effective and continuing decision-making concerning programs abroad. Delegation of authority to those overseas is undoubtedly wise, but participation by faculty members and administrators at home is also desirable.

Since many of the programs are limited to activities of interest to relatively few faculty members, it is important to associate with the program an active nucleus of those in the subject area. It is unrealistic to assume that all faculty members of a college or even of a large department will be interested, but a nucleus is necessary if the program is to avoid difficulty. To keep interest alive it is well to give the department members an active voice in policy decisions and perhaps even in the administration of the program (Adams and Cumberland, pp. 41–46; Adams and Garraty, p. 118).

The complications of launching and operating a program, including the necessity of liaison with a variety of other groups, often lead some persons to think only of getting the cooperation of leaders in American universities. The rank-and-file faculty member tends to be forgotten. The leaders often are more concerned with administrative details than with substantive issues, as in the activities of the Committee on Institutional Projects Abroad of the American Council of Education from 1955 to 1958 and after. When institutions get involved in a program without competence in the field or desire for more competence, and without some active nucleus of faculty support, they risk frustration and failure. Such programs need integration into the regular departments and activities of American universities.

Other Groups. Abroad, the involvement of personnel at the host institution varies even more widely than that at American universities. Most program plans are the product of a relatively few persons, often only the host-country director or dean himself. For example, the North Carolina State College textile engineering program in Peru was tied to one of the basic academic units of the National University of Engineering. While a certain dean remained in office support was forthcoming, but with his replacement it was withdrawn. At the University of Bologna, the rector was interested in the University of California program in public administration, but little interest was forthcoming from the faculty of law.

In some instances the American university has gone ahead without a host institution, making all the decisions and, in some cases at least, expecting host-country personnel to rubber-stamp these when and if they take over the organization. This was the pattern of the Pennsylvania program in public administration in Pakistan. Such lack of mutuality in American university relations with host institutions was not the rule, but smaller elements of it were present in more than half the programs. Such tactics were frequently unsuccessful, especially where host-country nationals were highly sensitive to outside assistance, sensitive to too much American influence, or not interested in the program.

Host governments can be either facilitative or restrictive. In most instances in the sample it was the latter. Governmental approval had to be obtained on almost all matters requiring additional expenditures, such as new professorships, departments, or institutes. Curricular revision often involved governmental agencies. The Nebraska program in Turkey required extensive government approval. In some programs the host institution was a governmental agency. Some of the American universities had contracted directly with the host government even though an American foundation or ICA was financing the program. Under AID (ICA's successor), such direct contracting will be more common. Emphasis is on a host government's general development plan and on channeling financial, commodity, and human resources to help it carry the plan out. More specific host-government planning and approvals will thus be essential, and as host governments develop competence, they will do more of their own contracting directly.

Some of the larger sponsoring organizations such as the Ford Foundation and ICA have evidenced division of opinion within their agencies relative to university programs. For example, they have both field and central office staff. Each has functional and area specialists, and officials with greater and lesser degrees of over-all responsibility. Some of these groups may favor one arrangement more than do the others. Under Harold Stassen, the top Washington leadership in FOA pushed university contracts, while some of the field offices were reluctant partners. In regard to any proposed contract, one group may be against, another for a university program. Because the future of a program may depend on smooth relations with the financial sponsor, both host and American institutions need to be aware of the varying degrees of support within the sponsoring organization before undertaking it.

A continuing contribution to program plans, objectives, and methods has been made by ICA and the large foundations, especially the Ford Foundation, in projects they financed. In some instances the American university reciprocated, contributing to foundation or ICA program plans, as in Pakistan (Ford Foundation with several American universities) and Bolivia (ICA with Tennessee). The relationship of the sponsor to American university and host organization has varied from assistance to supervision. On occasion, ICA has threatened severe sanctions against a host government or institution in order to assure the American university of the necessary financing or space. ICA normally has taken an active interest in the development of work plans, and indeed has reserved the right of approval. Where disagreements have occurred, they have not often been sharp. When ICA has exercised its right to veto plans, it has placed its professional judgment ahead of that of the universities. This has caused a good deal of disagreement in a few ICA projects, such as the Minnesota-Korea program. Occasionally the Ford Foundation has had a similar problem, as in one case in India.

Special relations with third countries have occasionally been established, but they have not frequently affected work plans or methods. An exception is in British Africa, where newly emerging nations are asking for technical assistance. Representatives of American and British universities have tried to develop certain joint plans for assistance to higher education in Africa. This pattern may be applied in many new nations in that continent. For the most part, the French have looked with much disfavor on American efforts in former French possessions, and cooperative development of plans has not taken place.

To some extent, decision-making in university programs has been conditioned by public reaction. Special community programs, including talks, films, and radio presentations, have been developed abroad and at home as a public service and a means of assuring community support. Student demonstrations and strikes have affected technical assistance program policies in Mexico and Japan. In Mexico, the effect was to terminate Mexican interest in the Texas A and M program. In Japan, a student demonstration against the Michigan program helped turn the program away from curriculum and teaching, and led it instead in the direction of research.

Need for Continuous Planning and Assessment

Planning is affected by the length and duration of a project, its repetitive character, and its diversity as well as by the number of centers of decision-making. Effective planning is more than central leadership and involvement of many persons. Effective planning requires that project activities be continually reviewed, especially in relation to the objectives sought. The objectives themselves often must be questioned to see if they are appropriate, or the most appropriate. Planning breaks down as often on the content as on the procedure.

Continual planning is particularly important in technical assistance programs because the objective is to accomplish specific objectives and then phase out. Objectives and the methods of accomplishing them need to be reviewed from time to time in order to adjust operations to changing situations. Most projects issue periodic reports of progress, setting forth the accomplishments to date and the hopes for the future. American and host-country groups separately meet and discuss next steps or objectives. Some university programs include periodic meetings between American and host-country personnel, although these meetings are often highly formal. Work plans are drafted and discussed. In India, regional and even national conferences of Indian and American personnel in agricultural education have helped to review plans, objectives, and methods. Elsewhere, new institutions such as Ataturk University have been created, and in effect are a living, adaptable plan in action.

The most common shortcoming in planning is the failure to provide for continual review of project objectives and methods by the several parties concerned. There are several factors that explain this shortcoming. First, the contract itself tends to rigidify objectives and even methods. In some instances, American universities and host institutions are bound by arrangements that do not fit currently perceived needs. There seems no graceful way out for individuals or groups. The project continues beyond a time when it can possibly be useful. The New York University program in law and public administration in Turkey is illustrative. Of course, some lag is inevitable between perceived needs, contract authorization, and adjustment of project goals, methods, and personnel. An alternative method would be more general contracts or grants, with permission for an American and a host institution to use the money in some related activity if the original objectives turn out to be impossible to accomplish or undesirable. At a minimum, the original agreement should facilitate the withdrawal and addition of institutions participating in the program and should provide a way in which objectives, methods, and personnel could readily be changed.

Second, the need for continuous planning is not always evident to personnel associated with new projects. American universities become more concerned with continuous review of objectives after a project has been running for two to four years. The problems of program planning become more marked at such a point. Yet some contracts or grants have even been renewed with little evaluation of accomplishments to date. Regular yearly or biennial analyses are rare. One recent instance of a tripartite (sponsor and the two universities) review of a program before contract renewal occurred in Indiana's program at Thammasat University in Thailand.

Third, in technical assistance programs, over-all planning of any kind may be politically impossible, particularly in those countries in which a project may affect a number of host institutions. A demonstration project may be acceptable to one host university, but opposition would arise if others were asked to participate. In India, over-all planning for agricultural education covering several states was not politically possible. It is also impossible for many American states. While the broadest planning may thus be outside the scope of a single project, within a project the host institution and the American university can seek to develop careful plans and adapt them to changes in conditions as the project goes along.

Basically, planning is not pushed very far in most instances because there is disagreement on the objectives to be pursued and the methods to be used. The decisions to be made are often very difficult, and a full rationale is seldom agreed upon. What institutions, if any, should be created and in what order? What are the limits of absorption of innovations? What are the official priorities in growth? What subject matter areas most need development? Should extension activities have higher priority than teaching? The list of possible issues is a long one. Premature planning may result in freezing situations that either the host or American universities may regard as undesirable. Though planning is consistent with much freedom of action on the part of program personnel, specific plans are identified only after both parties have come to agree on their desirability. To return to the Indian example, American and Indian university representatives would not agree if they were pushed to define an ultimate plan for the development of one or more Indian agricultural colleges. The Indians are not certain among themselves what objectives to seek. American outsiders have little basis for insisting on an American pattern for the host country. In some projects, the specific objectives gradually evolve and are not necessarily all agreed upon at any one time.

By definition, program success depends upon innovations. In most situations, the probability of change will be greater if a long-range, educational approach is used, involving administrators and faculty members. Forcible introduction of change is a short-run technique that may or may not result in long-range acceptance of innovation. Its major usefulness is in a few technical assistance programs where no host institution exists, pending its development. Where American or host institutions already exist, a broad base of decision-making usually makes the acceptance of innovations more probable, especially when their acceptance depends on the voluntary cooperation of many people.

Chapter 12

SELECTING THE TECHNICAL ASSISTANCE TEAM

One school of thought contends that only with good personnel can a technical assistance program succeed. Good personnel brings good performance while poor personnel brings poor performance. Another school of thought argues with equal cogence that given a good program, high quality personnel will be attracted to it. In fact, there is a mutual dependence. Good personnel and good programs are often found together, as are poor personnel and poor programs. Each helps to reinforce the other.

Exactly what constitutes good personnel varies from project to project, since no two projects have exactly the same needs in regard to quantity, quality, or kinds of talent. While allowance for such differing requirements must be made, many similarities of needs do exist among technical assistance programs.

A chief adviser or group leader who heads the field party abroad is the person on whom the success of the project most depends (Smith, pp. 78–83). He is in charge of a team of varying size, often five to ten, but occasionally smaller or substantially larger. In addition to the subject matter specialists, a project normally has an administrative officer who handles the dozens of details concerning housing, transportation, secretarial and special local help, shipment of equipment, goods, and materials, and communications. On the American campus, a coordinator helps direct the university's support of the project and serves as a liaison with the central office of the financing organization. In large programs he may be assisted by his own administrative officer. Sometimes he has an advisory committee of administrators or professors. Programs of technical assistance abroad may also involve some participation by members of the financing organization, although normally this duty requires only a small part of the regular time of a staff member. Host-country personnel seldom spend full time on a university technical assistance program. The key persons are the host-country director and his chief adviser.

Qualities Related to Job Success

Personnel requirements vary in accordance with the personnel structure of each program. Obviously the qualifications for the chief adviser of a one- or two-man project may be quite different from those in a large undertaking. There are also many diversities among the job qualifications within projects. The qualifications for chief adviser are not those for other project personnel, and the qualifications for host-country nationals differ from those for Americans. However, if a distinction is made between the qualifications for a specific job and the broad qualities related to success of the program, it is apparent that the broad qualities leading to success are similar in all jobs and programs.

Perhaps the point may be illustrated best if the qualities for a certain kind of personnel, American professors overseas, are examined in detail. The data available from the present survey bearing on job success are primarily derived from programs rather than from individuals. Questions were asked to ascertain the qualities sought by the program director and the qualities typical of the personnel actually recruited, as judged by those closely associated with the program. Qualities found in the more successful programs are the basis for the following conclusions.

There are three criteria for success in technical assistance programs abroad that are primary in importance. Each is a necessary ingredient to any substantial degree of success. Together they may even be sufficient to assure success in some instances.

1. The quality most related to job success for American professors overseas is professional competence. The other qualities are irrelevant unless the test of professional competence can be met. But professional competence is many-sided.

Mastery of subject is one element. A choice must be made as to the breadth and degree of competence in subject matter. Is a social scientist needed, or just an economist? If the latter, a public finance specialist or one in economic development? The process can be carried on almost indefinitely, until the specifications define the competence of a single man. In practice, highly specialized competence has not been a necessary criterion, since it is not often possible to predict in advance the exact requirements of an overseas position.

Professional qualification has another element, *competence in the role to be played.* A professor may be a good teacher, or a good researcher, or a good consultant, or a good administrator. Each of these requires a different manner of communication with host-country nationals. Relatively few professors achieve high competence in all four of these activities, although skill in two or three is frequent. Each of these major roles can be broken into smaller units. For example, the ability to teach undergraduates in a foreign setting is not the same as the ability to teach graduate students. The ability to give leadership to a group is not the same as the ability to perform the tasks of administrative officer. Underlying all the roles is the fact that professors in technical assistance projects are expected to be change agents to a much greater degree than they are at home. The roles in which a professor has competence ought to be those he is called upon to play abroad.

In addition, technical assistance requires that a person grasp the broader significance of what he and his counterpart are doing abroad, how the subject matter and role fit into the larger framework of society. In the case of a professor relating to higher education abroad, the desired quality is *competence as an educator.* Higher education is more than a combination of specialized subject matter areas. To be an educator requires knowledge of educational processes as a whole and an appreciation of the role that universities play in society. The professor who has taken time to understand the entire system of American education, for example, is much better qualified for an overseas post than a person who remains merely a subject matter specialist. If an educator-professor understands the relation of his specialty to one system of higher education, he is in a better position to become acquainted with the main features of the host-country's system and to associate with it. He may even be able to suggest modifications in both systems as the result of his experiences. Breadth of knowledge as an educator may be more important than specialized knowledge of a subject.

2. Each of the several elements of professional qualification have different applications or meanings abroad than they have in the

United States. A professor may be quite competent in each element at home, but overseas it is necessary for him to be able to *adjust professionally* to conditions in the host country. The role to be played will vary even if, for example, he teaches graduate students in both places. There will be special local applications of subject matter. And the place of higher education in the broader social framework will most likely be strikingly different. The American professor overseas is often called upon to perform unexpected roles on short notice. Many professors at American universities desire to be left alone to pursue their own objectives without interruption. Some of them chose university work in part because they wanted to be independent. Abroad, they will have to be somewhat different kinds of educators, working under markedly different conditions.

3. Programs in which personnel are *enthusiastic* about and *dedicated* to the task they are performing tend to be those that have a large measure of success in meeting their objectives. There is a two-way relation between enthusiasm and success; each tends to support the other. Some persons are not interested in assignment overseas, and others are more challenged by such an opportunity than they would be by a somewhat similar role at home. Those who go abroad should be centrally motivated by the task to be undertaken, rather than by concerns peripheral to the program. Whether the task be teaching, research, consulting, or administering, enthusiasm and dedication are second only to professional competence in importance in job success abroad.

In most instances, these three major criteria for job success must be accompanied by one or more other attributes if job performance is to be truly at a high level:

4. Special problems of *personal cultural adjustment* are present in an overseas assignment. Some individuals like conditions in the host country better than those at home, while others find adjustment difficult. The demands of each individual's personality are different, and so are each culture's expectations in regard to individual behavior. Thus, some traits of personality make a better impression abroad than others. Being friendly, getting along well with others, possessing good manners—personal traits such as these in the staff member and his entire family contribute to effectiveness on the job. Yet the ingredients that make for "being friendly," "getting along well with others," or "good manners" vary widely indi-

vidually and culturally. Aside from pleasant manners, culturally defined, the visiting American needs capacity to adjust to a strange environment. The problems of leaving home and of cultural shock are well publicized. For example, a willingness of the staff member and his family to put up with markedly different and often inferior living conditions is helpful. It is important not just that good adjustment may make more friends for the United States, but that it frees energies for the professional task at hand. It is, to be sure, no substitute for professional competence or enthusiasm and dedication as has been demonstrated by some university programs.

5. *Cultural empathy* implies not only knowledge, enthusiasm, and adjustment, but understanding, the ability to project oneself into another's position, and in general a great interest in things that are different from the way they are back home. It involves acceptance of the host institution's objectives and working for them without sacrificing American university objectives. Staying American and yet developing a feeling for the host point of view—this is the desirable quality. Faculty members with a high degree of cultural empathy will also be those who are themselves receptive to innovations. It is a trait that is appropriate for receivers as well as donors in cultural exchange. As W. H. Griffin has described it relative to Afghanistan:

> It goes without saying that few individuals born and raised in Western culture can after maturity develop complete identity with people of the East. To be effective in educational work technicians must, however, have a sincere desire to learn about and understand the host country and its people. This involves study of the history and culture. It involves bending a sympathetic ear to explanations of apparently enigmatic features of every day life. It means seeking opportunities to meet the local people on their own ground. It means ridding one's mind of the idea that in every way our own country is superior to the underdeveloped country. It means searching for the reasons why things are as they are.[1]

6. To all these desired qualities must be added the ability to get the job done or *facility at implementation*. An individual may be professionally competent in all senses of that term, he may adjust well professionally and personally, be enthusiastic about his assignment, and possess cultural empathy, but he may not have the drive

[1] "American Educators Abroad," *Journal of Teacher Education*, vol. 11, March, 1960, p. 34.

that is essential to completing a task, and completing it well. He may not enjoy finishing an assignment, "buttoning it up," like the doctoral candidate who is brilliant but never completes his degree. Even more than the doctoral candidate, the professor abroad usually has a time limit for his work. In technical assistance, to be sure, the personal drive for productivity must be qualified by the realities of the situation; innovation cannot be pushed too fast. There must be professional adjustment or a "sense for politics."[2] The American professor abroad must know how hard and how far he can push without injuring the objective he seeks. Technical assistance is often painstakingly slow. Yet the inner ability to complete an assignment underlies success in even the most sensitive job for the American professor overseas.

Other desired qualities pale in significance to these six. They may be important in certain special circumstances, but are not attributes generally necessary. For example, for what period of time should a person be available to carry on an overseas assignment? The answer depends on several factors, including the kind of program and the nature of its objectives. Continuity of personnel is not necessarily desirable, nor are long terms abroad, although the presumption favors continuity and long terms. Short-term assignments, however, can be effective with some members of a team when used in combination with long terms for other members, or when used with host institutions that have a high capacity to absorb innovations. In the University of Minnesota program in Korea, the medical, agricultural, and engineering phases of the programs use short-term personnel; it is reasoned that these fields already have been well established at the host university. In public administration, a new program is being developed with Minnesota's help, and it is thought essential that long-term personnel be sent. The truly outstanding person is always wanted for a longer period,

---

[2] The term is from Harland Cleveland, Gerald J. Mangone, and John Clarke Adams, *The Overseas Americans* (New York: McGraw-Hill, 1960), pp. 142–149. Five traits for effective overseas performance are listed by these authors: technical skill, belief in mission, cultural empathy, a sense for politics, and organization ability. In general, the findings here are similar, except for the present emphasis on professional and personal adjustment and the spelling out of the several aspects of professional competence, differences that perhaps are explained by the focus on individual projects in the present study and on overseasmanship in general by Cleveland, Mangone, and Adams.

no matter when he must cease his connection with a project; his less esteemed colleague may not be wanted beyond his original tour of duty. Turnover in personnel can favor innovation as well as hinder it, by bringing new forces to bear on a situation.

Special knowledge of the host country and of its prevailing language are qualities often sought. Area and language knowledge applicable to a given host country is not to be found among many professors in most fields. This is true even though some faculty members in the social sciences and the humanities may have specialized in one foreign area or another as graduate students and later as professors, and even though many faculty members may have had previous experience abroad as a tourist if not in a professional capacity. Area specialization, though it is not a part of professional competence as normally defined in most fields, is a desirable quality for the faculty member who goes abroad.

English is such a universal language, and so much is available in it, that unless a scholar has an area specialty, knowledge of a foreign language does not loom large in his search for employment in the United States. Abroad, also, command of English is highly advantageous. Except in French and Spanish-speaking countries, English can get the American professor far in discussions with host-country university personnel. Yet knowledge of the local tongue has both psychological and substantive advantages. It leads to closer rapport with the host-country personnel; it is an indication of interest in their culture. It will also facilitate informal communication on professional matters.

Age and experience are especially prized in the American professor abroad by some host-university representatives. Most other countries place greater value on age and experience than does the United States. In addition, if professors with known reputations are sent abroad, the host institution takes this as an indication of interest in the project on the part of the American university. Host-country nationals are anxious that an American university send well-known professors. In some cases their view is well taken, especially where a host university wishes top-level advice relative to a firmly established faculty or institute. Yet it is unrealistic to assume that only top persons should or can be sent abroad. Persons with international reputations may not be the best for a particular assignment, even if they are available. A strong desire for outstanding authorities may be incompatible with the aims of university programs in the long run. Few American universities can continually provide top-level experts from their own staffs. They could become mere recruiting agencies if the idea were pushed too far. Furthermore, experience is not just a matter of age or reputation— experience in the particular work that needs to be done under the program is the most significant element. This point is frequently not understood, especially in programs that have rather vague objectives.

As a rule, reputation as a subject matter specialist is the best-known quality, but it may not be the most important aspect of professional competence. Some countries advisedly ask for certain kinds of experience in seeking an American university affiliation. Experience at a land-grant university is an example, since this kind of institution might make a contribution if it were adapted to host-country conditions. In contrast, the experience of teaching law in Turkey may or may not be a qualification for directing research in law in Japan.

The qualities related to job success of American professors abroad are also applicable in the United States in large measure. Adjustment and cultural empathy are needed as a professor goes from one university to another, from one subculture to another. Professional competence, dedication, and an ability to get the job done are central requisites, just as they are abroad.

What, then, is different about working abroad? In terms of the qualities that make for job success, not much. Apparently some persons do succeed better abroad than in the United States, some succeed better in the United States, and others are equally successful or unsuccessful in the two locations. The difference in success is due less to any unique qualities of personnel needed abroad than to the fact that often a professor performs a task that is radically different from his task in the United States. The professor who goes abroad changes jobs, and the new job is often very different from the one to which he is accustomed. In the United States he has probably been a teacher-researcher-specialist. Abroad he is often a combination of consultant-administrator-general educator. Many professors cannot make this dramatic shift. Differences in job requirements such as this have probably had more to do with lack of job success abroad than the more publicized cultural shock factors.

Qualities Obtained in Personnel

No institution can be expected to recruit persons all of whom perfectly fulfill such all-encompassing requirements. Yet it is necessary to inquire how many of these qualities have been reflected in actual selections. The results, as judged by those associated with the programs, are modest.

The overwhelming majority of the American professors abroad had real professional competence of one kind or another as judged by their peers. Particularly, they had mastery of specialized subject matter. If there were few outstanding authorities among them, there were also few incompetents in the fields concerned. Most rated better than average within their professions at home. However, there were many square pegs chosen to fill round holes. Professors competent in one part of a discipline were called upon to fill a job abroad emphasizing a different part. More frequently, professors were asked to widen their horizons to discipline-wide or interdisciplinary dimensions. For example, a professor of political science from a Western state university became a social science specialist in a Middle Eastern university.

The greatest professional shortcoming of American professors abroad was their competence as educators; most had had little opportunity to reflect about higher education as a whole either at home or abroad before their assignment overseas. American professors seldom have had any formal training in American or comparative higher education. Except for those few who have pursued independent reading on the matter or who have served on university committees whose terms of reference have concerned broad issues of higher education, professors may not be prepared for this aspect of overseas assignments.

When research and teaching were the activities concerned, most of the professors overseas performed acceptably. There were notable shortcomings in administrative ability on the part of the chief adviser, and in consulting ability on the part of those expected to use that means. A consultant is of necessity "other-oriented"; few university professors excel in this trait. The typical Western state university political scientist sent to the Middle East not only broadened his field, but changed from a teacher-researcher to a consultant-administrator.

Of all the criteria, enthusiasm for and dedication to the professional task varied the most, project to project. Keeping professional objectives paramount amid concern with administrative red tape was sometimes difficult. Many professors and their wives developed what can be called the "2s, 2h syndrome." The syndrome is identified by the following symptoms: the victim constantly and almost exclusively talks about servants and souvenirs and about housing and health problems in the host country. An engineering professor and his wife from a Southern state university working in a South Asian country exemplified the 2s, 2h syndrome almost perfectly throughout several hours of conversation. Professional objectives were pushed into the background.

A majority of the professors abroad had good professional reasons for going, but these were not the only reason; in some cases they were completely absent. The range of motives is illustrated in the technical assistance programs in Indonesia. There, about a quarter of the American professors had religious or missionary-type motives such as to be their brother's keeper or to help less fortunate peoples to the best of their ability (Smith, p. 90). Such enthusiasm led some to make excellent personal adjustments with Indonesians. Among motives, many professors ranked high the pleasures and value of an overseas trip for themselves and their families, and the substantial increase in income that accompanied it. Some came over for professional reasons, wanting to learn about Indonesia as applied to their field, or desiring to teach or carry on research in their specialties. Some valued the friends they made, and others the prestige accorded them as professors in a foreign setting. Some were trying to escape from some unpleasant situation at home, such as marital or job difficulties, or they felt that they had been sent overseas in order to be pushed aside or placed out of the way. Such individuals are often looking for opportunities to go abroad. It is important, although not easy, to identify them in the selection process so that their applications can be set aside if their difficulties would be likely to interfere with job success overseas.

While professional competence, adjustment, and dedication were the most essential qualities for success of the program, other qualities contributed to the same end and were to be found in favorable quantity in fewer instances. For example, in Asia and Africa fewer than one in ten professors had fluency in the indigenous language, and most had limited knowledge of the area. Even in Latin America or in French-speaking areas, a minority of American professors had fluency in the second language adequate to lecture in it. A large majority of the professors were on their first overseas assignment and lacked experience in technical assistance. The professor and wife from a private Eastern university sent to the Middle East, who devoted a large portion of their day-to-day conversation to criticizing the host-country people, were startling exceptions to the rule. Yet real cultural empathy was characteristic of less than a majority of the American professors abroad.

The quality of host-country personnel, in the long run, determines results more than that of American personnel. The host-country staff must bear the responsibility for continuing the operation of the faculty, department, or institute. For the most part, host-country staff members exhibited more shortcomings in qualities related to achievement of project goals than their American counterparts. Particularly this was true of part-time staff members and the host-country project director. If the staff members served only part time they often had little interest in the program and the changes it was to introduce. They exhibited little cultural empathy toward things American and little enthusiasm for the project. They were mainly concerned with other matters. Normally a few persons had special interest in a project, but there were programs in which no discernible interest was present on the part of any host-country staff member, as in two projects in Turkey, one in Pakistan, and one in Mexico. At another extreme, there were a few projects in which the initiative and interest came mainly from host-institution nationals.

The host-country project directors were frequently on part time, and were appointed because of their ability, the prestige accorded them, or the political influence they enjoyed. They sometimes were poor administrators by American standards, failing to make decisions, to delegate authority, or to involve subordinate personnel in policy discussions. Their part-time status and high prestige on occasion resulted in a widening gulf between them and their full-time staff members (if any) who had been trained by American faculty members. This was apparent in a project in Italy.

Type of motivation as well as degree of interest varied. Some host-country professors accepted technical assistance programs of American universities for professional reasons. They wanted to develop a new aspect of their discipline, they prized the interchange of ideas that would take place, or they wanted American professors to demonstrate a different way of looking at things. Yet acceptance of American professors was often the result of a desire to fill vacant posts with free labor from abroad, or to obtain free trips to the United States. In a technical assistance program, the equipment obtained was sometimes valued more highly than the American professors. Fourah Bay College in Sierra Leone actually received ICA-financed equipment without the "necessity" of accepting American professors. Both equipment and professors were usually badly needed, but stress on material aspects of a program limited the innovations that could be introduced.

It is difficult, and somewhat unfair, to compare the quality of the personnel of the host-country institution with the quality of visitors from the American university. American faculty members were usually far more advanced in their respective disciplines than host personnel. However, there were teams of American professors who were not taken seriously by host personnel because the latter were of higher quality than the former; an instance of this took place in Pakistan.

American and host-country institutions have not approached an ideal standard in the personnel selected. In comparison with other groups operating overseas, however, consensus was that although on the average personnel associated with university programs fell somewhat short of the best, they were far ahead of the worst. The comparison was not undertaken directly by the present study, but opinions on the subject were expressed by those interviewed. For example, in technical assistance work, American universities were thought inferior in recruiting as compared with foundations which carry on programs directly. But the universities were believed to be doing a better job than ICA, although there were notable exceptions. The universities recruited better people than most of the private consulting agencies, in the opinion of those who discussed the subject. It should be kept in mind that universities usually do a different kind of recruiting than do other agencies; the latter are far less concerned with obtaining academic personnel. Since what is "better" may sometimes be thought equivalent to "more academically respectable," a standard unfair to ICA and the consulting firms may result. An academically qualified person is not necessarily the best choice for all technical assistance positions.

Improvement of the Quality of Personnel

There are limits beyond which American universities cannot improve the quality of personnel associated with their technical assistance programs. Many of the persons affiliated indirectly with the projects are not and never will be specially selected for the purpose. Some more or less select themselves. This is particularly true of some of the American campus coordinators. A university may have a choice not among various qualified persons, but between a self-designated person who takes the initiative and no program at all. Stanford and California, Chicago and Michigan State, New York and Harvard: all present instances of coordinators selecting themselves or of persons automatically given the responsibility because of other administrative positions they hold.

Staff members from the host country often are not specially selected for a program. Host-country professors who have seniority may be those with whom a technical assistance team will have to work if a project is undertaken. Some of the Indian programs illustrate the point well. There are thus practical limitations on the freedom to select, which in some instances may be so narrow as to throw doubt on the wisdom of entering into a program.

Nevertheless, universities employing present practices are not selecting the best among those who can be chosen. In several ways the personnel of university technical assistance programs can be improved in quality.

Systematic Identification of Desired Qualities. Specifications of desired qualities for American staff members abroad or host-country personnel has been haphazard and irregular; it was almost completely lacking in many instances. Those who select have images of the kind of person to be sought, but there is no formal list of qualities, with or without priorities.

In both the United States and the host country there are few candidates among whom to choose. It is felt that rules of thumb can govern choices among a handful of candidates—if indeed there is more than one. The shortcoming in this reasoning is that in some instances no one ought to be selected where personnel is as scarce as this. American and host-country institutions have erred in valuing fulfillment of quotas above the need for competence.

If specific criteria were adopted, the poorly qualified person who is "the best of the lot" would more often remain home.

One reason for lack of specifications is the informality with which all faculty personnel are recruited in the United States. Each university and department tends to have its own system. Only the rare department bothers to spell out the exact qualities it desires in a new faculty member, other than vague references to rank, salary, and subject matter specialization. Departments recruit for overseas positions in much the same manner. The "rub" is that a different combination of qualities is often needed for an overseas assignment. Since most departments have not had much experience in recruiting for assignments abroad, they may not recognize this difference if they do not spell out the qualities they are seeking. Specifications of the qualities sought would offer a guide not only for departments but also for potential recruits.

Enlargement of the Number of Potential Recruits. The usefulness of systematic criteria for personnel would be enhanced if there were more capable people available from whom to choose. As for host-country personnel, to increase competition for jobs may require a substantial increase in salaries paid to the relevant host-institution personnel, training of many more qualified persons, and creation of a new or enlarged faculty, department, or institute. In some countries, such as Japan, India, and Pakistan, there is a great surplus of qualified personnel in some fields.

American universities have found that the major personnel problems begin in the third or fourth years of a project, or when a second or third project in a single field is accepted by a university. For example, the University of Tennessee sent mainly its own staff members to Bolivia during the first two years of its project there, but thereafter had to look elsewhere for more recruits. The Tennessee experience has been repeated elsewhere, over and over again. Johns Hopkins has rather ambitious and unique overseas programs in Italy, Burma, and Indonesia. It has had some difficulty in staffing at least the last of these because the School of Advanced International Studies (SAIS), which is in charge of all three programs, simply does not have a large enough staff to keep the programs going with top-level personnel.

Broadly, scarcity of faculty members for service abroad can be avoided by concentrating programs in the stronger departments or universities and by developing interinstitutional programs. ICA has recently moved in the latter direction, and the Ford Foundation's use of the University of the State of New York is somewhat akin to an interinstitutional program.

A department that has a large commitment to overseas programs may choose among four policies. It may develop a separate foreign service of its own that can go from program to program, or expand its home staff enough to meet needs for personnel, or recruit on an *ad hoc* basis, or give up some of its programs.

Johns Hopkins has come as close as any university to creating its own foreign service. A separate little foreign service may be feasible for some of the major universities, although reliance on it would probably minimize the impact of technical assistance on the American campus and on its academic objectives. Universities would act as contracting or consulting agencies in this activity, not as institutions of higher education. Where academic programs abroad utilize nonacademic personnel in supporting roles, a university foreign service of such persons might prove useful.

Expanding the home staff sufficiently to meet certain personnel needs abroad may not only be possible and desirable for the program, but advantageous to the home department. Several universities have had this experience. The department of government of Indiana University used its public administration program in Thailand as a device for expanding and developing the department. Michigan State has similarly used its business administration program in Brazil.

The use of outside *ad hoc* recruiting has varied from virtually none at all to the selection of almost all personnel in this manner. At the time field research was undertaken for the present project, the Harvard business administration program at Istanbul and the New York University public administration project at Ankara relied primarily on specially recruited personnel. The California-Bologna and Nebraska-Ankara and Ataturk programs, on the contrary, used many faculty members from their home campuses. The Peabody teacher education and the Minnesota public administration efforts in Korea were largely staffed by outsiders, the Minnesota-Korean program in medicine, engineering, and agriculture by campus professors.

Hiring of outside staff members on an *ad hoc* basis can include various conditions of employment. The most common arrangement is to hire a person for a specified tour of duty and provide nothing further. Some universities have given outsiders permanent jobs, sending them overseas for their first assignments. In other instances the recruits have been promised a year's employment on the home campus on return, or help in finding another job. Such assurances may aid in recruitment and they may also help an outsider feel more a part of a university group.

Those institutions that have been willing to invest some of their own personnel resources abroad have tended to obtain better staff on an *ad hoc* basis, when needed. Association with the home staff sent abroad has offered attractions for potential recruits, and is a symbol of institutional concern for the program. Those institutions that have shown genuine enthusiasm for an overseas program, whether or not they have been able to send their own staff members abroad, have been more successful than others in *ad hoc* recruiting. For example, Peabody, being a small institution, has not had many staff members to send, but it has been able to recruit able persons, in part because of the energy and enthusiasm invested in the program on the home campus. Recruiting for overseas work is comparable in some respects to recruiting for the home campus. It is much more difficult for a less well-known institution such as Kentucky to recruit outstanding men for foreign service than for Harvard or California. Where the former type of institution succeeds, it must make a much greater effort; institutions of the latter type can more easily recruit able faculty members for service abroad. Association with the name Harvard, even on a temporary overseas basis, may pay handsome personal dividends.

Those institutions that largely send their own staffs abroad often have the most successful programs, though not always by any means. The successes may be explained in part by the fact that home recruitment signifies interest in the program on the part of the relevant departments. Such interest, plus a high level of competence in a department, characterizes a large percentage of successful programs. The chief adviser ought to be chosen from the university that assumes responsibility for a program. In this case the program will probably yield the largest possible benefits to the American university; and there will be more likelihood of program continuity and a greater probability that administrative liaison will be effective. In programs with many faculty members overseas, a nucleus from the responsible university will emphasize connections with the responsible university and facilitate more effective team spirit and cooperation.

A high percentage of home staff members among the group abroad does not always mean that the team will be of high quality or constitute an adequate staff for the job. Universities do not always send their best people. Some universities have sent retired or nearly retired persons abroad for little other reason than that they were no longer wanted at home. This happened in one of the programs in India. Younger staff members, not among the best in a department, have also been attached to programs abroad because they were thought good enough for a job overseas. This happened in one of the programs in Thailand.

A little more than half of the institutions in the sample assigned a cross section of the "best they had" to their programs abroad, judging by a comparison of the ranks of those abroad with the ranks of those at home and the opinions obtained in interviews. This pattern prevails, country to country and region to region. It also prevails among various subject matter fields and different kinds of programs. This is not to say that 50 per cent of the faculty members abroad were as competent as might be wished. It is to say that in this percentage of programs, American universities were represented by a typical group of their own professors at the several ranks, whether they were well suited to the task at hand or not. Usually, however, a cross section of the professors of a strong department is adequate for the needs of the program if there is dedication to the objectives sought and if the roles to be played are familiar. The requirements of most programs are not so stringent that only full professors of international reputation can fulfill them.

The release of staff members from a department may be painful. It interferes with teaching and other activities on the home campus. Students may suffer. Small departments or those that are just developing or expanding may find it especially painful to send faculty members abroad, even though the sacrifice may ultimately assist them in their expansion plans. Competing departments within or outside the university may gain advantage in the interim.

In order to avoid these unhappy consequences, some departments have made qualified staff members available for assignment abroad on only a short-term basis, as in certain programs in Peru and Korea. Used properly, short-term personnel can be highly effective, but usually some long-term personnel must set the stage for them.

If a program places too heavy a burden on the American university, it would perhaps be better that the host institution contract with a nonuniversity group, for recruiting services only. Many departments have turned down invitations to engage in technical assistance programs because of personnel shortages. More should do so unless their faculty members can and will serve abroad.

Recruitment and Selection Procedures. In addition to increasing the number and quality of faculty members among whom effective choices can be made, better personnel can be obtained for the technical assistance programs of American universities by better recruitment and selection procedures.

Recruitment carried out by the regular academic units is normally more productive of high-level personnel than that carried out by special groups or campus coordinators. One of the most remarkable programs from the standpoint of recruiting able personnel is the Ohio University project in Nigeria. In the early days of the project, good persons were identified for each job, for the duration of the project on a rotating two-year basis. The dean involved felt great interest, and several regular departments recruited from their own staffs. But there is no immutable principle here. Sometimes an individual department is of poor quality or is opposed to a program and has to be by-passed. In most such instances, however, the program should never have been started unless the department was an exception among several which were competent and interested. Cooperation between the program coordinator, his advisory committee, if any, and the relevant regular departments, with recruitment through the latter, will best assure competent personnel. The regular departments have closer contacts with faculty members and the profession generally; this gives them a natural advantage in personnel selection. Most of the personnel sent abroad is not recruited by the regular departments.

If well qualified academic personnel are desired, one way to obtain them is to emphasize high academic standards and objectives. Some of the recruiting appeals have lost sight of program aims. Practice is mixed, but the more serious aspects of an experience abroad are frequently underplayed. Faculty members are told how much money they will make, what a wonderful experience the family will have, how easy it is to employ servants, and how interesting will be the souvenirs they can bring back. There is nothing wrong in mentioning such items, but to give the impression that they constitute the main reason for going abroad, and that the professional or academic reasons are secondary, adversely affects the selection process. No university in the sample was guilty of telling faculty members that professional and academic objectives were unimportant. Most mentioned the real objectives and explained in detail some of the perquisites. The relative emphasis in a substantial minority of programs is revealed by the frequent comment of faculty members abroad: "The university did not explain to me what I was to do when I got over here." Such a comment reflects inadequacy in the recruiting process, the appeal used, and the kind of personnel it attracted.

Procedures for selecting American personnel in technical assistance programs are exceedingly complicated; nominations must be approved by the American university, the host institution, the sponsoring organization, and the host government. In addition, each organization may require approval, for example, by a selection committee, a department chairman, a program coordinator, a dean, an academic vice president, a president, and a board of university trustees. Some of these approvals are likely to be formalities, but they all take time. In some of the more complicated cases, it is necessary to allow eighteen months or more from the start of the recruiting process until the chosen person arrives overseas. Seldom is the process carried out in less than six. The period of recruitment cannot be much shortened, unless one or more organizations forego their desire to be consulted. Many universities have not made adequate allowance for the time consumed in recruiting personnel in the early years of a project. Institutions which have taken their responsibilities seriously have been forced to make adjustments in the first year or two.

Selection of host-country staff members is normally not a function of Americans. However, where new members are to be selected Americans have often given advice. In some cases, the advice has been useful, especially when the host country has been uncertain about the kind of persons most suitable for the new undertaking. Where a host-country director has been selected after American personnel are in the country, consultation has often occurred, but most American universities have judiciously underplayed their hands on this sensitive situation. The most positive role of American universities has been in selection of trainees who some day may become staff members of the host institution. Here Americans have commonly exercised a veto and have taken initiative in turning up qualified recruits.

Increase in Job Attractiveness. The outstanding individual who is challenged by the professional objectives of a job will, of course, be concerned primarily with the aims of a project and the resources available to accomplish them. They are discussed in detail in another chapter.

Having satisfied himself as to the professional nature of a project, the potential recruit will then turn to other aspects of the possible employment. Supporting perquisites are an essential element in a technical assistance program, although they should not constitute the main reason for going abroad. The desire to go abroad under such a university program is not alone enough to attract qualified persons. There are many drawbacks to participation in international programs, professionally as well as personal. Among the professional disadvantages are a loss of accustomed contacts during the period abroad, with adverse consequences for promotion, knowledge of job opportunities, participation in professional conferences, and perhaps even publication. Equipment, laboratories, supplies, and library facilities may be more adequate at home. Staff members should increasingly be given facilities and opportunities abroad such as resources to attend professional meetings on occasion, provision for publication, and rapid development of library and laboratories.

On the personal side, faculty members and families hesitate to go to countries where living conditions may be hazardous to health and housing may be inconvenient. Faculty members with school children, particularly those with children in high school, hesitate to go to countries where schools are deemed inferior. This eliminates from overseas assignments some professors who are in their most productive years.

Disadvantages such as these have been overcome in some instances by obtaining adequate faculty housing, providing good medical facilities, developing financial incentives, etc. These are important to the success of any international program. Their possible negative effect, if carried to an extreme, is attraction of persons who are interested mainly in comfortable and profitable living abroad and alienation of host-country nationals whose living levels do not begin to compare with those of their visitors. Extreme instances of this kind occurred in a minority of the projects, and were most frequent in the less successful technical assistance projects.

Preparation and Briefing. Ideally, an assignment abroad should be preceded by fairly long professional preparation. Some faculty members have spent from several months to a year or two in this way. Knowledge specially applicable to the country concerned, be it language, area, or subject matter knowledge, is obtainable in this manner. Professional competence can be enhanced. At present, selection procedures for faculty members often preclude adequate preparation, since they are completed only a short time before the reporting date overseas. The results achieved through briefing depend not only on the length of time available and the care with which the activities are planned, but also on the type of recruits. Effective briefing requires persons who in the broadest sense of the term are prepared for their assignment abroad. In a more fundamental sense briefing merges with on-the-job training, learning, and planning. In the more successful programs this fact was not overlooked.

The more extensive briefing activities have concentrated on program operations and objectives, the role of the recruit in them, area and language training, and details of living abroad. Good briefing programs can facilitate adjustment and heighten enthusiasm and dedication, area and language skills, and cultural empathy, the latter two of which are not typical of university personnel abroad. They have little effect on the academic or professional competence of individuals or their ability to see an assignment through to completion, two of the more important qualifications, but at least the former of which is usually found in professors overseas.

Professors who are to go abroad may be briefed by those who have returned from a previous assignment with the project. Facilities of the consulates or embassies are sometimes used, as are those of ICA or a large foundation. Conversations with host-country participants take place. In some African technical assistance programs, preliminary briefing in the metropole country has been undertaken; for example, Ohio University sent its whole team, including families, to the United Kingdom for briefing before they went to Nigeria. There is a tendency to lengthen briefing periods, but the six weeks' briefing of the Michigan-Waseda program is still highly unusual. Some project reports and a few days of discussions may be all that is provided; the prospective travelers are told to "play it by ear" when they arrive overseas.

By all odds the most extensive experiment in briefing programs was the Ford Foundation-sponsored summer briefing program in 1958 at Cornell, for all Ford-financed personnel going to Indonesia, including personnel from university programs. Language and area training was given to staff members and their families over the summer term. The results were immediately evident on their arrival in Indonesia, especially to the Indonesians.

This experiment is suggestive of a possible pattern that could be used for both university and nonuniversity program personnel. One of the great barriers to the development of special briefing programs is the small number of persons sent abroad at any one time by any one program. It is too expensive in time and money to organize an elaborate briefing program for a few persons. Pooling of briefing services for government, business, and university personnel would make possible longer and more intensive briefing.

Some of the larger centers for area studies could serve as central briefing stations, offering ten- to twelve-week sessions the year round for the country or countries in which they specialize. ICA has made use of such centers for training some of its personnel. The School of Advanced International Studies of Johns Hopkins has conducted seminars for ICA on development planning, Ohio State has organized one on advanced supply management, and the African Studies Program of Boston University has trained ICA staff members headed for Africa. Programs such as these, particularly of the Boston University type, could form the nucleus of combined training opportunities for personnel going abroad. The combined sessions could offer area and language instruction and give background information on the problems and mechanics of living overseas. For university personnel, special attention could be focused on the university systems of the countries concerned. For those playing special roles abroad, the problems associated with that role could be emphasized, such as those of a consultant in fostering change in a foreign environment. If repeated a few times a year, briefing center programs would also help to eliminate one shortcoming of the Cornell-Ford-Indonesia experiment, namely, the necessity of holding all personnel in the United States until they could attend a single briefing program so that a flood of new persons arrived abroad at once.

Briefing should be carried on both before and after going abroad. Several countries sponsor briefing sessions or institutes for foreign students and/or professors: India at the University of Delhi, Indonesia at Bandung, Italy at Perugia, and others. Extended over several weeks, these programs can help the visitor to meet his host and get to know his point of view, as well as impart language and area training.

Personnel procedures derive their significance and much of their effectiveness from the program itself. Given an attractive and challenging professional undertaking, the appropriate procedures can locate high-quality personnel. For an ill-considered program even the best personnel procedures may be of no avail.

Most of the personnel participating in most of the technical assistance programs of American universities have been of acceptable quality in the eyes of informed observers. With more attention to improved procedures, universities could obtain, on the average, a markedly higher quality of faculty member.

Chapter 13

ACHIEVEMENTS OF UNIVERSITY TECHNICAL ASSISTANCE ABROAD

Activities of American universities abroad must be judged by their results. The programs cannot be evaluated merely by the number of projects, the costs, or the number of persons involved. First, we must ask what the immediate objectives were and what innovations the effort has stimulated. That is the subject of this chapter. Then we must inquire whether these changes approached the chosen long-term goals, and, most important of all, whether the goals were well chosen. Such issues form the subject of Chapter 14.

The present survey observed programs in a single year of their operation. It may have been their first year, the second, or the *n*th year. To conclude that a project had little impact simply because little change was observed may be inaccurate. Change does not occur in neat yearly cycles. Opposition to some programs appears insurmountable for several years. All of a sudden, opposition may recede and change become evident. Consequently, it is difficult to judge the ultimate impact of a program from what is observable in the short run.

Some accomplishments can be identified or measured easily, while others cannot. Innovations in organization, laws, curricula, library holdings, equipment, numbers of students or staff and their formal training are among those more readily determined. By contrast, other innovations, often more fundamental, are exceedingly difficult to measure, such as changes in attitudes and beliefs, in the advance of knowledge, in student-teacher relations, and in the role or status of persons and organizations. Changes in intermediary groups (e.g., teachers or professors) under training are more readily

246

identifiable than changes in the groups which teachers or others may ultimately influence. In regard to changes in the latter or the so-called target groups, the present study has relied mainly upon the observations of staff members in the American or host organizations as well as upon the opinions of informed observers.

Even when innovations are apparent, it is not always safe to conclude that the American university exchange programs were responsible for them. It is impossible to separate sharply the impact of a university program from that of other forces for change. Nonetheless, we can report many changes that have taken place and even, perhaps, make tentative judgments as to the probability that a project begun will attain the objectives originally in mind.

Accomplishments in the Host Country

The major objective of technical assistance projects is the introduction of change in the host country. Though other kinds of achievement are possible, success in the impact abroad is necessary if a technical assistance project is to be a success as a whole.

Institution-building. About half the technical assistance programs originally were intended to build institutions and another quarter later developed this objective. Institution-building is a smaller part of activities abroad than these proportions suggest. Many of the projects with such objectives have also had direct-action goals. American universities have engaged in consulting activities with government agencies without attempting to institutionalize the process in the host-country universities, in government agencies, or other groups. They have conducted in-service training without creating an organization to carry on in the future. And they have themselves conducted research, without, as a rule, institutionalizing the process at any point. For example, Cornell in Peru worked with the Indian Institute in bettering the community of Vicos, but made no effort to set up village research in the Institute, although the American personnel carried out field research. The University of Tennessee program in Bolivia led to establishment of a special school at the university, but in-service training was not institutionalized within the government.

In technical assistance programs, direct action and the desire to show immediate results seem imperative at first. Later, university personnel come to feel that institution-building may be the principal contribution in the long run. Thus, the Harvard program in Pakistan shifted from direct help in preparation of a national plan to building permanent institutions for research in economic development and national planning.

New or newly modified host organizations run by host personnel were found by the present survey in a narrow majority of those cases in which projects had had institution-building objectives. There were four patterns for the new institutions. (1) In a few instances entire new universities were established, such as Ataturk University in connection with the Nebraska project in Turkey. In Ethiopia the Oklahoma State project helped establish an agricultural high school at Jimma and a college at Alemaya. (2) In a few other instances regular faculties or departments were developed as integral parts of a university, for example at several Indonesian universities. (3) More commonly, special institutes or schools were established and attached to the universities but with a status different from that of the several normal faculties. The public-administration school at the University of San Andres in connection with the Tennessee program had a special status. (4) A practice equally frequent was to establish independent institutes or organizations to carry on narrowly defined functions. The vocational school in heavy-equipment training in Mexico followed this pattern. Patterns (2) and (3) were followed in institution-building within government agencies. Universities have helped establish national planning commissions, as did Harvard in Pakistan and Iran. In Peru, the Cornell project gave life to a special organization, the Indian Institute, and the Harvard nutrition project helped the department of nutrition expand its activities greatly.

The timing of such new or modified institutions as were created has varied from project to project. On occasion, the institutions were established before the American university program began, and the project was designed to develop and nourish them. Thus the Kampala Technical Institute in Uganda was strengthened by the Delgado Trades and Technical Institutes' program. In other cases institutions were created either at the beginning of the program or were developed after considerable work by American and host-country nationals. Numerous institution-building projects remain unfulfilled, though planned for a distant future. Institutionalization of the process of keeping the Liberian law code current had not occurred in the Cornell-Liberian program under which Cornell had prepared a code.

There have been some striking successes. The teacher-education program of Ohio State University in India, in association with Indian government officials, assisted some 53 active departments of extension services in 54 secondary-school training institutions, whereas there had been only 23 when the project began. In Turkey, permanent training units were established or strengthened in connection with the New York University program in commercial education and the Spring Garden program in automotive mechanics. The vocational training school in Mexico, created in connection with the University of Michigan project, is a unique type of institution for both Mexico and Latin America. Most such training takes place on the job, but this school has full-time employees, high standards, and engages even in some theoretical work. An Institute for Research on Productivity has been established at Waseda University in Japan under another Michigan program. An Economics Research Center at the Catholic University of Chile was set up in conjunction with the Chicago project.

There have been frustrations. Legal obstacles have been encountered in establishing an organization. More important, there have been difficulties in arousing the interest of host-country nationals in assuming leadership and direction. After several years of effort, the University of California has not persuaded the Italians to take over the public administration institute at Bologna, although technically an Italian is in charge. The business administration program of Harvard at Istanbul and the public administration program of New York University at Ankara have not been able to get Turks interested in creating or administering new or modified organizations. In many countries American universities have tried to promote a land-grant college type of organization for universities, including the unification of extension and experiment-station activities with the teaching of agriculture and related subjects. There has been almost no success in obtaining inclusion of extension activities. Of the many institutions in seven countries in the sample, in which one or more agricultural programs were in operation, only three had made any noticeable progress toward accepting innovations vaguely similar to an American agricultural college in other respects—the Terai Agricultural University in India, Ataturk University in Turkey, and the agricultural college at Alemaya in Ethiopia, all completely new institutions (Hart, p. 81; Adams and Garraty, pp. 132–133). Even in these instances the land-grant pattern was not accepted in a form anywhere near that which the

Americans desired. In public and business administration, and in agriculture and related fields, American university personnel have recommended structures that correspond rather closely with American practice, without much adaptation to local circumstances. Frustration is more likely under such circumstances. An Ethiopian agriculture administrator trained in the United States observed:

> Is the American system of unifying extension services with agricultural colleges best? This depends in part on the psychology of the farmers. Apparently the American farmers fear the hand of the central government and feel that placing agricultural extension under the United States Department of Agriculture would mean government control of the farmers. What is the psychology of the Ethiopian farmer? Many farmers feel that the Emperor is generally interested in their welfare so no matter what man comes around from the central government, he is looked upon as being helpful.

New or modified institutions were the result of many forces, of which that of the American universities was only one. The new universities and faculties in Indonesia arose primarily from an Indonesian drive to establish such institutions. American universities, along with ICA, the Ford Foundation, and many others are helping them toward their goal. The Terai Agricultural University is the result of the efforts of dozens of Indians and Americans over a period of many years; the contribution of American university programs was a minor factor. Nevertheless, host-country groups have wanted some assistance in institution-building and the American universities have helped supply it.

The final test of these new or modified institutions lies in the future. Will the innovations be permanent; will they meet the needs of the host country? A substantial minority of the new or modified institutions was not assured of permanence. Though formally run by one or more host-country nationals, these institutions were in reality stepchildren supported largely by American assistance. Whether local financial and personnel resources could be found after the American university program ceased was questionable. Whether the institutions would be given a status sufficient to permit them to carry on their functions was in doubt.

Courses and Curricula. Modification of teaching techniques and changes in courses and curricula are the most common objectives of university technical assistance projects. Occasionally old curricula have been followed at new institutions and new curricula implanted at old institutions. Changes in courses and curricula are more frequently sought in existing university programs than is institution-building. A large majority of projects in Indonesia, India, Italy, Turkey, Peru, and Bolivia had this objective, for example in sanitary or textile engineering in Peru, public administration in Bolivia, agriculture, teacher education, or home economics in India, and economics, teacher education, engineering, or medicine in Indonesia.

Innovations were introduced in most of these instances, although as a rule not as many as the Americans would have liked. At least one new or modified course taught by a host-country national or some new curricular requirement was found in a majority of programs with such objectives in the sample. Even among a few of the small projects for research or professor exchanges, modifications of curricula have occurred in the host country.

The scope of some of the more extensive changes is illustrated by the Tennessee program in home economics in India. Before the program got under way, the dean of the Tennessee school of home economics made a trip to India and as a result of her study recommended several major changes, including work in foods and nutrition, home-economics education for rural extension workers, in-service training of existing home-economics staff, and graduate work in institutional management, in child development, in home management, and in teacher training in home economics. The Tennessee program led to a thoroughgoing revision of home-economics curricula at six of the eight institutions concerned. They adopted more general curricula with less specialization and substantial graduate work. In Indonesia many projects began with substitute teaching by Americans; curricular revision gradually assumed importance, particularly the development of a more general basic curriculum for the first two years of university work.

Innovations in courses and curricula have been introduced in many different ways. In some cases American and host-country professors shared in the development and teaching of new courses. In a few cases, as in public administration programs in the Philippines, Pakistan, and Bolivia, American professors more or less carried on by themselves, organizing the curricula and teaching many of the courses. Later the teaching was gradually turned over to host-country nationals as they gained experience or came back from graduate work in the United States. In still other programs, the role of American professors was confined to advice on such matters.

In some countries, influence from American universities concerning curricula is strongly resisted. Americans have had to be careful not to suggest curricular changes directly in Japan because of national sensitivities. In countries such as Turkey curricular change is so dependent on legal and administrative approvals that it has come slowly, but most of the projects included it. Ankara and Istanbul universities have strongly resisted changes in curricula and course content, although special training centers not affiliated with old Turkish universities have introduced some changes. So has the new Ataturk University.

The new subject matter introduced into courses and curricula has varied. In some projects in Japan, Turkey, and Germany an attempt was made to stimulate interest in general American studies or in certain subjects found in American legal education. Courses in American law, history, and letters, and in American social, economic, and political institutions were taught by professors from the United States in the hope that they would become part of the regular curriculum. The tangible results of these programs are few indeed. As for the Georgetown program in Frankfurt, little follow-through can be expected after the one German-born American law professor finishes his work. Turkey has not evinced much interest in American law courses. The joint law school program in Japan has had more impact. Several years of American studies programs at Tokyo, Kyoto, and Doshisha universities have stimulated some interest, but chairs in the subject had not been created at the time of this study. At Tokyo University there was still some opposition to a chair in American studies, the neutralists favoring one in international relations instead. Though few formal American studies courses or curricula have sprung from technical assistance programs, the programs have increased the attention given to American topics.

American universities are playing a greater role abroad in some fields of study than in others. They have contributed to many innovations in agriculture, teacher education, and the applied social sciences. The United States is also considered a leader in home economics, medicine, public health, engineering, and the basic sciences, but in these, fewer innovations have been introduced, in large part because of fewer programs per field. The liberal arts and the humanities have not been prominent in American university technical assistance programs; they are areas in which American higher education is not regarded abroad as a leader. Some programs for the teaching of English as a foreign language have prospered, and many programs include this as one objective.

Technical assistance programs have aimed at the establishment of curricula that will broaden general education of host-country university students; traditionally, higher education abroad has required much earlier specialization than in the United States. The programs have also aimed at application of knowledge to practical problems. Moderate and about equal success in meeting these two contrasting but mutually reinforcing objectives is evident. Successes in these aims have been more numerous in curricula emphasizing vocations and skills than in those of the professions or fundamental disciplines. Participants returning to India from the Kansas State and Illinois programs in agriculture found that in their teaching practical problems interested them more than before. An aim of university programs in technical assistance in India has been to reorient agricultural higher education toward the needs of the rural population, and to relate it to research and extension work. The development of home-science work in India not only has helped promote a new discipline that implies much for the role of women in Indian society, but has contributed to broadening the concept of home-science education.

Teaching Techniques. At least some innovation in teaching techniques has been the objective of most technical assistance programs. In a broad sense the aim has been to make methods of teaching more democratic, providing a relation between professor and student more like that in the United States. This objective has largely been unrealized. A practice here and there may have been changed, but professors in no country or major university have accepted in any substantial degree American professor-student relationships either in the present or as a goal. A majority of the host-country professors involved denied that there had been any effect on their teaching techniques, even in programs that specially stressed this objective. Only a third of the professors of one Chilean and two Peruvian faculties reported any influence on their teaching methods under the North Carolina, North Carolina State, and Chicago programs. Although the first of these programs had particularly emphasized teaching techniques, the percentage reporting innovation was not noticeably higher than in the others (Adams and Cumberland, pp. 78–79). Some change, however, was reported in each program.

The discussion technique in its various forms is a commonly proposed innovation, yet lectures to large classes remain in effect to almost as great an extent as formerly. There has been some introduction of case methods in law and in business and public administration. Of the programs in the sample, only in two instances out of ten was the case method with local materials actually put in practice in these fields by host-country nationals, at the time of this study. The joint law program in Japan had been most successful in encouraging greater use of case materials by local scholars. Seminar discussion in the American manner of give and take is still rare in most of the countries in the sample, and the combining of lectures and discussions is no greater than before, with isolated exceptions. Emphasis on memorization of lectures continues.

The use of reading materials to supplement classwork has also been a central point of many projects. Marked improvements in host-country libraries have resulted from at least half the technical assistance projects. Libraries have been increased, physical facilities improved, availability made easier, and librarians trained. In the long run, library improvement could be an important influence on changing teaching techniques, for with materials readily available, students would not have to rely solely on the lecture for information. Also, students could be informed before they go to class, and have something to discuss intelligently. However, the library facilities of Europe have not led to the prevalence of discussion techniques on the Continent. At present, the additional library facilities in less developed countries are being used to some extent, although the language problem creates difficulty in some countries and part-time students cannot make much use of libraries. Textbooks that are something more than printed lectures are gradually appearing. The use of textbooks and outside readings in classes associated with technical assistance projects was still scanty compared with that in American classes, but some increase occurred in one or more classes taught by host-country nationals in a majority of the programs.

Laboratory and field work has been introduced by American professors in some of the technical assistance projects. Where introduced, it has supplemented the theoretical work of the lectures. Since well-equipped laboratories are not often found in the less developed countries, much equipment has had to be sent abroad. The equipment has been gratefully received. In India, four of twelve high-level host-institution professors associated with the Kansas State and Illinois programs felt that additional equipment and books were the most important contributions of the university programs. The four did not on their own initiative even mention the participants or visiting American professors (Hart, pp. 59–60). Most overseas technical assistance programs included the sending of some equipment, but provision of equipment did not always result in any increase in laboratory or field work. The physical presence of the equipment was valued because of the prestige it brought, yet its actual use by a professor might be thought detrimental to his prestige.

A variety of other techniques were introduced with rather small success. Term papers or supervised student research was accepted as practices in a few instances. Special written examinations during a course were tried on occasion, but as a whole American examination methods have not been welcome. The use of audiovisual aids was promoted widely; at advanced levels of teaching they have had little impact, although they became important in a few more elementary courses in postsecondary institutions. A special aspect of a few technical assistance projects has been the development of extracurricular activities. Occasionally one or more American faculty members have helped organize quasi-professional associations, clubs, athletic events, and similar activities.

Long-range change in teaching methods will depend upon the extent to which the small number of innovations now accepted spreads to other professors and courses. There is no evidence that this process will be rapid. Broad changes in teaching techniques apparently take place only over many years. Most of the programs may have influenced one or more members of the host faculty or affected one or more of the courses, but only a few had any perceptible influence on most members of the host faculty or any effect on most of the courses.

Study Habits. Two main problems in less developed countries are the poor study habits of the students and the lack of competent faculty (Smith, pp. 28 and 40). Poor study habits can be improved to some extent by better teaching techniques. The availability of study space and library facilities is helpful. However, study habits are intimately related to the nature of the examination system in the host institution and the part-time status of students, so that substantial improvement cannot be expected until these have been changed. They are relatively untouched by the bulk of American university programs.

Training and Experience of Faculty Members. Nearly all the technical assistance programs of American universities recognize a need for improving the training and experience of host-country faculty members. Particularly where such faculty members have already done advanced work in their fields, American staff members abroad may help to achieve the desired result. Contributing to the development of host-country staff members overseas was a continual responsibility of most American professors abroad either on an *ad hoc* basis or at a more organized in-service training level.[1]

Where host-country staff members had had a substantial professional background, the major problems were administrative or organizational. In reviewing the programs in Mexico, Peru, Bolivia, and Chile, Adams and Cumberland observe:

> An issue that came up . . . was that the U. S. university staff member in the host country was so occupied with administrative work that he did not have the time necessary to prepare in-service work and carry out the training. A more common difficulty involved in-service work with university teachers who were part-time faculty. The faculty members simply did not have the time or the inclination to spend time in the work. Teaching was a sideline with many of them, and the time spent in in-service training would so distract them from their regular occupation that it would be financially unwise. A third, and fundamental, problem in the upgrading of personnel within an institution is the development of incentives for obtaining the new knowledge. Whatever work was done by the Harvard group in training chemists in the Department of Nutrition in Lima was working against the undeniable fact that marked improvement in the work would not bring concomitant improvement in salary.

They conclude:

> Generally speaking, the study of the projects involved indicates that in-service training is a weak link in the chain of technical improvement; there are too many conditions which impair its effectiveness. This problem is greater, perhaps, in a government organization where there is

[1] See Chap. 8 for a discussion of participant training of faculty members.

neither civil service nor merit system, than it is in a university where teaching is done specifically because the individual likes to do it and wherein his problem is one of time (Adams and Cumberland, pp. 61–62).

Target Groups. In some technical assistance programs, the objective in the host country has been to train the ultimate users of the knowledge or "target groups" either alone or in conjunction with the teaching of teachers or "intermediaries." Beyond the learning of subject matter derived from taking any course given by any instructor, it is difficult to determine what the impact on target groups has been. Some of the students have been inspired to go to the United States for further study. Most have remained in the host country; the course or courses under American professors are simply part of the many aspects of their education.

The number of host students receiving some kinds of training was increased in many instances through the use of American professors. Without American professors in Indonesia, little undergraduate teaching would be available in certain fields, and without American professors special training programs for public servants would not exist at either Bologna or La Paz. The training of target groups has also been augmented through the training of host intermediaries. The number of students in sanitary engineering in Peru has been sharply increased at the National Engineering University at Lima (Adams and Cumberland, p. 179).

These are quantitative statements. As for the qualitative impact on target groups, neither Italian nor Bolivian public administration was noticeably affected by the programs at the time of this study. The joint law school program in Japan has no impact either on raising the low status of lawyers or on the likelihood of permanent changes attributable to the American influence. Yet, in some projects important innovations have been made among groups not directly associated with university education in the host countries. The Cornell-Peru project in anthropology stimulated Indian village development. Teaching methods in the secondary schools in India were affected by the Ohio State project. The special objective in the Ohio State project was to emphasize secondary education for vast numbers of Indian children, not just for the relatively few who go on to the universities. In Liberia, the Cornell law codification project had affected the users of law—executive departments, big businesses, lawyers, and law schools. Since the law codification, Liberians feel that a greater respect for their country exists.

Research and Publication. Research and publication have been central to a few technical assistance projects and have played a supporting role in many others. At best, the record is spotty. Frequently, research has been put aside as of low priority, and the staff members, both American and host country, have concentrated on other things. In the New York University program in Turkey, not one textbook in Turkish public administration was produced for use during this project, although such a book would have been an important teaching aid. Two of the technical assistance programs that emphasized research resulted in substantial publications, however: the Chicago-Chile project in economic development and the Michigan-Waseda program in business administration. In general, more than two-thirds of those technical assistance projects in which research was secondary had failed to produce much of significance at the time of the study, while three-fourths of those in which it was a major objective produced something of value.[2] It is surprising that research has not been included among the more important objectives of many projects.

Research most often leads to innovations in the host country only if the research is applied. Research was used on occasion in teaching or as background information for public policy decisions. Case studies of public administration in Israel and Vietnam were used in this way. The results of research were not always pleasing. Disappointment was sometimes expressed because research was too theoretical, or of value to certain groups though not to others. In the Michigan-Waseda program in business administration in Japan, a few critics said that the research carried on as a demonstration was valuable mainly for big companies who could carry on their own research. Similar criticism was incurred by the Oklahoma State project in Ethiopia, which has helped to develop improved methods on large farms. Basic research projects are intended to gain new knowledge which has wide applicability, not necessarily of special use to the host country.

Making Friends. Nearly all international programs of American universities aim to make friends for the United States. As in the popular song, the assumption seems to be that "the more we get together the happier are we." American faculty members are sup-

---

[2] This compares very favorably with all research programs, whether technical assistance related or not, of which only a majority showed substantial results. See Chap. 7.

posed to be better at making friends than tourists, businessmen, and members of the Armed Forces. The present project was not able to collect systematic data on a topic as broad as this, but those interviewed believed overwhelmingly that professors did make friends for themselves and for their country while abroad. The net effect was very favorable. The impression that most other Americans make abroad is also favorable, although the feeling varies according to the groups concerned. The general population in host countries makes no distinction between the image of American professors and the image of American residents and tourists, but they like these groups better than American servicemen. The academic communities in a host country usually have a poor opinion of the tourist and the more frequent contacts with American academic personnel often lead to a more favorable attitude toward them. To the extent that second-rate American staff members have been passed off as American "experts," the image of American higher education suffers, as well as the image of the United States. One of the technical assistance programs in Pakistan and another in Turkey were unpopular because of the poor quality of the staff members. In addition, academic personnel who know little of the country to which they go and do not take the trouble to find out do not make favorable impressions.

Personal relations among faculty members at home have not always been pleasant and sometimes have led to serious conflict. American faculty relations with host-country nationals have not been any worse—or any better. Disagreements are encountered from time to time as the result of clashes in personalities, but they are not frequent. Yet unfortunate choices of personnel for assignment overseas have more serious consequences than poor choices at home. Some of the unfit representatives sent abroad have led observers to despair.

Said an American university professor after a year in Europe, "I wonder if an American university program overseas does any good. I cannot see that the anti-Americanism in the world has been affected by such programs one bit." Judgments such as these are based on exaggerated expectations. It is unrealistic to assume that less than a thousand professors in technical assistance programs can fundamentally alter images of the United States around the world. However, it is not unrealistic to assume that professors have a special impact on relations with their contemporaries abroad. As a whole, they do a good job within this limited area. In one case, in Ethiopia, an Oklahoma State staff member was even given a major decoration by the host government on the completion of his six-year assignment.

One of the best possible results occurs when professors become expert in the other country in their several disciplines, and the two institutions develop lasting affiliations. These objectives have not been generally attained, but as a rule friendship between American and host-country scholars has improved. The programs have undoubtedly furthered internationalization of disciplines. More complete exchange of professional information and observation of differing approaches to fields of learning have taken place. It is far too early to determine the long-range impact of new professional friends, of continuing institutional contact with American higher education, and of the internationalization of the various disciplines, but growth of attention to American topics in regular courses will be part of the results. American university programs encourage such a trend, although they are only one influence in this direction among many.

Foreign Attitude toward American Programs. One indication of the way host-country nationals feel about American university programs and American university personnel is that often they seek more contacts of the same sort. However, most of them would also like more contacts with universities in other countries as well. "There is a fear that American universities may become too active compared to those from other countries" observed a Canadian vice chancellor. In practice, the desire abroad is for more programs. Even in such a sensitive nation as Japan, the president of Hokkaido University used an ICA contract with the University of Massachusetts as one reason why he should be returned to office in his campaign for re-election.

Host-country groups have accepted American university programs in principle far more than they have accepted substantive innovations growing out of them. Substantive innovations by the host subgroup or institution abroad have seldom spread to others. The innovations introduced at the Seoul National University as a result of the University of Minnesota program have not spread appreciably to other national universities in Korea. In India, innovations affecting agricultural colleges have not markedly spread from those who work closely with American universities to those who do not. Within host institutions, there has been some spread of interest in change from faculty to faculty, or from faculty to administrative units, such as those in charge of registration and record-keeping, but this has not taken place on a large scale.

Programs and innovations are welcomed more by those who are internationally minded or interested in America to begin with than by those who are not. On the other hand, the impact of a program may be more sweeping when an international view is lacking at the start. Part of the objective of ICA and the foundations in financing these programs has been to encourage professors in other countries to look outward as well as to their own resources. Those who have already been doing so have been reinforced, and those who have not done so have had a new experience. Of the American studies programs at the three institutions in Japan, the greatest effect was felt at Kyoto precisely because the other two universities were more internationally minded to begin with.

Objectives and Accomplishments in the United States

In most cases American universities participating in technical assistance projects overseas have set no objectives at the home campus. Most of the impact at home has been accommodative— i.e., adjusting administratively and otherwise to a project—rather than substantive. Offices of project coordinator have been established, secretarial and other personnel hired, lines of authority designated, and sometimes advisory committees set up.

Few other changes were planned for or introduced, for example, in regard to teaching or the pattern of courses and curricula. Faculty members returning from abroad have normally gone back to teaching the same courses as previously, perhaps introducing some new examples but yet covering the same subject matter. If several members of a department have gone abroad, not much of their teaching load can be concentrated on the few courses directly related to their overseas experience. In many subjects, too, teaching abroad and in the United States is fundamentally the same; no regional aspect is present.

Within the humanities and social sciences, area studies are most intimately related to host countries and their problems. Strangely enough, area studies at American universities have not played an important role in most technical assistance programs, and few area studies professors have gone abroad under them. This is largely due to the fact that technical assistance has been requested in many subject matter areas but not in regional or host-country studies. The overseas programs have been a major factor in developing a comparative approach in some fields, such as comparative education or comparative public administration.

In most fields outside the humanities and the social sciences the nature of the subject matter precludes the introduction of many geographical considerations in courses at the American university. The call for courses in medicine, engineering, or agriculture on a regional basis is not great enough to induce many institutions to specialize in them, and the wisdom of such specialization at the home campus is open to question. Tropical building engineering was a specialty encountered by the staff members of Northwestern University in the Sudan, but few students at Evanston would be interested in it. However, examples of problems encountered in building in the tropics have become more frequent in courses at Northwestern conducted by faculty members who served in the Sudan. On occasion, overseas programs have contributed something to curricula in colleges of medicine or agriculture. Thus the School of Tropical and Preventive Medicine of the College of Medical Evangelists has a program in Tanganyika which gives faculty members valuable field experience for courses back home. In agriculture, where the host-country geography and climate are similar to that encountered at the American university, experimental work of advantage to the American institution can be carried out. However, American professors have introduced at home very few practices of host-country universities.

The main effect of the projects on American students has been to deny them access to certain professors while the latter are serving overseas. In a broad sense, of course, experience abroad adds to the richness of the professor's background. On occasion, graduate students have participated in the programs and this has sometimes been of special value to them. However, few institutions have used the programs to give graduate students an opportunity to pursue specialties or collect data for theses. Only three of the programs in the Latin American sample did so. The University of Chicago used its program in economic development in Chile to involve American-based graduate students and faculty members. Some graduate assistantships have been available on home campuses in connection with technical assistance programs, but they have often been held by students with no special interest in the program. California wished to expand its Italian program in public administration to include research in Italy by American graduate students, but financial support was lacking. The Harvard nutritional experts were unsuccessful in furthering their research objectives through their project in Peru.

The general impact of the programs on American university campuses, though usually not a formal objective, has occasionally been real. A single program is likely to have more effect on a small campus than on a large, sprawling university. If a large university is going to marshall its international resources, it must do so in more ways—through an international faculty, a substantial number of foreign students, and individual as well as group exchange. However, institutions as large as Nebraska and Oklahoma State have found it possible to use their technical assistance programs for making contributions campus-wide and even community and state-wide. Turkey and Ethiopia have become the focus of much attention in those states. Oklahoma State has even gone so far as to have annual Ethiopia days. Prominent Oklahomans from all over the state come to Stillwater. One of the features of the occasion is a large banquet, usually addressed by some prominent Ethiopian—the Emperor himself in 1955. The general impact of the programs at home has been enhanced in several instances by extension personnel at land-grant colleges.

These are exceptional examples. For the most part, little systematic use is made of the experience abroad of returning professors. Most professors observed that few of their colleagues seemed to care about their overseas experience. Some had not even been asked to speak to any campus group. Community talks were, if anything, more frequent than campus appearances, in part because certain organizations were always looking for speakers, and university speakers bureaus provide a liaison. Wives of staff members gave a number of community talks. In the case of programs that had been under way for some years, those first returning often made some appearances, but those who followed later found that the saturation point had been quickly reached.

Influence on American campuses has been surprisingly small. While inadequate financial support for special activities was responsible for some of the lack of impact at the home campuses, a more general obstacle was that the programs were not normally closely tied in with other academic interests or with the regular academic departments. The Cornell-Liberian program, though successful in accomplishing its objective, providing a code of laws for Liberia, was not of concern to anyone at Cornell beyond those immediately involved. The Pennsylvania research program in Mexico, which involved technical assistance, was not tied into the activities of the University of Pennsylvania at home. Most programs have affected only a minority of the members of any one department. They are not central to the day-to-day thinking or problems of most academic personnel.

Part of the impact of the programs on American universities has been evident as the programs or their goals have been expanded or contracted. More and more American universities have been willing to engage in the programs. Those institutions that have participated in one have often been willing to take on another. Some institutions have developed reputations at home and abroad as international- or technical assistance-minded universities.

Some projects have been expanded beyond the intention of the originators or have contributed to lasting cooperation between two universities. The Texas A and M program at Antonio Narro was discontinued formally, yet the two institutions are still cooperating informally. In the University of Michigan training program for Mexican operators of heavy equipment, a relationship to the program in Ann Arbor was at first envisaged. It was felt that

. . . the Mexican center could serve as a laboratory for teaching methods in vocational schools; experience there could be transferred to the United States scene with, it was hoped, considerable economies resulting in vocational training at home. This objective was completely lost; if there was any experimentation it is not reflected in the reports, and there was no coordinated plan for using the Mexican experience in United States schools. Furthermore, the two deans envisaged the project as an opportunity to establish rapport with other Mexican institutions which could in turn lead to the establishment of programs "at a higher academic level," but this objective, too, apparently was abandoned (Adams and Cumberland, pp. 220–221).

Some of the technical assistance programs have reinforced the language competence of faculty members directly involved and given them more specific understanding of another culture and more international involvement. Impact on their family and profession was also observable. Most of the professors considered going abroad an advantage for their families, although this varied somewhat with the post to which they went, the age of their children, and general family adaptability.

While a majority of faculty members who have been abroad do not see any immediate professional gain and a number of professional losses in the time spent overseas, at least a minimum of professional impact has occurred in most instances. Individual faculty members have published articles and books on subjects related to their overseas assignments, when their experience was relevant to their specialties. Foreign experience has been advantageous to professors seeking new opportunities abroad, and administrators of the programs have also qualified themselves for other job opportunities.

All international exchange programs of American universities extract a price. Manpower is scarce, and the time and energy that any individual has to devote to professional pursuits are limited. A professor abroad is making no contribution at home. The use of personnel resources is costly, and the returns must equal the cost if the overseas programs are to be considered successful. The present project did not examine the many alternative activities in which professors might engage. However, unless the innovations achieved by the technical assistance programs are substantial, they will not be worth the cost. No program in which desirable innovations barely outweigh the undesirable is likely to be a wise investment of personnel resources because of the sacrifices of alternative uses of the personnel.

Long-range values cannot be measured after a few years of experience with technical assistance programs abroad. Observers and persons directly participating feel that programs with modest results are worth the cost. They point to the necessity of gaining experience and to the fact that many of the objectives to be achieved cannot be quickly realized. Most programs of American universities are products of the 1950s. Perhaps by the 1970s it will be possible to measure their effectiveness in achieving long-range results.

Most of the shortcomings in the programs can be attributed to inexperience by all concerned. It is necessary to recognize and overcome these defects. About half the universities encounter serious difficulties in their programs during the first two or three years. Some programs are discontinued, others improved. Rarely has a university been asked to leave a country before its contract expired, as happened once in Cuba. Most programs of longer than five or six years' duration are able to meet many of their objectives with an economy of resources. They also are able to choose objectives more realistically. It may be unwise for universities to engage merely in short-term, isolated projects.

Professors from England, France, the Soviet Union, and other countries are engaging in many technical assistance activities, although in a form somewhat different from the program device used by American universities. They, too, have made mistakes. For example, the Soviets have erred in sending some poorly qualified people to India in engineering, England has erred in not responding to urgent calls for help from certain South American countries, and France has sometimes sent its second-best professors abroad. No university system has a perfect score. However, if American universities wish to continue to make contributions to and receive benefits from technical assistance programs, it would be well for them to remember that they have no monopoly. If they fail to profit from their experiences of the 1950s and greatly to improve their programs, they may find that doors will close, that others have taken up a good share of the responsibility for technical assistance abroad and the benefits flowing therefrom.

Chapter 14

LONG-TERM GOALS IN TECHNICAL ASSISTANCE ABROAD

Even if it were possible separately to identify all the innovations flowing from a university technical assistance program, the significance of the findings would depend upon more than absence or presence of innovation. The innovations gain their significance only in relation to certain criteria. Then, too, the significance of a university project is related to its value as compared with the work of other agencies such as foundations, governments, international organizations, consulting firms, religious bodies, or professional associations. Some would also be concerned with the question whether American higher education is doing more, or less, technical assistance work than universities from other relatively developed countries such as Australia, Canada, England, France, Germany, or the Soviet Union. Finally, the use of university resources in these programs must be justified in comparison with their possible alternative uses at home or abroad.

Importance

Numbers. American university technical assistance programs are numerically impressive in several ways. Although comparative data are spotty, there is no doubt that American universities engage in more *programs* and send more professors abroad under them than universities from any other country. American faculty members abroad under university technical assistance projects represent about a third of all American faculty members abroad.

At a few institutions, the projects play an especially important role in sending faculty members abroad. Prairie View and Michi-

267

gan State, for example, find that technical assistance programs account for a high proportion of their staff overseas. Though these universities are exceptions, many departments, schools, or colleges are in a similar position. Usually, however, these programs account for only a small proportion of the total of professors abroad at any one university. Indeed, most universities have no technical assistance projects. In the words of the president of a Middle Western university prominent in international activities,

The technical assistance programs of an American university are the frosting on the cake as far as its international emphasis is concerned. The basic element in a university's international emphasis is the character of its faculty. Is its faculty interested and competent in the international and comparative aspects of its work? If an affirmative answer is given to this question, many devices for supporting and furthering that interest are more important than international programs. It is a university's policy in regard to such items as leaves for travel abroad, encouragement of foreign students on the campus, area and foreign language study, and willingness to hire professors from abroad or with a refugee status that does the most to further an international orientation of a university. Examine how a university marshalls its financial support for travel to or from overseas through its regular funds, alumni support, Fulbrights, Ford grants, pre- or post-doctorate fellowships, and other sources, and you will see the real character of an institution's international flavor.

Underlying Goals. In regard to their *general* goals, the technical assistance programs of American universities do indeed represent frosting on the cake. Groups other than universities play the major role in the achievement of some of them, and noninternational program activities of the universities are major to the achievement of others. It has not always been clear exactly why technical assistance participation by American universities is essential to goal accomplishment to any large extent.

In 1957–58, the Institute of Research on Overseas Programs asked the coordinators of all university international programs for the reasons that led their universities to enter upon the programs (Inventory, pp. 320–321). Sixty-eight per cent of those in charge of government-sponsored technical assistance projects replied that a desire to support the objectives of United States foreign policy was one of the two main reasons. Such goals as creating friends for the United States, furthering mutual security, and combatting communism helped to explain the origin of the programs. Seventy-one per cent of the same program coordinators said that one of the two main reasons was the development of some aspect of the host country, such as the expansion of a university and its curricula, the modernization of the government or the economic system, or the raising of the standard of living. Of the coordinators of technical assistance programs not financed by the United States government, 44 per cent chose support of foreign policy and 50 per cent chose helping to develop the host country as the first two major reasons for their programs.

A much larger percentage of coordinators of nongovernment-financed than of government-financed technical assistance programs listed as objectives the advancement of knowledge and the strengthening of the United States university. One-third of the former identified the advancement of knowledge among the first two reasons for their undertakings, and only 19 per cent of the latter. Similarly, 22 per cent of the former emphasized strengthening their own universities and only 12 per cent of the latter did so.

As a whole, the interviews conducted by the Institute staff accord with these findings. Though United States government officials gave somewhat more weight to the foreign policy goal, the interviewees as a whole, whether American university representatives or employees of government or foundations, agreed that the prime two factors which accounted for university contract programs were, first, desire to help development in the host country, and second, particularly in government-sponsored programs, a desire to do what was possible to help American foreign policy. The two types of responses were connected. Most felt that a key point in current United States foreign policy was assistance to other countries in development, and this fact helps explain the frequency of reference to foreign policy. It was significant that foundation-financed programs were regarded as somewhat more diverse in character and somewhat more centered on broad intellectual goals and on the aims of the American university. Host-country nationals closely connected with the programs responded in much the same way, stressing somewhat more development objectives, and making a greater distinction between government-financed and foundation-financed programs as to association with American foreign policy objectives.

How important were university technical assistance projects in relation to these basic goals? Few persons would suggest that any phase of foreign policy is substantially determined by university technical assistance programs. Be it the development of friendlier relations, specific support of the American position in world affairs, or assistance in mutual security, these American university programs play a supplementary role only. The supplementary role may have its importance; the programs may be more significant on occasion than their numbers or scope would indicate. Academic personnel are leaders of opinion and may exert widespread influence. But in most countries American contribution to, or competition in, the cultural field is carried out principally by other means, and the cultural aspect of foreign policy is usually a minor one.

Most of the university technical assistance programs are in fields of major importance to host-country development. For example, in Peru, American university programs were designed to improve water supply (North Carolina), the textile industry (North Carolina State), Indian village development (Cornell), and nutrition (Harvard). On occasion, programs have dealt with central problems of economic development such as the Harvard programs in Pakistan and Iran, and the Chicago project in Chile. As a whole, the programs represent long-range investments in institutional development rather than in means of increasing production in the short run. Though the programs concern important development problems, they are not, and are not intended to be, the major element in American technical assistance to most countries.

In a few countries educational assistance is a major aspect of American foreign policy and of host-country development; there university programs may play a large role. Indonesia is one of these. Seventy-two, or about 44 per cent, of the foreign professors in Indonesia in 1958–59 were from the United States, and 63 of the 72 were members of university contract teams (Smith, pp. 51–52). Indonesia obtained about 70 foreign professors by means of individual contract, 12 from Colombo plan resources and 7 from UNESCO. American university programs ranked second only to individual contracts as a means of meeting Indonesia's urgent needs for professors from abroad. Since the American professors were concentrated in certain fields and at certain institutions or faculties, the significance of American university programs was even greater in subjects such as economics, engineering, and medicine, and for three or four host institutions.

Intellectual goals such as discovery and acquisition of new knowledge were not closely associated with most technical assistance projects. Quite naturally, therefore, the programs contributed little to discovery and acquisition of knowledge in any one field, and only little to the international and comparative aspects of subjects. Intellectual goals were often overshadowed by other objectives such as service. Universities have not been quick to utilize the technical assistance programs for research, even where this was clearly possible. Nor have they looked upon these programs as means for improving themselves. American universities have, in this part of their activities, been transmitters of knowledge, not creators.

Among the other underlying goals of the programs was that of confronting American professors and host-country students and faculty members with alternative values, to permit them to obtain a first-hand understanding of the diversity of the cultures of the world, with special attention to their own fields of study. Some hoped the programs would contribute to world peace and understanding. Some desired to hasten the development of pluralism, of respect for others. Underlying most of the programs were desires to further freedom and world interdependence, to extend democracy and to be one's brother's keeper. No one has pretended, of course, that the programs are the sole or the major means to such ends.

To summarize, the technical assistance programs of American universities play a contributing not a dominant role in the achievement of most of their own underlying goals. Whether foreign policy goals or those of higher education are considered, the programs are not principal factors. This is also true of world peace, host-country development, the advancement of knowledge, and the strengthening of American universities.

Are they necessary or especially desirable means of achieving a part of these broader goals? The answer depends in part upon an examination of the more specific objectives or means of the programs. These specific objectives have implicit in them an assumption as to what constitutes good education at the university level. There is lack of agreement on this subject among the several systems of higher education of the world, and there are even differences of viewpoint within systems of higher education.

Specific Means. Apart from the rather general goals that lie behind the programs, there are a great variety of specific means or objectives. Respondents pointed out that such projects as the writing of a textbook in teacher education, the beginning of extension methods in agriculture, the teaching of a course in engineering, or the advising of a government official in public health were involved in the projects. It was through such means as these that the broader goal of helping to accelerate national development in the host country was to be achieved.

The specific objectives are at least as revealing of the nature of the projects as general goals. Some of the specific objectives have nothing to do with higher education in the host country. While a majority of them are connected with higher education, they seldom are centered on the whole system of higher education in the host country. Only infrequently do they deal with the development of a single university as a whole, as did the Nebraska project in Turkey.

The specific objectives of a university contract are typically restricted to one or two fields such as textile engineering or one or two techniques such as audio-visual education. In the large majority of programs, American universities are essentially technical aids of ICA or of the foundations in helping other countries toward national development. What is sought is the use of the university's technical experts rather than the backing and support of the university as an institution of higher education. University staff members go abroad because of competence in either technique or subject matter. Even in the most eminent programs, the tendency is to look for American professors who are outstanding as individuals. Their knowledge of their fields and their methods of making that knowledge available to others and of acquiring new knowledge— these are the qualities sought, surely these are the elements, it is said, that must be brought to the host country in order to hasten its process of national development.

Another characteristic of the specific objectives is that certain practices of American universities are considered good patterns for the host institution. Such practices are thought to be independent of the nature of a university as a whole, and good in and of themselves. If a practice cannot be introduced into the host institution as it is found in the United States, the tendency is to introduce as much of it as possible rather than to develop a practice tailored to the needs of the host institution and country.

Whether it be an institute of public administration, a land-grant agricultural college, or a teacher's college, the American pattern is thought to be the right one to follow as closely as possible if national development is to be furthered.

In addition to the emphasis on technique, subject matter, individual professor, and American practice, the specific objectives of the university contracts are above all else concerned with training manpower in the host country. They aim to add to the pool of trained personnel abroad either directly or by training the trainers.

Evaluation of Means. It is doubtful whether the aims of national development can be most fully attained with such limited concepts of the role of universities in the host country as these specific means or objectives of technical assistance imply. Certainly, experience in the United States does not bear out this assumption. In the United States, the universities as a whole not only are sources of trained manpower for the private and government groups who play a direct role in development, but also are leaders in the realm of ideas. In turn, many institutions including universities help to provide ideas in a form that is useable by the farmer, by the businessman, and by the government. The universities are not uniform, patterned machines that through competence in technique and subject matter turn out trained manpower. Several kinds of universities exist; collectively they are forums where competing theories are displayed; they are market places of ideas. American universities are free institutions of higher learning, contributing fundamentally to the growth and development of a free society. They *educate* as well as train.

If there is any justification for asking a university to undertake a complicated, time-consuming, resource-absorbing function such as an overseas technical assistance project, it must lie in the unique qualities of a university and the manner in which these qualities are relevant to the objectives of technical assistance. A university is by nature a social institution performing an essential function for society. Underdeveloped countries seek to accelerate national development. They turn to the United States for help not only because it has financial and material resources that are essential to them. They also turn to it because the United States has a record of remarkable national development, a process that continues even today. They should study the record of our development to see if there is in it anything that would be applicable to their situation.

They should not copy exactly either the techniques used in the United States or the kind of development it has achieved. Rather, they should understand the process of development in countries such as the United States and the role of various institutions in the process, and they should adapt to their situation or goals any ideas that would be useful.

Here is where, somehow, the university contract program has gone off the track. Instead of engaging in a useful mutual self-analysis, self-observation, and demonstration of the process of national development in the United States and the host country, American universities and host institutions have focused their attention on subject matter and technique. The American university has provided ready-made nostrums, cures for all evils under all conditions. The American form of democracy, the American form of private business, and the American form of higher education are viewed not as examples of but as *the* way of national development. Worse still, the larger framework in which institutions work tends to be forgotten, and detailed techniques and practices, thus separated from the context that gives them meaning, are held up as the way in which national development can be achieved.

In technical assistance the United States has neglected the role of universities in national development and has concentrated on particular segments of higher education. A new textile engineering curriculum, a revised public administration program, a new medical education plan, or the creation of a home economics department—all are a part of American higher education, and therefore all are presumed good for underdeveloped countries. Similarly, the case approach, the seminar method, the land-grant college formula—these are all part of American higher education and so, it is assumed, represent appropriate exports to development-conscious countries.

Many such innovations may be desirable and appropriate. Yet they scarcely have meaning by themselves. Without a framework they are mere pieces of a puzzle. They do not even distinguish between a university in a free society and one in the Communist world. Are the needs of a society for higher education the same regardless of its dedication to freedom? The Soviet Union needs experts in administration, textile engineering, the seminar method, and the others. What, then, distinguishes the United States from the Soviet Union? What indeed, except the function that a free university plays in a free society! These techniques, these subject matter specialties must be related to a concept of a university as a whole. In turn, the concept of a university must be related to a concept of society. This the technical assistance programs of American universities have almost completely failed to do, whether they be run by a Harvard or a Podunk, whether they be financed by ICA or a foundation. There is little justification for spending university resources on technique-oriented programs. Techniques can be transmitted in many ways—by government employees, consulting firms, or foundation-hired experts. However, only a university itself can give a live demonstration of a free university in action. Only it can illustrate the relation of subject matter, technique, and practice to a living, tangible whole. Only it can illustrate the relation of the individual professor to higher education as a whole and the dependence of training manpower on the realm of ideas.

The failure of technical assistance in higher education to be much more than assistance in subject matter, technique, and practice is not alone the failure of sponsoring organizations. The host countries themselves have been responsible in part for the misuse of technical assistance from American universities. They have wanted the fruits of American development efforts without being willing to pay the price. In some instances, they have wanted rapid business development and have thus turned to the American collegiate schools of business for a clue as to how to accomplish it. Yet their universities have not been willing to establish such programs as regular units or faculties nor have the business communities been willing to make the necessary changes in their patterns of family ownership or operation. These countries have desired to retain some of the old ways, but at the same time to receive the benefits of new ways. They have wanted to meet their crucial need for more trained manpower without making many changes in higher education as a system. They have been expecting quick competence in subject matter and technique to solve their problems painlessly. They have viewed universities in the United States condescendingly, except in a few technical areas. Host-country universities have resisted reconsidering their function in society. They often reject outright the notion that American

universities provide a useful example. They have been content
to remain the educational vehicle for the few, and to make little
modification of their contribution to national development.

American universities themselves must share responsibility for
accepting as satisfactory the technique and subject matter idea of
technical assistance. They take for granted the concept of a
university as a whole and the role of a free university in a free
society. Professors seldom reflect formally about such matters.
They are, after all, essentially specialists in particular subjects.
When sent abroad, they proceed as specialists in much the same
manner as at home. They are surprised when they find that expertise in their particular fields is not adequate to meet the needs
of a host-country university. A University of Kentucky professor
in Indonesia commented, "For the first time I am beginning to appreciate the many university services available at home that help
us carry out our teaching assignment, such as the registration procedure, the library, and even the activities of the business office."
Other American professors have discovered that before much
progress can be made abroad in engineering, agriculture, teacher
education, or other areas, such matters as the examination system,
the relation of students to a university, the full-time or part-time
status of the staff, or the pattern of degrees must be considered.
More fundamentally, their experience has made them realize that
the role of the professor abroad is different from that in the United
States. This affects receptivity to change or the results obtainable
from such matters as high competence in the subject or a new way
of teaching. The different roles assigned to a subject matter field
within a university and to a university within a society also affect
the outcome.

In short, experience of American universities with the technical
assistance programs to date has been that any large number of innovations in practice, technique, or subject matter depend upon
innovations in higher education as a whole and in the relevance
of its objectives to the needs of the society. The personnel sent
abroad by American universities has not been made aware of these
facts. Even more serious, the great majority of the programs of
university technical assistance have never had fundamental objectives formulated for them. Rather, the formal objectives have
been at the level of practice, technique, and subject matter. Without any advance agreement with the host-country institution that

more basic objectives are being sought or will have to be explored, it is difficult for the American university and its personnel to proceed from the specific to the general, from the superficial to the fundamental. American universities and sponsoring organizations have allowed host institutions and personnel to expect far-reaching results from superficial change.

There is no single magical system for universities. Higher education systems in England, Canada, and the United States, to take three examples, follow somewhat different lines, and all three systems help supply the needs of national development and of democracy. Other general patterns could be useful. It is important for the host country not to look upon American higher education as the pattern, but as one pattern that has worked under certain circumstances. University technical assistance projects can usefully be limited to one or two fields, but they cannot accomplish their aims unless the relation of the field or fields to the university and to society as a whole is examined carefully. And if mere imitation is to be avoided, a comparison will have to be made of the conditions that underlie the American or other systems with those that underlie the host-country system.

The Future of University Technical Assistance
Abroad Programs

There is a continuing need for American universities to engage in technical assistance abroad. However, a more precise set of criteria for such university activity is called for, and a new basic philosophy.

Criteria of Relevance. Two major criteria of relevance for university technical assistance programs overseas emerge from this study. First, a negative criterion: Nonuniversity contracting groups or government agencies or foundations themselves should carry out as many of the technical assistance programs as possible in order that scarce university resources may be preserved. Such a criterion is essential for effective United States policy in higher education in the present university emergency. The distinctive usefulness of university contracts is largely in situations which call for a team engaged in institution-building or for continuing institutional support, and in which assistance from a university is required or highly advantageous. University support may be required (1) because of the reliance that must be placed on the use of university personnel, (2) because the assignment falls in that part of higher education in which only universities have had experience, or (3) because universities as institutions and professors as individuals have a unique level of prestige in the host country or a unique nonpolitical character that permits receptivity to their suggestions lacking in the case of others.

Second, a positive criterion: Universities should engage in those programs and only those programs that are related to their own institutional objectives. University integrity and balance must be maintained. University competence abroad must be paralleled by university competence at home. Furthermore, universities need to take steps to integrate the projects into their regular departments. If such integration is not possible because of faculty resistance or for other reasons, universities ought not engage in the projects concerned. Otherwise, universities act as mere contractors, not as educational institutions.

If such criteria were rigidly adhered to, at least a third of the projects under university auspices would be eliminated and perhaps two-thirds or more of their personnel would be conserved for other purposes. University projects and personnel, in appropriate circumstances, could be replaced by projects and personnel of other organizations. University participation is not required in many aspects of the present programs; technical and subject matter personnel can be found elsewhere. This is less true of foundation-financed projects than of those financed by ICA. Some of the programs rely on excessive numbers of American professors abroad. If the institution of innovation by the host country is accepted as a prime objective, it would seldom be necessary to send more than four or five professors, almost never more than six or eight. A reduction in the number of present projects and in the size of the university teams overseas would help the universities develop programs of higher quality by reducing the heavy administrative burdens, making the staff abroad appear less like miniature USOMs or embassies, and permitting greater care in sending abroad only highly qualified personnel. Large operational teams with their tendency to introduce strictly American ideas would be avoided. Such a course would also enhance the ability of American universities to experiment with new kinds of technical assistance programs.

The provision of substitute professors should not be confused with the more basic goal of lending technical assistance. American universities do not have the manpower to provide professors for the underdeveloped countries of the world. The present university technical assistance programs overseas should be sharply reduced in number, in size, and in scope.

Action by Sponsors. If American universities are to demonstrate to host-country personnel the role of an American university in the United States and if they are to be permitted to be as effective as they can be abroad, four major steps need to be taken by sponsoring organizations in regard to university technical assistance abroad programs. Changes must be made in regard to co-optation, selection, operation, and evaluation. If substantial reliance on universities is to continue, both government agencies and the foundations should develop more effective relations with them. Representatives of the sponsoring agency should sit down with representatives of the universities concerned to plan the major forms of participation and the appropriate general objectives for future programs. This goes well beyond the conferences so far initiated by ICA with the Committee on Institutional Projects Abroad of the American Council on Education, which have largely been confined to financial and contractual details and to ICA and university administrators. Foundation or ICA representatives and university specialists in higher education and in subject matter fields need to be brought together more regularly than through a chance meeting in Washington or New York, or through informal contact at a professional meeting. These persons could in time provide useful suggestions as to possible objectives of the programs. In turn, administrators of universities and sponsoring organizations could develop general policies concerning the operation of the programs. General criteria of relevance for university contracts, together with general policies concerning their operation, laid down in advance and revised from time to time, would help avoid the serious risks of American universities in undertaking tasks that are ill-conceived or not thought through and that they cannot fulfill because of a nationwide shortage of staff. It is a standard procedure in administration to establish a means for continuous development and review of policy with clientele and contracting groups. Foundations and ICA should not be exceptions.

Sponsoring organizations play a leading role in selecting the

American universities to participate, since in technical assistance programs university self-selection is not frequent, and the host country cannot often identify universities that might be qualified and interested (see Chapter 11). At present, selection is carried out casually. Some foundation or ICA employee makes a contact with someone he happens to know at some university, or a letter is broadcast to a dozen universities asking if they are interested. Personal contact and the casting of the large net are supplemented by *ad hoc* advice from a variety of sources.

Sponsoring agencies urgently need to review their methods of selecting American universities. One promising innovation would be for major sponsors to find a few outside consultants in each major subject matter field, whose responsibility would be to keep in contact with university personnel and advise the sponsoring agency on the selection of universities. Perhaps the sponsors could allocate more of their own staff time to making contacts with prospective American universities. Selection panels made up of representatives of sponsors and university or professional groups could review prospective contractors for particular assignments abroad. Another possibility would be for major sponsors or, preferably, the universities themselves to form consortia of universities with some common resources for and interests in technical assistance. These consortia could then undertake one or more projects in the appropriate fields as desirable, sharing the burdens of staff support but also sharing in the professional advancement such programs would bring to their staffs. They would do their own "selecting." Whatever the ultimate solution, the need for action is immediate because of the large number of projects involving universities, the need for distributing demands upon university resources as broadly as possible, and the desirability of encouraging a high level of performance abroad through selection procedures. Recently a university that turned in what was described by ICA representatives as the worst job in its field was selected for another contract in a closely related field in another country. No stigma was attached to this institution for failure abroad, in part because of the poor method of selection.

A third needed change is more appropriate relations between university and sponsor. Day-to-day sponsor supervision of an inter-university contract or of any other program that is basically a project in higher education is inappropriate and offensive. American universities at home suffer no such indignities. Both host and American universities must be given the freedom to develop and experiment. Although their activities in higher education touch every part of society, their activities are separable and need not involve daily coordination. With ICA contracts, such independence in operation is all the more essential in countries that are sensitive to United States interference in their affairs. The new AID program envisages greatly increased assistance by universities and other contractors in highly sensitive areas such as host-country development programming, and operational independence from AID will be essential in such instances.

Fourth, a more thorough periodic review of the programs and a more careful consideration of the extension of the contracts is needed. Currently, day-to-day supervision is about the only regular kind of review that takes place, and even it occurs in only a part of any program. Of course, universities are required to submit periodic reports; and *ad hoc* program reviews by sponsoring agencies occur from time to time. There is need for biennial program reviews by representatives of the sponsoring organization, the university, and the host-country institution. Such reviews cannot be made adequately by the familiar traveling junketeer from each of the three groups. Reviews should also be carried out from time to time by persons not immediately involved, for a period of several weeks, with frank and candid evaluation and criticism submitted to all three parties, including their highest echelons. An isolated example of an outside review occurred with the Oklahoma State program in Ethiopia. It was conducted by the dean of agriculture at the American University of Beirut. Contract renewal should depend on favorable reports from these periodic reviews. There should be no softness in judgment because the sponsoring agency is afraid to hurt the feelings of a powerful university president or to make an unpopular decision. An outside evaluation would minimize this problem. Such an evaluation would encourage each project to identify its objectives and revise them as the project evolves and host-country needs change or are better recognized.

New Kinds of Programs. These are suggestions for improving the existing pattern of university contracts overseas. However, the pattern itself is defective in concept.

ICA and to a lesser extent certain foundations look upon American universities as merely means to their ends. No recognition of university aims and objectives is present. Consequently, the contracts for technical services abroad tend to be narrow instruments, defining the job a university is to do overseas very strictly. ICA contracts, especially, are neolithic. They usually are for services in a single subject matter. No money is allocated for the American universities' research objectives or for their programs at home. The universities are looked upon with suspicion, even with fear.

While authorities speak of the great need for more manpower for the technical assistance effort and more know-how, ICA and some foundations do little to try to alleviate the shortages. They continue to parcel out overseas technical assistance in little packages. They ignore the relationship between regular university activities and technical assistance needs. They have been cynical when universities have asked for broad contracts. An ICA official emphasized: "The universities are dishonest. They come to us claiming competence to do a job overseas. Then they turn right around and ask us for research money. Either they don't need to do research or they're not competent." The ICA habit of looking upon universities as just another set of contractors has resulted in its failing to recognize that universities can potentially do much to relieve the shortages of personnel and know-how in technical assistance through their regular and special teaching and research activities. ICA has put a drain on universities instead of trying to develop their resources.

A sharp about-face is called for. The concept of positive contracting must be introduced. Contracts with universities are not just a necessary evil; viewed broadly, they are a great asset to the nation in technical assistance. Universities must be treated as complete institutions with their own integrity and balance, which must be maintained. Contracts or grants not only must be consistent with university objectives but must contribute to them. New research undertakings, new international emphases in the several disciplines, new international educational programs for young Americans, new training programs for Americans going abroad, new multipurpose and multisubject matter programs abroad—these are a few of the possibilities. If contracts and grants included such items, many universities that now shy away from them would gladly participate. Thus the contract resources available to the sponsors would be increased and know-how and personnel resources of all kinds would be augmented.

New concepts of contracting should be coupled with new concepts of relating to host countries. If it is assumed that the basic reason for involving universities in technical assistance programs is to bring higher education to bear more effectively on the needs of national development in the host country, certain requirements are evident. Among the more important is recruitment of American professors who are centrally interested in their fields in relation both to a country's national development and to a system of higher education—a system based on academic freedom and one that contributes to the growth of other democratic institutions.

There are not enough persons interested and knowledgeable in these areas, even about higher education in the United States. There are many experts on chemistry in American universities, but few who can relate the contribution of university chemistry to development of the United States in the past hundred years. There are fine specialists in public administration, even comparative administration, yet few who can show specifically the relation between the academic work in public administration and national development in the United States in the past five to seven decades. There are thousands of professors in the United States, but few among them who appear to have thought about the relation of the American university system as a whole to national development, much less to have carried out research on the subject. Here and there some have made beginnings. There are some studies of the land-grant college system that contain needed information. But there is nothing comprehensive, even for a single field.

Similar knowledge about the host country is required. There are even fewer data on higher education and national development in the host countries, although some of their more active planning commissions or official bodies of inquiry have made useful general beginnings. Before American experience in higher education can have much meaning for a host country, university teams abroad must have knowledge concerning the history of development and the role of higher education in it, the relation of higher education to the society as a whole, the national development objectives and the possible contribution to them of higher education and its component parts. It would not be necessary to undertake the entire task at the beginning. Much of the work could be carried out field by field, by those with special interests and competence.

Once the patterns of higher education and national development in the two societies are outlined, it is for the host country to decide whether there is anything in the American experience that might fit the local culture, its traditions, and its aims. Is mass education at the higher level desirable? Is the American pattern of applied curricula useful? Can universities maintain their independence and yet work closely with government and community groups? To the extent that adequate data contribute to decision-making, these and many similar questions could be answered more rationally when the data were available. To the extent that understanding of a successful system in being stimulates action, decisions supporting innovation would be encouraged.

American universities have no panaceas to offer host countries. We do have our own remarkable experience as a demonstration of what one nation did, but we have exceedingly few data bearing on it. It is possible that the problem of relating higher education to national development in the United States in the nineteenth century, or even today, is entirely different in kind from that in underdeveloped countries. The present university contract system assumes that we have answers that we do not have, that competence in subject matter and skill in techniques constitute a force for change that alone they do not and cannot exert. We need to recognize more fully the limited applicability of the present system, its peripheral or supplemental nature. It would have more meaning if it were part of a new central pattern for technical cooperation in higher education.

Important changes in higher education take a long time and may require painful changes in the society as a whole if education is to make useful contributions to national development. Success in interuniversity technical assistance programs will depend on the desire by a host-country government and host institution of higher learning and its staff members to maximize the contribution of the institution to national development. This desire should not spring merely from a promise of equipment or quick trips to the United States or around the world. Only if the host feels the need deeply should the possibility of a program be contemplated. American universities lose and no one gains when programs are forced upon host-country groups, as occasionally they are at present. American universities should stop wasting their precious resources by sending a team of university professors in the hope that they may be able to work a miracle. A single higher education consultant of ICA or of a foundation, or a single Fulbright professor can help develop initial interest in major change, not only with less waste of resources, but leaving behind him more respect for American universities. Omitting programs that are not taken seriously by the host country doubtless will mean far fewer programs at first, but if they are omitted, American higher education can contribute far more to the development of nations that are genuinely interested.

More and more, countries have or are developing basic structures for higher education and personnel to staff them. Some, such as India and Pakistan, even have a surplus of personnel in many fields. Where structures and personnel permit, a new kind of university program should be established. This model program should begin with recognition by the host-country institution and government of a need to relate higher education more fully to national development and/or a free society. Such a desire may be restricted to a small part of the institution, or may extend throughout it. In any event, those who had such a desire would make contact with an American university having similar interests, and two or more professors from each institution would be designated to make a thorough exploration of the relation of higher education to national development in the fields of study designated, first in the United States and then in the host country. Such a study would probably take at least full time for a year or more, perhaps up to a year in each country. At the end of this period, a report would be forthcoming that could be a useful guide to the host-country institution, and also would be equally valuable to the American university, to scholars all over the world desiring to learn more about the topic, and to practitioners desiring to chart courses of action. During and after the research process, policy discussions at the host institution could be arranged so that the closest possible relation could be established between research findings and policy decisions. In this manner basic innovation would be encouraged.

The period of time for the basic study could be shortened or lengthened depending on the clarity of existing national-development goals, the extent of background research that led to their establishment, whether new institutions are to be established or old ones changed, and the relative shortage of university personnel in the host country and the United States for the undertaking. It would be essential that host-country nationals participate willingly and as equals with the Americans, even though some host professors would not be able to spend as much time as the Americans. Undoubtedly there would be numerous countries and many institutions where professors with high prestige would refuse to be involved even on a part-time basis. In that case, if they fairly represented the institution, there would be no use in a university contract in any case. Nothing would be lost.

After serious study of universities and national development, the host-country institution may conclude that to achieve development objectives it requires some special help in subject matter and technique. The host institution would then know for what purpose such competences were needed and what results were to be expected, a lack in most current programs. And the acquisition of such competence could come quickly and meaningfully and by many different means if the major objectives were clarified. In some cases, the host institution would not need help in implementing its decisions. In most instances one or a few advisers might be necessary.

Such a program is not glamorous, and it may not make effective window dressing, but it is intellectually honest. In its deliberate, long-range pace, it emphasizes that real improvement in higher education cannot take place in one or two years. In its emphasis on finding out the facts before making decisions, it both sets a scholarly tone, and in its own way points up the usefulness of an empirical approach to knowledge. Fundamentally it assists the host institution in identifying and selecting new goals.

The new program here suggested would be especially appropriate where technical assistance, as such, is desired in higher education. In many countries there is no desire for the changes implied by the term "technical assistance." In such cases, the most effective means of cultural relations in higher education would be joint research projects by American and host-country professors or the one- or two-way exchange of professors. By these means both American and host-country institutions could benefit from the contacts with each other, augmenting the knowledge and insights of both and presenting, indirectly, many ideas for innovation. The line between technical assistance and cultural exchange is indeed a thin one.

The new suggested program for relating to host-country nationals is only one of many possible alternatives. However, it would be in striking contrast to existing university programs of technical assistance abroad in at least five ways. The present programs emphasize the "foot-in-the-door" approach in convincing host-country nationals of the desirability of change; the new program would provide a more intellectual approach as befits universities. The present programs try to force change by direct American administration of host-country institutions or parts thereof from time to time; the new program would be based on the assumption that host personnel must desire change before a substantial program is inaugurated. The present programs are often emergency and short-range in character; the new program would emphasize deliberate speed and long-range aspects. The present programs assume that substantial host-country educational structures and trained personnel do not exist; the new program would recognize that they increasingly do and will exist. Above all, the present programs assume we have knowledge we do not have about what is best for the host country; the new program would be based on acquiring necessary knowledge before action.

Universities are institutions of higher learning. Their distinctive purpose is education as well as training. Education requires that one go from what is known to what is unknown and that new knowledge be gained. American universities can help fulfill the historic mission of universities by joining with their contemporaries overseas in pushing back the boundaries of the unknown in regard to the relation of higher education to national development through both new research and teaching programs. Such action would redound to the mutual benefit of universities in both countries as well as contribute to the future of mankind. Universities would be developers of resources rather than just sterile resources to be bought and sold in the contracting market place. In the meantime, American universities can leave to others much of the less exacting task of technical support for overseas programs.

Chapter 15

AN AGENDA FOR AMERICAN UNIVERSITIES

American universities have drifted on the seas of international exchange programs without rudder and direction, without compass and destination. There have been exceptions. Yet, by and large, the international exchange programs of American universities have been creatures of the moment, improvisations rather than long-range commitments. They have lacked a fundamental philosophy, a fundamental relevance to the university and its objectives.

Basis for Participation in Programs

The first step in developing criteria by which universities may decide whether to participate in foreign programs and if so, in which programs, is an assessment of their own resources and aims. American universities are confronted with insufficient financial support and a scarcity of qualified personnel, at a time when the demand for higher education is rapidly expanding. How may they best allocate their limited resources? Unnecessary activities must be eliminated if additional burdens are to be carried. International programs must compete successfully on their merits for the limited resources of an institution.

Allocation of Resources at Home. The allocation of resources in American higher education is in some ways unique. Most university systems in other lands have not departed far from the image of the classical university. The classical university, whatever its shortcomings, at least has a clear central focus. It is aimed at the search for truth, at the discovery and conservation of knowledge for knowledge's sake. Its teaching purpose is to develop, at an

288

advanced level, the ability of its students to reason clearly and to think independently. It admits a relatively small group of students, presumably constituting a future elite. Both teaching and research are rather abstract or theoretical.

The American university system at the beginning was modeled after the European. But the classical university and its objectives were inadequate for the needs facing the United States. Knowledge for knowledge's sake, thinking independently, and reasoning clearly were important, but were not enough to help the development of a vast pioneer nation. University graduates needed skill in performing specific tasks in society. Research, like teaching, was to be increasingly applied to the solution of problems confronting ordinary people. Knowledge was to be made available to the largest possible number. The influence of the frontier and the development emphasis accompanying the agricultural and industrial revolutions resulted in demands that universities keep the needs of society in mind. This approach to higher education spread until it influenced private institutions about as much as public ones.

Even the old liberal arts colleges modified their programs somewhat, but the great changes in American higher education came with the appearance of new and specialized small institutions and the large, complex universities. There is now at least one kind of small institution for almost every vocational need. The large universities have grown until they have become supermarkets of education, displaying a rich array of products.

With the introduction of the idea that universities should carry on socially useful activities in regard to knowledge, the doors were opened wide to the acceptance of new activities. Today, a complete listing of the activities carried on by universities in the United States would be staggering. The number, variety, and scope of courses and degrees continue to expand. For example, a student expecting to be an administrator no longer must major in the social sciences, or in political science or economics. Instead, if he selects his school appropriately, he may major in public administration and, within it, municipal administration, or if he finds that too general, he may concentrate on municipal fire-protection administration. The business-minded student need not major in economics. He can major in business administration, or, within it, in office management, hotel administration, or mobile home administration.

Much staff time at universities is now spent on noncredit teaching. Many universities compete with evening classes of high schools in offering elementary courses in foreign languages, homemaking, or typing. A few universities now offer to organizations of citizens a rather complete set of services, including central secretariat, office space, and advice from staff members. Universities have become centers for many types of conferences, to the discomfiture of commercial hotel interests. Faculty or administrative staff members may roam far in numerous extension activities or other services. In research, a wide range of projects, from the most theoretical to the most practical, are to be found, perhaps without relation to each other. Universities offer a large variety of late afternoon and evening events such as concerts, lectures, or films. They aid the extracurricular activities of students, over a wide range. Large resources are involved in intercollegiate athletics and other public relations activities.

At one extreme, a handful of proponents of service have become so imbued with the idea that they have proclaimed that there is no longer any room for the ivory tower at the modern university! At the other extreme, some proponents of the liberal arts colleges have defended most aspects of classical education. A more moderate approach prevails, for the most part. For the present discussion, the main point is that higher education as a whole and nearly every institution within it are faced with the necessity to develop objective and clear criteria for selection among programs, for allocating scarce resources. Once socially useful activities are admitted, on whatever scale, how can a university distinguish between those activities that are appropriate for it and those that are not so that it does not assume too many responsibilities?

Who is to say that helping the petroleum industry is less socially useful or less appropriate to a university than a curriculum in applied mechanics? On what basis is a university to choose between a course in industrial sociology and one in home economics? Can the social usefulness of research in packaging be defended as well as research in agricultural productivity? The American university has tended to lose a discriminating standard and an integrating principle by adding the socially useful concept to that of the classical university. Under the former concept, a university can engage in any activities that are related to knowledge alone or to useful knowledge, and yet carry out a function appropriate to a university. Nevertheless, criteria of relevance can, and must, be developed.

Universities can confine themselves to that kind of socially useful knowledge and its application that has some theoretical content, and leave to other organizations areas of nontheoretical knowledge. If the distinction were applied, some of the current activities of universities would disappear. A course in typing has little theoretical basis; or a course in social dancing. If extension and conference activities had to meet this test, a sharp reduction would take place. Some highly applied research would have to go, also.

A second criterion may be more specific and consequently more usable. The pragmatic test can be applied: are there other organizations in society that can perform the activity just as well? Other agencies can equally well conduct many activities such as applied research, extension, conference, and noncredit teaching now undertaken by universities. Some of the vocational curricula could be transferred to trade schools or to the in-service training programs of government or industry.

Undoubtedly other more discriminating and precise criteria of relevance could be developed. However, the more specific the criteria proposed, the less likely it is that they will be appropriate to all institutions, considering the latter's variety.

Application to International Programs. The criteria of relevance for university activities at home should also constitute the criteria for their activities abroad, unless the international programs are to be mere appendages. If the criteria for programs adopted by institutions of higher education center about theoretical knowledge and the absence of other organizations able to perform this function, many of the present international programs of American universities would be outside a proper university focus. In technical assistance, universities engage in rather detailed chores in nontheoretical areas, and compete with several other organizations that do the same kind of thing very effectively. Not only do some of the student programs lack theoretical content, either basic or applied, but some compete with the educational tours conducted ably by nonuniversity groups.

Beyond these rather general considerations, it is difficult to establish many specific criteria for the international exchange programs of all American universities because there are many kinds of institutions. Each university, college, school, or department can and should establish its own criteria, however. At small institutions, criteria can be established that are meaningful for the entire university. At the larger institutions, most of the selection of criteria must of necessity lie with smaller academic units such as the departments or schools, since large American universities are seldom unified bodies.

In the last three or four years, at least 30 to 40 universities have begun to plan for international programs which can involve an entire institution, college, or department. This policy has resulted from the large number of programs, the desirability for some degree of coordination, and an effort to expand what has been termed the "international dimension" on the home campuses. One of the most common patterns to emerge has been for a director, dean, or vice president to assume responsibility for international activities of all kinds. This is the pattern at Rutgers and New York University. Michigan State has aimed at university-wide coordination through a dean of international programs and, in several of its colleges such as agriculture, business and public service, and education, through college-wide coordinators. At Texas the foreign student adviser has wide responsibility in the international area. The Harvard Business School has a general international program coordinator. The department of government at Indiana University has developed a departmental plan.

As the number of programs further increases, more general planning at institutions or parts thereof will probably ensue. Whether this will mean a closer relation of the programs to on-campus activities will depend on whether the special directors or deans work through the regular academic units instead of developing separate empires. The emergence of special directors or deans is to be deplored to the extent that they administer programs of peripheral concern to an institution, programs that do not meet the criteria of relevance, or programs that are not integrated with the regular academic units. A few directors or deans serve a highly constructive purpose by acting as central coordinators and by applying criteria of relevance to the selection of programs and to the clarification of their objectives.

The many differences among colleges and universities in the United States do not preclude cooperation among them. A few consortia of universities have already developed in student-abroad, Peace Corps, and ICA activities. More will undoubtedly be forthcoming as institutional objectives in the international exchange programs become clearer. Consortia can also play a leadership role in defining more precisely various criteria of relevance.

Many other devices can be utilized for exerting leadership in framing *general* criteria of relevance for groups of universities or colleges. For example, special associations of universities can examine appropriate objectives for international exchange programs for their members, as the American Association of Land-Grant Colleges and State Universities has done in the technical assistance field or the Association of American Colleges in study-abroad programs. Universities with special kinds of programs can band together for program and support purposes, as those with technical assistance programs have done in the Committee on Institutional Projects Abroad of the American Council on Education, and those with study-abroad programs have done through the Council on Student Travel. Private groups such as The Experiment in International Living and the Institute of International Education exercise both leadership and service functions. Each professional association is coming to have its international committee.

At an official level, the Board of Foreign Scholarships for the Fulbright program and the United States Advisory Commission on Educational Exchange have influenced government policy. The Committee on Exchange of Persons of the Conference Board of Associated Research Councils has effectively represented the several professional associations in connection with IES programs. No ICA advisory bodies for universities have existed to assist in agency-wide substantive policies, nor have foundations used such devices.

Despite these many existing vehicles, the Ford Foundation's Committee on the University and World Affairs in its report, *The University and World Affairs,* has suggested yet another:

What is especially needed is a new organization, based upon American universities and colleges, but able to take into account broad national needs. It would provide a mechanism through which universities and colleges can consider together educational planning, the development and employment of educational competence in world affairs, and the systematic cumulation and appraisal of growing educational experience in world affairs. It would facilitate communication for these same ends with agencies of government, business and foundations in the United States, and with the institutions of other nations.

In relation to the government, the organization would provide a source of independent and authoritative advice on matters such as the development of educational institutions abroad, educational exchange, and the support of American university programs for developing American competence. Government funds allocated for these purposes, however, would be made available directly to the educational institutions, which would accept responsibility individually or in cooperation.[1]

The proposal has the merit of retaining the individual universities' direct contact with sponsors. It has one major, perhaps fatal, drawback. No one instrument can or should presume to speak authoritatively for American higher education. No "chosen instrument" is suitable, given the desired diversity of universities in the United States. American higher education's many voices, large and small, private and public, professorial and administrative, should continue to be heard effectively, not silenced or coordinated into a single chorus by an elite group. What is needed is more experimentation by American universities in international exchange programs, not authoritative pronouncements of university policy for all. The new organization could be one voice, however, and an important one.

These and other organizations can and should contribute to policy making by both universities and sponsors. They can and should paint the broad picture. They can contribute immeasurably to clarity of thinking. Yet *specific* criteria of relevance will continue to be identified primarily, if at all, by individual institutions and their component parts. To be meaningful, such criteria must be relevant to each institution's peculiar needs.

The importance of establishing criteria of relevance is illustrated by the experience of institutions accepting or rejecting international programs. Some smaller colleges and universities have rejected opportunities to engage in international exchange programs, and almost all larger universities have done so on occasion. Lack of faculty interest, lack of community or alumni support, and scarcity of resources are three prominent reasons. A fourth reason is lack of academic merit in the programs. This is in part a key to the other three, since if the academic relevance were clearly established, more interest, support, and resources might be forthcoming.

In those instances where universities or parts of universities with clear and unified objectives at home have undertaken projects abroad, the results have tended to be much better than the results obtained by universities with unclear or scattered activities. A

[1] New York: Ford Foundation, 1960, pp. 77–78.

Smith or a Middlebury, with clear academic objectives, can carry on effective student-abroad programs. Some small colleges, with vague and uncertain academic objectives, have difficulty. A University of California Medical School, being relatively precise as to its criteria of relevance, can carry out a successful technical assistance project in Indonesia; some business and public administration schools, even at well-known universities, have difficulty, in part because of their diverse activities and aims (Garraty and Adams, chap. 5 and Appendix; Smith, p. 73; Adams and Garraty, pp. 15–17, 24–26, 129–131).

Those universities that have accepted international programs as an integral part of the work of their academic units at home have been much more successful in their international programs than those universities that have just taken the programs as "another" function. However, there is little reason for integrating international exchange programs into the regular colleges or departments if academic criteria of relevance are not used at the beginning to select appropriate programs. Even advice from the faculty may not be useful. Thus, over half the coordinators of the programs report to the central administrations of their universities rather than to the regular colleges or departments. And nearly half the coordinators do not have any policy or liaison committee in the departments or colleges (Inventory, pp. 44–45). Many international programs of American universities are as peripheral to the objectives of the departments as are many university off-campus activities or many of the isolated, applied research projects. Like them, international programs are independently organized. They are ignored by most of the faculty, and sometimes actually resented or opposed.

The frequent lack of a test of relevance has serious consequences overseas as well as at home. One of the aims of many of the university programs in technical assistance is to convince host countries that their concepts of higher education are too narrow, and that their desire to make a maximum contribution to national development can be fulfilled by taking on additional activities. The experience of American universities is supposed to demonstrate the advantages of such a plan. Instead, many American universities carrying out diverse international projects give a demonstration of how such activities lead to confusion of academic with nonacademic objectives, and consequent loss of a unifying principle in a university. If this is the American system, host-country institutions want none of it. There are also serious consequences in the case of student-abroad programs. Unless American universities can relate them to the central purposes of a university, they are likely to deteriorate into mere foreign tours. Students are shortchanged and the prestige of American universities suffers.

The lack of clear educational policies at home is often compounded by lack of clear objectives abroad, and together they lead to university participation in inappropriate foreign programs, or to lack of success in those chosen. Multiple objectives are the rule, rather than the exception, for international programs, and failure to establish priorities among them leads to further difficulties.

Multiple Objectives. Nearly all programs have multiple objectives, and the result is that frequently there is some conflict among them. While few instances of outright incompatibility of the several objectives are to be found, conflict does result from disagreements as to emphasis or priority. The Cornell anthropological programs in Peru and India were viewed primarily as research programs by the Americans and projects significant in development by host-country groups. No clear decision was made as to priorities. In the University of Chicago program in Chile, different groups desired different degrees of emphasis on research and on the teaching of Chileans. Hokkaido University wanted its students and staff to learn the latest American techniques in agricultural science; the University of Massachusetts wanted to show the Japanese how an American land-grant college works and its contribution to national development. In research programs, Americans have often been principally interested in basic research, host-country groups in development or in the training aspect of the research. Technical assistance programs have often included American stress on organizational change or on new techniques of teaching, while host-country groups have been more concerned with their students learning a subject. Student-abroad programs have not involved much disagreement on objectives between American and host-country groups, since the latter have not played a major role in most of these programs.

Americans or host-country nationals do not always agree among themselves. Sometimes members of a foundation or government agency agree with neither the American nor the host institution.

Disagreement on objectives takes place within as well as between groups. Leaders of higher education tend to stress national policy or institution-wide objectives, while professors may seek professional, departmental, or faculty aims. Procedures under which programs have been developed without faculty knowledge or consent have accentuated such differences. For example, Turkish leaders imposed on their university staffs both the Georgetown language program and the New York University–Ankara law program. Within financing organizations there are differences between central and field offices or between geographical and subject matter specialists. Both American and host-country students and professors who go abroad often see project aims differently than do their colleagues at home.

Even the simplest international exchange program involves several groups and subgroups, and each of them tends to use the program to achieve one or more objectives. For example, a small student-abroad program will be affected by the interests of the students who participate, their academic advisers, the faculty members, various members of the administrative hierarchy, and donors, if any. Like American university exchange programs, those of governments, foundations, and foreign universities also involve several groups and multiple objectives. The question is not whether multiple objectives exist. The relevant questions are whether the interplay of groups and objectives has tended to make the program function poorly and whether among the several objectives there are clearly discernible, important, and suitable reasons for participation by an American university.

Unstated Goals. The unstated motives behind a program often help to explain differences in objectives. The most prevalent informal motives have to do with personal and institutional prestige. This is more true of student-abroad programs and technical assistance projects than of programs with religious overtones and a few of the research projects. Prestige-seeking seldom runs counter to formal objectives but may de-emphasize them. Prestige may flow from participating in a program but not from achieving its objectives. Often some of those concerned are not in a position to know whether a program is highly successful.

Closely related to prestige is a desire for preferment among various influential groups. It was a factor in requests by Waseda and Keio Universities for business administration or industrial management programs (to gain support of the business community) and in promotion by ICA of a textile engineering project in Peru (to do something desired by American-financed textile companies and thus gain or keep their support for the ICA program).

The variety of informal goals is great. In at least one student-abroad program and one technical assistance program the motive of the American university was to let a faculty member do what he wanted (i.e., head up a project) as long as he did not involve the rest of the institution. Some technical assistance projects were prompted by the desire of some host-country personnel to influence or replace some of their colleagues against the latters' will; a technical assistance project may be the opportunity or "excuse" they need. Financial motives may underlie a project. A few private American universities have found that sending students abroad is cheaper than educating them on the American campus, especially when it is necessary to expand physical facilities. Some host institutions have accepted technical assistance programs of American universities in order to get the money involved, and some host governments have accepted them in order more fully to justify requests for other types of economic aid or technical assistance. There is also some politeness underlying a considerable number of programs. The responding institution does not want to hurt the feelings of the originator, and agrees to a cooperative arrangement without any real enthusiasm for it.

Multiple objectives and unstated goals are normal aspects of any university exchange project. The aim must be to understand them, assign priority among the several objectives, and know what to expect from the informal and unstated motives. This course will facilitate the accomplishment of the formal objectives as well as promote harmony in a project which is worth understanding at all. Accurate expectations are products of candor, close association, and careful research and reflection. In turn, candor, intimacy, and reflection are augmented over time so that emphases and priorities can be established among the several identifiable objectives. All of this assumes that selection of a program has been based on the suitability of its objectives, that those participating attach importance to these objectives, and that a flexible arrangement can be established for altering objectives from time to time as new ones appear and old ones fade in significance.

Clarity of Objectives. One of the most striking aspects of the international programs of American universities is the lack of clear, consistent objectives. Clarity of all objectives was characteristic of only a minority of the programs, although lack of clarity of any objectives was characteristic of very few. This is as true of the student-abroad programs as it is of the technical assistance projects. It is as true of the religious programs abroad as it is of the participant training programs in the United States. Even some of the small two-way student or professor exchanges or some of the research programs have lacked focus, although they are far less subject to this criticism than the others. Their objectives, like their size and scope, are rather modest.

There is little agreement among American universities on the appropriate objectives for each kind of project. Some universities will emphasize one, some another objective in basically identical programs. ICA officials have with justice complained that they do not see where competence claimed by universities begins and where it ends. Activities by American universities in student-abroad programs or in participant training programs in the United States show a similar dispersion. These activities range from formal class and research work to the organizing of a tour of Paris and a trip to an American automobile factory. Sometimes the emphasis on touring seems greater than the emphasis on classwork or research.

The lack of clarity of objectives in international programs (as well as the lack of criteria of relevance for American university participation) is equally characteristic of sponsoring agencies and host-country institutions. Sponsoring agencies place temptations in the path of universities in the form of preferred grants or contracts. Many of the grants or contracts could just as well be offered to other groups such as consulting firms or educational tour conductors. Sponsoring agencies are unsure in their own minds as to what activities are appropriate for universities. While it may be unrealistic to ask them to develop a policy on this matter when the universities themselves lack one, their own objectives could be sharpened considerably; similarly with the host-country organizations. They could inquire more thoroughly into the relevance of a program for an American university. The host university could question the usefulness of employing its facilities and resources in connection with a proposed student-abroad program, or a host government could question the utility of a university consulting contract. Here again it is unreasonable to expect host-country groups to establish criteria of relevance for the projects of American universities, but not to expect host-country groups to think through their own aims clearly.

Even if all three major groups separately specified their objectives, there would remain difficulty of agreement among them. This is perhaps the central problem of programs involving all three groups. Among the broad aims of programs are to further the world affairs education of American students, help host-country groups, and stimulate international or cross-national research. Underlying these are varying emphases on foreign policy and advancement of knowledge, world peace, and the strengthening of American universities. Several of the aims and underlying emphases may be listed as goals in a particular program, the three major groups not pausing to determine priorities, or to consider possible conflicts, among them. The process of listing aims at the outset of a project is often an appeal to values, rather than part of a rationally conceived plan relating specific program objectives to the broad goals.

Aside from the possible conflict of multiple objectives and the existence of goals that had best remain unstated, there are several reasons for the lack of clarity in the formal objectives. Many of the international exchange programs of American universities are so recent that clarity of their stated objectives suffers because of inexperience or incompetence of the university personnel. More frequently, university personnel complained of lack of time and resources at the beginning for substantive matters such as program objectives; administrative problems absorbed all concerned. Also common was plain uncertainty; objectives could not be stated exactly because goals were not identified. Uncertainty in goals encourages wishful thinking; goals are stated in such a sweeping manner that their achievement is impossible. Some projects are frankly exploratory, with experimental operations, activities, or methods. Part of the purpose of an exploratory project is to define an area of cooperation more precisely.

At the beginning of a program, the participating organizations tend to postpone identifying specific long-range objectives, making a choice among them, or establishing a priority. It is felt that after the program is in operation it will be possible, on the basis of greater knowledge, to choose more exact general objectives, reconcile differences, and remove uncertainties. It is argued that rigidity is to be avoided, at least at first. There is some truth in this view, but there is also a large element of wishful thinking. Differences do not necessarily become resolved by the passage of time, and institutions that have not concerned themselves with general objectives in the initial stages are unlikely to do so after a project has begun. Even projects for exploring objectives must recognize this frankly.

The goals of every project are indeed subject to alteration as a project evolves. Yet such changes do not necessarily clarify goals. Often they lead to greater diversity and generality. A project may take on additional functions as it goes along, which may or may not be closely related to given specific objectives. Some of the long-range goals are of necessity general and abstract. Student-abroad programs are designed in part for impact on the students' lives after college, and technical assistance programs for ultimate diffusion of innovations within a society.

Clarity of objectives can be achieved more readily in some projects than in others. The aims of most research projects are rather easily stated; they are limited and specific. It is rather simple to define the objectives of technical education projects, such as those in Turkey of Spring Garden Institute in automotive maintenance or New York University in commercial education. Whether American students abroad or host-country students in the United States are involved, the objectives of liberal education are more difficult to state than those of technical education. Many broadly based technical assistance programs have objectives that elude concrete definition. Defining the specific objectives of a project designed to help reorient a system of higher education or one designed to change business administration practices is not a simple matter.

There are several consequences of the failure to develop clear-cut objectives with identifiable priorities. First of all, a large measure of drifting is likely to occur, with a lack of direction in the activities undertaken. Secondly, a certain dysfunction is likely to set in, one part of the project working at cross purposes with another part. In the third place, unrealistic or outright undesirable objectives may be sought. Finally, the means-end problem is accentuated. Thus, American universities have emphasized short-range aims and specific means rather than long-range and general objectives. The specific activities in which student and professor engage apparently come to carry their own justification. It is sometimes assumed that if a student goes abroad to study for a year this will necessarily result in a superior education for him, particularly in international affairs. It is sometimes assumed that if a professor goes abroad under a technical assistance project he will necessarily contribute to the acceleration of national development in the host country. In such instances, the specific means are confused with the more general ends or a causal relation is attributed between the means and the end that does not necessarily exist. There is a lack of information about what means are most likely to result in certain ends.

Technical assistance, student-abroad, and other programs affect the prestige of American universities by the failures or successes achieved and the image of American universities portrayed. A growing minority of the 184 universities with international programs seems to enjoy merely being preoccupied with all the activities attendant upon them, as if institutional and individual prestige depended upon such preoccupation. Among some reference groups within the United States, the mere number of programs a university has lends prestige to it, especially in the short run. In the long run, and especially in the host country, other factors prevail. If projects are executed capably, additional prestige may be forthcoming for the individual university or for the American university system as a whole, but failure abroad will injure both. Criteria of relevance and clear objectives can contribute to the long-range success of the programs and improve the reputation of American universities.

Alternative International Involvements

Most universities have opted not to participate in international programs. Some of these may achieve international objectives in other ways. Few universities have the resources to engage in more than one or two international programs of any one kind, and no university engages in programs of every kind. There is a selective process at work, a series of choices to be made. It is important to make the best choices.

Selection among Kinds of Programs. There are three types of programs, one of the main purposes of which is a contribution to education at the American university, and three other types designed chiefly to make a contribution to groups abroad. In the first category are the American student-abroad programs, the group-research abroad programs, and a variety of small one- or two-way exchange programs. In the second category are the two technical assistance programs, the participant training programs in the United States and the programs which involve sending of American professors overseas, as well as the various religious programs to further Christian education abroad.

The international activity with the greatest value to most American institutions in the long run is the student-abroad program. In its present form, this program is a very limited instrument of higher education. With easily introduced modifications, it could become a major factor. It can be adapted to the objectives of many kinds of institutions, to the needs of many different kinds of students. It can be closely relevant to academic goals and may be carried out with the highest of standards. It deserves the careful attention of universities and their faculties, and of sponsoring agencies.[2]

Projects for group research abroad for which an American university accepts institutional responsibility have recently expanded in number, but they are not and probably never will be the main instrument for research abroad by American scholars. On an individual basis, research abroad has been an important part of many disciplines almost since their origin. For example, professors of agriculture and the biological sciences have long undertaken field research overseas, as have those in the humanities. Social scientists and scholars in related areas have greatly increased such research activities since World War II. Among the reasons have been the rapid development of the disciplines, the desire to learn more about comparative aspects of the subject matter, and search for a social science that is not culture-bound. Physics, chemistry, and astronomy have already become completely world-wide, international disciplines.

Where continuing research by a group of scholars in a country is necessary, the university project has been used, as with the University of Michigan in Japan. Where special arrangements with the host-country government or institutions are necessary, as at present in archeological research by the University of Chicago in Egypt, the university project is helpful. Where comparative research is

[2] See Chaps. 4, 5, and 6 for a detailed discussion of these programs. The findings of the present study are fully supportive of the conclusions on study abroad of the Committee on the University and World Affairs. See its *Report* (New York: Ford Foundation, 1960), p. 19.

required in several countries simultaneously, the university project is a natural device, as with the multicountry research of Cornell in anthropology.

The likelihood that institutional research abroad will expand depends on the future of research. It seems likely that much more research in the future will be carried on overseas by American scholars, and by groups rather than individuals. Multicountry, comparative studies are in their infancy.

Special arrangements with host-country scholars or institutions and special permission from host-country governments will also be more common aspects of overseas research. Particularly in the less developed areas, the subjects of overseas research are increasingly related to the expanding national and international development plans of the host countries. Government authorities wish to be assured that research will be of maximum help to national development, or at least not inconsistent with it. Hereafter few American scholars will be able to carry on research abroad successfully without consulting with local scholars. To do so would be both impolite and unintelligent.[3]

For many years, a third type of international program of American universities has always operated as a minor part of the activities of the department, college, or university in which it has been located. This is the one- or two-way exchange of a few students or professors between an American and a host-country university. The diversity of the financing of these programs is greater than for any other type of international program; sources include special student funds, endowments, special contributions, university funds for scholarships and visiting professors, foundation awards, and, mostly on an *ad hoc* basis, government grants such as Fulbrights. Several purposes are sought by those who use the device. Some of the exchanges are on an institution-wide or college-wide basis, others are along strictly departmental lines. The former often are expected to encourage interest in another country on the part of the university at large, and the latter often are designed to develop competence in a particular subject matter, such as a foreign language or history. Both department- and institution-wide exchanges are frequently related to area studies.

The small one- or two-way exchange programs do not seem as

[3] See Chap. 7 for a discussion of research programs and small exchanges.

glamorous or important as the huge student-abroad or technical assistance programs, and yet in a number of instances they have received almost as much attention by American students and faculty. One way to encourage wide participation in such a program is for persons at the respective universities to take the initiative in raising part of the money, and to rely on outside funds, if any, for a part of the total costs. In cases where there are local fund-raising campaigns, many people on campus and in the community feel involved in the program. A second way of encouraging meaningful participation is to integrate such programs with the work of regular academic departments. University-wide programs often lack focus. Those programs that are connected with a department are normally tied into regular academic activities of a university. In the latter case, students and faculty make special efforts to meet and talk with the host-country national during his year's stay or to listen to the reports of the American sent abroad after his return. There are more organized efforts for impact on the American campus in some of these programs than in many of the large ones. They should be encouraged. The best of them can be of equal benefit to the host-country institution and the American university.

There has been considerable discussion of the value of permanent affiliations, university to university. The small exchange programs represent the most likely form for a permanent affiliation. Such affiliations are an attractive variation of international programs, but their success depends more on the initiative of departments and individual professors and students than on the initiative of top-level administrative leaders, although at least a minimum financial contribution from the university or the exchangees is needed. It would appear that most of the successful long-range affiliations are based on the common intellectual interests of university personnel in certain fields rather than on vague sister-institution-to-sister-institution considerations.

Large-scale university technical assistance is embodied in two kinds of technical assistance programs: technical assistance abroad (the sending of American professors overseas) and the participant training program in the United States (the sending of host-country nationals to American universities for work appropriate to their needs). Though the major impact of technical assistance programs is supposed to be felt abroad, they can be of advantage to American

universities as well. Most American universities with such programs have not realized the potential advantages to themselves of
engaging in these programs.

Some phases of many of the present university technical assistance abroad programs could be carried on by other groups or, in
other instances, could be dropped in favor of longer-range institution-building objectives. Technical assistance abroad programs
could and should be adapted to support more directly the long-
range objectives of both the American and the host institution.
Under such circumstances, some new programs would be required,
emphasizing research into the relation of higher education with national development, the objectives each institution desires to seek,
and the way in which cooperation between the two institutions
would help achieve these objectives. New programs like these
could be tailored in size to the personnel and other resources of the
two institutions and could provide a flexible basis for long-range
cooperation.[4]

The proper role for an American university in participant education and training varies with the connection, if any, to technical
assistance abroad programs. Participant education and training is
in one sense a supplement to, and in another sense a substitute for,
sending American professors abroad. If the host institution desires
to increase the number of its faculty members or the competence
of its current staff, it will find that participant programs offer a
better opportunity for education of host-country staff members than
technical assistance abroad. In a host country, no group of American professors, however competent, can by themselves give as balanced and forceful a demonstration of the subject matter in which
they specialize or the methods of teaching, research, or extension or
the way the American system works as can be given at an American
university. To be more effective in bringing about change in the
less developed countries, participant training needs to be coupled
with sending one or a few American professors abroad to prepare
the host-country visitors for their participant experience, and to
assist follow-through on their return home. In the more developed
host institutions, there is little or no need to combine participant
training with training or consultation in the host country. In such
countries each device may be effective by itself.

[4] See Chaps. 9 to 14 for an extended discussion of the technical assistance
abroad programs and Chap. 8 for the participant programs.

However, the sending of a small number of American professors abroad should be no substitute for agreement on objectives. For example, no group of American professors abroad can help out much if the host institution has so little commitment to the undertaking that it is not willing to permit its returning participants to teach or have status as staff members; this has happened in several projects. Nor should the American professors abroad become involved in trying to make up for teacher shortages in host countries by acting as substitutes, except in rare instances. The needs are too great, and the supply of American professors too short.

Whether degree programs or not, participant programs need to center on academic material, courses, or experiences. Admission standards should be high and should be determined by the admitting university; at least it should have a veto. Few or no special courses for degree participants would have to be offered by a university. If their coming and going is planned to coincide with university terms, even nondegree in-service trainees might fit into one or more regular university courses or seminars. Many universities may have to take a hard look at their permanent offerings, however, to see whether they are adequate for American as well as for foreign students. Relating higher education and academic disciplines to development problems is a focus increasingly needed.

American universities will find other international involvements desirable from time to time. Among these, religious programs are not likely candidates. Nationalism and its relation to religion as well as the changing relationship of American religion to American higher education makes an increase in these programs improbable.[5]

It might be desirable to encourage taking groups of students from abroad to study at American universities, apart from technical assistance objectives. Yet one of the peculiar handicaps of United States universities is that they are distant from other countries, and the costs of coming to this country are prohibitive for most students or professors from abroad except from Mexico and Canada. Therefore, under present financial arrangements large-scale movements of students to the United States as counterparts to the American student-abroad programs are not to be expected except possibly from Mexico and Canada, and occasionally from Europe. The Monterrey Tech two-way exchange with 10 American universities and the regular sending by a German institution of several students to the University of Cincinnati are illustrative of the possibilities. European universities have many short-term exchanges among themselves that cannot be matched with American institutions because of distance and cost. In the future more short-term programs providing foreign students with only partial immersion in the American university system should be developed if adequate financing is forthcoming.

A sizable proportion of graduate student and professor travel to the United States from abroad will have to continue to be financed from American resources. In doing this, Americans should make certain that programs of the broadest possible advantage are available to all qualified personnel from the scholarly community abroad. On some American campuses, foreign students distinguish between educational opportunities of the "haves," those who come under the participant programs, and the "have nots," those who come independently. The distinction in educational opportunities between the haves and have nots should cease.

Mutuality. It is common to refer to all the international exchange programs of American universities as interuniversity affiliations. Such a reference is inaccurate for at least three reasons. First of all, in some of the programs no institution abroad is involved in any substantial way in formal relationships with the American university. One out of every three or four student-abroad programs and one out of every five or six research-abroad programs have little or no host-institution involvement. In the second place, a number of those programs in which host institutions of some kind play a role do not involve host universities. Some of the student-abroad programs are related to *ad hoc* cultural organizations and occasionally even to lycées. One-fifth of the research and technical assistance programs are related to government agencies in whole or in part. Finally, the word "affiliation" is misleading to the extent it implies mutuality. Mutality in many of its aspects is not a formal or informal objective or an actual condition in most programs.

In a very broad sense a measure of mutuality in program operations has been achieved by the international exchange programs of American universities. American faculty members and students go abroad; host-country faculty members and students come to the United States. The balance is not perfect. More students go abroad than come to the United States (approximately 3,500 compared with 2,000); over 1,000 American faculty members go abroad and less than one-fourth as many foreign faculty members come to the United States under the university programs (Inventory, pp. 36–42).

If each American university engaging in international programs is considered separately, the mutuality of program operations is much less. One hundred and twelve of the one hundred and eighty-four institutions with programs have only one of them, often providing for a single-directional flow of personnel, as in an American student-abroad program. Institutions with only one technical assistance project may merely send their own faculty members abroad, or may also include provision for participants to come to the United States. Among the 17 institutions with five or more programs, none have achieved a balance of sending and receiving students and faculty members. Nor has this objective been included in the programs.

Of the more than 80 programs in the sample of the study, only 11 had substantial mutuality in two-way exchange of professors, students, or information. All 11 were with institutions in Japan, Europe, or Mexico, educationally highly developed regions or countries as compared with most others in the sample.

Long-range affiliations are more likely to be consummated among institutions of a similar nature. By far the greater number of American university programs do not involve similar institutions abroad. Of course, the institutions or faculties of no two systems of higher education are identical; important differences of size, purpose, resources, and development exist. Institutions or departments may vary in professional competence, public support, continuity of personnel, traditional functions, autonomy, and the role that vested interests play (Adams and Cumberland, pp. 152–160). There may be differences in the status accorded any two institutions and their personnel in their respective countries. In formulating a program, there are problems of finance, personnel, and interest in affiliations. Even though a matching of race and regional interests was present, Lincoln University did not find Ghana University College desirous of establishing mutual exchange. The mere size of the large student-abroad programs prevents much reciprocity. The purpose of technical assistance is in the main non-reciprocal, although the hope has often been expressed that mutual exchanges would grow out of them.

There are forces that help bridge such gaps, such as the inter-

national professional spirit that helped to bring together representatives of ICA, the host university, and North Carolina in a sanitary
engineering project in Peru. As the internationalization of various
fields of higher education proceeds apace, more opportunity for
mutual exchanges will exist. Such a development may be evident
in another five or ten years, but is not to be expected in most fields
before then. In another five or ten years the relative stage of development of universities and, it is hoped, the resources available
to them, will be more equal, country to country. In the meantime,
relations which benefit both parties can be devolped, even though
they are not exactly mutual.

A large degree of mutuality or reciprocity has not obtained in the
donation and receipt of culture items. It is true that American
universities and their personnel both donate and receive items of
culture, as the result of the programs. A few genuinely two-way
exchanges occur as far as culture items are concerned. Yet in some
of the programs with mutual operations the United States university
was considered the prime donor, the host institution the prime recipient, although a two-way transmission of culture items was
clearly intended and in part provided. This was true of the joint
law school program in Japan, the Stanford and Michigan American
studies programs in Japan, the Chicago-Frankfurt faculty exchange,
and the joint Michigan and Columbia law school program in Turkey. The transmission of culture items in most of the programs
with one-way operations has tended to be in a single direction.
The overseas branch and the large student-abroad programs intend
mainly that American students shall be the recipients and their
instructors, or host-country personnel, shall be the donors. Two
exceptions are the large mutual student exchange of 10 American
universities with Monterrey Tech and the UCLA student program
in India. The UCLA students contribute information about the
United States and in turn learn much about India, and the Monterrey Tech program is completely reciprocal. Technical assistance
programs and those with some religious emphasis are also unidi-
rectional for the most part. Naturally, no program involving contact between persons from different countries can be entirely one-
way in its cultural influence. Furthermore, the net flow of a project
may not be reflected in the impact on any one person or group.
The professor who goes abroad may well be affected by his experience much more than any one person with whom he comes into

contact. Distinctions need to be drawn between professional and personal, planned and unplanned, formal and informal changes. Innovations that are planned, formal, and academic or professional for the most part constitute the stated objectives of the university programs even though an individual may be more affected by the unplanned, informal, and personal innovations.

Though mutuality of operations cannot be expected in each university program, a greater degree of reciprocity in the donating and receipt of culture items is possible. Nor is there need to wait for five or ten years for this development. American universities can derive many more valuable culture items in technical assistance programs simply by becoming interested in such items. So, too, with study and research programs. Host institutions can benefit much more if they will only be interested. As long, however, as one-way large study-abroad programs remain peripheral to host institutions, the host institutions will receive but little from them.

Programs Compared to Other International Involvements. There are some alternatives to international programs of American universities. The valuable experience a professor receives by being abroad under a technical assistance project could in part be obtained by an individual research grant overseas. His contribution abroad could be made by giving him a leave of absence to serve on an ICA or other project. The values of the student-abroad movement could in part be achieved through the introduction of courses in the social sciences stressing the comparative aspects of the disciplines, and through the use of foreign guest lecturers, plus the encouragement of individual foreign student enrollment and the contact with foreign cultures that it brings. It is for each university and department to choose those devices that best support its aims. Some institutions will find that many international programs fit their needs, others will find that few or none do.

There is no reason to assume, a priori, that universities have an obligation to engage in a wide variety of international programs. Most American universities include international or world affairs education, international and cross-national research, and cooperation with those from other countries among their goals, but no university can afford to accept a stereotyped formula for achieving them. Each must construct a plan that is most suitable to its resources and to its specific teaching and scholarly objectives. The present study has not found any single combination of international programs or other devices that would seem best for all institutions. With these qualifications, it would seem highly desirable:

1. for all universities to bring to the attention of their own *qualified* students a variety of alternatives for study abroad, including programs with different objectives from which students could select if they so desired, and to assist the students in going abroad whether the program is administered by the university or not;

2. for more universities to undertake study-abroad programs, and of a wider variety, thus increasing the desirable alternatives available to qualified students;

3. for some universities to encourage reverse study-abroad programs for foreign students in the United States, subject to the limits of available financing;

4. for all universities, consistent with their resources, to be receptive to individual scholars and departments at their institution who wish to initiate group research and small-scale student and professor-exchange programs in the fields of their specialization, with broad implications for international scholarship and long-range scholarly affiliations in the various fields of study;

5. for all universities with adequate graduate facilities to be receptive to participant programs centering on regular degree work and for some to administer nondegree but academically relevant programs in areas of their specialization;

6. for some universities to develop a new aspect of academic specialization at home available to all foreign and American students, emphasizing the relation of subject matter specialization to higher education and the relation of both to national and international development;

7. for all universities which have technical assistance programs, abroad or at home, or are in the future approached concerning them, to review them critically in regard to their appropriateness to a university and the clarity of their objectives;

8. for some universities to experiment with a new approach to technical assistance abroad that would emphasize studying the relationship of higher education to national development and the adequacy of alternative means of furthering the relationship.

Finally, all colleges and universities must be ever conscious of their obligation to transmit and advance knowledge. The giving and receiving of knowledge are no respectors of national boundaries. American universities need to look forward to a new era of far greater mutual interchange with scholars and institutions abroad. Be this interchange one of ideas alone, or of student and scholars as well, be it individual or administered by a university or some other group, the interchange is crucial. No institution of higher learning can afford to be isolationist if it is to be true to its name as a university.

Chapter 16

AN AGENDA FOR
FOUNDATIONS AND GOVERNMENTS

Any agenda for policy changes in university programs must include all participating organizations, even though the initiative comes from the American universities themselves.

Host-country Institutions and Governments

In more than two-thirds of the international exchange programs of American universities one or more of a wide variety of host institutions are involved. Host-country governments play important roles in supporting many university programs. Their policies affect the outcome.

Host-country institutions have good reason to develop their own criteria of relevance in deciding whether to participate. This is especially true when they initiate a program or when they are to be major recipients of culture items from American universities. In the latter case, host institution commitment to the objectives of the project is essential if the project is to be a success. After they have identified criteria of relevance, host institutions can begin to spell out objectives and methods. Many host institutions lack concern for carefully considered, well-laid plans. Although sponsoring organizations have erred on the side of financing vague and uncertain projects, they do at least normally require a minimum amount of planning. Host institutions must comply if they wish outside financing. Grants are not often given without commitment by the host institution to invest some of its resources as well, especially where the host institution initiates the proposal.

In the future, an increasing proportion of the international programs of American universities should, and probably will, involve active participation by a host-country institution. There must be more reciprocity, if the programs are to have a lasting place. Both parties will have to grapple with the thorny problems of adopting clear long-range objectives and careful selection of means. Even though objectives be defined and agreed upon, there will remain, as the program develops, the necessity of providing means of revising them from time to time to the mutual satisfaction of the two cooperating organizations. In any active program plans must be made more specific as the program evolves and new needs continually identified.

Agreement is often difficult to obtain, even in regard to student-abroad programs. Host-country universities seldom have planning mechanisms as effective even as those of their American counterparts. The American idea of academic administration does not prevail. Furthermore, clarity in these matters is less appreciated abroad than in the United States. An agreement on ends is elusive and can seldom be reached quickly. The parties must first get to know each other, identify the area of cooperation, and make plans for it. This process takes time; some existing projects were developed much too rapidly.

Even with as much time as anyone would care to spend, the two universities may find it difficult to agree on the priority of objectives. If they have widely different needs or desires, agreement may be impossible; in this case a program ought not be undertaken. Cooperation in the social sciences, the humanities, and related fields may be especially difficult in newly independent countries or those not committed to political freedom. Countries that place their ideology above objective thinking will not find institution-wide cooperation with free universities compatible with their aims. Limited programs will have to suffice, by-passing the more sensitive areas.

Host-country governments often are related to American university-exchange programs in their role as the legal superiors of the host universities. Occasionally they have helped finance the programs, or one of the government agencies has actually been the host institution. Host-country governments differ widely in their willingness to facilitate university exchange. At one extreme they give every encouragement; at the other, they have exceedingly negative attitudes. A few host governments have not been above playing against one another the United States government, an American foundation, and an international agency in technical assistance. This process is not a rational use of alternatives but a game to see which agency can be forced into financing what frequently is an ill-conceived undertaking.

Notwithstanding all the discussion about desire for rapid development, few host-country governments vigorously support change. They see no role for cultural exchange other than that it is a "good idea" to broaden the experiences of students and professors. American university cooperation with universities abroad can scarcely fulfill its purpose without a marked change in policy by many host governments. A desirable policy would include the promotion of cultural exchange not for "broadening" persons by means of trips abroad, but for the major role it can play in the advancement of knowledge to the end of world-wide development.

American Foundations

American universities and host-country institutions have welcomed support from foundations as an alternative to governmental sponsorship. If free universities and independent scholarship are to be preserved at a time when large outside financing is required, it is important that alternative sources of support be available so that no one group solely determines university policy.

Foundations, deliberately or otherwise, help to fill some of the gaps left by the several agencies of the United States government in university programs. They extend grants to American and host-country universities which do not or will not participate in government programs. They extend grants in subject areas that are not covered by any government program, or in which host governments do not want to get involved with the United States government. They support some American student-abroad programs and small exchanges; only seldom does the government directly subsidize such activities. Government agencies have also been reluctant to support programs exclusively for research; most of these are foundation financed. Because of the limited number of devices available to a government agency in regard to international programs of American universities, some projects are terminated before their useful life has ended. Often it would be desirable to continue them on a smaller or a somewhat different basis. Foundations have filled a need here: for example, the Ford Foundation grant supporting the University of California's work at the University of Bologna after ICA bowed out, or the Rockefeller Foundation grant to the Institute of Public Administration at the University of the Philippines to obtain assistance somewhat similar to that it formerly received from the University of Michigan–ICA contract program. If the United States government were to establish a new, unified policy in university international exchange, foundations would find fewer gaps left by the government program. At least, they would be less influenced by the inadequacies of government policy and could more freely pursue their traditionally independent role, experimenting with new programs in new areas as their interests and resources warranted.

Nevertheless, foundation policies in supporting international programs of American universities need revising as much as those of the United States government or of the universities themselves. The university programs supported by foundations are not, on the whole, any more effective than those supported by the government, judging from the programs in the sample for the present study. It may not be entirely fair to compare all foundation-financed programs with all those financed by government, since each total is differently distributed among the several kinds of programs. Two kinds of programs, however, those involving research and those involving some measure of technical assistance, are sufficiently supported by both to justify comparison. In neither kind are programs financed by foundations more successful in achieving their objectives.

This is somewhat surprising, since many host-country nationals are more receptive to a foundation-financed program. Furthermore, it may involve less red tape and thus minimize annoyance. Apparently such advantages do not counterbalance some disadvantages incurred in programs sponsored by foundations.

Many foundation-financed programs suffer from inadequate field contacts both in the planning and in the review stage of a program. Without field offices, foundations find it difficult to keep abreast of developments in host countries and thus properly to analyze a project proposal or to review the progress under way. Foundations have used special consultants and occasional travel by staff members to gather information relevant to university programs. Such checks tend to be *ad hoc* and spasmodic. At no time does a foundation possess as many facts concerning the host-country situation and the university program as USOM is likely to have in regard to its university contracts. During the entire course of a university program abroad, a foundation representative may visit it for a few days. Those visits are normally hurried and provide no basis for a thorough review.

The experience of the Ford Foundation suggests that wherever possible the foundations should appoint representatives to provide analyses of prospective and on-going university programs from the field. The overseas development division of the Ford Foundation has established several field offices. Other divisions of the foundation have not done so. The university technical assistance contracts made by Ford in Indonesia and Pakistan, where such offices are located, seem to be far more successful than the university contracts in Turkey and Italy, where there are no Ford offices. ICA experience is similar. Where no USOM field office has existed, universities have often performed very badly, as in Haiti a few years ago. Partly it is a matter of contact from time to time. Partly it is a matter of placing the university project in the perspective of a broader policy or set of priorities. The function of field representatives should be to assist in both the planning and review stages, and to be available for consultation or advice should the universities desire assistance. In addition, they can keep the home office informed of developments in the host country and supply essential data for decisions by the sponsoring organization. Where field offices cannot be established, foundations should increase the frequency and duration of field trips by their own staff members or by consultants. Field representatives should not engage in day-to-day supervision of universities; this has been a shortcoming of government-financed programs. Foundations seldom commit this error, however.

Both foundations and government agencies should review thoroughly university-exchange programs at least once every two years. In these reviews representatives of the foundation, the American university, and the host institutions should cooperate with outside observers or experts, who should make candid reports to those involved and their superiors. The sponsors would then be in a better position to judge the value of each project they sponsor, the justification for its extension, and the criteria for future applications for grants.

Foundations, like government agencies, tend to operate within certain program areas. The charters of many foundations are specific in the terms of reference for administrators and boards. Even when charters are general, foundation executives usually try to delineate their fields of interest. A foundation cannot prudently spread its limited resources too thin. University-exchange programs are not necessarily the best means to carry out the objectives which foundations choose. They may be very poor means. Not often does a foundation adopt the policy of promoting the international programs of American universities as such. Rather, these programs become means to other ends. The foundations use universities to serve their own social objectives rather than contribute to the objectives of higher education. Even the larger foundations have done so, despite formal policies maintaining the contrary.

American universities have the prime responsibility for ensuring program effectiveness regardless of the means of financial support. Since effectiveness in accomplishing objectives depends in large part upon the university which undertakes the task, the decision of a foundation or government agency as to whether it is going to give a university a contract or grant is of crucial importance. A part of this decision is a determination by the sponsor of what requirement the university is to meet in laying down clear, long-range goals and objectives and specifying the means to be taken to achieve them. Foundations and government agencies have been about equally successful in solving these problems.

A foundation or government agency may vote a grant with the assurance that objectives are clear and certain, and then find a lack of support at the university required to put the project into operation. In the course of obtaining this support the objectives of a project may undergo a metamorphosis. It is difficult to distinguish between, on the one hand, the outstanding university, department, or able scholar and, on the other hand, the assurance of broad support for a program by a group of scholars or by one or more departments. There is no easy way out of this difficulty. More thorough acquaintance with a university and the type of personnel likely to participate would help. So would resisting pressures for selection exerted by government agencies for political purposes and preferential treatment for the alma maters of foundation board members.

The United States Government

In international exchange the policies of the United States government exert great influence on the nature and scope of the activities of university personnel. The Fulbright and Smith-Mundt Acts, the university contracts of ICA, and smaller government programs have accounted for a large proportion of the going and coming of students and scholars. The great expense incurred in travel requires support outside the universities. Government funds are the largest source of outside financing. Also, the United States government has a major interest in international exchange because it affects foreign affairs. The national government has a deep concern with training of Americans for overseas assignments, understanding of international problems by Americans, understanding of the United States by foreigners, promoting friendship for the United States, and accelerating development of countries in the free world. International exchange of American university personnel can contribute to these objectives. In particular, the many programs throughout the world for which American universities have accepted institutional responsibility can so contribute; on occasion these institutional programs have been related so closely to government objectives that both the universities and the government have confused the role of the university with that of a government agency.

Nevertheless, the foreign policy of the United States has never placed as much emphasis on higher education or cultural affairs as have some European countries, primarily England and France. Indeed, cultural affairs have been a central aspect of French foreign policy, if not of British. The emphasis dates from the days of their great colonial empires and the philosophy of the "white man's burden" in bringing the benefits of Western civilization to other areas. Cultural activities and universities have been more central in the French and British societies than in the American.

Shortcomings of Present Approach. The policies of the United States government affecting university exchange are marked by several shortcomings, perhaps reflecting lesser emphasis on higher education and cultural affairs. Agencies of the United States government with foreign policy responsibilities, like all government agencies, have tended to concentrate on short-range goals. Each year a government agency must justify itself before Congress or run the risk of losing some of its appropriations. In the eyes of Congress, programs with short-run payoffs can give more tangible evidence of accomplishment than long-range, less readily measurable programs. Yet higher education is essentially long range and does not fit well into the crash or emergency programs of government agencies under pressure.

American universities training participant students from abroad have been expected to do so in a few months, at least no longer than a year. No time was to be wasted on the earning of "useless" degrees. Even where the degree-earning objectives were accepted, foreign students who could meet few prerequisites for admission to graduate study and who frequently could speak little English have been expected to complete in nine to twelve months studies that normally take an American student 15 months or longer. American universities have been expected to send faculty teams for technical assistance overseas almost by the next plane after the signing of a contract. Little or no time or money has been authorized for the highly useful language-and-area training and other preparation or for ascertaining long-range objectives and appropriate means to achieve them. From the day university teams arrive overseas, they have been besieged by requests from ICA officials for monthly, quarterly, and semiannual reports of progress. Emphasis has been placed on the accomplishments already achieved and the prospects for further impacts. At weekly staff meetings the chief advisers of university teams have been asked to report the universities' progress just as progress is reported by each of the USOM division chiefs.

The infrequency with which government funds have been available for student-abroad programs or small exchanges of faculty members or students reflects both the interest of the government in short-range programs and its lack of interest in higher education as a whole. These programs are not geared to any one subject matter. They contribute to the education of students in the long run or to the further development of faculty members. Neither objective can be readily measured; its significance is not immediately apparent to budget examiners or congressional committees.

If educational exchange in higher education is to rise or fall by its short-range results, it can claim little support. The work undertaken by universities may not take effect for several years or even for decades. Emergency training programs can of course be developed by universities, but to build a permanent policy on them is to endanger the basic role of universities in society. Continual diversion of university resources to short-range programs can have serious consequences. Universities and, more particularly, their international programs, do not play as immediate a role in our national defense as do nuclear weapons, or as immediate a role in our foreign policy as economic or military aid. Nor are they nearly so costly.

If long-range goals are considered, the international programs of universities can have important consequences. The advantages to the United States of these programs lie not in making friends, not in putting down some imminent Communist threat, not in supporting the latest statement of the Secretary of State. There has been entirely too much discussion at this level. Rather, the potential advantages lie in strengthening American and foreign universities and in augmenting their contribution to the world fellowship of learning. If, and only if, such things are accomplished can these institutions contribute more effectively to national and international development, a more favorable climate of international affairs, and world peace.

Both the Fulbright and ICA university programs are criticized widely overseas on the ground that they are dictated by the United States government. "We don't make any decisions," said a host-country member of one of the European United States Educational Foundations (Fulbright Commissions). "Everything is handed down from the State Department through the cultural affairs officer. We're rubber stamps." After discussing his own country's program in higher education abroad, an official of the French Foreign Ministry observed, "You Americans consider such programs to be valuable principally for political or propaganda purposes. You keep them tied closely to the State Department. That's why receptivity to your programs is so low compared to that of the British Council." These are extreme statements, only partly true. Yet credence is lent to them by the tendency of government agencies to claim credit for any achievements brought about by university international exchange.

"Though it sounds paradoxical, the gain of the exchange program may be the finest propaganda because it is not propaganda— it is education." [1] Is the purpose propaganda or education? If it is higher education, the goals could be achieved more readily if the program were administered in a manner that benefits higher education rather than the special objectives of the Department of State. "I have many fine associations with USIS personnel," one Italian remarked, "but you Americans are going to have to remove exchange activities from government agencies and place them in an independent organization. Regular government agencies have too many handicaps and are too objectionable to those with whom you seek exchanges."

The world power of the United States is used in its own self-interest on most occasions. Foreigners have an understandable fear of that power. They fear that it will be used in a manner that will unduly affect their own lives, and will influence decisions that are essentially matters of internal concern. University leaders and faculty members are particularly sensitive about outside interference in their affairs.

Another evident shortcoming of the present situation is that neither in legislation nor in administration has the United States government pursued a unified policy in respect to international university exchange. Among the agencies participating have been the International Cooperation Administration, the United States Information Agency, the International Educational Exchange Service, the Department of Defense, and, most recently, the Peace Corps. In addition, the United States Office of Education, the United States Public Health Service, and the United States Department of Agriculture have had large special interests in the matter. The number of agencies active in international exchange reflects the many-sided nature of higher education; it has a functional import for such fields as agriculture, public health, and education, as well as its broad international aspect. The United States government has no general policy toward international exchange in higher education. It has pieces of policies, each piece relating to the special concern of one government agency.

There has been much discussion of the need for the coordination of the international cultural activities of the United States govern-

---

[1] Quoted in International Educational Exchange Service, *International Educational Exchange Program, 1948–1958* (Washington: Department of State Publication 6647, August, 1958), p. 55.

ment, as in the Morrill report in 1956 in regard to one area.[2] Since
that time several steps have been taken to assure such coordination.
The Cultural Planning and Coordination Staff in the Department
of State was created for this purpose. One of its first reports was
designed to help eliminate conflict and duplication in the exchange
of persons and programs of three national agencies.[3] In 1958,
Robert H. Thayer was appointed Special Assistant to the Secretary
of State for the Coordination of International Educational and Cultural Relations. And in 1961, President Kennedy appointed Philip
H. Coombs the first Assistant Secretary of State for Educational
and Cultural Affairs. The new Assistant Secretary was given the
specific responsibility of coordinating the international educational
and cultural affairs of the United States government. For the first
time an office exists that has the power of settling disputes among
agencies in this field.

Coordination, however, is not a suitable goal in and of itself. No
amount of coordination of the many cultural activities of the
United States government can meet the need. Coordination of a
series of inadequate programs does not remove the basic difficulties, and may accentuate them. The steps taken toward coordination of cultural activities to date overlook three major needs:

1. Inadequate distinction is made between short-range and long-
range aspects of the program, between such things as concert and
lecture tours and university educational exchange. Each has an
entirely different set of needs.

2. The immediate and direct subservience of the cultural program to the political policies and special political objectives of the
State Department remains.

3. The present bits-and-pieces program continues, a program that
requires universities to conform to the particular demands of each
agency. There is no program making government support available to universities in order to further programs that fit their needs.

Until these shortcomings are remedied, it would be wise for

    [2] J. L. Morrill, "A Proposal for the Coordination of the Exchange of Per-
sons Programs of the International Educational Exchange Service and of the
International Cooperation Administration" (Washington: Department of State,
May 1, 1956, mimeo.), 43 pp.
    [3] "Coordination of the Educational Exchange Program of IES, Exchange
Aspects of the Technical Training Activities of ICA, and Certain Cultural
Activities of USIA" (Washington: Department of State, December, 1957), 24
pp. It has since become simply the Plans and Development Staff.

universities to be wary of too much involvement with the government in international exchange. Until action on such shortcomings is forthcoming, further coordination of government activities in university exchange may place the universities in a more untenable position than ever, and allow them even less freedom of decision than they have had.

A Proposed General Policy. If the United States government's policies of cultural exchange in higher education are to have a sound basis, universities must make the first move, by developing suitable criteria for embarking on projects. At present, governmental groups have no guidelines from them. The government should expect no single voice. University pluralism and independence must be retained. Once criteria for various kinds of programs are identified by a number of institutions or groups of institutions representing different kinds of universities, Congress and the various administrative agencies will be in a position to consider in what respects their policy can support the needs of higher education, and vice versa. The present study leads to the conclusion that three major elements must be present in any policy that is adopted.

First, the unique qualities and requirements of university international exchange need to be understood and recognized. A distinction is imperative between international cultural affairs that centrally affect higher education and those that do not. The distinction rests partly on the size and scope of the activities in which universities play a central role; the extent is large enough to warrant separate attention. Partly the distinction is justified because the universities are of such central importance to a free society that their international exchange activities warrant the development of a separate policy.

More fundamentally, higher education exchange is separable because it deals with a distinctive group of institutions, the goals of which are markedly different from the goals of government agencies or of the press, private business, or other private associations. Universities, by their very nature, must have a large measure of independence if they are to make their maximum contribution to society in the dissemination, preservation, and acquisition of knowledge. Detailed coordination of their activities with those of other groups may be harmful. Their goals are of necessity long range. Concert and lecture tours are one-shot affairs. So also are many other international cultural exchange activities. University international exchange can build a foundation in a manner that even exchanges of leaders in government, business, or the press cannot. The knowledge universities gain and the educational devices they employ are expected to be institutionalized, preserved, and made available to future students and society in general.

The arguments for coordination of higher education with other cultural affairs are largely organizational and political. The new Bureau of Educational and Cultural Affairs in the Department of State has one set of educational and cultural programs, and so there seems some reason to continue and expand it. The United States Information Agency has another group of educational and cultural activities. Understandably, each agency sees a need for more, not less. Politically, those who feel the United States has made too little an effort in educational and cultural affairs wish to see a new enlarged, coordinated program.[4] It is seldom asked what the proper role of universities is and how that role can best be carried out. The welfare of universities at home and abroad is thus subordinated to organizational and political considerations.

The distinction made at present between educational exchange and educational technical assistance programs is not appropriate, and is actually harmful. In the long run, certainly within a decade, it may lead to unhappy consequences for American universities. Technical assistance, particularly as universities administer it, is really a form of education; at the same time higher education can be considered technical assistance from the university to those who benefit from the education. If technical assistance be regarded as a process of helping others by extending their knowledge and thus stimulating innovation, its similarity to education becomes apparent. American professors going abroad engage in the same kinds of educational activities, even though they are labeled technical assistance, that some American professors carry out at home. The American student abroad is considered part of an educational exchange program, whereas the participant coming to the United States to earn a degree is considered part of a technical assistance program. There is no logic in these artificial distinctions. This is well illustrated by the Johns Hopkins University program at

---

[4] A forceful presentation of the case for coordination can be found in Walter H. C. Laves, *Toward A National Effort in International Educational and Cultural Affairs* (Washington: U.S. Advisory Commission on Educational Exchange, 1961), part VII.

Bologna, which was considered to be a technical assistance program by some Italian government officials, although American students can progress toward a degree by participating in it.

One effect of classifying some educational exchange as technical assistance has been that extra sums could thereby be obtained for these activities. This has had an unfortunate effect because it has encouraged stress on a very small part of higher education as a whole. It has resulted in overemphasis of vocational training, and so has reinforced the fears of host-country nationals that American universities do not have high standards of learning but think of themselves merely as vocational schools. If all phases of higher education were more evenly balanced in international exchange, host-country nationals would understand American universities more clearly, and would better appreciate the role that vocational specialization plays.

The distinction between technical assistance and educational exchange is patronizing at best. For the time being, the less developed countries accept it, however reluctantly. In the long run, scholarly exchange will be seriously curtailed if the distinction is not eliminated. Host-country nationals cannot for long tolerate a state of affairs in which an American professor teaching at their universities is believed to be giving them technical assistance while a professor from their country teaching at an American university is believed to be engaging in educational exchange. The distinction between technical assistance and university exchange reduces the mutuality of the process. Emphasis is on giving, not receiving. Thus American universities give Japan technical assistance, though no thought is given to receipt by American universities of help from Japan in such areas as mathematics, physics, or chemistry, where Japan has a surplus of personnel and American universities a shortage (Bronfenbrenner, chap. 7).

The distinction between educational exchange and technical assistance has yet another unhappy facet. Within ICA, education in the broad sense of the term has been lost. Education has had a narrow professional ring: teacher education, vocational education, audio-visual education, and the like. No one at a responsible level has ever been concerned with the broad educational approach to technical assistance. Universities become occasionally used tools, nothing more. The same defect was evident in AID, as initially proposed to Congress. Planning, economics, commodities, financial assistance, and development research all had recognizable homes, but development education had none.[5]

Second, a government policy needs to be developed that will assist the universities at home and abroad in furthering their objectives. The present policy is based upon the assumption that the universities must change their activities to support each of the government's specific requirements. The latter is an invitation to the bits-and-pieces policy which prevails. The former points to the development of a general policy which could facilitate international exchange programs of the widest possible variety both in American universities and in higher education abroad. It rightly assumes that in most instances the selfish interest of United States foreign policy lies in supporting the aims of universities in international educational exchange rather than imposing artificial and restrictive government goals upon them.

The needs of all faculties for international exchange should be met, be they in the fields of agriculture, engineering, or arts and science. International exchange should extend to all subject matter appropriate to a well-rounded university. It should apply to exchanges between American universities and host-country institutions, whether the latter are located in less developed or highly developed countries. And it should include both one- and two-way exchanges. Emphasis on techniques should not preclude emphasis on long-range objectives, and emphasis on teaching and extension should not preclude emphasis on research and university administration. Such a policy would bring the greatest returns to both the American and the host-country university systems and thus would be of the greatest long-range benefit to the United States.

Government support should be made available to universities in such a manner that they have the widest possible choice of the devices of educational exchange in higher education. There should be no restrictions of devices based upon presumed importing or exporting of knowledge. Support for bringing students to the United States for study should be included, but so also should support for sending American students abroad; support for sending American professors abroad would be important, but so also would support for bringing professors to the United States. There should be no artificial stress placed upon institutional programs, or any artificial stress put on the individual aspects of exchange. Indi-

---

[5] See *An Act for International Development, A Summary Presentation* (Department of State Publication 7205, June, 1961).

vidual grants could lead in time to group applications, and group programs could in time stimulate individual applications. It is essential that individuals and institutions have direct access to the sponsoring agency and not have to work through some intermediary or chosen instrument or organization unless they so desire. The East-West Center of the University of Hawaii and various consortia of universities are examples of intermediaries. They are highly desirable, but not as exclusive agents. With such an array of devices, the policy would give no competitive advantage to the large university over the small, the group application over the individual, and the export program over the import.

In the group programs, emphasis should be placed upon development by institutions of their own proposals, on a broad multipurpose scale, after giving careful attention to the long-range goals and means selected. Group proposals, if accepted, should be implemented by means of general grants to universities, not detailed contracts. As the National Science Foundation has observed, "Basically, the psychological relationship between the recipient institution and the government, implicit in the awarding of a grant, is more in keeping with the concept of maximum freedom of action for the scientific investigator." [6] And, we might add, it is more in keeping with the concept of maximum freedom of action for universities and university scholars generally.

Third, university international exchange should be effectively insulated from the political policies of the State Department. Though complete separation may be impossible, university international exchange should not appear to be just another branch of the State Department. Exchange should be placed on a long-term basis. The universities and their scholars should have a major role in determining specific policies. Government red tape and restrictions which characterize present exchange should be eliminated.

The importance of insulating university international exchange from the Department of State is underlined by recent events. Under the impetus of the New Frontier, the Assistant Secretary for Educational and Cultural Affairs has moved to examine the entire governmental program in this area. This step was long overdue. Some of the many reports of consultants have pointed up the need

[6] National Science Foundation, *Government-University Relationships in Federally Sponsored Scientific Research and Development* (Washington: Government Printing Office, April, 1958, NSF 58-10), p. 33.

for respecting the integrity of universities as institutions and of
supporting university objectives. In contrast, some other recommendations have called for a unified cultural and educational
"attack" by the United States government in its foreign policy.
One school of thought has repeatedly asserted that now, at last,
education, culture, and science are "instruments of foreign policy"
to be joined with political and economic activities in sustaining and
directing the position of the United States in world affairs.

Such assertions are reckless and unwise. If this is the direction
in which the New Frontier is moving, the relative inaction of the
previous eight years would be preferable. Universities should not
be tools or instruments, similar to political and economic devices,
for United States foreign policy. To go in such a direction negates
the very nature of higher education. American universities would
lose respect around the world and most would at best be unwilling participants.

Path of Implementation. There are many ways to implement
an exchange policy like that envisaged in the foregoing pages.
New responsibilities for private organizations can help. For example, the hands of the Conference Board of Associated Research
Councils and the Institute of International Education could be
strengthened in regard to the programs of the Bureau of Educational and Cultural Affairs (formerly the International Educational
Exchange Service). Both groups could also provide a number of
services to American universities overseas, independent of the State
Department.

The development of regional centers for cultural exchange presents a further possibility. An East-West Center for higher education contacts with Asia and a hemispheric center for contacts
with Latin America could be the prototypes of centers for other
regions. If they were devices to involve many interested American universities rather than just the University of Hawaii and the
University of Puerto Rico, respectively, they could become major
instruments for the distribution of government funds to universities and university personnel for exchange purposes.[7] Involvement
of many interested universities might carry with it some representation in the governing of the centers.

[7] See "Report of the Committee of Consultants to the Board of Regents,
University of Hawaii" (Honolulu: June 14, 1961, mimeo.), for suggestions concerning the East-West Center.

Many other private organizations have been suggested. Action by private groups can provide one layer of insulation for university international exchange from government agencies. Yet the fundamental inadequacies of government policies remain. The Department of State has brought strong pressures upon the East-West Center at the University of Hawaii. The Board of Foreign Scholarships of the Department of State has reversed the Conference Board of Associated Research Councils from time to time. No private organization can provide a program basically better than the government agency concerned allows.

At a governmental level, there are three broad choices for action. At a minimum, the several existing agencies could broaden their programs and make them more compatible with university goals. These would include (a) the university contract and higher education programs of AID (ICA), both for technical assistance abroad and for participant training at universities in the United States, and its research and staff training programs, (b) most of the Fulbright and Smith-Mundt programs of the Bureau of Educational and Cultural Affairs and some aspects of its other programs, such as grants to specialists and leaders in higher education and contact with international agencies in matters of university international exchange, (c) the university-related activities of the United States Information Agency and the United States Information Service, (d) some aspects of the program administered by the United States Office of Education under the National Defense Education Act, (e) some aspects of the Peace Corps, and (f) the programs of the Department of Defense related to higher education overseas.

Rigidities of contracting and program content could be eliminated. AID and other agencies could adopt procedures that would give universities and university scholars some voice in policies for exchange programs. The Bureau of Educational and Cultural Affairs (CU) has more of these procedures than any other agency at present, given its Board of Foreign Scholarships and United States Advisory Commission on Educational Exchange plus its arrangements with the Conference Board of Associated Research Councils and the Institute of International Education. Even CU needs more effective devices. CU could help separate university activities from other cultural affairs and AID could help separate university activities from other technical assistance.

The broadening and improving of existing programs would lead to a second course compatible with the first. A point of government-wide coordination could be established. The Assistant Secretary for Educational and Cultural Affairs is one such point. A new proposed United States Advisory Commission on International Educational and Cultural Affairs, reporting to the President, is another, if its advisory jurisdiction were extended government-wide.[8] An interagency committee, reporting to the President, is a third.

The major difficulty with these two proposals, even in combination, is that none of the present agencies can suitably administer a broad program of university international exchange because their central concern is with other matters. The bits-and-pieces approach will continue to prevail. None of the agencies are centrally concerned with building up the resources of universities in general in the international area. ICA always had a negative attitude toward university contracting. The Peace Corps has developed a positive one, seeing universities as highly desirable contractors. Despite these differences, neither agency has sought to increase the capacity of universities. They assume that universities are to be used, not strengthened.

A third choice thus presents itself. Ideally, a separate agency could be established for all aspects of university international exchange supported by government. If transfer of all activities proved impossible to adopt and implement, the new agency could be restricted to coordinating those programs not transferred to it and administering a broad complementary program by itself. Such an agency might well become part of a new national unit concerned with higher education, if and when it is created. Under such circumstances, no longer would each agency be able to implement its interest solely in the propaganda side of exchanges, or in the foreign policy side, the technical assistance side, or the national defense side. The government's interest now stops at these points. No longer would higher education exchanges be promoted separately in agriculture, teacher education, medical education, and other fields. A new general program would be developed that would be more than a combination of current small ones.

A single agency could take one of several forms. The government corporation and the foundation are two prototypes. It should have its own presidentially appointed board for developing policy

[8] See U.S. Senate, Committee on Foreign Relations, *Mutual Educational and Cultural Exchange Act of 1961* (June 14, 1961), p. 16.

within the congressional mandate, a board that should include some outstanding leaders and scholars from American higher education and that would report to the President periodically. It should establish close liaison with American universities and scholars by means of advisory panels on policy and selection committees in several special fields. The procedures of the National Science Foundation (NSF) are suggestive: it uses a wide variety of techniques to assure its autonomy and to involve universities and scholars in its policy decisions. Among these are the broadly representative National Science Board, regular advisory committees in each subject area, special panels, ad hoc advisory groups, rotational positions in the NSF itself, and liaison with professional associations of scholars and with associations of universities and colleges.

The new agency should not be subject in matters of policy or administration to such government agencies as the Department of State, the International Cooperation Administration, the United States Information Agency, or the United States Office of Education. It should be as independent in status as the Congress will allow, with due regard for the fact that it would have custody of public funds.

The new agency should enjoy equal autonomy at home and overseas. Its overseas offices should not be subject to day-to-day embassy supervision. Offices should be established in capitals and principal regional centers around the world. They should take over and expand the function of the United States Information Service (USIS) in regard to information concerning American universities. New services could be offered to American universities and to host-country students and scholars, such as improved examinations in English proficiency and various tests of intellectual ability—for example, appropriate cultural modifications of the Graduate Record Examination or the Miller Analogies Test. The offices could become active in recruiting able students for study in the United States.

At the same time, the overseas offices could provide some services to students and professors from the United States. They could help with appointments for interviews, scheduling lectures and conferences, and itineraries for American students and professors abroad. Some assistance concerning such necessities as housing, medical care, and transportation would facilitate the academic work of the overseas Americans. American students and scholars should not be given commissary privileges or diplomatic license plates, or share in official government administrative support. However, all Americans from academic ranks should be treated alike, eliminating the unwarranted differences in the services available, for example, to ICA and Fulbright university professors abroad.

Advantages of General Policy. A single, flexible, independent policy of university international exchange is feasible. It falls within traditional patterns of American government; numerous devices are used by Congress to give independence to certain agencies and policies. There could be no more important area for safeguarding autonomy than higher education. Traditionally, even public universities in America have substantial independence from the units of government from which they obtain support.

A new, broad program in university international exchange would not be too costly. It would be a minor part of expenditures abroad. In 1957 only $21.4 million, $26.6 in 1958, $29.4 in 1959, and $31.4 in 1960 were expended for the entire educational exchange program administered by IES. The expenditures by ICA for university contracts were similarly modest—$8.9 million in 1957, $21.9 in 1958, $11.5 in 1959, and $12.5 in 1960. In total, the figures for both programs are far less than 2 per cent of the $3,050.0 million expended under the Mutual Security Program in 1960. The program envisaged in these pages could be implemented with a $30 to $40 million increase in university international exchange costs over and above that which the several separate agencies are now spending on portions of it. These additional funds should be spent on modest additions to resources available to foreign students for study in the United States, a large expansion of support for American students studying abroad, marked increases in small one- and two-way exchanges of faculty members, and a considerable increase in research abroad.

If such financial support were assured, both university-sponsored and individual exchange would take on new dimensions. Universities could obtain funds for institutional programs in areas in which they have competence, experience, and a desire to be active. Once again the universities could "be themselves." The new policy would affect universities primarily by encouraging them to think through priorities in international exchange and by providing them with part of the financial support needed to implement their several policies. The international exchange programs of

American universities would grow, but would no longer be subject to the imbalance and artificial barriers of present government policies or to the disadvantages of a close connection with foreign policy objectives, narrowly conceived.

Universities would gain freedom in several ways under such a new policy. For the first time they could play a major role in framing subpolicies of the government under which their foreign programs operate. These subpolicies would support as wide a range of individual and institutional exchange activities as possible, each individual and institution being free to apply for support for chosen activities in competition with others. Universities would gain not only freedom from restrictive government practices, but also the freedom that comes from the ability to obtain support for a desired objective.

The United States has no monopoly on knowledge, no monopoly on educational experience. Americans can benefit from intellectual exchange among nations as much as the nationals of any other country. Strong universities have always been fundamental institutions in free societies. In order to maintain their strength, they must reach out for fruitful contacts with students and scholars in other countries. In this process, the United States government can be of great assistance.

In sum, the Congress should establish a policy of broad support for university educational exchange. A unified policy should be established that eliminates the present distinction between educational exchange and technical assistance, that relates international exchange to the needs of American and host-country universities, and that includes whatever devices of exchange are useful to that end. To administer the program, at least in its basic essentials, a separate agency should be established of a semiautonomous character, in which representatives of American higher education play an important part.

The policies of all the major participating organizations in the international exchange programs of American universities need to be modified to make the programs more effective. The first requisite is for American universities to develop criteria of relevance—in groups, individually, and through smaller academic units such as schools and departments. Host institutions and governments also need to develop criteria of relevance for their own participation in university exchange. The United States government and foundations can then in turn adjust their policies of support for university exchange to be consistent with such criteria, although each sponsor will naturally wish to have its own distinctive policies.

In the energy and resources they have invested during the past fifteen years, American universities have done far more than universities of other countries to further institutionally based programs for the sending or receiving of students and professors to or from abroad. This is a record in which they can take pride. That the achievements of the programs to date have been modest is due less to the defects of university international exchange or the ineptitude of any of the parties concerned than it is to the inexperience of all in programs of this nature, and the fact that long-range objectives are involved, the accomplishment of which is likely to take many years.

International education, the discovery of new knowledge through cross-cultural contacts, and assistance to others are goals of prime importance. American universities should not be deterred from reaching them by the difficulties encountered. Efforts to attain such ends should be redoubled.

APPENDIX: DEFINITIONS, RESEARCH MODEL, AND PROCEDURES

The fundamental objective of the present research project was to examine the impacts university programs have on institutions and individuals abroad and also the impacts they have on institutions and individuals at home. Impacts were to be examined as to their extent, the factors or variables related to them, and the criteria or sets of criteria that could be and are used to assess them.

Definitions

Throughout its course, the study concentrated on the substantive innovations or impacts brought about by the programs. Little attention was given to problems of administering the projects, except where they impinged directly upon substantive achievements. There are many kinds of success: success in organizing a program, success in financing it, success in recruiting able personnel. Herein, the term "success" unmodified refers to success in achieving substantive results. How many or what kind of substantive results make for program success? No large program can be expected to accomplish all its objectives in an equally satisfactory manner. The writer believes that to be successful any international exchange program of an American university should accomplish at least one of its major objectives. Where other universities or other organizations engage in similar programs, one may speak of success in a comparative sense. Under such circumstances, a university doing well relative to the achievements of others may be considered successful.

A program may be a success, but this fact alone does not make the program appropriate for an American university. Three factors contribute to such appropriateness. Does the program have a direct academic relevance, a relevance for higher education? Does the program have some contribution to make to the American university or its personnel, as contrasted with a contribution only to those abroad? Is the

337

program of such a nature that organizations other than universities could not carry it out as well? The more affirmative the answers to these questions, the more appropriate a program is for an American university.

Another part of the initial task of definition of the Institute of Research on Overseas Programs (IROP)—the organization at Michigan State University established to carry out the research—was to specify clearly what constituted a university program and to conduct an inventory of such programs. Previously, there had been no nationwide data on this subject. With the publication of *The International Programs of American Universities* in 1958 this task was completed. This inventory provided a classification of the programs and identification of six major types.

More formally, an *international exchange program of an American university* is an exchange for which an American university or subdivision thereof accepts institutional responsibility. There are many ways in which such institutional responsibility is accepted. Often a contract or grant is received from a financing organization. A formal agreement with a university or other organization in a foreign country is frequently reached. These contracts, grants, or agreements may be in the name of the university or in the name of a college, department, or other academic unit. A number of agreements are informal rather than formal in character and are not written, but where any agreement or understanding exists, a program was considered to be in effect for purposes of the present study.

Exchange activities vary as to how long they continue in force. In order to have been considered a program, some recurrence of the exchange was necessary. For the purposes of the present study, an exchange activity that continued longer than a single year was considered to meet the minimum requirements of a program. Those programs in operation for less than twelve months in any one year, such as a summer study-abroad program, but which continue for that shorter time year after year were, of course, included in the definition.

In the present volume it was sometimes necessary to use the term "program" in referring to activities other than the international exchange programs of American universities. For example, a foundation program or a program of the United States government may or may not be related to a university international exchange program. Likewise, there are many other university programs than those of international exchange. It is hoped that the context made the meaning clear. The terms "program" (unmodified), "international program," or "university international exchange program" were used interchangeably. On the other hand, the term "international exchange" is more inclusive; university programs are merely a part of the total activity of international exchange of university personnel.

The literature of international education is replete with references to *exchanges,* sometimes meaning exchange of things such as equipment exchanges or information exchanges, and sometimes meaning the exchange of persons. In the present volume exchange referred to both persons and things. Of course, exchanges may be one-way or two-way. They may involve sending a faculty member or student abroad or receiving a faculty member or student from abroad or both. The term "exchange" has been used here in its most general sense, and when more specific meanings were intended, one-way exchange or two-way or mutual exchange were the terms employed. Exchange is sometimes confused with the purpose of a program. For example, international exchange and international education are occasionally thought to be synonymous. On the other hand, technical assistance programs are often not considered to be exchange programs although they involve the sending and receiving of persons or things. Used herein, exchange referred to all programs, regardless of purpose, that involve the sending and receiving of persons or things.

Throughout the present volume, the term "university" was synonymous with *institution of higher education* unless the context clearly indicated another, more restrictive meaning. Thus the term "American" or "United States university" refers to all institutions and branches listed in the directory of higher education of the United States Office of Education. Similarly in describing events abroad, when the term "university" was used it refers to any institution of higher education in the country concerned unless the context clearly indicated another meaning.

Several other terms were used interchangeably. "Programs" and "projects" were so used. "International education" and "world affairs education" were, also; likewise, "sponsoring organization" and "financing organization"; and "professor" and "faculty member." "Faculty" was used in its European sense as equivalent to a college in the United States. "Staff" or "staff members" of a university include faculty members and administrative officials and these two terms also refer to the professional employees of nonacademic organizations. "Host country" refers to the country to which or from which an exchange is operating at an American university and does not imply directly or indirectly any foreign indorsement of the program or official acceptance or participation.

Research Model

A second step was an examination of the several types of programs to see if a preliminary statement of a central or common project model was possible. There are some difficulties in analyzing projects of as great a diversity as the international exchange programs of American universities. The activities carried on are exceedingly numerous and different. The personnel and nonpersonnel operations are varied. In size they range from small to very large. In time duration they last from two years up to an indefinite period. There are many kinds of persons associated with them through several types of organizations. Sources of financing are many. Objectives of the programs are almost legion. Essentially, the problem of finding a common denominator is the identification of a project model that is equally applicable to the three policy areas of international education, technical assistance, and international or cross-national research and that may be applied to any of the six major types of programs.

Despite their seeming and real diversity, the several types of programs are part of a common process nonetheless. The central aspect of this process is some innovation or change. When a given innovation or change has taken place the project may be said to have had an impact. Innovations or changes can be classified in various ways. There are changes that result from the transmission of culture items such as a technical instrument, a teaching technique, or a general idea. Other changes result from the creation of culture items, such as the development of a new breed of cattle or an analysis of the economic potential of a country in regard to its land and mineral resources. Whether through the discovery of new knowledge or the transmission of existing knowledge, a university exchange program is centrally focused on stimulating change or innovation. Innovations vary in the weights of their impacts. Some imply great or radical change in terms of past practices, attitudes, or knowledge. Others require little fundamental change. They vary also in number; there are fewer innovations resulting from some projects than others.

To bring about some kinds of innovation requires organization. A university program or project is essentially an organization of various human and material resources intentionally set up to bring about innovation.[1] It is usually temporary, but may be permanent. In the case of the transmission of culture items, there are donors and recipients. The donor is the individual or aggregate of individuals engaged in the process of transmitting culture items. The recipient is the indivdual or aggregate of individuals for whom the culture items are intended. In the case of the creation of culture items, a third category is introduced, namely, the creators. The items they discover may later be transmitted by donors to recipients. Of course, within any project, the same person or group may be at once the donor in regard to certain culture items and the recipient in regard to others. Normally, the main direction of the

---

[1] Adams and Cumberland, p. 104. The model here discussed borrows heavily from Adams and Cumberland (pp. 100–150), and from Frank Pinner, "Preliminary Ideas for Research Design" and "Research Plans" (Institute of Research on Overseas Programs, July 31, 1957 and August 28, 1957, mimeo.). The latter two papers constituted a preliminary statement of model for the research design developed by the Institute.

flow or flows is evident. For example, in American student-abroad programs the flow is mainly from professors abroad and from the host-country environment generally to the students. The students are primarily recipients. To put it in terms of activities, normally those who teach are primarily donors, those who study or seek additional professional expertise are primarily recipients, those who carry on research are primarily creators, those who engage in consultation are primarily donors, and those who receive consultative advice are primarily recipients.

Not only do donors and recipients tend to reverse their roles in relation to each other from time to time in regard to different sets of culture items, but also some recipients assume the role of donors in regard to third parties or groups. Such individuals or groups can be considered culture carriers. To some extent any recipient is a culture carrier. However, there are individuals or groups that are specifically allocated such a function in some international exchange programs. For example, a technical assistance project abroad may concentrate on training the host-country faculty members in a new technique or new subject matter so that the faculty members can make use of these new culture items in transmitting knowledge to their students. The host-country faculty members are thus culture carriers by design. Culture carriers are especially important in technical assistance projects, since they produce a spread effect. The training of trainers or even the training of the trainers of trainers is often viewed as the only way in which the limited resources available for technical assistance can be put to the maximum use. Such an idea fundamentally relies upon the central role of the culture carriers in diffusing culture items they have received directly or indirectly from abroad.

Projects vary in the extent to which they make use of culture carriers. When they do make use of them, it is possible to speak of the culture carriers as being the intermediary groups or individuals. When they do not make use of them, the project contacts the main recipient (or target) groups or individuals directly. More specifically, United States students abroad are primarily target groups, but they are intermediaries insofar as they have an impact on the home campus. Many small one- or two-way exchanges of students place the exchangees primarily in an intermediary role, to bring knowledge and experience of another culture to the home campus. Most small exchanges of professors result in the professor contacting target groups, i.e., students, directly.

The transmission and receipt of a culture item by means of an American university project can result in two different kinds of innovation or change, namely, change related to the content of the project and change resulting from the very fact that a project exists. The former may be called substantive innovation and the latter accommodating innovation. Examples of the former would be the acquisition of new facts by a student or the mastery of a new technique by a staff member or employee. Accommodating innovations include adjustments in office space, acceptance of new administrative responsibilities, altered salary scales and other costs, and temporary or permanent organizational changes in the American or host university. The distinction between substantive and accommodating innovation needs to be emphasized because frequently discussions of impact of international programs of American universities have concentrated on accommodating impact; particularly is this true in regard to technical assistance programs and their actual or potential impact on American campuses.

Once a culture item is transmitted and received, some change is bound to occur. Innovation can either be accepted or rejected by the recipient, or partly accepted and partly rejected. If innovation is accepted, the project may proceed more or less according to plan. If it is rejected, change or readjustment is, in turn, forced on the project itself. This is especially evident over the long run. Innovations also often have wave effects, one innovation causing another. Once an innovation is made, there is often a need to readjust various on-going patterns to it, and these in turn may cause further readjustments. The more radical the change, the more likely it is that substantial successive readjustments will have to be made.

Most of the changes that occur can be viewed as changes in either groups or individuals. At the individual level, changes may occur in behavior or actions, in skills, in attitudes and beliefs, and in cognitions or informational levels of people. As a result of innovations such as these, the role of a person relative to other individuals as well as his role in formal groups may change. There is a similar cluster of possible innovations in regard to groups. The actions taken and to be taken by a group, the state of its physical and social technology, and its information level on matters of concern may all be affected. So, too, may its role in its environment. A number of the international programs of American universities represent role departures both for the American university and the host-country institution. In some instances, individual or group status has increased, in other cases it has declined. Often it has increased with one group or set of individuals and declined with another.

Essentially, the model briefly outlined here for analyzing the international exchange programs of American universities is a communication model. As such, it can be greatly expanded by borrowing from contributions to communication theory.[2] While some communication

[2] See, for example, Karl W. Deutsch, "On Communication Models in the Social Sciences," *Public Opinion Quarterly*, vol. 14, pp. 356–380, 1952; and John T. Dorsey, "A Communication Model for Administration," *Administrative Science Quarterly*, vol. 2, pp. 307–324, 1957, especially his discussion on learning nets.

models have centered attention on decision-making, there is no reason why such models cannot be used equally well to center on innovation. The innovations with which the present study is concerned occur as the result of the transmission of culture items and the transmission is essentially a communication process. Likewise, in turn, the acceptance or rejection of innovations involves communication and also decisions.

Research Procedures

The development of other aspects of the research design followed a preliminary statement of the model. Included were the spelling out of various classifications and the development of several interview guides. The design was completed and field research began in the late fall of 1957. The present research project on the international programs of American universities was carried out for IROP by 11 social scientists over a period of four years. Altogether, perhaps 15 to 16 man-years were invested. Represented were virtually all the social sciences: political science, economics, anthropology, psychology, and history. Of the 11, eight carried on research primarily overseas, two in the United States, and one equally in both locations.

The design called for a study of the impact of the international exchange programs of American universities in selected countries and at selected universities. The fact that the research project of IROP was primarily oriented toward the programs of universities had important consequences for the research procedures followed. Basically, the choices of universities, countries, programs, and interviewees were all influenced by the desire to study representative programs of the six major types. Interviewees were identified not on the basis that they represented an adequate sample of all American professors, university administrators, or students, for example, but rather primarily on the basis as to whether each group of them represented a suitable pattern of informants for a particular international program. No attempt has been made to total the responses of all interviewees on certain matters, since the interviewees were chosen in relation to individual programs and not as a cross section of informed individuals for all programs. It has been possible to total data in regard to each program and thus to speak of the proportion of programs in which certain practices or opinions occur.

There were a number of sampling choices that confronted the research project. Since the innovations of the international exchange programs occur both at universities in the United States and abroad, some sampling of projects in both locations was necessary. Unfortunately, it was not possible to select a single set of programs that adequately represented different kinds of American universities and foreign countries and different types of programs. Consequently, two independent samples were chosen, one of American universities and another of foreign countries. Programs within each were then selected for field research. The selection of separate American university and foreign country samples had the distinct advantage that it facilitated study of the innovations associated with all programs of each American university in the sample, including an examination of the effects of multiple programs where they existed. It also made the conduct of research abroad considerably easier and more effective, since language and area competence was necessary in conducting such research, and the specific cultural contexts of the international programs abroad obviously were of substantial importance.

The countries selected were Mexico, Peru, Bolivia, Chile, Korea, Japan, Indonesia, India, Turkey, Italy, France, Germany, Lebanon, Egypt, Sudan, Ethiopia, Nigeria, and Liberia. At least a few interviews were carried out in each of five additional countries in Latin America, six in Europe, seven in Africa, and five in Asia. The interviews in these additional countries were intended purely as supplements to data collected elsewhere and were not complete studies in themselves. The criteria used in the selection of the basic sample of countries were essentially five. First, the sample was to represent countries with widely different systems of higher education; second, the countries were to be in varying stages of educational development; third, they were to reflect varying degrees and kinds of economic and political development; fourth, they were to represent some of the major cultures; fifth, a suitable group of American university international programs should be represented. Other criteria inevitably influenced the selection such as a desire to study large and small countries, those allied with the United States and those not, and of course the practical criterion of matching countries and the capabilities of qualified and available staff members. No sample of countries can be truly representative of multiple criteria such as these, but the sample for this study did reflect a wide variety of kinds of conditions from country to country under which university programs function. It was this kind of variety that was being sought in order on an exploratory basis to compare the innovations resulting from the different types of programs under varied conditions.

The pattern of programs sought by IROP in the countries selected was one that represented programs of all six types adequately and reflected other program characteristics as well. For example, both new and old programs were represented in an attempt to understand the time dimension and its effect; large and small programs were studied; technical assistance and nontechnical assistance programs; student and faculty member programs; one-way and mutual exchanges; government-financed and nongovernment financed; general and specialized programs; programs representing the different subject matter fields; study, teaching, research, and consulting programs; and programs of varying economic and political significance, potentially. In some countries, it was possible and desirable to examine all projects; in several instances a sample had to be selected.

The American universities at which interviews were conducted were selected in two ways. At least a few interviews were held at each of the American universities administering the programs in the overseas sample. Second, a sample of American universities was chosen for special interviewing, quite apart from the overseas sample. Some 28 universities with programs and five universities without programs were selected, the former by choosing the university administering every nth program, the universities ranked in descending order of the numbers of programs they respectively conducted. All the programs of the 28 universities were studied by means of field and documentary research in the United States. University officials were questioned concerning program objectives and philosophy as well as methods and results. Universities without programs were studied as a contrasting group, to see if different trends were ascertainable.

The kinds of persons to be interviewed in connection with each program were centrally determined as much as possible before field research began, although additions had to be made in the course of the research. First of all, there were a varying number of persons in charge of each project; the coordinator or program director on the American campus, the principal American university representative abroad, if any, the program director or officer in charge for the sponsoring organization both in the United States and abroad, and the person in charge for the host-country organization. Second, the administrative superiors of the persons directly in charge of the program for the American university, financing organization, or host-country institution were interviewed as to their perception of the program. Third, the American and host-country staff members and students who were the exchangees were interviewed, although on occasion student exchangees were so numerous that a small sample had to be selected. Fourth, those with whom the exchangees regularly worked were included, such as the professors of student exchangees, or the new colleagues or a sample of the students of professorial exchangees. Finally, a few interviews were held with those indirectly affected by a program, such as a foreign student having contact with an American student who was abroad or a wife who accompanied her professor-husband overseas, and those in a position to be informed observers such as the cultural affairs officers. Over 2,000 interviews were carried out in the United States and abroad under the Institute of Research on Overseas Programs' project. Most of the interviews were structured but provided respondents with ample opportunity to express their observations in as free a manner as possible. Interviewers took notes during the interviews, dictated an account from their notes, and the typed versions of the interviews were available to all project personnel, although not to others.

In any group research project such as IROP's, it is probable that complete uniformity in the data collected from country to country cannot and perhaps should not be achieved. In any event, the present project did not result in collection of completely uniform data, yet the common research guide facilitated the collection of data on similar matters and in roughly similar ways.

In the present project, impact, or the innovation or change brought about by project activities, was determined principally in two different ways. Through documentary and other sources the extent of certain changes in the donor and recipient groups and individuals was ascertainable, such as the creation, modification, or abolition of courses and curricula; the number of students specializing in certain subject matters; the number and qualifications of professors allocated to certain assignments; entrance requirements; briefing arrangements; changes in organization structure; and reports and publications issued. Documentation of such matters made it possible to determine rather exactly the presence or absence and scale of such changes. However, there are many aspects of impact that are not the subject of documentation. For example, changes in attitude and cognition are seldom clearly documented. Are students who have been abroad more or less disposed toward participation in international affairs? Are they more or less favorable to United States foreign policy? Are they more or less interested in academic achievement at home? Did they cause the persons with whom they came in contact abroad to become more or less favorable to American higher education? More or less favorable to the United States? There is virtually an unlimited number of such questions. No amount of documentation can establish the facts clearly in regard to them, although some reports may allude to changes of this character that have taken place, such statements reflecting opinions of the writers of the report or opinions of associates who may be quoted. In order to obtain data on such matters as changes in beliefs or in the level of information, interviews with the persons involved were held. What changes in the person's or group's orientation had occurred? What new values were being sought, what new attitudes were there, what additional information was now available? What modification of old habits or practices had taken place? In effect, these interviews were partly designed to elicit self-analysis by the interviewees as to the innovations occurring with respect to themselves and the organizations to which they respectively belonged. The reactions of interested observers about the nature of the impact were also obtained, and in addition, all persons associated with a project, American and host-country nationals alike, were asked to examine the impact of the program on groups other than their own and on persons other than themselves. In this manner, data identifying many changes that occurred during the life of a project and even after it was completed were obtained, limited though the information may be.

The identification of innovations was only a part of the research quest. An attempt was also made to obtain data that would lead to conclusions concerning causal relationships. Were the innovations brought about by the project? Would they have occurred if the project had never existed? What outside influences were there? If the innovations were related to the project, what particular features of the project, what individuals, were most responsible? Relating projects and project methods and personnel to specific innovations is rather simple in some instances and extremely difficult in others. It is simple regarding most accommodating innovations, and exceedingly difficult in regard to substantive innovations among target groups and individuals. Data on causal relationships were collected in the same manner as descriptive data on innovations, namely, by interview and from documentary evidence. In a number of instances, there was consensus among informants as to cause and effect, but such consensus was not always taken at face value. It is much easier to obtain data leading to a description of the innovations occurring during the life of a project than it is to obtain data leading to causal conclusions concerning whether the project or a part of it was responsible for the innovations.

There were shortcomings in the plan of research if a complete picture of the impact of the projects was to be obtained. First, the projects should have been viewed over a span of time of sufficient length to enable the researchers to observe the innovations taking place; alternatively, two periods of observation two or more years apart might have served the purpose adequately. Second, certain control groups should have been selected in order to compare the innovations occurring where university programs existed with the innovations occurring in similar situations where university programs were not present. Unfortunately, financial limitations prevented either course of action, except for random interviews and the collection of some documents in connection with groups that could have been used for control purposes. However, even without these additional dimensions, the study resulted in collection of a substantial number of data.

A BIBLIOGRAPHICAL NOTE

The several publications stemming from the studies of the Institute of Research on Overseas Programs, Michigan State University, listed in the Preface of the present volume, join a growing body of literature on the foreign relations of American universities.

The new Agency for International Development (AID) which has replaced ICA is generally described in *An Act for International Development, a Summary Presentation* (Department of State Publication 7205, June, 1961). Annual summary presentations to Congress on the Mutual Security Program have been made in the past by State, Defense, ICA, and the Development Loan Fund. Annual reports to Congress, such as the *Mutual Security Program, for the Fiscal Year 1960* (Department of State Publication 7099, January, 1961), have also been issued. All these documents make some reference to the university contract program, placing it in the perspective of the total assistance effort. A new research role for universities and other groups is outlined in the Report of the Development Assistance Panel of the President's Science Advisory Committee, "Research and Development in the New Development Assistance Program" (May 24, 1961). The report of the President's Task Force on Foreign Economic Assistance, Group on Contracting, "Positive Contracting for AID: Marshalling and Strengthening the Nation's Resources for International Development" makes recommendations on university and other contract programs, their philosophy and procedures.

The International Cooperation Administration has been the source of several publications on its university and education programs. AID will undoubtedly continue some of these. The Office of Contract Relations has issued a statistical quarterly report, *ICA-financed University Contracts. Technical Cooperation through American Universities* (n.d.) is generally descriptive of the contract program, as is its predecessor, *American Universities in Technical Cooperation* (FOA, 1955). Each of ICA's technical services (health, agriculture, etc.) have issued brochures from time to time describing programs in their areas, including university programs. *Technical Cooperation in Education* (1956) and *Review of Mutual Cooperation in Public Administration* (1960) are typical. The participant training program of ICA in which American universities have played an important role has been described in *Participants in Technical Cooperation* (1957). See also the Foundation for Research on Human Behavior, Ann Arbor, *Training Foreign Nationals in the United States,* a report of a seminar, 1956.

The Peace Corps has concluded several major contracts with universities. "Educational Institutions and the Peace Corps" (April 1, 1961) describes initial policies. "The College and University Affiliation Program" (leaflet, n.d.) of the U.S. Information Agency contains a list of affiliations and a brief description of the USIA-inspired affiliation program.

The new Bureau of Educational and Cultural Affairs (CU) has made extensive use of consultants and task forces to review its programs and plan for the future. Of special interest is Walter H. C. Laves, *Toward a National Effort in International Educational and Cultural Affairs* (U.S. Advisory Commission on Educational Exchange, 1961). Of the hundreds of pages of mimeographed materials prepared for CU largely for its internal use, the "Report of Working Group on the Application of Technology to Educational and Cultural Affairs" (June 30, 1961) and "International Educational and Cultural Policies and Programs for the 1960's: Philosophy, Objectives and Illustrative Programs: Synthesis and Recommendations" by J. E. Slater (July, 1961) are of major relevance. Several regional reports were also prepared. In regard to new legislation, see U.S. Senate, Committee on Foreign Relations, *Mutual Educational and Cultural Exchange Act of 1961* (Report 372, 1961) and *Section-by-Section Analysis of the Proposed Mutual Educational and Cultural Exchange Bill* (1961).

The several exchange programs of the Department of State have been the subject of a number of reports by the former International Educational Exchange Service. *Swords into Plowshares* (1956) examines the first ten years of the Fulbright program. *Twenty Years After: Two Decades of Government Sponsored Cultural Relations* (1958), by Francis J. Colligan, provides a brief history. *The Widening Circle* (1957) is an account of public-private cooperation in exchange. *American Grantees Abroad under the International Educational Exchange Program* (1957) is a research report on geographical and institutional distribution of grantees. IES also published semiannual reports of its Smith-Mundt (U.S. Advisory Commission on Educational Exchange) and Fulbright (Board of Foreign Scholarships) programs which will undoubtedly be continued in some form by CU.

The IES programs have been the subject of many studies and reports. "A Bibliography of Evaluation Studies," listing 35 titles, has been issued by the Evaluation Branch of CU. Regional and country programs are the subject of the several IES reports generally entitled *Program Planning Analysis of Educational Exchange and Related Exchange-of-Persons Activities* (varying dates, 1955–57). The Conference Board of Associated Research Councils in addition to periodic reports has issued *Educational Exchanges: Aspects of the American Experience* (Report of a Conference, 1956) and numerous reports such as that of Gordon MacGregor, *The Experiences of American Scholars in Countries of the Near East and South Asia* (April, 1957).

A number of publications have been concerned with coordination among government programs in the field of exchange. Included are *Federal Government Agencies and International Educational Exchange* (Inter-Agency Committee on Technical Training Programs, Exchange of Persons, and Overseas Cultural Activities, March, 1956), *A Proposal for the Coordination of the Exchange of Persons Programs of the International Educational Exchange Service and of the International Cooperation Administration* by J. L. Morrill (Department of State, May 1, 1956), and *Coordination of the Educational Exchange Program of IES, Exchange Aspects of the Training Activities of ICA, and Certain Cultural Activities of USIA* (Cultural Planning and Coordination Staff, Department of State, December, 1957). An annotated list of government agencies active in exchange was also prepared by the last-named group. The U.S. Office of Education, one of the government agencies in the field, has issued Paul S. Bodenman, *American Cooperation with Higher Education Abroad* (1957), which reviews both governmental and nongovernmental programs.

UNESCO's publications *Study Abroad, Teaching Abroad,* and *Vacations Abroad,* issued periodically, contain information of an inventory nature for those going abroad from the United States and those coming here as well as exchanges not involving the United States. The Pan American Union has issued publications dealing with exchanges in Latin America. See, for example, *Opportunities for Summer Study in Latin America* (1957) and *Exchange of Persons,* a semiannual bulletin. A special Expert Committee of the International Association of Universities prepared *Formal Programmes of International Cooperation between University Institutions* (UNESCO, 1960).

Foundations have supported many university programs but have issued few reports concerning them directly. Foundation annual reports contain some information, and the several editions of *American Foundations and their Fields* (American Foundations Information Service, Raymond Rich Associates) indicate fields of activities of the many foundations. The Carnegie Foundation for the Advancement of Teaching has published a summary of a discussion by its trustees, *The College and University in International Affairs* (1960). The Report of the Ford Foundation's Committee on the University and World Affairs, *The Uni-*

versity and World Affairs (December, 1960), is a major contribution to thinking in this area.

The Institute of International Education publishes an excellent monthly, *Overseas* (formerly *IIE News Bulletin*). Its annual *Open Doors* is the basic reference on statistics of American university exchange. *The Handbook on International Study: For Foreign Nationals* (1961) and its companion, *Handbook on International Study: For U.S. Nationals* (1961), are basic orienting volumes. *Forty Years of Educational Exchange, 1919–1959*, contains a review of four decades of work plus the usual annual report. The biennial National Conference on Exchange of Persons issues many useful mimeographed papers on conference topics. IIE has established the Committee on Educational Interchange Policy. Its publications are: *The Goals of Student Exchange* (1955), *Geographic Distribution in Exchange Programs* (1956), *Chinese Students in the United States (1948–55)* (1956), *Orientation of Foreign Students* (1956), *Expanding University Enrollments and the Foreign Student* (1957), *Hungarian Refugee Students and United States Colleges and Universities* (1957), *United States Medical Training for Foreign Students and Physicians* (1957), *The Foreign Student: Exchangee or Immigrant?* (1958), *Hungarian Refugee Students and U.S. Colleges and Universities: One Year Later* (1958), *Academic Exchanges with the Soviet Union* (1958), *Twenty Years of United States Government Programs in Cultural Relations* (1959), and *College and University Programs of Academic Exchange* (1960). The last in the list has a very useful bibliography.

The American Council on Education has been interested in both educational exchange and technical assistance. *The Educational Record*, its periodical, has contained several articles of interest. Its Commission on Education and International Affairs has issued mimeographed *Minutes* from time to time and Reuben Lorenz, *Problems of Cost and Programming of Foreign Visitors on the American Campus* (May, 1961), a report of a special subcommittee. ACE's Committee on Institutional Projects Abroad, mainly concerned with ICA contract programs, has released *Annual Reports*, an occasional periodical entitled *Education and Foreign Operations*, and annual summaries of their conferences, the November, 1960 conference report being entitled *The Role of American Higher Education in Relation to Developing Areas*. Several other ACE committees are also concerned with international exchange. Michael J. Flack prepared *Sources of Information on International Educational Activities* for ACE in 1958.

ACE is the publisher of several volumes growing out of a project directed by Howard E. Wilson and sponsored by the Carnegie Endowment for International Peace. Beginning with Wilson's *Universities and World Affairs* published by Carnegie Endowment directly in 1951, the series includes the following eight ACE volumes: Howard E. Wilson, *American College Life as Education in World Outlook* (1956); Cora DuBois, *Foreign Students and Higher Education in the United States* (1956); Cyril O. Houle and Charles A. Nelson, *The University, the Citizen, and World Affairs* (1956); C. Dale Fuller, *Training of Specialists in International Relations* (1956); Fred Cole, *International Relations in Institutions of Higher Education in the South* (1958); John Gange, *University Research on International Affairs* (1958); Richard N. Swift, *World Affairs and the College Curriculum* (1959); and Howard E. Wilson and Francis J. Brown, *American Universities in World Affairs: A General Report* (forthcoming). The Carnegie Endowment also issued a series of mimeographed reports on Universities and World Affairs during 1952–53.

Each university with major technical assistance programs overseas or in the United States has issued periodic reports, generally mimeographed. A growing proportion of them have also issued evaluations of their activities after several years of experience. Several analyses have been made of groups of university programs abroad, including *Technical Cooperation in Latin America: The Role of Universities in Technical Cooperation* (National Planning Association, July, 1955), and Jerome Jacobson and Associates, *The Use of Private Contractors in Foreign Aid Programs* (U.S. Senate, Special Committee to Study the Foreign Aid Program, 1957). Philip M. Glick, *The Administration of Technical Assistance: Growth in the Americas* (University of Chicago Press, 1957) includes discussion of university programs in relation to United States government and international technical assistance. See also Milton J. Esman, *Needed: An Education and Research Base to Support America's Expanded Commitments Overseas* (University of Pittsburgh Press, 1961), and William Y. Elliott, *Educational Training for Developing Areas* (Harvard University Press, forthcoming).

Information on religious programs abroad can be obtained from *New Horizons* (United Board for Christian Higher Education in Asia) and *Asia Colleges Newsletter* (Council on Christian Higher Education in Asia), two periodicals. The Missionary Research Library, New York, has issued several brief reports, mostly mimeographed, such as "Protestant Colleges in Asia, the Near East, Africa, and Latin America," by W. Plumer Mills (1955), as well as its *Occasional Bulletin*.

Most of the American universities with study-abroad programs have published their own descriptive account of their activities and several of them have made evaluation studies. Illustrative, but in no sense exhaustive of the former are: *Junior Year: Munich, Frieburg, 1961–1962* (Wayne State University), *Vienna Summer School, 1960* (Hope), *Our Cultural Heritage, A European Travel Course, Summer 1960* (Montana State), *Foreign Study Plan for Dartmouth Students Majoring in French,*

German, or Spanish (n.d.), Francis M. Rogers, *American Juniors on the Left Bank* (Sweet Briar, 1958), and *Hollins Abroad, 1960*. Some evaluation or critical reviews of the programs or reflections on them include Elizabeth Leonard, "Selected General Education Outcomes of a Foreign Travel and Study Program," doctoral dissertation, Pennsylvania State University, 1959, and "Foreign Study in Teacher Education at Adelphi" (*Adelphi Quarterly*, Summer, 1959); Irwin Abrams, *Study Abroad* (U.S. Department of Health, Education, and Welfare, 1960—containing many useful references); Howard P. Smith, "The Effects of Intercultural Experience—A Follow-up Investigation," *Journal of Abnormal and Social Psychology*, March, 1957; C. Robert Pace, *The Junior Year in France* (Syracuse University, 1959); Donald J. Shank, *The Junior Year: A Critical Look* (IIE, 1960); the *Smith Alumnae Quarterly*, Fall, 1960 (devoted to the Smith programs abroad); and *A Report on the Semester in Italy* by John Clarke Adams (Syracuse, 1960).

The Council on Student Travel is a good source of information on study-abroad programs; in addition to its *CST News*, it publishes other items from time to time; for example, *Asia, Africa, Latin America: Expanding Educational Travel* (1961), which includes a list of programs in these countries. IIE has issued *Programs for U.S. Undergraduates in Other Countries, A Survey of Present and Proposed Programs* (1960), the most recent listing and classification of programs. See also the March, 1961 *IIE News Bulletin*, "Summer Study-Travel Programs." Activities of The Experiment in International Living in assisting study-abroad programs are outlined in its brochure, *Cooperative Overseas Programs* (n.d.). The Association of American Colleges, the Council on Student Travel, The Experiment in International Living, and IIE have jointly sponsored two conferences on Study Abroad. *Academic Programs Abroad* (IIE, May, 1960) and *Transplanted Students* (IIE, 1961) emanated from them.

Foreign students in the United States are the subject of a several-hundred item bibliography in *Research in Programs for Foreign Students* (National Association of Foreign Student Advisers, 1961). NAFSA's *Newsletter* contains current information. NAFSA has begun a research series, of which *Research Studies in Inter-Cultural Education*, by Werner Warmbrunn, 1960, was the first. Among the more ambitious studies of foreign students is the series of mimeographed reports generally entitled *The Effects of an Orientation Program for Foreign Students*, by Stuart W. Cook and Associates, New York University, 1957. Claire Selltiz, Cook, June R. Christ, and Joan Havel have collaborated on *Attitudes and Social Relations of Foreign Students in the United States* (University of Minnesota Press, forthcoming). The University of Minnesota is also the publisher of a series of studies sponsored by the Social Science Research Council and including Ralph L. Beals and Norman D. Humphrey, *No Frontier to Learning: The Mexican Student in the United States* (1957); John W. Bennett, Herbert Passin, and Robert K. McKnight, *In Search of Identity: The Japanese Overseas Scholar in America and Japan* (1958); Richard D. Lambert and Marvin Bressler, *Indian Students on an American Campus* (1956); Richard T. Morris, *The Two-Way Mirror, National Status in Foreign Students' Adjustment* (1960); Franklin D. Scott, *The American Experience of Swedish Students* (1955); and William H. Sewell and Oluf M. Davidson, *Scandinavian Students on an American Campus* (1961). See also Jeanne Watson and Ronald Lippitt, *Learning Across Cultures, A Study of Germans Visiting America* (Institute for Social Research, University of Michigan, 1955). Edward C. Cieslak's *The Foreign Student in American Colleges: A Survey and Evaluation of Administrative Problems and Practices* (Wayne State University Press, 1955), and Homer Higbee, *The Status of Foreign Student Advising in U.S. Universities and Colleges* (Institute of Research on Overseas Programs, Michigan State University, 1961), examine selective aspects of foreign student problems on the American campus. Two issues of *The Annals* of the American Academy of Political and Social Science are also valuable: "America Through Foreign Eyes" (September, 1954) and "The Rising Demand for International Education" (May, 1961). John T. and Jeanne E. Gullahorn have written widely on foreign students, including *Foreign Student Leaders on American Campuses* (National Student Association, 1958).

Outside the present study but closely related to the world role of United States universities are programs of training for Americans going overseas on American campuses. The President's Task Force on Foreign Economic Assistance included a group making a report (1961) on training for Americans going abroad, with major recommendations concerning the possible role of American universities. The Legislative Reference Service, Library of Congress, authored *Survey of Selected Institutions of Higher Education with Study Programs Preparing Students for Work Abroad* (U.S. Senate, February, 1961). Harlan Cleveland, Gerald J. Mangone, and John Clarke Adams have written more broadly in *The Overseas Americans* (McGraw-Hill, 1960). A Ford Foundation-sponsored conference at Princeton in November, 1960 on "Training Americans for Overseas Technical Assistance" was the occasion for several mimeographed papers on the subject. Several universities engaging in these programs, such as Boston and Johns Hopkins, have issued brochures and reports on them. More generally, area studies are reviewed in U.S. Department of State, Bureau of Intelligence and Research, External Research Division, *Area Study Programs in American Universities* (1959).

INDEX

Academic standards, faculty appointment, Anglo-American, 37
  Continental and Latin American, 37–38
  recruitment of technical assistance personnel, 240–241
  selection of participants, 140
  student-abroad programs, 94, 98–100
Achievements, technical assistance programs, 246–266
  in host country, acceptance of aid, 260–261
  course and curricular changes, 250–253
  establishment of target groups, 257–258
  in faculty training and experience, 256–257
  improved study habits, 255–256
  institution-building, 247–250
  making friends, 258–260
  in research and publication, 258
  in teaching techniques, 253–255
  in United States, 261–266
  curricular changes, 261–262

Achievements, technical assistance programs, in United States, language competence, 264–265
Adjustment, participant, 140–141
  technical assistance personnel, cultural, 226–227
  professional, 225–226
Administrative problems, student-abroad programs, 105–107
  technical assistance programs, 194–196
  university-sponsored, 174
Advice and consultation, technical assistance programs, 166–170
  forms of, 168–169
  individual, 188
  "land-grant philosophy" in, 167–168
  relation to teaching, 169–170
  scope of, 166–167
  techniques of forcing innovation, 169
Advising, student-abroad programs, 107–108
Agency for International Development, 218, 281, 327, 331
American Friends of the Hebrew University, 90
Association of American Colleges, 293

355

Association of Land-Grant Colleges and Universities, 157–158, 293

Board of Foreign Scholarships, 331
Boards of trustees, American universities, 36
Book exchanges, 126–127
Briefing programs, 106
for participants, 150
technical assistance personnel, 243–245
Bureau of the Budget, U.S., 157, 176
Bureau of Educational and Cultural Affairs, 324, 326, 329–331
Business-sponsored technical assistance, 174–175

Campuses, decentralized, in foreign universities, 23
Colleges in special relation, University of London, 20–21
Commercial student-abroad programs, 90–91
Committee on Institutional Projects Abroad, 178, 217, 279, 293
Committee on the University and World Affairs, 3, 293
Competence as criterion for technical assistance personnel, 224–225
Conference Board of Associated Research Councils, 330–331
Council on Student Travel, 65, 106, 293
Courses, for foreigners, European and Mexican universities, 63–64
language or cultural history, student-abroad programs, 72
participant, 137–138

Courses, participant, English-language, 142
technical assistance innovations in, 250–253
Cultural empathy, criterion for technical assistance personnel, 227, 233
Curricula, American, effect of technical assistance on, 261–262
changes resulting from student-abroad programs, 72
European and American compared, 14–15
revising for student-abroad programs, 97–98
technical assistance innovations in, 250–253
resistance to, 252

Decision making, technical assistance programs, 214–219
American university, 214–217
faculty and, 215–216
host-country, 217–218
sponsoring agencies, 218–219
Degrees, participant, 138
Department of Agriculture, U.S., 134, 157–159, 189, 191, 323
Department of Defense, U.S., 176, 323, 331
Direct grants for technical assistance, 188–189
Discussion technique, technical assistance innovation, 254
Dissertation-research programs, 88
Doctoral student-abroad programs, 87–88

Economic Cooperation Administration, 157–158
Education, general and specialized, 15–16

Educational institutions, roles in international affairs, 2–5
Employment practices, universities and, 30
European-Mexican emphasis, student-abroad programs, 104–105
European United States Educational Foundations, 322
Examination, absence in European systems, 48
in British system, 48–49
Exchange defined, 338–339
Experience, criterion for technical assistance personnel, 229–230
Experiment in International Living, 90, 106, 293

Faculty members, American, 32
advising-consulting-extension activities, 35
as advisors and consultants in technical assistance, 166–167
cooperation with student-abroad programs, 94–97
exchange, number of, 5
foreign, 32–39
part-time, 32–33
effect on university operations, 33–34
and exchange programs, 34
relations with students, 39–42
roles and statuses, in British tradition, 37
in Continental systems, 36–37
teaching, research, and extension activities, 34–36
training and experience, improving by assistance programs, 256–257

Faculty members, full professors, status in foreign universities, 38
opposition to technical assistance, 215–216
relations between, and international exchange, 38–39, 259
national differences in, 37–38
scarcity of, recruiting, 236–237, 239
technical assistance and, 194–196
small exchange programs, 127–128
as technical assistance personnel (see Personnel)
Fellowships, 128–129
Field trips, participant, 151
Financial motives, exchange programs, 298
Financial problems, student-abroad programs, 107
of university-sponsored technical assistance, 174
Ford Foundation, 154, 176, 179–180, 184, 188, 198, 210–212, 219, 237, 244, 250, 293, 317–318
Foreign Operations Administration, 158, 207
Foreign policy, support as goal of technical assistance, 268–269
Foundations, 316–319
fields of interest, 319
need for continuous policy revision, 317–318
sponsoring roles, 313–317
in technical assistance programs, 160, 176–188
effect on university-host relations, 184–185
nature of programs, 176–177
relations with universities, 179–180

Fulbright program, 5, 131, 304, 319, 322, 331, 334

General education, as prerequisite to year abroad, 83–84
  in sophomore year abroad, 83–84
Goals, of international exchange, multiple, 296–297
  need for clarity in, 299–302
  unstated, 297–298
  of technical assistance, evaluation of, 273–277
  future, 277–287
  general, 268–271
  advancement of knowledge, 269
  educational assistance, 270
  and host-country needs, 270
  intellectual, 271
  support of foreign policy, 268–269
  specific, 271–273
  characteristics, 272–273
Government, control of universities, 28–30
  host-country, policies on exchange, 315–316
  relations with universities, 26–31
  United States (see United States government)
Government-sponsored technical assistance, 176–188
  effect on university relations with host, 180–187
  number and organization, 176
  university relations in, 177–180
Governmental Affairs Institute, 138
Graduate study-abroad programs, 87–88
Group Study Abroad, 107

Handbook on International Study: For U.S. Nationals, 107
Health services, central, lacking in foreign universities, 23
High schools, 13–15
Higher education, American, 18–19
  year-by-year plan, effect on student-abroad programs, 83–84
  Continental versus American systems, 41–42
  differing systems, need for understanding, 49–55
  foreign systems, 19–21
  general versus specialized, 25
  role in technical assistance, 275–277
Host country, attitude toward American aid, 260–261
  government policies on exchange, 315–316
  need for improved relations with, 283–285
  technical assistance achievements in (see Achievements)
Host institutions, lack of clarity of objectives, 299–300
  matching to American university, technical assistance program, 204–205
  policies on exchange, 314–315
  relations with, and expansion of student-abroad programs, 102–104
  mutual objectives and, 103–104
  role in selecting American university, 213–214
  selecting for technical assistance, 207–209
  technical assistance personnel, motivation of, 233–234

Host institutions, technical assistance personnel, past performance of, 233–234
project directors, 233
selecting, 241–242
Housing accommodations, 106–107

Independent study abroad, 91–92
Individual technical assistance, 188–189
Information exchange, 129
Institute of European Studies, 90
Institute of Inter-American Affairs, 157–158
Institute of International Education, 57, 65, 107, 293, 330, 331
Institute of Research on Overseas Programs, 108, 160–161, 268, 338, 343–346
Institute for Social Studies, 86
Institution-building in technical assistance programs, 247–250
difficulties in, 249–250
institutional patterns in, 248
success in, 249
Inter-American Institute of Agricultural Sciences, 175
Interinstitutional cooperation, student-abroad programs, 101–102
International Confederation of Free Trade Unions, 135–136
International Cooperation Administration, 5, 34, 38, 45, 51, 120–121, 135–138, 141, 154, 156, 158–159, 161, 163, 171, 174–188, 190–194, 197–213, 218–219, 234, 236, 243–244, 250, 260–261, 272, 279–282, 292, 297, 310–311, 318, 320–323, 327, 334

International Educational Exchange Service, 120, 323, 330, 334
International educational programs, nature and types, 2–10
need for appraisal, 10–11
International exchange programs, and differing student-professor relations, 42–43
difficulties due to university organization, 24–25
extent of, 4–5
and faculty differences, 32, 34–35, 38–39
importance of, 1–2
mutuality in, 308–311
and national patterns of secondary education, 12–13
nonpersonnel, 8
role of U.S. government (see United States government)
sacrifices needed, 265
small (see Small exchange programs)
and understanding national differences, 49–55
university in, 288–313
approach to, 311–313
choosing among alternatives, 303–313
cooperation by, 293–294
criteria of relevance, 291–296
definition, 338
effect on prestige, 302
growth, 5–7
multiple objectives of, problems involving, 296–297
need for clarity of objectives, 299–302
roles, 289–291
success or failure of, 294–296
types of programs, 7–10
unstated goals of, 297–298

International friendship as objective of technical assistance, 258–260
International Programs of American Universities, 108, 338
International YMCA, 114
Interuniversity affiliation, future of, 305
and mutuality of exchange, 308–309
technical assistance and, 192–193, 260
Instruction techniques, national differences, 46–48

Junior-year-abroad programs, early, 56
emphasis on liberal arts, 78–79
fields inappropriate for, 81–82
interinstitutional cooperation in, 102
and lack of educational resources abroad, 82
other than liberal-arts oriented, 80–81
possibilities of expanding, to more institutions, 80–81
to other fields, 81
requirements for, 78–79

Land-grant colleges, 155, 157
Languages, faculty competence, effect of technical assistance abroad, 264–265
instruction in, student-abroad programs, 73
in preparation for sophomore year abroad, 84
technical assistance personnel and, 229, 232–233
Lecture systems, 46–47, 253

Liberal arts curriculum, junior-year-abroad programs for, 79–80
Libraries, central, lacking in foreign universities, 23, 254

Material and equipment provision, technical assistance programs, 171–172, 254–255
Missionaries, 113–114, 119
Morrill Act, 155
Motivation, American technical assistance personnel, 232
host-country technical assistance personnel, 233–234
unstated, international exchange, 297–298

National Defense Education Act, 331
National Science Foundation, 329, 333
Nonpersonnel exchange programs, 8

Office of Education, U.S., 157, 195, 323, 331
Office of International Labor Affairs, 136

Participant technical assistance programs, 7–8, 134–152
effect on American universities, 144–146
examples, 135–136
extent of, 134–135
field trips in, 151
future of, 305–306
kinds of, by administrative organization, 139–140

Participant technical assistance programs, kinds of, by course structure, 137–138
degree-granting, 138
by locational arrangement, 138–139
by rank of participants, 138
related to technical assistance abroad, 136–137
by training method, 140
by training objective, 137
selection of personnel, 140–143
special courses in, 147–148
special noncredit, 146–149, 151
staff for, 140, 143
successes of, 143–144
Participants, failure after return home, 144–145
impact on American campus, 145–146
junior and senior, 150
length of stay, 140–141
motives of, 142
selection, procedure, 141–143
standards for, 140
utilization after return home, 144
Participating organizations, need for clarity of objectives, 299–302
sponsors, future roles of, 279–281
technical assistance, 199–214
agreement on objectives, 202
American, number of, 200–201
financing, 199–200
host-country, number of, 200
problems involving, 201–202
originating, 202–203
selecting, 204–214
American university, 205–207
host institution, 207–209

Participating organizations, technical assistance, selecting, matching of institutions, 204–205
procedure, 209–214
Peace Corps, 292, 323, 331, 332
Personnel, participant, selecting, 140–143
for participant programs, 140, 143
for research-abroad programs, 123–124
small exchange programs, recruitment, 131–132
technical assistance, 223–245
ability, for cultural adjustment, 226–227
for professional adjustment, 225–226
age and experience of, 229–230
cultural empathy, 227, 233
enthusiasm and dedication, 226, 232
facility at implementation, 227
increasing job attractiveness for, 242–243
kinds, 223–224
knowledge of host country and language, 229
length of service, 228–229
motivation of, 232
past performance of, American, 231–233
host country, 233–234
preparation and briefing, 243–245
professional competence, 224–225
recruiting, 191–192
reputation of, 230
selecting, 235–245
American, 241
host-country, 241–242

Personnel, technical assistance, selecting, identifying desired qualities, 235–236
increasing potential for, 236–240
outsiders versus staff members, 237–238
procedures, 240–242
Planning technical assistance programs, 220–222
Point Four program, 3, 134, 157
Political activities, foreign students, 44
Prestige as goal in exchange, 297
Private student-abroad programs, 90–91
Protestant ethic, American university system and, 41
Public Health Service, U.S., 157, 189, 323
Public reaction, technical assistance programs, 219

Recruitment, technical assistance personnel, 236–240
outsiders versus staff members, 237–238
procedures, 240–242
Religious exchange programs, 8
combining study and technical assistance, 114
faculty exchange and technical assistance, 115
financing, 116
future of, 307
history of, 112–113
objective and achievements, 117–118
personnel selection, 116–117
prospects of, 118–119
secularization of, 119
small, 115

Religious exchange programs, summer-abroad type, 114
university relationships, 115–116
Reputation, criterion for technical assistance personnel, 229–230
Research, lacking in foreign universities, 34–35
and publication, technical assistance programs, 258
student, as technical assistance innovation, 255
in technical assistance programs, 170–171
Research-abroad programs, 8–10, 120–126
beginnings of, 120
direction of, 122–123
examples of, 120–121
future of, 303–304
host-country fear of, 125–126
initiation of, 121
results of, 124–125
role of ICA, 120
selection of host institution, 122
staffing, 123–124
Rockefeller Foundation, 184–185, 198, 317

Scandinavian Seminars, 90
Scholarships, 126
foreign, student and, 43
for study abroad, 107
Secondary education, American and European compared, 13–16
national patterns, 12–17
American, 13–15
foreign, 13–16
Small exchange programs, 8–10, 126–133
combined faculty-student, 128

Small exchange programs, extent of mutual participation, 129–131
  faculty, 127–128
  fellowships in, 128–129
  financing, 131
  future of, 304–305
  history of, 126–127
  information, 129
  long-range, 133
  objectives, 132–133
  organization of, 131–132
  student, 127
Smith-Mundt program, 5, 320, 331
Sophomore-year-abroad program, 83–86
Special participant programs, 146–149
Sponsoring organizations, lack of clarity of objective, 299
  relations with universities, 280–281
  selection of universities, 279–280
Student-abroad programs, 7, 9–10
  academic standards and criteria, 98–100
  advantages, 78
  commercially sponsored, 90–91
  and curricular and course changes, 72–73
  disadvantages, 77–78
  early, 56–57
  effect, on international relations, 73
    on total academic experience, 73–74
  examples, 58–62
  expanding, 100–111
    administrative difficulties, 105–107
    financial and advisory problems, 107–108

Student-abroad programs, expanding, by interinstitutional cooperation, 101–102
    location as problem, 104–105
    and relations with host institutions, 102–104
    student-selection problems, 108–110
  faculty cooperation in, 94–97
    importance of, 97
    reasons for lack of, 95–96
  freshman and senior years, inappropriateness of, 82–83
  graduate, 87–88
  growth of, 57
  impact on hosts, 75
  independent, 91–92
  junior year (see Junior-year-abroad programs)
  major objectives, 73, 76
  number and importance, 57–58
  organizing for, 62–66
    origination, 62–63
    selecting host relationship, 64–65
  other than junior year, 83
  personnel selection, campus coordinators, 68
    field directors, 67
    host-country staff, 66, 68
    students, 68–71
  present importance, 303
  principles of, 93
  privately sponsored, 90–91
  relation to regular academic work, 97–98
  short-term, 86
  sophomore year, 83–86
    length of, 84–85
    prerequisites, 83–85
  summer, 88–90
  types of, 76–77
Student leadership, foreign, 44–45

Student organizations, foreign, 44–45
Student-professor relations, American, 41
effect of overseas programs, 262–263
effect on exchange programs, 42–43
foreign, 39–42
Student strikes, 45
Students, American, academic life of, 40–41
effect of student-abroad programs, 73–75
exchange, number of, 4–5
foreign, academic and social controls on, 40
roles, 43–45
in United States, 134
motivating in student-abroad programs, 95–96
national differences in performance, evaluating, 48–49
in small exchange programs, 127
for study abroad, personal adjustment of, 69–71
qualities needed, 69
selecting, 68–71
problems of, 108–110
Study Abroad, 107
Study habits changing through assistance programs, 255–256
Summer-abroad programs, 88–90
advantages, 88–89
noncredit, 89–90
organizing for, host-university responsibility, 63–65
with religious emphasis, 114

Target groups as aim of technical assistance, 257
Teaching, national differences in, 45–49

Teaching, American versus European, 46–47
evaluation of student performance, 48–49
relation to cost, 47–48
technical assistance programs, demonstration, 164
direct, 163–164
modification of tradition techniques, 164–165, 253–255
opposition to techniques, 165–166
Team approach, technical assistance, nonuniversity, 189
university, 167, 189
Technical assistance programs, 4–5, 7–9
achievements (see Achievements)
activities, advice and consultation, 166–170
material and equipment provision, 171–172
research, 170–171
teaching, 163–166
alternatives to university, direct grants, 188–189
individual, 188
nonuniversity teams, 189
characteristics, 153
continuous planning and assessment, 220–222
early, 155–156
examples, 161–163
formation of, decision making in, American university, 214–217
other groups, 217–219
importance of prior contact and knowledge, 197–199
selecting participants, 204–209

Technical assistance programs,
    formation of, selecting partici-
        pants, procedure, 209–214
    future of, 277–287, 305–306
    goals (see Goals)
    interuniversity affiliations from,
        192–193
    numbers, 267–268
        cost and, 153–154, 160
        origin of, 154–155
    origination of, 202–203
    participant (see Participant tech-
        nical assistance programs)
    personnel (see Personnel)
    recent, 156–160
    related to participant programs,
        136–137
    special competence of universi-
        ties, 189–191
    sponsorship, 173–188
        business, 174–175
        foundation versus govern-
            ment, 175–177
        effect, on university-host
            relations, 180–188
            on university-sponsor
                relations, 177–180
        international agencies, 175
        university and host-country,
            173–174
    suggestions for improvement,
        281–287
        of contracts, 282–283
        of host-country relations, 283–
            285
    technique and subject idea, fail-
        ure of, 275–276
    university administrative prob-
        lems, 193–196
Technical Cooperation Administra-
    tion, 157, 158
Textbooks, 254
Training, participant, 137, 140
"2s, 2h syndrome," 232

UNESCO, 107, 126
United States government, present
    exchange policies, 320–325
    lack of coordination in, 323–
        324
    propaganda orientation of,
        322–323
    short-range nature, 321–322
    proposed exchange policy, 325–
        330
    cost of, 334
    implementation of, 330–335
    role in international exchange,
        320
    technical assistance programs of,
        156–160
United States Information Agency,
    176, 323, 326, 331
United States Information Service,
    331, 333
United States Operations Mission,
    176, 179, 181, 186, 192, 209,
    318, 321
Universities, American, approach
    to exchange, 311–313
    control in, 36
    democratic objectives, 16–17
    foreign perception of, 49–52
    interest in international edu-
        cation, 2–5
    international exchange pro-
        grams of, 5–10
        choosing, 303–313
        cooperation in, 293–294
        definition, 338
        objectives and goals, 296–
            302
        relevance of, determining,
            291–296
        success or failure in, reasons
            for, 294–296
    matching to host institution,
        204–205
    nature of, 18–19

Universities, American, numbers
    and types, 18
    organization, 24–25
    receptivity to exchange, 53–
        54
    roles of, 289–290
    criteria for, 290–291
    selecting for assistance pro-
        gram, 205–207
    autonomy of, 27–29
    classical, 288–289
    colonial, 21
    definition, 339
    and employment practices, 30
    European, restricted nature of,
        16–17
    foreign, advising-consulting-ex-
        tension by, 35–36
    changing roles of, 20–21
    faculty roles and statuses, 36–
        39
    nature of, 19–21
    organization of, 22–24
    national patterns and innova-
        tions, 21–22
    number and size as characteris-
        tics, 21
    relations with government, 26–
        31

Universities, in technical assistance
    programs, criteria for, 277–
        279
    government- or foundation-
        sponsored, host-institution
        relations, 180–188
    relations with sponsors,
        177–180
    personnel recruitment, 192
    roles, 273–274
    special competence for, 189–
        191
    as sponsors, 173–174
    sponsor's part in selecting,
        279–280
University and World Affairs, The,
    293
University Religious Conference,
    114, 117–118

Vacations Abroad, 108

Washington International Center,
    149
World affairs education, nature and
    importance, 3–5

Zengakuren, 44–45